Humanism and Secularization

Humanism and Secularization

From Petrarch to Valla

RICCARDO FUBINI

Translated by Martha King

DUKE UNIVERSITY PRESS   *Durham and London 2003*

© 2003

Duke University Press   All rights reserved

Printed in the United States of America on acid-free paper ∞

Typeset in Bembo by Tseng Information Systems, Inc.

Library of Congress Cataloging-in-Publication Data appear

on the last printed page of this book.

This book was originally published in Italian as *Umanesimo*

e secolarizzazione da Petrarca a Valla

(Rome: Bulzoni, 1990).

Contents

─○○○○─

Acknowledgments

It is usual for the authors to acknowledge the debts incurred in the course of their work according to criteria that may be likened to a musical *crescendo:* beginning from the lesser and ascending to the most close acquaintances, from colleagues and friends to the most distinguished representatives of the academic world. This time, on the occasion of this English edition of my book *Umanesimo e secolarizzazione,* I would like to invert this customary order. At the very roots of the project there is one person in particular. For many years duration, for the sensitive understanding of my historical researches, for the never-failing attention—in short, for his true friendship—I must remember here first and foremost Ronald G. Witt. Thank you, Ron!

The work of translation has been long and laborious. Emily O'Brien, very young at the time, was the first to take it on; her contribution was later revised by a professional translator, Martha King. As far as I can judge, the text resulting from this cooperation seems to me duly homogeneous, and reading over again my old writings in their new English dress, I would no longer be able to distinguish Emily's youth and enthusiasm from Martha's experience. If shortcomings or obscurities still remain, the reader will not be wrong in attributing them to the writer and to his poor knowledge of English.

As far as the translation is concerned, the first chapter, "Consciousness of the Latin Language among Humanists," is an exception to the remaining parts of the volume. Since Emily was then engaged in her own scholarly work, the translation was undertaken by Gloria Ramakus. Unfortunately, a short time thereafter, Gloria fell ill and died, and the revision of the text was carried out by Amanda George and the writer. It may be the right occasion to remember here this courageous woman, so well known and admired by all participants of the I Tatti community, both for her generous, if sometimes provocative, political passion and, above all, for her undertaking legal studies later in life. She became a lawyer in New York in order to protect the rights of the more disadvantaged members of society.

Lastly, the numerous adaptations of the writing for editorial preparation of this volume have necessitated the recourse to various computer applications and thus to the assistance of the younger generation. I do not know how I would have managed without the help—sometimes impatient, sometimes compassionate—of my sons. I wish particularly to thank Renzo and Andrea (since Federico no longer resides in Florence). To them, together with Maria, go my most affectionate thoughts.

This is surely not the place to speak of my intellectual and academic debts. These are implicit in the Introduction and in the essays themselves that make up the book. Just one aspect, but an essential one, must be mentioned here. I maintain that Ron has been particularly supportive of me, because we are both descendants, even if by different paths, from the lesson of the intellectual movement that old German scholars defined as "Historismus." To say how much of this concept is outdated now is clearly beyond my scope. Yet the insistent and sometimes ungenerous criticism of one of the last exponents of that school, Hans Baron, is an unmistakable sign of how vexed the problem still remains. The thought with which I would like to conclude these preliminary lines is much more simple and essential. The scholarly tradition from which my Renaissance studies derive (here I testify for myself only) is concerned with content rather than form, with ideas rather than erudition, with moral issues rather than literary virtuosity. I do not know how many people will agree with me on this point. I suspect that all together we would have difficulty in winning a presidential election, albeit a presidential election at the RSA only. Let these humanistic essays, in their more diffusive English edition, be dedicated to all people who will share with me such an honorable minority.

Humanism and Secularization

Introduction

The essays collected in this volume are the products of various occasions and are also widely separated in time. Consequently they cannot be considered by the standards of unified discourse; and yet I would venture to claim they all share a single theme.

Such a unity is notable in the title, especially in its boundaries and chronological parameter, "from Petrarch to Valla." It is also important to clarify from the beginning that I do not use the term "humanism" in a generic and indeterminate sense, and still less according to a standard definition that presumes one version more "authentic" than another. The studies here are of a historical nature and therefore incompatible with standardized and unhistorical paradigms, however valuable and useful they may be. In other words, if these studies are not systematic, and if they follow partial points of view wherever they lead, they are nevertheless arranged according to a specific perspective that culminates in Valla and finds its necessary antecedents first in the work of Petrarch and then in the elaborations of his legacy by Florentine humanists (primarily Leonardo Bruni and Poggio Bracciolini), and to some extent by humanists in Venice and especially in Lombardy, such as Pier Candido Decembrio and Cosma Raimondi, to whom I pay some attention.[1] My primary aim is to identify an ideological movement that develops out of Petrarch's work and that is given its most precise and structured configuration by the aforementioned authors of the first half of the fifteenth century.

To speak of defining an ideological movement naturally implies proposing a method suitable to the task. The links between humanist texts and their sources are not always evident at first sight. According to traditional scholarship, it would seem that each text has a story of its own, and that, on account of this, the modern exegete ought to limit him- or herself to an investigation of what I shall call the vertical ties connecting a given text to its classical sources. The underlying assumption of this approach is that it is important to ascertain the level of knowledge of the "ancient" and the capacity to reproduce it. No less meaningful and important, however, are what I call the horizontal ties linking contemporary texts or those of the same general historical period. An analysis of these relationships is more difficult, and not only because of the dearth of lexicons and in some cases even of edited texts. A reference of this kind was almost always left implicit, being signaled to the sensitive reader by the allusion to, or literal citation of, certain expressions and characteristic connections; it can be conducted on the model of a common citation of an ancient author, or on an original expression; it can signify agreement as much as an elaboration (even radical) of some propositions, or even a disagreement and a reversal of thesis. In essence, it is a fabric of cultural and ideological relations that can be reconstructed by textual comparison more effectively than with epistolary or other kinds of documentation, if they exist. Such a methodology should at the very least make it possible to map the most fundamental features of an intellectual movement, and thereby transcend mere static paradigms and the search for general principles.

For a single example, only once in Poggio Bracciolini's letters is the work of Petrarch mentioned, according to the index in Harth's edition. And yet, checking from his letters two other explicit occurrences of his name, we learn that Poggio had carefully acquired Petrarch's opera, and that he saw in him a model of the self-taught man. Therefore, Petrarch was quite present in the background of Poggio's work, and a comparison of Poggio's writings with Petrarch's comments provides us with an essential criterion of interpretation, not only of Poggio, but also of his contemporaries who will be discussed here. Like Poggio, they too, for their good reasons, were accustomed to using Petrarch's name only infrequently and reluctantly.

Such insistence on Petrarch's influence also requires the explanation of an important term in the title of this collection, that is, the concept of "secularization." This term is not intended to denote any kind of an all-embracing *Weltanschauung*. Still less is it to be understood as the opposite of "religiousness," even though in the sphere of secularized culture religious devotion seems weakened and at times even absent. This investigation is not concerned with religious sentiments (or even with those irreligious), but rather with indirect cultural aspects. The opposite of "secularization," as it is defined here, would be "prescriptive," to be understood in the sense of a culture that obeys canons established by the common agreement of ecclesiastical, ethical, and educational institutions. Petrarch's great accomplishment was to point the way (in the words of Leonardo Bruni, a good witness, "he opened the path") for a new culture that could break out of the authoritative and publicly sanctioned structures of late scholasticism, that is, of a culture especially intent on the systemization, or itemization, of inherited knowledge and age-old norms. Viewed in this light, Petrarch's famous and highly personalized catalogue of "my own favorite books" reveals its amazing potential of opposition and provocation.

Chapter 2 treats this theme in detail. While it is a tentative experiment in methodology, the chapter can be considered both the centerpiece of this collection and the essential path for essays that follow, for illustrating and verifying analytically the approach I propose in this essay. It is this trail that links Petrarch's discussion on the Church Fathers with his scornful condemnation of Valerius Maximus and, with that condemnation, of the contemporary technique of the *exemplum* and current styles of preaching (the same that Poggio pursued in his polemic against San Bernardino); but also, more generally, his scorn of the modules of ancient ethical stereotypes, on which Valla would later exercise his radical criticism.

The real dilemma was not so much the opposition of an ancient abstract paradigm and a Christian one but rather the manner of confronting authority *tout court*. It finds its clearest expression in Valla's *De vero bono*, in the context of the twofold and parallel debate about Cicero and Augustine alike, in which I presume to recognize the interpretive key to this controversial work.

Actually the Christian tradition (and primarily the Church Fathers), precisely because it held canonical authority, was the most direct target of the polemic. It constituted that very untrespassable barrier, according Archbishop Pizolpasso's warnings to Decembrio ("whoever assails a wall he does strike his own head himself"); while Decembrio answered opposing his own truth, which "is to be given preference over all authorities."[2] However, as we can easily understand, such polemical themes as a rule were disguised, as a tactical device to avoid indictment but also for the more intrinsic reason of an ongoing ambivalence. As a point of reference, Augustine is no less important for Petrarch than he is for Valla. Nobody could fail to acknowledge that the Augustine of the *Confessions* (as well as the *Enarratio in Psalmos*) was essential to Petrarch; but no one could claim that the character of Augustinus called upon to be Petrarch's interlocutor in the *Secretum* is the same *Augustinus magister* of the ecclesiastical tradition. The dilemma would be found again in an even more radical form in the work of Valla a century later. Here, a kind of retaliatory exchange takes place between classical philosophy and Augustine's "Christian doctrine," resulting in the elimination of the entire doctrinal and ontological system of each, according to the old controversial device by Christian apologists of *proprio mucrone confodere,* piercing someone with his own sword. Therefore, it would be more accurate to say that such an approach to Augustine (although we could go so far as to include other Christian authorities, not to mention Sacred Scripture itself) is aimed at challenging the trends of contemporary scholasticism. Only by a misinterpretation—of both the matter and its Latin expression— one would state that the *studiorum summa conformitas* that, according to a Petrarch's saying, would link him with the authoritative Augustinian friar Dionigi of Borgo San Sepolcro is to be understood as a declaration of the congeniality of studies. This way one would confuse a thing with its opposite: an individualized culture, liberated from enforced cultural institutionalism, and a typical and eminent exegete of the "great authorities" of scholasticism, such as Dionigi typically was. Once again, an even more pronounced discrepancy (and a greater confusion) would arise when Valla's interventions in theological matters were compared to, or even identified with, the official and principally Augustinian-based theology of the age.

If a clear distinction is not made between scholasticism (and the related tendency in the late Middle Ages to gather encyclopedic collections of knowledge) and the rival trends of humanism, the contrast would presumably look like one of competing disciplines within the broader ambit of a common scholarly institution. The eminent individuals who constitute the focus of the essays in this book were indeed indisputable protagonists of an influential and important intellectual movement, but it was a movement of a noninstitutional nature. The opposition Valla encountered—and ultimately failed to overcome in his attempt to introduce into a common scholarly background a substitute for the traditional scholastic method—is a good indication of how severe the break had become. This is a culture of few but distinguished initiates who coexist in various ways with a much broader institutional base rich in various evolutionary solutions and compromises, as well as with a more traditional scholasticism and other more or less related and concurrent trends of ecclesiastical and theological studies. An ancient text recovered in its entirety, like Quintilian, for example, can be well-circulated and become a general resource for the teaching of rhetoric, but not for the reading and the very personal conclusions Valla draws from it. These conclusions, therefore, should be contemplated in quite another setting, especially in those passages where Quintilian's name is cited authoritatively by Valla primarily for polemical purposes, in order to justify more boldly personal propositions.

For these very reasons, the proposal to reduce the dissension to a mere difference of opinion among disciplines and methods of teaching—authors against the arts, rhetoric against dialectic—cannot be accepted without serious reservations. Even more misleading would be to assume the polemic against scholastic Aristotelianism as the main feature of the humanist movement, to the point of furnishing its real identity. The anti-Aristotelian polemical motives from the time of Petrarch to Valla's are well-known, and this is not the place to review them. Aristotle is twisted into a symbolic representation of the most arid doctrine of the new dialecticians and is thus contrasted with the copious Ciceronian eloquence. Such is the characterization Petrarch presents in his invective *Contra eum qui maledixit Italie* and elsewhere. Valla echoes him, in typically emphatic fashion, in *De vero bono,* setting himself against the "wretched and pallid dialecticians," so that even Marcus Tullius would be too much of a "philosopher" and not enough of an "orator." Yet no anti-Aristotelian polemic can explain Petrarch's attacks on the Papal curia, on Patristic compilations, on the "labyrinth" of canonists and theologians, and on Valerius Maximus and religious preaching. Moreover, however ingenious the interpretation, no "rhetorical methodology," not even the most daring, can be linked to Valla's doctrine that "pleasure" is the sole motive for human action. The "humanists" (and I use this general term reluctantly and only for convenience) were in turn reproached by their opponents for their rhetorical facility, to be understood negatively as a lack of speculative rigor. Thus, Alonso of Burgos accused Bruni of using rhetoric to relativize the sound principles of ethics, while from a juridical and philosophical standpoint Lauro Quirini rebuked Poggio in similar fashion for relativizing the idea of "nobility," a concept certainly more profound "than could be discussed by eloquent men." Once again, however, beyond the commonplace (typified since antiquity) of an opposition between rhetoric and philosophy, there is something else: a distrust of doctrinaire principles on the one hand, and the accusation of relativizing the norms of individual and social conduct on the other. In short, Aristotle is used to personify the scholastic system, in spite of the fact that such system by far transcends him, and, moreover, its origins largely predate the rise of Aristotelianism in the thirteenth century. The anti-Aristotelian and antidialectical polemics are also a way to conceal and to legitimize the transgressive will to measure themselves, more or less boldly, against the very sources of scholasticism, the "great authors" and the Church Fathers. A historiographical investigation, therefore, should identify this hidden side, and attention to the practice of implicit reference will also be essential to the purpose.

The clearest trait of an intellectual movement that asserts itself with the insignia of its anti-traditional challenge is provided by the mutual connection of a truly Petrachan imprint of three principle components: the linguistic-exegetic concern (roughly the ground of traditional trivium), and the historiographical and moralistic concerns in their various mutual connections. Surprisingly enough, the last of these, morality, has received the least attention and will consequently enjoy a privileged position in these essays. They will briefly consider its essential formulations in Petrarch but will concentrate especially on Poggio, perhaps the most representative author on the subject, and will conclude with an investigation of Valla's radical conclusions. The piece titled "The Consciousness of the Latin Language" (chapter 1) may be considered an exception to the principal topic of this collection, inasmuch as it was written at an earlier time, differing in both occasion and priority of interests. Its conclusions, nevertheless, are directly relevant to the fundamental concept of secularization. It not only deals with a humanist consideration of language that goes so far as to affirm its independence from the normative categories of grammar and rhetoric of the scholastic tradition; also, and more importantly, this independence goes along with the rejection (especially by Valla) of the linguistic ontology of the Isidorean lexicographic tradition.

(These issues are highlighted in the *Postscriptum* discussion concerning the recent book of M. Tavoni, not published here.)[3]

As I wrote above, I have not intended to propose a paradigm of humanism in my discussion of the humanist movement from Petrarch to Valla; indeed, quite the opposite. Existing simultaneously and in competition is a patristic humanism that finds its most authoritative voice in Ambrogio Traversari, as well as a genuine expression in the letters of Francesco Pizolpasso.[4] But if only in passing, another important aspect in the developments in humanism must be hinted at here. There was a sudden interruption in continuity of the most radical issues that are the focus of this book. The principal motives can be recognized in Valla's consequential radicalism, in the subsequent inquisitorial trial of 1444, and then, on a broader scale, in the papal restoration by Nicholas V (1447–1455), who aimed at both promoting and controlling cultural initiatives. This will be seen, through the essays presented in this volume, in the tone of impotence and uneasiness that appears in Poggio's writings in old age, or, on the other hand, in the reactions provoked by Valla's *De vero bono*. For a fuller consideration of these issues, I should like to refer to my own summarizing essay of the developments of Quattrocento humanism published elsewhere.[5] Therefore it would be misleading to look upon the cultural and ideological features discussed in these essays from the perspective of the latter half of the Quattrocento and its various trends as, for example, the textual philology of Poliziano, the ethical treatises of Pontano, Paolo Cortesi's rhetorical Ciceronianism, or even Giorgio Valla's Platonizing encyclopaedism. In other words, although decisive and influential in various ways, the humanist movement represents on a whole and in its most original motives an interrupted tradition, so that the uncertainties and lacunae existing in modern historiographical interpretations have been in some way affected by its rapid development, followed by an equally sudden interruption and realignment within an orderly discipline (Italian culture of the late Quattrocento is, in fact, largely characterized, as its principle feature, by a general program of reorganizing school-teaching).

In conclusion, let me recount a personal experience. I was first introduced to the themes treated in these essays through the edition of some of Poggio's unedited writings, to be published as an appendix to the reprint of the *Opera omnia*. There I observed Poggio's way of dealing with citations from sacred and profane authors. Before the publication of the reprint, it had been almost impossible to consult Poggio's works outside of a few specialized libraries: an indication, without a doubt, of a general lack of interest as well as of critical and historiographical concern. I began with Poggio and with Poggio I should like to conclude. P. O. Kristeller, among others, has observed that every scholar, however great his adherence to objectivity, cannot help but bring with him some of his own preferences. It is not my task to judge my own objectivity; nevertheless, by concerning myself with an author surely polemical and militant, yet fighting for an ideal of independence, colloquial attitude, and tolerance, I take pride in having assumed the defense of a good, indeed, an excellent, cause.

1

Consciousness of the Latin Language
among Humanists
Did the Romans Speak Latin?

———— ⌘ ————

A typical and well-known aspect of the humanist movement is its constant attempt to connect the renewal of liberal disciplines with the subjective consciousness of such an undertaking: a consciousness represented by a new periodization of history that acknowledged the era of decadence and eclipse of liberal arts in the centuries between antiquity and the present age and finally resulted in the glorification of a cultural rebirth that manifested itself almost miraculously in the course of a few decades. Equally typical was the importance attributed to linguistic exegesis and reconstruction, which was conceived of as preliminary to the restoration of all the arts. Thus the period of decadence and cultural rebirth almost recapitulates the apparent corruption and rebirth of the Latin language and rhetoric. In other words, in addition to research by grammarians, rhetoricians, and philologists, there is a reflection, a specific way of thinking about language. This does not consist, as scholars of times past have emphasized, in the exaltation of Latin over Italian vernacular—this was a contraposition that scholars today recognize to have been overdramatized—but rather essentially in the revision and rejection of the middle-Latin traditions.[1] Such condemnation, however, if one considers it attentively, is not the same for all writers, as there were a variety of attitudes, especially concerning the more or less pronounced degree to which the break in cultural tradition was perceived; and in these, differing cultural programs are reflected.

Within this framework it seemed important to me to consider those germinal thoughts that are concerned more directly with language (meaning the consideration, even if only in a rudimentary way, of the nature and history of Latin, independent of or collateral to grammatical and rhetorical speculation, as positive historical evidence), which arise from about the third or fourth decade of the fifteenth century, during a period which scholars, at least in the past, were accustomed to regarding as the transition from "empirical" methods to "scientific" philology.

What significance such discussions had in the framework of that culture, and how these related to the contemporary renewing of the teaching of grammar and rhetoric, is the subject of this inquiry. It is my belief that this perspective is historically more appropriate than an approach that emphasizes the precursors of any given theory or of any given scientific discipline developed in the following period on the basis of different cultural assumptions, or than the monotonous search for justifying the use of the Italian vernacular. Another consideration, more general in character, sustained me in this study: I mean the significant rôle played by linguistic speculation within the complex whole of a culture, especially in the processes of renewal and reform. As a macroscopic example, let us look at the science of glottology, surely one of the most typical and original products of the Romantic age. But as more modest yet meaningful case, there are the investigations on language during the fervor of erudition in Italy at the beginning of the eighteenth century,[2] or, by contrast, the relative vacuum in this area that existed in the decadent Baroque period in Italy.

This is obviously true of fifteenth-century humanists. The texts that were taken into consideration, even though of comparatively limited importance, and even though collateral to much broader and exacting enterprises, offer one of the most typical indications of the new directions of contemporary culture. In plainer terms, they are among those writings whose very existence could not even have been conceived in the immediately preceding era, in the times of the so-called prehumanists or the first generation of humanists.

To emphasize this point it seems necessary to me to return, even if briefly, to the concepts that were basic in traditional thinking about language, so that it will be easier to follow the developments through which we arrive at the humanist perception of the decadence and rebirth of good learning and eloquence, and, with it, at the premises from which a new theme emerged as a topic of the debate.

The first humanistic debate on the nature of Latin goes back, as far as we know, to 1435, when Leonardo Bruni and the College of Apostolic Secretaries (namely, Antonio Loschi, Poggio Bracciolini, Cencio Rustici, Antonio Fiocchi, and Biondo Flavio) discussed the topic in the Papal waiting room. Two epistolary tracts, one by Biondo and a response by Bruni, followed.[3] The theme under discussion, in the words of Biondo, was "either ancient Romans were accustomed to speak with the unlearned people and rough crowd in that tongue which today we call 'mother' or 'vulgar' speech, or according to the rules of grammar, that is, in the language we now call Latin."[4] The first thesis was held by Loschi and Rustici and embraced by Bruni, while the second was defended, together with Biondo, by Poggio and Fiocchi. According to Biondo,[5] they were not dealing with an extemporaneous theme of conversation but with a question that kept presenting itself to learned men of the period, with ambivalent arguments on both sides, but still lacking a real and suitable basis in order to pose the problem, which is in fact what Biondo intended to do in his essay "On the Words of Roman speech."

This preliminary account points to a first consideration: that the dispute did not turn on providing the justification of a particular thesis (for or against the vernacular or for or against this or that kind of ideal Latin eloquence) but that the dispute itself was significant, as if it were testing the consistency of traditional concepts conventionally accepted up until that moment, such as the notion of the mother language and the grammatical one, of rough versus eloquent speech. The dispute projected these concepts into the past or better still compared them directly to the Latin texts, above all Ciceronian texts, which were becoming the prototype and model of cultural excellence.

Scholars have subscribed to Schuchardt's authoritative statement: "(In this dispute) both parties were right since both were wrong." Once it was admitted that there was a difference between learned and spoken language, in the absence of methodical criteria on which to judge linguistic matters, the disagreement could only turn on the degree of difference and on the meaning of the word "language" itself. Thus "the dispute was entirely on the names, not on the substance."[6] Now, apart from the excessive antihistorical severity of such criticism of method, it is important to emphasize how Schuchardt came to understand the common base, the common cultural background within which the debate arose, and, consequently, the impossibility of imposing a clean break between the opposing parties. But before beginning the discussion about the different levels of perceptiveness and rigor in dealing with the theme, or about the basis upon which one or the other thesis rests, it is worth emphasizing the importance of the question that then arose: How did people talk in ancient times? Herein, no doubt, lies the newness of the discussion, even though it is obvious that both terms of the problem pre-dated the raising of the problem itself. As Schuchardt keenly pointed out, the question from the beginning was not so much to formulate a theory but to place the accent on one or the other point of view present in a common cultural situation. Schematically speaking, one can say that the ambiguity came from considering language from either a grammatical perspective or a rhetorical one. Thus, on the one hand, there was the opposition between regulated and nonregulated language, natural speech, common to everybody, and speaking as we have been taught in school. On the other hand, there was the polemic, starting with Petrarch, against teaching rhetoric in the schools (actually, the *dictamen*); against an excess of sophistication, in the name of a freer and more varied eloquence that would ideally bring back the spontaneousness of everyday language.[7] Still, while the desired extension of Latin usage and education widened the separation between learned men and the uncultivated populace, this very concept suggested the opposing idea of a single language, without competitors, suitable for every occasion, no matter whether as a reality or only as a fiction.

Almost direct evidence of this ambivalence exists. Bruni's position that "among ancient Romans there was a kind of speech proper to plebes and common people, quite different from the learned one, which would be generally adopted in subsequent centuries"[8] has usually been attributed to his insistence on the medieval concept of grammar as "a series of rules established *a priori*," as a convention prepared by learned people.[9] Leaving aside such an indiscriminate idea of "medieval grammar," I only note that Bruni understands "grammar" in its etymological sense as the "art" whose object is writing, with a tendency toward assimilating it to the styles of individual authors.[10] Thus it is not a question of generic medieval legacy, but rather an example among others of the difficulties inherent in the attempt to return to ancient cultural models while living in a different age and against a different cultural background.

However, the fact remains that in its extreme formulation Bruni's thesis must have seemed a paradox right from the beginning (as is shown by the immediate reaction it provoked). Furthermore, if we understand Biondo's comment correctly,[11] it must have seemed in contrast with the opinion implicitly accepted by preceding generations: for this very reason Bruni's thesis was meant to open the discussion.

In any case, it is certain that before this time the issue was never an object of explicit interest: "I reject all those kinds of disputes according to which I heard many words and sentences said by many people against Leonardo's opinion. To tell the truth, I was by no means interested in it," as Carlo Marsuppini expressed himself later in Poggio's *Disceptatio convivialis,* in words that appear to be a real opinion instead of a dialectical device.[12] In truth, if we set out to look for immediate or distant precedents in terms of one thesis or the other, we will end up with the same uncertainty as Biondo's or Bruni's contemporaries when the discussion began.

Reference to Dante's *De vulgari eloquentia* is at this point almost unavoidable, not because it is directly pertinent to the topic at hand but rather because of the connections other scholars have established, and of the too hasty deductions they have made. To me, instead, the issue must be described in terms of an indirect relationship, rather than a direct and continuous one. In any case, we should keep in mind that in conceiving the existence of a vulgar Latin, or, one should better say, a permanent bilingualism, it is impossible for us, as far as Dante's times are concerned, to recognize something approaching a historical theory, except by means of some incidental inferences.[13] This is certainly not the place to discuss the *vexata quaestio* of Dante's linguistic ideas, and his mythical premises in the philosophy of language. It is instead important to focus clearly on the linguistic premises within which Dante moved and to which in turn his concept of Latin should be related.

Surely we cannot say that Dante was in any way lacking in historical curiosity. With accents that are still appealing to the modern reader, he showed sensitivity and consciousness of the continuing variation of languages through history; he knew how to indicate with scientific precision both large and small linguistic regions; he could recognize and distinguish groups and families of languages, and his curiosity was attracted by their common origins and different development: "Now we must dare the reason we are endowed with, when we wish to inquire about that on which there is no established authority. The question is about successive variations of a language which, at its very beginnings, was one and the same."[14]

But the process of investigation that Dante used cannot be understood in any other terms except, generally speaking, as etymological: that is, seeing what is common in diversity, explaining the past not by independent comparison of evidence but through the data supplied by the present itself. Thus, in the same way in which Dante established the kinship of German languages by the common affirmative particle *jo,* and the common foundation of the "threefold idiom" (or, *idioma tripharium*) in the similar use of the term *amor;* likewise, as far as Latin is concerned, Dante recognizes its very nature as an unnatural language, stable because of the sanction of grammatical rules, commonly understood above idiomatic differences, and he explains its origins by these very features. Inasmuch as it is a "secondary" language in respect to vernacular (or mother) languages, it originally rose in opposition to the latter, as an artificial and conventional tongue; since it was common to many peoples in the past as well as the present, it was formed and accepted by a common convention, with the further and not strictly required justification that it remedied the Babelic confusion of languages. It would be easy to infer that, differentiating at least from a genetic point of view the Latin from the "threefold idiom," Dante had to have been thinking about a particular moment in history in which poets and writers generally expressed themselves in a language that was different from the one usually spoken.[15] But this would mean attributing something extraneous to Dante's way of thinking, and hence supposing logical and historical developments in his linguistic ideas that in fact did not occur.

Within the context of the first book of the *De vulgari eloquentia,* in fact, both Latin and the "threefold idiom" are the objects of different and unconnected ways of thinking, and not even the author is concerned to connect them. In particular, the mention of Latin is only incidental to the author's aim of recognizing the existence of an illustrious Italian vernacular in opposition not to Latin, but rather to its sister languages, French and Provençal. Seen in this light, Latin, inasmuch as it was a conventional language that seemed to have come to a dead end, reappears with a new aspect, as the model to which Italian comes closest ennobling itself:[16] an assertion that is almost the introduction to the precept of book 2, that great poetry requires regulated art and language, and that therefore it must follow its models closely: "The vernacular versifiers differ from great poets who follow the rules, because the great poets write their poems according to regular language and art, while versifiers write casually, and for this reason it happens that the more we imitate them closely, the more rightly we compose our poems. Thus, if we aim at learned work we must emulate their disciplined poetry."[17]

In other words, if on the doctrinal level regularity is a specific attribute of a conventional language and is contrary to the natural fickleness of human language, then on an artistic level, which is the most important to Dante, regularity is thought to be transferable into "vulgar eloquence," and Latin, at least in its illustrious authors, from a "secondary" language becomes the model and the subject of emulation.

Thus does Latin become a part of Dante's linguistic thought not as an autonomous element endowed with its own characteristics and its own history, but as subject to its relationship with the vernacular, his own vernacular: a relationship that appears in turn as a distinction, as competition and emulation, as an ideal communion. Latin is the language of grammar, but it is also the language of writers of tragic poetry, and it is the goal of artistic elevation; it is the conventional immobile language, "perpetual and incorruptible," meant by its very nature to express the concepts of the mind. But the vernacular "by its own goodness" can do no less, and thus in a certain way becomes a substitute for Latin. It is the language intended to perpetuate both sacred and profane records, common to many people, but it was also the language peculiar to the Latin people, as Virgil demonstrated in all its power, and which Cicero defended against its detractors, supporters of Greek "grammar," just as Dante defended Italian speech, *lo parlare italico,* against those who upheld the language of Provence. In a sense, we may say that the absolute conventionality of Latin is in Dante a concept that exhausts itself in the contrast with the absolute spontaneity and fluidity of the vernacular. This assumption also works in reverse. Given the indisputable certainty of the goodness of the vernacular, once the attempt to recognize its qualities on the lips of the *terrigene mediocres,* the average countrymen, failed,[18] these qualities become pigeonholed according to the different gradations of rhetorical styles, the standard for which was no longer found in the vernacular itself but in the artistic works and in the rules of rhetoric. Therefore the requirement for the existence of the "illustrious vernacular"—that is, the highest expression of the language's very nature, and thus of the soul of whoever speaks it—should be to diverge in turn from the mother language[19] and to identify itself immediately with "tragic style." A hiatus is evident between the thesis of book 1 and the precepts of book 2 (and of the others that should have followed according to the author's intentions), or, perhaps, it would be better termed a leap of logic, which manifests the despairing attempt to "think about vernacular rhetoric within the framework of a linguistic theory,"[20] without a basis for impeding the unperceived and tautological tendency of one term to assimilate the other. But Dante's intention was clear: he meant to claim for the vernacular the dignity of dealing with noble subjects and dictating the conditions under which this should happen with all the sanction of art.

The problems that Dante tried to resolve arose independently with his contemporaries and successors. Dante's linguistic thought, within the terms in which it was expressed, led to a deadlock with no further possibility of development.

A more obvious and positive solution existed as far as the vernacular was concerned. There was a language that had been adopted by a literature whose teachings were recognized by everyone: this meant that this language, Tuscan, lent itself more than any other to the discipline of the art, so as to make known those intrinsic qualities of attraction and communicability that had long ago been assigned to Greek, and more recently to French: "The Tuscan language is more adaptable to grammatical rules than other languages, and for that reason is more common and understandable."[21]

Latin, faced with a reality that expected to be disciplined by art and grammar, appeared only as the mere cultural baggage that was required in order to become a good rhymer.

In this way the identification of the language with the product of a given people and place was strengthened. It is significant that Antonio da Tempo, when dealing with vernacular poetry, emphasizes his preference, even though still not exclusive, for the Tuscan language as language, prior to the consideration of any stylistic refinements: "At the end of this work one may ask oneself why we use words from the Tuscan more than from other dialects in our rhymed poetry. Our response is quick: because Tuscan (. . .). But we do not deny for this reason that we can also adopt other languages, or dialects, or ways of speech."

Thus, especially after the end of the fourteenth century, it became commonplace among Florentines to praise their own language, "the sweetest mother idiom" (*dolcissimo edioma materno*), "the rich and polished Florentine idiom" (*l'edioma fiorentino sì rilimato e copioso*). The quality of Tuscan (also with respect to its capacity for expressing difficult concepts)[22] was exemplified in the work of Dante, Petrarch, and Boccaccio—the so-called Three Florentine Crowns—which, while unparalleled, at the same time acted as to sanction, and witness for, the language itself. In short it was a sort of discovery, confirmed by authoritative testimony and supported by the sentiment of municipal pride, of the possibilities inherent in the nature of one's own language, enabling it to receive all kinds of learning, with no need of further justification.

However, it is obvious that we are dealing here with a narrow perspective: a codification of one type of vernacular literature, the pride in one's own country and its traditions. Latin, quite independently of the systematics of Dante's thought, is still the language of grammar, and above all it is the language of heroic meter and ornate style. Thus Latin and vernacular were still distinct at essentially two levels of style, two successive degrees of rhetorical refinement, corresponding to the traditionally different relationship and dignity of speakers and their publics (language of clerics and language of laymen; of noblemen and scholars or artisans; of men or women; language of the mature, language of youth).

Yet, as we see from Boccaccio's rationale for justifying the adoption of the vernacular in the *Divina commedia*,[23] such a sharp distinction proved to be unstable. On the one hand Boccaccio, in order to purge Dante of the suspicion of ignorance, introduced the legend of an early conception of his poem in Latin and admitted that "there is much more art and gravity in speaking Latin than in the mother tongue";[24] while on the other, he compares Dante to Homer and Virgil ("which—i.e. vernacular poetry— he was in my opinion the first among Italians to exalt and hold in high esteem, like Homer among the Greeks and Virgil among the Latins")[25] and recognizes elsewhere the achievement of the most profound poetic meanings through rhetorical artifice, independent of any linguistic guise (or *cortex*, the bark).[26] Beyond the dissension as to the usage of Latin or vernacular, Boccaccio was not as interested in linguistic matters as he was in the process of elevation of the literary discourse through art, through the willing commitment to conform to the dignity of the argument and of the interlocutor; and finally through the exemplary discipline to which the ancients subjected themselves in order to reach the end: precisely their own "diligence,"[27] which now so humbled modern men and intimidated Boccaccio himself at the mere mention of Cicero.[28] Thus there were two species of human language: the natural one, common to all, and often "rudimentary and strange" (*rudis et exotica*), and the language refined by art, "adorned, florid, regulated by strict rules, which only a few expert and willing men are able to achieve."[29] This last kind of expression was that required for social convenience, and, in its highest form, for prayer to God,[30] and whenever it was necessary to keep passions of the soul under control or to make use of it as an instrument of persuasion. But at this point a new reason for perplexity, according to Boccaccio, comes to the fore: once a language has been elevated to the summit, will the author still find public response? Was the humble style really devoid of any power? "To deny that an eloquence constructed with Ciceronian tools is more efficacious than uncultivated speech, is quite stupid. But uncultivated speech may sometimes have some effect."[31]

This is one of the arguments used by Boccaccio to justify Dante,[32] but it is also illustrated in the speech by Menenius Agrippa to the Roman people to convince them to come down from the mountain, "having moved them because of the truthfulness of the speaker more than with his eloquence."[33] This passage is worth noting because it shows clearly the continual uncertainty of the writer between the rhetorical level in a technical sense (the "attenuated" figure, according to the *Rhetorica ad Herennium* 4.7.11, is that "quae demissa est usque ad usitatissimum puri sermonis consuetudinem," in other words, which express the small things in everyday language), and the linguistic level; between the two "kinds of human speech" (*species humane locutionis*) and the figures of rhetorical elaboration (*oratoria elocutio*), and where in short the concepts of classical rhetoric, so to speak, are borrowed in order to weigh the merits and respective functions of Latin and the vernacular in the contemporary historical situation.

The image of solitude and antique ruins—where an ambitious eloquence "is apt more to terrify than to warn the people" (*non monitos sed attonitos facit*)—of the fickleness of human destiny (it is Fortune who addresses the author), takes us back to Petrarch and to his concept of the separation of the two eras, of that "immense people" which, in the poet's evocation, seem to rise once more from the ruins toward a new and independent life.

We should ask ouselves to what degree such a new sensitivity modifies the terms of the language question. Scholars have often insisted on Petrarch's contempt for the vernacular, so as to place the *Rime* out of range of justification,[34] and on his exclusive idolizing of Latin. But Petrarch's attitude in reality was more subtle than it might appear. Because of his very emphasis on the contrast between the educated and the uneducated, in the end the linguistic question was deliberately avoided and reduced to terms of subjective experience. The dignity of language is understood by Petrarch as an index of the nobility of the soul ("the one depends on the other"), sharing its own feelings, impatient of grammatical bonds and of fixed models. The three rhetorical gradations in style, moreover, will only have a relative value, aside from any abstract rule. Thus the Latin language reacquired its living mobility, even if only in relation to subjective experience, disregarding historical reality.

And the vernacular? There is an interesting passage in which Petrarch legitimizes vernacular lyric through the discovery of its very roots in antiquity: "This kind of poetry, which by fame was born not many centuries ago and reborn among the Sicilians, in a short time was extended throughout Italy and beyond: this same kind of poetry was in the past cultivated among the most ancient Greeks and Latins. In fact we learn that the Attic Greeks and the Romans usually employed only rhymed poetry."[35]

But, as a more general rule, the very reason for Petrarch's refusal of vulgar speech does not depend on its inherent lack of artistic capacity but simply on its belonging to the *volgo*. In other words, it depends on the fear of trusting his own fame to a literary tradition that was still unstable and devoid of a regulating discipline. These are indeed not in themselves original concepts, but in this way Petrarch could eschew any doctrinal strictness and express his mind through a kind of autobiographical myth.[36]

As noted above, the dignity of language was for Petrarch the sign of a "free" (*ingenua*) condition of the soul, which one can find among the ancients, while contemporary life in all its poverty seems to impose an unsurmountable hindrance to it. Therefore, while deploring the loss of so much antiquity, Petrarch understands the corruption of institutions, mainly the linguistic ones, only as a part of a more general failing of customs and noble moral intentions,[37] hence unworthy of any particular attention in and for itself. There is a passage of Petrarch's that, on the contrary, would seem to hint at the vulgar as playing a historical and objective part in this corruption. It identifies three gradations of the dignity of speech, of which the present age just manages to achieve the humblest, and rarely rises above it: "That which is below does not consist of any degree of noble speech but rather it is a diffusion of words deserving of plebians and peasants and slaves. And although it took root through usage over a thousand years, nevertheless over time it will never reach the dignity which it does not possess by nature."[38]

But the occasion of this comment was the author's refusal to accept the nomination as Apostolic Secretary and adapt himself to the chancery's style ("this one, which people call a style, is not really a style at all").[39] Thus, in the meaning of this "speech worthy of peasants and slaves" (*agrestis et servilis effusio*), Petrarch includes both current speech and a mode of writing that relies on preestablished rules of style and is aimed at a practical (and therefore *servilis*) end. Likewise his insistence on the coarseness of popular speech is in the end no more than a pretext to include in this very notion the culture of contemporary schools and law courts: a culture no less "vulgar" than the former, sharing with it the same ignorance and contempt of the illustrious collections of antiquity.[40]

To the Latin commonwealth of noble spirits, Petrarch opposes the "vulgar speech" of "uneducated people." But what discriminating criteria does he suggest? What instruments should we employ in mastering the language? All this he kept implicit. What counted was results, and all the work involved in preparation remains hidden from the reader. Grammar was the affair of students ("what is more ridiculous than an old man intent on these matters?"),[41] against which Cicero and Virgil, "the fathers of Roman eloquence," argued in their own time; language was by its very nature fickle,[42] and imitation consists in free choice from different models.[43]

It was Salutati who was to spend an entire life breaking through this Petrarchan silence. To the same degree that Petrarch had reduced the linguistic question to the terms of subjective experience, Salutati was trying to formulate the facts of the situation objectively. In the guise of a rigid antinomy, on one side we have the example, unchangeable and unattainable, of antiquity: "unsurpassed antiquity maintains its position, and remains fixed on the battlefield with its banners";[44] and, on the other, we see modern usage, "which has no substance, but which moves easily from its roots, uncertain and variable, quite inconsistent, so that it cannot and must not be compared to the constancy of antiquity and to its linguistic usage, nay to reason."[45]

But what is the explanation for such distance? Salutati does not conceal his own perplexity in answering: "thus, because of the weakness of human nature, or because of the difficulty of learning, or because labor bore no fruit, or because—as I am more inclined to believe—greed turned human souls away, in our times the study of eloquence is too neglected, and by now kings and princes do not write in Latin, but in French or in other vernacular languages. I do not dispute that this kind of speech may also be supported by some kind of art, but I am angry that there is an opinion that it is less laborious to follow the uncultivated mother language than scholarly discipline."[46]

What had been lost was the ancient "truth and consistence of the discourse,"[47] the majesty of eloquence that has its roots in the rational soul of man: whether we are dealing with "modern sloppiness" or with the "cadenced sonority of friars' preaching"[48] in the construction of speech, or with "absurd" habits, such as chanceries' usage of the plural form of the second person, *vos* (instead of the singular form, "thou," *tu*), which is the same in French, and seems to Salutati almost a final attempt to extinguish Latinity.[49]

It seems now that Salutati's concern was to discover linguistic truth, and hence a rhetorical opportunity, the measure of which would be the light of reason itself: "On this subject, one thing is what men do, and quite another is what men believe they should do. But take your mind off your senses; or rather, to say it in a better way, take off the custom you learned through your senses; bring your thoughts back, or rather run with your soul to those times in which no nation, no men, when dealing with a single subject, used anything but the singular form."[50]

Thus, in a more general way but in the end still in the same abstract perspective, it seems that ancients have exhausted any possibility for perfection, so that we are incited to study them, rather than moved by a futile ambition to emulate them: this, by the way, was the actual direction of Salutati's cultural programs.[51]

But beneath this recognition there was a fatalistic vision of an overall process of decadence. This was represented not by an immediate contrast, in black and white, the purity of the past compared to the corruption of the present, but in the guise of a continuous line, even through alternating phases, of a progressive, almost necessary degradation from the ideal of eloquence as represented by Cicero and the times in which he lived. This process, overlooked at its very beginning, had become more and more evident and extensive, so as to make the increasingly circumscribed and rare exceptions stand out, placed on undeserved pedestals by unaware contemporaries: "Surely in ancient times literary studies of every kind reached such a high level of eloquence that posterity even though it made an effort to imitate, and even though it did so zealously, could not preserve such majesty and such a height of eloquence. There were a few over time who seemed to emerge above their contemporaries, in a way they were considered by inexpert people to have reached such excellence."[52]

Thus our deploring of the indolent and uneducated times in which we live becomes a calmer reflection on an overall historical trend, independent of the intellect or the will of individuals, where the predetermined goal of reaching an ideal of eloquence is at the same time the standard for measuring the ever greater distance that has come to interfere with it, as well as the increasing difficulty that is created in reapproaching it. The task indicated by Salutati was, therefore, while concentrating one's own research on ancient models, to measure at the same time one's own capacity in respect to them, without ignoring the evidence of centuries of tradition—of which Salutati claimed to be part and heir—of alternate yet inadequate attempts, so that one could redirect one's endeavors according to the results of such consciousness.

Beyond the profession of modesty at the conclusion of Salutati's reasoning (*ego michi non placeo,* "I do not like myself"), we recognize a precious acknowledgment of an inability to embrace in a comprehensive way the multiple elements that make up the *facultas dicendi,* "the faculty of eloquent speaking," which at first glance seemed to rest on rigid and rational premises. General assumptions such as the paradigmatic and unchangeable character of the models, or the absolute superiority of the ancients over the moderns, appear nonetheless disproportionate in respect to the particular motives of Salutati's linguistic discussion.[53] Actually such general assumptions reveal their own precarious nature and derive no justification from his fragmentary linguistic observations, from his uncertain historical orientation, and from his difficulty in establishing a precise relationship between the form and content of eloquence, between art and rules and the undeniable arbitrariness of individual choices. Here too— and it is no novelty—the linguistic consideration tends to resolve itself into the rhetorical one (according to which, as we have seen, decadence cannot take any form but that of a history of rhetorical approximations); but he acquires a more acute awareness of the difficulty, so that Salutati is induced to cover the path in the reverse direction and move, not from language to art, but inversely, from a rhetorical ideal to the more humble and episodic observations of the elements that constitute speech, apart from any immediate prospect of strengthening the circle.

It is interesting that, contrary to the common opinion of the times, Salutati asserted that prose had priority over poetry in eloquence, because, being freer and much more complex, it was more difficult and thus wide open to a more ample range of observations:[54] "The ornaments of speech which some believe to be a matter of rhetoric alone have many other implications, and are the result of innumerable observations."[55]

Thus, implicitly, we are presented with the problem of the validity of grammatical instruments for establishing a rhetorical discipline of composition. In theory, for Salutati, grammar preserved the objective basis of *ianua scientiarum,* the door to all other sciences, within which the various elements of speech found rules and reason.[56] But in particular applications, such as in questions of orthography, to which he frequently returned, Salutati could not hide the fact that, in his own need for discipline, he was working on empirical ground. Etymology, which should furnish the first step ("everyone may write as he prefers, as long as he have the right notion of the origins"),[57] reveals itself, as was suggested by his lexical sources (Hugutio, Papia, Balbi, etc.), to be no less uncertain than variations in handwriting, leaving a broad arbitrary margin for various hypotheses and separating etymological considerations from orthographic-grammatical ones.[58] Therefore, except for the cases where analogic or euphonic reasons are given, the final word is that of *usus,* the usage, that is to say, to the indiscriminate tradition of the erudite: "So will the custom of all age, and with it the usage of learned men: that usage through which arbitrariness we obtain the rules and the law of speech."[59]

Analogous to the interpretation and the choice of words and the determination of their own "meaning" (or *significatio*), Salutati prescribed keeping equally to etymological propriety and to the "usurpation" of custom: "We must keep in mind propriety according to the origins . . . and (at the same time) we must not for any reason ignore the appropriation that is generated by usage."[60]

Such insistence on the grammatical category of custom (or of "usage," we do not distinguish here) is significant first of all as an index of a reluctance to let go of form and meaning as established by tradition, as well as of all that is familiar to the present age.[61] In conclusion, Salutati, having taken classical models as his objective and realizing the distance that separated them, as well as the enormous job that still remained in the purifying of style, in practice stopped halfway down the road and finished by reclaiming modern-day rights and customs. A salient reason for this was Salutati's great admiration for Petrarch and the need he felt to defend and exalt him when compared to the ancients, from whom he undeniably differed. In this light the general contrast between the fixed ways of the ancients and the uncertain variability of the modern disappeared, or at least became more tenuous, and a different perspective began to take form, modifying and in a way contradicting the previous view. In other words, we are talking about justifying in some manner that fickleness that seemed to signal the inferiority of modern men.[62] Eloquence is thus an exceptional conquest, much more arduous and rarer even than wisdom itself, to which it is inseparably connected: but precisely for this reason it is the work of privileged individuals,[63] as unattainable in their own times as in the present; and since eloquence cannot be conceived without wisdom, the one must adapt itself to changes in the other, becoming part of its relativity, constantly superseding former eras through the work of those that follow.[64] How finally may we compare pagan wisdom with Christian, where the dignity of the subject makes up for the eventual failure in style, which in its time was cultivated and carried through to perfection in order to compensate for the uncertainty of absolute truth? The practice of eloquence also responded to civil customs that are no longer the same: but after all, what is eloquence if not the appropriate expression of what we know and what we have to say? "Everyone must be eloquent enough in that which he knows, unless he is quite foolish and ignorant."[65]

Thus the comparison between the two eras, even from the point of view of rhetoric, ends up as idle talk: "Whatever is well spoken, even though it is spoken variously, is eloquent anyway."[66] Cicero pointed to an orator's vice *a vulgari genere orationis atque a consuetudine communis sensus abhorrere;* "to take his distance from the common way and custom of speech," and the Latin writers themselves perfected their art by innovating respect for that which was for them the tradition of antiquity.

It should be noted here that Salutati is now going beyond linguistic boundaries proper; for example, he did not claim any place for the vernacular as an innovative language in respect to Latin: if anything, he claimed dignity for vernacular composition in itself (such as Dante and Petrarch, but also he used religious eloquence as an example). More generally speaking, the stress was on freeing, so to speak, such terms as *mutatio,* the change, or *consuetudo,* the custom, from the negative connotations of decadence and arbitrariness, in an effort to recognize and determine that degree of autonomy which, on the whole, modern cultural works are able to claim in comparison with the ancient. However, the claim that modern writings "outdo antiquity, or at least savor of it" is not only impossible to attain but not even legitimate, so that it is impossible to accept the principle of imitation unconditionally: "I have always believed I must imitate antiquity not simply to reproduce it, but in order to produce something new . . . but it is one thing to reproduce and another to imitate."[67] The language used by Salutati was still Latin, even if he did not follow ancient customs to the letter: "these are anyway Latin words, not so wholly distant from antiquity."[68]

These assumptions of historical relativism are meant, we should remember, as a polemical self-defense and a defense of tradition that he was aware of representing, faced with the requirement for greater classicist rigor manifested by his younger followers, in particular Bruni and Poggio. Salutati's wavering between ancient and modern usage had become, in effect, for his disciples, the matter of a clear-cut choice, according to the issue that Bruni summarizes in exemplary fashion in the very beginning of his *Dialogi ad Petrum Histrum*. Upon invitation by Coluccio to exercise the *disputatio*, the good old scholastic custom of disputing, to cultivate as much of the cultural Latin legacy as had somehow survived, Niccoli instead stresses polemically how much had been lost, how every liberal art had deteriorated, almost to the point that its original and authentic features were no longer recognizable, so as to lead, "in so great a disaster of all disciplines," to a disdainful reticence.[69]

In other words, we can recognize the decisive turning point that occurs through the awakening of a clear perception that the loss of ancient works represented a qualitative, not a quantitative factor, and that a restoration, not a correction must take place, by isolating sources of ancient culture from the subsequent traditions.

In such perspective the evaluation of great modern literary works is far less important than the silence that programmatically (and polemically) is maintained on the cultural world surrounding them. The recognition of language as an instrument in relation to a particular subject matter becomes the acknowledgment of the language itself as the main vehicle of culture, which in antiquity found expression in all the liberal arts, while nowadays it is reduced almost to the point of complete extinction. The question, therefore, is no longer to ask ourselves what use the ancients made of language—in a constant more or less mortifying comparison with modern usage—what the secret of such eloquence was, but rather to inquire as to the quality of ancient language itself, of the eloquence that antiquity expressed through that usage. To abolish the term of comparison of modernity would be to open the field to generalization, and with that, to plain and simplified solutions, cutting out traditional issues and grammatical or rhetorical subdivisions, without much need to modify substantially the terms.

Especially characteristic, following the contempt inherited from Petrarch for grammatical studies, is the emphasis on "usage" as a general principle of linguistic choice. But which usage, what are the criteria of choice and discrimination? "Because linguistic liberty, rules, or conventions are established by usage, whoever can testify to that usage more effectively than most learned and expert men, those who have been recognized for their eloquence? The corrupt usage by unlearned people must not be called usage, but abuse. If we cannot find another reason to explain certain words, then we must consider the usage by excellent men as reason."[70] The error (in this case the confusion between *fastidire*—"to get annoyed"—and *fastidium parere*—"to cause annoyance") comes from not being able "to take the mind away from the vulgar custom of speech."[71]

Reducing grammar to exemplification of language was correlated to the need for a precise individualization in styles, and the issue led to the tendency to absorb different notions, such as grammar and rhetoric, usage and linguistic choice, in the actual context of individual writers. On the other hand, elaboration by illustrious Latin authors could not be invoked by using the criteria of good linguistic usage, unless it was agreed to consider them not only for their individual excellence but as a sign of the excellence of an era, therefore emphasizing the historical notion of corruption.

This does not mean, even though the lines of demarcation were clear-cut, that in Bruni's thought there did not remain some vagueness between a historical-institutional vision of the linguistic process and an individual and particularistic concern, as a residual of the uncertainty of perspective pointed out in Salutati,[72] excepting the fact that by greatly simplifying the terms themselves, he intended not only to announce the fact but to define it and give it an explanation, laying the problem bare against its historical background.

In this regard we may recall Bruni's well-known concept of the rise and fall of the Latin language as it was tied to the outcome of republican freedom, whose incitement was able to predispose skilled men to the liberal arts. This doctrine interests us here especially in regard to the well-defined image of an era of perfection of the Latin language, considered, if not within its autonomous institutional reality, at least in strict relationship to determined institutions and civic customs.[73] But precisely because the process of perfecting Latin has been generalized in the broadest vision of an era of particular stimulus and growth of creations by gifted writers, Bruni must have perceived, as far as language was directly concerned, the existence of a customary language below the "usage" of the educated people: thus the problem was now to define in some way such a different dimension of spoken language.[74] Hence comes the statement, somehow summary and indeterminate, of the existence of a bilingualism in the most classical era of Latin: a statement that is introduced beyond any concern for the structural or genetic character of language, as a simple enunciation of a fact. Bruni supports his thesis through a twofold kind of reasoning: first paying attention to and gathering documentation of the existence of expressions or single words that in some way attested to a double usage;[75] and second, much simpler, relying on the analogy with the present age, on relationships between learned and unlearned men, on language endowed with grammatical inflection that could be acquired through scholastic discipline and current usage of the mother language (whose own value, by the way, could be independently recognized). It would seem paradoxical that at the very moment of the most vivacious polemic against grammatical systems, Bruni emphasized precisely grammatical rules in order to set the boundaries between the spoken language and that of erudite men. However, rather than from an abstract doctrinal apriorism, the problem came from an empiric attitude, a sign of sharpened historic-linguistic perceptiveness. Thus, on the one hand, grammar became no more than a means for purifying Latin expression, making it impermeable to the infiltrations of the underlying vernacular (and in this regard vernacular reappears as a parallel kind of language); and, on the other hand, grammar was reduced without any further explanation to the linguistic context of the writers, a function of the expressive values of a language polished by genius, that is, a cultural fact rather than a technique in the strict sense of the word.[76] Thus, the definition of grammar was not so much at the center of the question raised by Bruni: it was really the objective difficulty in understanding the Latin language as an organic whole, at a moment in which the support of Scholastic doctrine had failed, revealing its inadequacy to grasp the inner meaning of the language itself and establish a direct relation with the authors.

———∞∞∞———

In taking up the discussion with Bruni, Biondo immediately placed himself on a different plane with respect to his interlocutor. He was not a militant Latin writer ("I recognize that I lack such skill for eloquence"); he did not aim at eloquence, but rather at objectivity in determining facts, that is to say, establishing "that ancient people actually maintained the usage of Roman speech" (*quo Romanae facundiae . . . servatum a priscis usum ostendi oporteat*). Thus the language passed from a subject to the object of observation, and for the first time the institutional aspect was at the very heart of the question, along with rhetorical or philological concerns. The originality of Biondo's treatment is to be found precisely in the constancy with which he held fast to this perspective and in his consciousness of method with respect to the theory he proposed. Further along in the text he affirms: "I would like you to keep in mind that I organized my discussion in regard to words and not rhetoric, speech and not literary composition, the cortex and not the marrow of the art."[77]

We can well understand the difficulty in which the author found himself here in his commitment to effect a comprehensive vision, over and above the partialities of the debate. Since the time of antiquity, the term *latinitas* was meant as a rhetorical ideal attainable through stylistic elevation of language and the screen of grammatical art; faced in modern times with the existence of vernacular speech, it became a proper synonym for grammatical discipline (hence *loqui grammatice* meant precisely "speak Latin"). In what measure then was it possible to ignore this rhetorical meaning of "latinity" in determining an institutional dimension? How could one avoid, in reasoning about language, differences in tone and levels according to current use being identified with the customary grammatical and rhetorical notions on which linguistic thought was traditionally based?

Rather than tackle the problem directly, Biondo avoided it and held fast to traditional conceptual schemes on the one hand,[78] while on the other, avoiding any commitment to general statements, he reasoned on the basis of the only historical evidence. First of all, Biondo had to clear up the conception of "vernacular speech," whose existence alongside Latin had been asserted in the dispute to be the somehow indeterminate qualification of *vulgare quoddam,* a certain kind of vulgar speech. We cannot of course expect here an open statement of its complete autonomy, like any other language, with respect to Latin. Biondo's definition is a negative one (*omni latinitate carens,* a speech wanting in any kind of latinity), even though in subsequent references vernacular speech shows itself in a more neutral way, as the customary kind of speaking typical of modern times ("this kind of vulgar speech of our times, whose excellence I recognize among Florentines");[79] further, its close affinity to Latin cannot be negated ("the very great kinship and similarity of the vulgar and Latin tongues").[80]

Beyond these variations, the reasoning on which Biondo first relied was the awareness of a disparity which, though present in the minds of modern men, did not exist among the ancients:

> No one should have any doubt that if it had been spoken in another language, which I admit you may call "vulgar," what later has been rendered in this Latin prose according to the requirements of the oratorical art, M. Cicero, Quintilian, Q. Asconius Pedianus, and many others who were so scrupulous in referring every slightest detail about orators, would allude in some way to this diversity of language. This precisely happened in our own and in our fathers' time, when, after reducing the "Comedy" of the Florentine Dante, or the beautiful tales of Boccaccio according to the strict rules of grammar, we affirm that they were translated into Latin.[81]

Thus the vernacular, whether or not intended as a derogatory term, whether meant to be subordinate or parallel to the grammatical language or preserving its relationship to Latin, represented first of all a reality different from Latin, for the simple tautological reason that it called itself "vulgar" and not Latin.

Biondo uses an analogous procedure to formulate and develop the central question. Taken as given the existence of a Latin language common to all, in which "a few learned men have been greatly superior over the multitude of the unlearned," how would it be possible to determine the degree of difference (*in quo quantumque differentes fuerint*)? The source is Cicero of the *Brutus* and the *Orator,* and his discussions about the making of a good orator and on the legitimacy of the criteria for "anomaly" and "analogy." This is where testimony to tonal variety was underlined—tones more or less refined, more or less elaborated—in which Latin found its expression in the Roman oratorical tradition. Here also was the appreciation of orators who used correct language by instinct rather than because of any literary education; or the praise of a good domestic education for the purity of diction.[82] But what escaped Biondo (or possibly did not interest him here) is what has been defined as the very heart of Ciceronian rhetorical thought: "the aspiration for a form of purism based essentially on the taste of what in linguistic patrimony is more suitable and more elevated."[83] According to Biondo, the boundaries between scholarly and nonscholarly language remain instead defined by the observance of norms that are imposed by the independent elaboration of an elite, as the results of doctrine and art:[84] "That way of speech that the Romans had in common in ancient times was improved by some men through the cultivation of good arts and letters."[85]

In this way there was a risk of returning to the concept that a clear distinction existed between the two forms of language. But precisely because Biondo keeps himself outside the linguistic process, which was marked by grammatical and stylistic elaboration, he can free himself from doctrinal rigidity and base himself once more on the facts. The orators, he suggests, customarily had to use a *medium,* that is, an "average language," not definable as such on the ground of the usual classification of the three rhetorical styles, but on the contrary in relationship to its capacity to communicate with the public, who in the common vocabulary could well have understood the speeches they heard, even though unaware of the technical devices of the art, just as it is possible for someone to understand a language without being able to speak it correctly.

Such a capacity was widely demonstrated by the popular favor surrounding orators, poets, and fiery speakers; none of them would have been accessible to the crowds who came to listen to them if nothing but the vernacular translation were available, where the intrinsic value of the art would inevitably be lost: "All that in poetry was wit, sweetness, vigor would be corrupted and finally lost in translation, just as wine turns to vinegar whenever it is decanted into an unsuitable jar."[86]

These observations are noteworthy for the perceptiveness they convey concerning the basic unity of the language throughout its history, implying the idea that an entire population, not only a narrow scholarly tradition, is the repository of literary reputation. But to return to the argument, we observe that Biondo defines the uniqueness of language not according to the formative process of scholarly rules, and revealing its foundation in the qualities inherent in the nature of the language itself; but he relates everyday language to the established rules: a language certainly less disciplined and therefore not easily qualifiable, but not so different that the capacity for comprehension and appreciation are compromised.

Thus there existed a "pure" Latin, a legacy belonging to everyone, and a "scholarly" one belonging to the select; a Latin formed by the rules of grammar ("from which I carefully kept the populace away"), and one that was more current, empirically comparable to the former but not so substantially different from the very language that modern scholars define as "literate": "My opinion is that the uncultivated populace neither learned rules nor did they know them by nature or good custom according to which they could make their speech congruent in every part with grammar; nevertheless their Latin was not so different from variations and declinations and other parts of grammar that it does not seem to us, and in effect is not, the same "literate speech" that learned men of our own time know, and only in a modest way."[87]

But such a distinction between the two domains, the strictly grammatical one and the other more generally linguistic, still seems rough, so that the inflexibility with which one appraises the first cannot but be applied in the evaluation of the second. To the system of rules set up by "grammatical language" corresponds the *latinitas perpetua,* that is to say, the continuity over time of the language spoken by Romans, different in tones but always one and the same since its very beginning as an institution proper to the Roman commonwealth. Hence the problem of corruption emerges, in a different guise from that of cultural decadence: "I wonder for whatever reason, for whatever historical event it happened that we have exchanged our vulgar speech for the common universal usage of Latin" (*qua ratione, quibus temporibus causisque factum est, ut vulgaritatem hanc nostram cum universae multitudinis latinitate . . . permutaverimus*). Thus for the first time the concept of a catastrophic outcome for Latin becomes explicit with a precise cutoff point in time, which of necessity coincided with the barbaric invasions and the fall of the Roman empire.

The thesis is formulated through generalizing and by taking literally the terms of linguistic purism. As in the time of Cicero, the Roman language had to protect itself from external influences, so with the invasions of the Goths and Vandals the contamination must have been generalized:[88] "After Rome was taken and began to be inhabited by Goths and

Vandals not only one or two men were stained, but everyone was polluted and completely corrupted, and little by little it happened that instead of Roman latinity we have this vulgar speech adulterated and mixed with barbaric speech."[89] In this way the vernacular might be defined as "adulterine" and "semi-barbarous" not only in the guise of a disparaging metaphor but because between it and Latin's eras were literally the barbarians who established the dividing landmark for the two epochs.

Biondo's tract undoubtedly marks an important moment in the history of humanistic culture. A positive relationship between language and history was established, a periodizing date was set as a guideline that excluded any kind of myth and maintained an unusually scrupulous adherence to the complex date of reality in order to differentiate past and present.

The apologetic introduction that Leon Battista Alberti added in 1437 to the already completed third book of the *Libri della famiglia* is proof of what we are saying. Alberti too is now taking sides in the dispute over spoken Latin, but with an aim of his own. Agreeing with Biondo's thesis, he intends to legitimize his own literary use of the vernacular as the modern and everyday language. His intention was not only to spread its use but to elevate it through the refined work of writers to the dignity once enjoyed by Latin.

Likewise Filelfo, asked in 1451 by Sforza Secondo for his opinion "about this language of our times, which some call 'Tuscan,' others 'vulgar,' still others define as the 'mother tongue' or 'illiterate,'" returned without any further discussion to the confutation of Bruni's thesis, that "Latin language was a spoken language, and not a grammatical one."[90]

It should be noted that Alberti (just like Filelfo in a later letter on the subject to Lorenzo de' Medici)[91] simplified Bruni's thesis by identifying the supposed ancient vernacular with the modern one (Alberti: "*sempre in Italia essere stata questa qual oggi adoperiamo lingua comune,* that the common speech we use nowadays was a language always existed in Italy; Filelfo: *eadem qua ipsi nunc utimur,* the language we nowadays use), thus being the first scholars to consider Bruni's letter—and in this consideration the scholarly tradition would follow—as an opinion on the origins of the Italian language. Actually the matter under consideration was Latin, in its dual rôle, as a language belonging to its people and as a language of culture in all its expressive vigor and in its civilizing capacity. These were not simply two points regarding the same phenomenon but two different ways of thought and two different historical perspectives, and it was difficult to establish a relationship between the two. Latin was the mother language, and the language that the ancients themselves thought needed perfecting through the *institutio oratoria,* the instructions to orators; it was the language in common use, and the language that had been able to impose itself for use; a language corrupted by external and unexpected events, and a language that declined because of the withering of its genius, now miraculously revived in its primitive eloquence.[92]

Biondo's tract, with its usual sobriety and balanced criticism, appeared somehow neutral in character, posing the question but without drawing all its conclusions. This is an aspect that surely contributed, along with obvious claims to priority, to its being apparently ignored (at least in open citations), even though it provided arguments that would be widely repeated and developed by scholars like Guarino, Poggio, Filelfo, and later F. Florido Sabino, who would deal with the theme in almost the same terms.[93] But the reference point in the continuing dispute on language was still Bruni's letter, the memory of which lives on as a dialectical moment and also as a proof of existence, even though sporadic and circumscribed, of a continuous line of followers still witnessed by Bembo's *Prose.* Evidence is also furnished by the works of Benedetto Accolti (in his *Dialogue* on the excellence of the men of his age) and Angelo Decembrio (*Politia literaria*), both written around 1460. In these writings the reference to the dispute on Latin is only incidental to the main argument, but nonetheless this very reason gives us an opportunity to understand why such an opinion was held.

Accolti's aim was to defend the "dignity" of modern times with respect to antiquity,[94] weighing the relative fame of both eras. Among the greatest reasons for the renown of antiquity, which seemed now to be so reduced, was unquestionably eloquence, insofar as it was stimulated by civic and judicial competition. But was this actually a reason for the excellence of a historical era, or rather the achievement of a few geniuses? "[A]nd this was a very reduced number, who lifting themselves far above the common herd of orators, worked hard and left the orations they had published to posterity."[95]

The orations reported by ancient historians were as closely based on reality as the orations given by Bruni's characters in his *Florentine History.* Even if in the last years of the Roman republic letters flourished particularly, "all other citizens, whenever they were giving advice on public affairs, did not in my opinion differ from our own way of speaking."[96] Thus Accolti remained faithful to Bruni's vision of eloquence as a conquest of individual genius rising above the common rule, even though he was less preoccupied than Bruni had been for more strictly linguistic reasons. From Bruni, *Vita di Dante,* Accolti draws the following remark: "To me it is not important whether one speaks Latin or the mother tongue, provided that he speaks with gravity, ornament and abundance."[97]

Decembrio's theme, instead, is "Which method and order should we use in order to refine and improve our library?";[98] and in particular what place should be assigned to vernacular works within this hierarchical order, according to higher or lower degrees of stylistic refinement. Essentially Latin was considered as a style that had attained standards above and beyond the multiplicity of spoken languages, while varying from author to author.[99] On the contrary, works written in the vernacular ("the books of Dante, Petrarch, Boccaccio and others written in Spanish or French which have been brought to our country") deserved the title of literary compositions only among the common people, a type of literature proper to the "idiots," *conterraneo tantum usu loquentes,* who were speaking only in their own vernacular: "In fact from which ancient author have we learned that he ever wrote a work in the mother tongue?"[100]

The opinion of whoever suggested the existence of a single Latin language of both learned and of common use gained no support: "if we consider the very great difference there is in style among the writers, it would follow that no school teacher or preceptor existed among the ancients, while we see that the ancients often cite their existence. Otherwise they could easily have learned it in everyday speech and among the plebeians."[101]

But beyond the question of language, it was important to Decembrio to place Latin in opposition, precisely because it was a product of art, to the complex and extended heritage of the Middle Ages,[102] tracing a clear-cut and distinguished line in the structure of the ideal library, in the guise of a tangible and somehow rigid expression of that model of an individual and free taste that had been inherited from Petrarch.[103] In the end the vernacular authors could not but be counted with whoever *a veterum more dissentiant,* who were discordant from the ancients' custom.

A different argument, advanced by both Guarino and Filelfo in integrating Biondo's confutation, is in the analogy of Latin to Greek, since

Greek is a parallel grammatical language that still existed in spoken form. For Filelfo the relationship between "language" and "grammar" (or *litera-tura*) was a question yet to be defined in general, the domains of which he insisted on maintaining separate, as distinguished by learning and lexical choices rather than degrees of grammatical correctness.[104]

For Guarino (1449) "grammar" was simply a science elaborated to protect language from barbarisms and solecisms, criteria which, he pointed out perceptively, could not in any way suit the vernacular: "and for this very reason by no means shall we call that language Latin."[105] Nonetheless Latin remained on its pedestal as a privileged language, of which the grammatical phase signaled the highest moment in an organic evolution. From this point of view it was no longer a language belonging to Latins, but the "daughter" of Greek, a definition which, although it was drawn from the *Etymologiae* of Isidore of Seville,[106] takes us back to the personal experience of Guarino himself and his conviction that the teachings of Manuel Chrysoloras were the spark that originated the miraculous rebirth of ancient eloquence.[107]

Among the other analogous tracts, Poggio's contribution (1450) stands out as a more decisive step, so to speak, in the "de-rhetoricization" of Latin. It is worth noting that the writing of the *Facetiae* was nearly contemporary, and that the author explained that its intent was to experiment "whether one can say in a suitable way many things that were considered difficult to express in Latin . . . , inasmuch as it was not possible to use any ornament or abundance of speech."[108] The rhetorical intention ("this writing exercise will be of use to the doctrine of eloquence") ended up coinciding with the need to extend the use of the language by making it manageable on different levels, while enlarging its lexical base.

The tendency to consider the language primarily from a lexical point of view followed, conceiving of it therefore as the natural product of usage by a specific people:

> I ask you what origin do you think this language that you call Latin had, that is the so-called language of grammar. I believe that this is nothing more than that which was used by the Latin peoples, and that it originated with them, and that it was used by those people who were said to be Latin, from which the language got its name . . . We must therefore hold that this language was commonly used, in the same way in which French, German, Italian are the languages

spoken by the French, German and Italian people . . . In addition Latin is made up of words with which Latin people constructed their speech . . . "Almost everyone spoke Latin in an appropriate way inasmuch as they were used to speaking that language: even if they did not want to, they could not speak any other language but Latin."[109]

Thus the modern forms of Latin that have survived, as well as providing proof of antique usage, could have served to integrate some details regarding literary knowledge of the language ("in conversations in Rome I learned many new words, of which earlier I was ignorant").[110]

Poggio's tract is composed for the most part of a long series of citations that demonstrate the uniqueness of language, while dealing more briefly with the variety of structures and styles according to the requirements of culture and art. Poggio defines "grammar" as *scientia eloquii,* the science of speech, meant to confirm and impose discipline in controversial cases ("learned men judged by reason while others arrived through usage")[111] and to fulfill the function of guardian of the properties of the language. Thus the term *loqui grammatice,* speaking according to grammar, summarized generically those qualities for which a speech by an educated person could be distinguished from everyday language, so long as there is a common base insofar as the propriety of terms was concerned: "those who spoke in a simple and uncorrupted way achieved the reward of eloquence."[112]

Filelfo rebelled against such naturalistic views and paradoxically associated Poggio and Bruni with the same error (in spite of their opposite conclusions), insisting, as we have already seen, on holding onto the distinction between language and *literatura,* the grammatical speech. But much more interesting was Valla's criticism, founded not on episodic exemplification, but on a reexamination of concepts and terms.[113]

First and foremost, Valla was the first to become aware of the fact that *latinitas,* the ideal of a pure Latin speech, meant in the ancient authors a value rhetorical in nature, a superior standard in the language determined by its highest expressions (which is precisely the subject of the *Elegantiae latinae linguae*): a term in respect to which grammatical choice represented only a preliminary moment and remained in a subordinate position:

> You see that to speak according to the true spirit of Latin (*latine loqui*) is a matter for orators and learned people, which is something more than speaking according to grammar. For this reason *latine loqui*

is placed among the virtues of rhetoric, in a way that grammar is appropriate to common speech, while latinity is appropriate to eloquent speech (*ut grammatica sit locutionis, latinitas elocutionis*).[114]

In the debate with Poggio the difference in degree of awareness was particularly evident, inasmuch as it was reflected in the exploitation of the same passage of Quintilian,[115] sufficient for Poggio to distinguish summarily between thoughtless usage and grammatical "reason," while Valla is able to give an interpretation more intrinsic to Quintilian's context. He grasps the real meaning of the latter's caution against any strictly analogical criteria and in a more general sense against every abstractly normative determination: "[Quintilian] does not base himself on reason but on example . . . There is no law of language but only observation, so that nothing else has produced analogy but custom. When I say analogy, I understand almost all that is based on reason in grammar . . . You can see how difficult it is to attribute reason to grammar, which you would prefer to be entirely constructed on reason."[116]

The relationship between the different styles of speech therefore was not seen in terms of whether they were more or less appropriate: the language was in effect posed as a given fact, *veluti in suo cuiusque civitatis numismate*—in the guise of a coin proper to every single city—explaining whose "reason" would be futile. Rather it was seen as a process of elevation within a common linguistic area: "I do not understand why you say 'in a more correct way' (*emendatius*). One could have spoken in a more ornate, sublime, eloquent way, I admit, but not in a more Latin way. Latin was common to all Romans just as today every town has its own vernacular."[117]

The perspective within which Valla placed himself may be seen as analogous to that of Bruni, in the sense of evaluating the language according to its highest elements, with respect to which spoken language is given in any case a lower status. But unlike Bruni, Valla considered the linguistic process in its own autonomous reality, and thus also as a continuity within which the problem of isolating and defining the essential moments was proposed. Therefore he refused to identify the corruption of language by the barbarians as the cutoff point between Latin and the vernacular: the language actually spoken in Rome, as well as in every latinate territory ("It does not happen any other way in all of Italy, Spain, and France which have some kinship [*cognationem*] to our language"), was still Latin, even though it was transformed, and not another language in which a trace of antiquity could still be found.[118] The upshot of this point—on the issue of the differences between the languages of orators and of the common people—is that in the discussion the reference to the present situation shifts from a mere term of reference to the term of relationship. The grammatical knowledge of language, which enables the understanding of poets and orators, in any case required study; the heart of the question, however, was that what the ancients easily attained from childhood in two years within an institutional framework, required in modern times far greater labor by mature men. In this way the question of language as it was spoken in ancient times lost relevance, and the problem shifted rather to asking why such a change took place. How is it that now we find it so difficult to acquire knowledge of Latin? How is it that the voices of "literate" speech are no longer recorded and listened to as they once were? How is it that the grammatical structure of language changed so dramatically? The example of Spain is analogous:

> I ask myself why the Spanish people, if once they spoke according to the rules of Latin [as is confirmed by plurals ending in -s: "that there is no better evidence that these people once spoke Latin"], have not preserved the declension of cases and participles, gerunds, and supines, or the use of derivation except in a few cases, or many other things prescribed by grammar. Where did the articles come from, those articles which are in use in Rome and in Italy, and in France?[119]

The question remains unanswered, of course. Valla's contradiction should especially be pointed out: after having negated, with respect to grammatical method, the legitimacy of imposing reason on the rules of language, and after having refused to find an external cause for the change, he did not limit himself to ascertaining what happened but also tried to find out why it happened.

It is a contradiction, however, that has its own roots and historical necessity and can be explained by keeping in mind the radical intention of restoration on the part of the author of the *Elegantiae*. There was more to the polemic against ancient and modern grammarians than simply the question of the opposing methods of observation and abstract normative construction. It also meant placing the "true" language in opposition to the deformed one, opposing usage not only to reason but opposing one to another more authentic reason, almost as if he were fighting his own more immediate adversary, the logicism of medieval grammarians, on their own ground. Hence an ideology proper appears and lends sense and strength to empirical research without imposing itself. The "elegances" of Latin language are not only formed by examples endowed with a particular rhetorical suitability; they are also essays of right interpretation of the intrinsic properties and capacity of the language itself. Therefore it was possible to identify this very "reason," as well as the conceptual error of whoever would deviate from it.[120]

In other words, if thought has to be brought back to linguistic usage, that usage cannot be recognized except through internal logic and its exact determinations. In this sense Vallian "usage" appears to us to be more a term of polemical reference than a spontaneous changing reality. One can therefore understand how the intuition of the vernacular as a product of an intrinsic transformation of Latin justifies itself on the one hand as a part of an organic understanding of linguistic phenomena, in which all the characteristics (morphological, syntactical, semantical) acquire precise recognition. On the other hand, however, this remains a somehow random issue on the margins of the polemical task of a linguistic restoration. Whence the perplexing question: "If we are not backwards, but equal to the ancients, how does it happen that people cannot in any way preserve, indeed achieve and imitate the sound of Latin words?"[121]

But on the whole Valla's perspective was entirely consistent. Focusing on Latin in its true form, he saw scholarly degeneration and popular transformations as nothing but two aspects of the same historical vicissitude departing from correct expression: "Certainly the language that is now used by Romans should be called Latin even though it has degenerated very much from the ancient one. We see that the same thing happens to the language of those who speak according to grammar: a language that you call "Latin" but which is so different from the ancient one that only with difficulty would Cicero, should he rise from the dead, understand."[122]

Thus we may profit from the experience of the vernacular to know Latin better, either by contrast highlighting its characteristics—in the same way in which the identification of *aliorum errata,* the errors by other writers, may be of use to "those who wish to learn Latin"—[123] or by recognizing analogically certain constants of linguistic behavior,[124] and with it the proper sense of current expressions.[125]

In this light the concept of the "gothic language" hinted at by Biondo acquires the extensive meaning of a polemical metaphor. The real "Goths" and "Vandals" were the grammarians, the rhetoricians, the commentators, who jointly worked "in order to unteach Latin . . . not teaching anything else except to speak Gothic;"[126] and sometimes the same "errors" in common speech seem to result, almost as if they were derivations of a relationship of cause and effect, from conceptual arbitrariness of scholars, as for example in the well-known confutation of Boethius about the meaning of "persona":

> I establish that such "qualities" are in God, and I say that these are "persons" who cannot but be in Him, and this means "quality," not "substance" according to Boethius, who taught us to speak barbarically. Perhaps from here people were induced to speak this way: "three persons are waiting for me," "I see two persons," "this man is a good person." Once this kind of language was unheard-of, and today no one speaks this way unless he is quite uneducated.[127]

On a different occasion (*Oratio in principio sui studii*, 1455),[128] and according to a broader historical outlook, Valla did not fail to identify the fall of the Roman empire as a fundamental reason for cultural decadence. The linguistic community, coincidentally with extension of the political commonwealth, gave the essential conditions for the increment in all disciplines by the unique opportunity it offered to skilled and learned men in Rome, and especially from the provinces, for competing with and emulating one another, in the very way in which the introduction of money as a means of exchange had opened the way to commerce and prosperity: "In fact by nature it happens that nothing can progress and increase if it is not planned, elaborated and refined by many people, above all particularly if these people rival each other and compete for praise."

With the fall of the empire, "upon which Latin language relied" (*quo lingua latina nitebatur*), as in a return to a natural economy, language necessarily divided itself into ancient particularisms, and consequently there was a decline in the arts: "Whoever wrote works of any value in grammar, dialectics, rhetoric? Which orator was born in these times worthy of the name? Which historian, poet, jurist, philosopher, theologian is comparable to any of the ancients?"[129]

The Oratio was dedicated to developing a thesis, presented by the author as unheard of: "that the very survival of these sciences was due to the Apostolic See,"[130] pointing to the Church as the principal saviour of the direct Latin tradition in Europe. We should recall here that in a famous passage of the *Elegantiae* Valla had attributed the same role of safeguard to the books of the *Digest,* notwithstanding the abridgments inflicted by Justinian's codification and the "barbarity" of the commentators: "Thus, through continuous study of the *Digest,* Latin has in some way been saved and honored, and in a short time will regain its dignity and richness."[131]

Obviously this does not mean a revaluation of the ecclesiastical Latin tradition, just in the same way as the violent rejection of the commentators' juridical learning corresponds to the exaltation of the *Digest.* But in both instances there was the important recognition by Valla of the fact that the Latin tradition was a continuity, thanks to ecclesiastical and juridical institutions, which because of their own needs had guarded the authenticity of the sources, and therefore its cultural potential.

In conclusion, Valla was able to enlighten, if indirectly, relevant aspects of historical truth because of his mature and original awareness in developing the most important principle of humanism, conceiving language as the very basis and source of culture. Thus, despite his radical attitude of breaking with tradition—or rather, precisely because of it—Valla was able in the end to identify the essential core of a historical continuity.

From Valla's assumptions we get the impression of something like a circle closing, through a coherent composition of the elements that constituted the terms of the debate. This was a composition fit to clarify what cultural premises demanded. But it need not be pointed out that we are dealing with an ideal conclusion rather than with a historical one. The discussion of spoken and written Latin in ancient Rome continued to develop over the following century, from Lorenzo the Magnificent to Alciato, Bembo, Florido Sabino, Castelvetro, and Cittadini,[132] even though actual new contributions to the topic were rare. It is obvious that now the subject of Latin was subordinated to the fundamental topic of the codification and definition of the vernacular, both for the question of its origins and as a term of reference in the dispute on language.

In this last respect, it is not only a matter of the historical issue of the evolving cycle that Latin had now completed, giving way to the new language of the vernacular ("the corruption of things is the real reason for the generation of others") and the principle that "grammar is born of language, and not the language of grammar."[133] We can also observe the transposition into the dispute on vernacular of the very same terms argued with regard to Latin—the concept of the language as the irreducible peculiarity of a nation, or as a common basis imposing itself on various particular idioms; as a natural product, or a cultural one.[134]

Otherwise, along with continuity, the emergence of other elements revealing a dramatic change in perceptiveness and cultural climate must not be ignored. We refer particularly to the organic and cyclical conception of language,[135] or to the renewal of an abstract Aristotelian terminology (upon which, for example, was constructed the too-celebrated work of Cittadini),[136] all of which are opposed to the essentially pragmatic spirit of the humanists of the fifteenth century. In the same way, because of greater experience, the broadening of linguistic concerns and increasing interest in modern languages raised philosophical problems and issues of comparison and more or less mythical genetic connections among them, which the humanists through their research concentrated on Latin had been able to elude.

In conclusion, we can now estimate the contribution of the discussions I have examined here. First of all, they give us precious evidence with regard to the problem of periodizing humanism. This is true either as far as the subjective definition on the part of the actors themselves is concerned—we recall that the disparaging metaphor of the "gothic" ages has its origins here before being generalized in the history of the visual arts—or as a landmark of a decisive turning point with respect to scholastic tradition, and as a typical expression of a given cultural climate.

If we finally consider the evolution of humanism in Italy during the second half of the fifteenth century—namely, the rigid prescriptions of Ciceronian rhetoric, or eclectic preciousness in style, an artificial search for strange modes of writing in the most obscure and decadent areas of Latin—where ultimately an even more sophisticated linguistic erudition joins with a literary and scholarly withdrawal, then we are better able to understand the epocal significance of the emergence of an embryonic historical-linguistic thought just in the middle of the transition from one rhetoric to another.

2

Humanist Intentions and Patristic References
Some Thoughts on the Moral Writings
of the Humanists

Even at the risk of going over ground already well covered, let me begin this discussion with an observation. Quattrocento humanists often
quoted Christian authors openly or covertly in their own writings, not
so much for the religious significance but because they represented a cultural tradition understood to be in conflict with the classical one, adopted
as a model and methodological guide. I refer especially to Bruni, Poggio,
Valla, and Biondo, who frequently cited the Church Fathers to confirm
and defend their own classicism, or more precisely, their own secular-
ism. These references fall into two categories. The first are those that aim
to demonstrate, in opposition to theological and canonist denials, that
the Church Fathers acknowledged the use of classical authors. The arche-
type of such acknowledgment must be considered St. Basil's brief treatise
De utilitate studii in libros gentilium, which Bruni translated to support his
thesis.[1] In the second category are those works that directly attack writers
of apologetics and their respective condemnation of pagan writers, as in
the case of Lorenzo Valla's hostile treatment of St. Jerome's famous dream
("You are a Ciceronian, not a Christian!") in his Proem to book 4 of the
Elegantiae. These references can also be implicit, not only in the development of the argument but also in the title itself. *An seni sit uxor ducenda,* the title of Poggio Bracciolini's short dialogue celebrating his own
marital happiness, is an obvious counterposition to the argument that St.
Jerome and, on his authority, a broad medieval tradition, had confirmed:
"Non est . . . uxor ducenda sapienti," a wise man should not get mar-

ried.[2] At other times, the argument is more subtle, and even insidious, as when Biondo Flavio referred in his treatise on Roman institutions, *Roma triumphans,* to the authority of St. Augustine, mentioning him just in the beginning and the end of the work: "which (Rome) the blessed Aurelius Augustinus desired to see triumphant."[3] His intent was not to insert his own historical vision of Rome into a framework of Christian Providence as much as it was to conceal in some way the informing spirit of his text, which he knew to be incompatible with that of the *De civitate Dei.* In fact, when discussing the civic virtues that were the foundation of Rome's grandeur, Biondo attacks those who, "philosophizing only with words, since in the matter itself they are far from real philosophy," were kept from truly recognizing Roman virtue by their condemnation of the Roman love of praise, that is, by their tenacious attachment to Augustinian tradition.

At this point I shall not expand with further examples. Instead, I would like to advance an initial set of considerations in order to establish a more precise line of investigation. The passages cited above are sure indications of how a pure and simple restoration of the ancient culture was unimaginable for a humanist of the fifteenth century without taking Christian and ecclesiastical traditions into account. Consequently, the militant writings and the earliest expressions of humanist culture were clearly marked by the polemical spirit against tradition. How can Valla's *Elegantiae,* to cite only one of the most obvious and important examples, be understood without considering, in addition to the authors on whose basis his rules are formulated, the corresponding usages of medieval Latin he punctiliously sought to correct?[4] In short, I deal with texts that carry the imprint of the polemical climate during which they were written. Therefore it will not be enough simply to identify textual citations, following a pattern compatible with other kinds of inquiries, such as on Trecento encyclopedias and *florilegia,* or on the grammarians, philologists, and exegetes of the late Quattrocento; but we must especially understand the context in which the citation is introduced, the representative and symbolic value it assumes, and the cultural issues and ideological positions it evokes.

In short, it has to do with an avant-garde culture, establishing itself outside a definite institutional base,[5] conscious of its separate existence and marked by the refusal of age-old scholastic and ecclesiastical traditions. As a consequence, this culture acknowledged itself through simplified metaphorical or ideological formulations, such as the well-known concept of the "rebirth" of scholarship from the "rust" (or "shadows") of the past, or of the contrast between "learned" and "unlearned," which to Leon Battista Alberti appeared to be determined by a law of nature itself.[6]

Culture, as is well known, is tantamount to education and morality, a morality that is nourished by exhortation, that is to say, by rhetoric, with its storehouse of authorities and exempla. Therefore a transition like that we are considering from one cultural style and tradition to another also involves a change in the forms of morality and, reciprocally, in the way of dealing with the authorities and examples. It is no coincidence that Étienne Gilson, concluding his discussion of medieval philosophy with an exposition of Leonardo Bruni's pedagogical treatise *De studiis et litteris,* with its recommended series of good authors, observes, "We have most assuredly entered a new world." To which he immediately adds, "through a continuous evolution rather than a revolution."[7] It seems to me, however, that the question under consideration—the emergence of this new, reticent, and tendentious way of mentioning the most traditional *auctores* as a sign of the emancipation of a secularized and antischolastic culture, and the value attributed to a morality found outside religious discipline and without adherence to institutions—cannot be viewed as part of a continuous evolution. Consider, for example, the defense of poetry (and the study of letters generally) from the accusations of theologians. For Salutati, to mention only his last writing in answer to Giovanni Domenici's *Lucula noctis,* the defense of poetry is still based on theories of the traditional triuvium and quadrivium curriculum of the arts, and consequently as a celebration of poetry, joined with Sacred Scripture by the same kind of allegorical exegesis, both moral and doctrinal, and therefore on the same high level as theology itself. While for Bruni, in the above-mentioned proem to the translation of Basil, the importance of the studies summarized by Cicero in his definition of *humanitas* no longer needs justification, and whoever denies the importance is himself ignorant: "But it usually happens to those whose natural dispositions are somehow dulled, that they are not strong enough to contemplate anything lofty or admirable, and since they themselves can approach no part of the humanities, they do not even consider that others should do so." Where Salutati required thirty-five pages to develop his argument (moreover, left unfinished) in the Novati edition, his pupil and follower Bruni needed but one, and one so important as to leave its mark on the promotion of humanism, as well as on its subsequent programs of study.[8]

In addition to its rejection of the institutionalized *artes* of scholasticism, what is especially characteristic and significant about this cultural transition is the abandonment of allegorical interpretation, as is particularly evident in Bruni's *De studiis et litteris,* where the parallel traditionally drawn between poetry and Sacred Scripture is reduced to irony: it would be less harmful to read the pleasant poetic love stories about Venus and Daphne or Aeneas and Dido than the "real" stories about Samson and Dalila, Lot's daughters, David, or Solomon.[9] In other words, with the rejection of allegory the tie was broken that united secular and sacred studies, however artificial and extrinsic it might be. But, at the same time, Bruni was distancing himself from the illustrious tradition of Florentine and fourteenth-century culture in general, as personified by Boccaccio, whose work Salutati had continued, at least in this field of scholarship.[10] The importance of Bruni's attack on Boccaccio cannot be underestimated. In fact, it is this disassociation from Boccaccio and his times that principally drives Bruni's polemics in *Dialogi ad Petrum Histrum,* namely against his assumptions to bring Dante and Petrarch together on a single exalted level and in consequent conventional presentation of the two poets. Bruni's difference of opinion with Boccaccio with regard to Dante is still more obvious in the biographies of the two poets that he undertook later.

"It seems to me," Bruni remarks, "that our good Boccaccio, the sweetest and gentlest of men, wrote the life and ways of such a sublime poet as if he were writing *Filocolo* or *Filostrato* or *Fiammetta.* He becomes so impassioned in the sections dealing with love that he neglects the serious and essential parts of Dante's life, passing over them in silence, mentioning trivial matters and saying nothing of the more weighty ones."[11] In the same vein, and still with Boccaccio in mind, Bruni introduces a digression that concerns not only "the nature of poets" but also their name, "by which the substance may be understood." He explains that "the word 'poet' is Greek, which is to say, 'a man who makes.' " As is known, Boccaccio, in *Genealogia deorum* 14.8, took (by way of Petrarch) the etymology of "poesis" from Isidore. It did not come from *poiò,* "I make," but from the mythical *poetes:* "From their accomplishment they were called *poesim* or *poetas,* which in Latin is *exquisita locutio,* 'refined speech,' and those who composed were called *poete*": an etymology consonant indeed with the subtleties of the medieval *dictamen.*[12]

There has been of course extensive scholarly discussion of Bruni's depiction of Petrarch (I need mention only Hans Baron's basic observations), in which he is no longer portrayed so much as the greatest poet and master of Christian virtue, as he had been described by Boccaccio and Salutati, but rather as the man who "restored the *studia humanitatis,* which had been forgotten until now, and which showed us the way we could learn."[13] Guided by Bruni's own testimony, I will simply point out how he, by setting aside Boccaccio's heritage as well as his own justificatory cultural guidelines and by strengthening his ties with the circle of humanists in Padua (as indicated by the *Dialogi* themselves, which by no coincidence were dedicated to P. P. Vergerio),[14] had gone back in a direct and critical fashion to Petrarch's propositions, drawing from them inspiration for cultural renewal.

A cultural transition like that which took place in the course of a few years, from the end of the fourteenth to the early fifteenth century, can be explained only as a revival and reinterpretation of the cultural polemics that Petrarch had directed against his own time.[15] In other words, just as, when discussing the methodical writings and polemical devices of someone like Valla or Biondo, we must go back to Bruni's propositions, so too we can understand Bruni's work only as a direct development of Petrarch's cultural legacy.

In fact, returning to Petrarch again after a certain familiarity with Quattrocento humanism, and at the same time comparing his cultural and ideological statements with those most typical of his time, even those represented by authors whose epistolary evidence shows their closeness to him, one is continually struck by the complete isolation—regardless of how many admirers and collaborators surrounded him—in which he formulated his most fundamental arguments. It is also remarkable that it took more than half a century before his ideas were understood and embraced again, exerting a powerful influence over an epoch by then far from his own.

Petrarch's assault on the fundamental ideas and *auctores* of that varied complex we conventionally call "medieval culture" (a term, by the way, based on the polemical generalization outlined by Petrarch and after him by his fellow humanists) was direct and frontal. There would be nothing like it again until Lorenzo Valla launched his attacks on scholasticism in the following century.

Heir to a tradition that has come to be known as "prehumanistic," in which a literary education was seen as a complement to a legal career, often a kind of badge of honor and superiority in civic life, Petrarch shattered the unity of law and letters by abandoning his legal studies at the University of Bologna, thereby accentuating his break with tradition while violating his father's will.[16] With this decision he also turned his back on the particular approach to learning expressed in various *compendia, florilegia,* and lexicons, texts with a taste for compilation and categorization typical of scholars of the *Digest* and Sacred Canons. Figures such as Geremia of Montagnone, as R. Weiss has so aptly shown, fall into this category, as well as Petrarch's own friend, Guglielmo of Pastrengo, who drew his inspiration, at least in terms of structure, for his *De viris illustribus* and *De originibus rerum* not only from the *Digest* but also from St. Jerome's *De viris illustribus* and Isidore's *Etymologiae.*[17] About the latter work, we know of Petrarch's ironic marginal notes, not to mention his explicit reluctance to make use of it;[18] and as for biographies, he condemned the compilations and encyclopedias of *Vitae,* against which he set up his own select gallery of Roman heroes.[19] By attacking scholasticism, legal culture, and the encyclopedic tradition, Petrarch seems to align his purpose ideally with the tradition of the great learned clerics of the twelfth century. In fact, many of his admirers actually considered him a cleric sui generis, on account of his unusual learning and eloquence: "For to me, you are in heaven—not in the place of God, but as one who points the way to God," as Francesco Nelli, prior of the Santi Apostoli, wrote to him.[20] But in *Familiares* 4.15, where Petrarch's criticism is directed at the famous professor of canon law, Giovanni d'Andrea, and more generally "against those who display knowledge not their own, plucking others' little flowers" (*contra ostentatores scientie non sue ac flosculorum decerptores*),[21] Petrarch first of all attacks d'Andrea's opinion (which was but the general one), which exalted St. Jerome as the first "among sacred doctors," or in other words, which recognized in his works the foundation of Christian Latinity and doctrine. (Another one of Petrarch's correspondents, the Dominican Giovanni Colonna, author of his own *De viris illustribus,* hailed St. Jerome, "the doctor of doctors," as his primary model.)[22] Nor was this an isolated occurrence. By returning to a classical model and by giving preference to active instead of contemplative, philosophical, and religious virtues, Petrarch in his *De viris* completes a process in some sense analogous and inverted with respect to St. Jerome's *De viris,* in which Jerome had measured himself against Suetonius.[23]

Apart from what has been said about the conceptual novelty and provocativeness of Petrarch's *De viris,* in the *Rerum memorandum,* immediately preceding the famous passage in which he describes himself as "located at the border between two peoples" (*in confinio duorum populorum constitutus*), the last of the moderns to experience intimately the classical legacy, Petrarch concludes with a puzzling statement: "but how many famous authors of antiquity do I remind, so many shames and infamous deeds I recall."[24] What are these *pudores,* these "shames" associated with the *delicta,* the "crimes" of the moderns? I had first considered *pudores* in the active form, in keeping with its classical definition, as *timor iustae reprehensionis,* the fear of just censure. But this reading needs correction: no doubt that in this context the word is used in the sense of "infamy, shame," and therefore in a certain sense a hendiadys with the *delicta.* Even though the expression is still somewhat vague, it certainly does not contradict the fact that Petrarch was blaming Christian traditions, or more precisely, the canonical norms that had institutionalized the Church Fathers' restrictions against using classical writers, as the reason that so many classical works had not been transmitted.

The paradigm of such norms was St. Jerome's dream, in which he makes amends and vows to resist the allurements of pagan literature. Petrarch challenges this prohibition in more than one instance. In a letter to Giacomo Colonna, the bishop of Lombez (*Familiares* 2.9), he observes, "My Augustine was never dragged to the tribunal of the eternal judge in his dreams, as was the case with your Jerome; he never heard himself charged with being a Ciceronian, as was Jerome who promised never again to touch the writings of the pagans," and—as Petrarch adds ironically—"you know how diligently he avoided all of them, especially those of Cicero." With these words Petrarch answered Colonna, who had reprimanded him because he "embraced Augustine and his books with a certain degree of good-will, but really [he] did not give up the study on poets and philosophers."[25] This statement clearly shows Colonna's skepticism concerning Petrarch's genuine adherence to the Augustinian context. Admittedly, in the letter to Giovanni d'Andrea the debate focuses not on the relationship between the Fathers and classical literature but on whether preference among Church Fathers should be given to Augustine or to Jerome. However, apart from the doubts expressed by the bishop of Lombez, we know from Petrarch's own confessions made in the letters of his later years that, after a period of youthful rebellion and exclusive devotion to pagan literature, he learned to appreciate sacred texts by reading Augustine's *Confessions.* Writing to Donato Albanzani, Petrarch explains: "That book was my way into sacred literature. As a proud and pompous youth I long avoided it as humble and unrefined and inferior to secular letters because of my excessive love for the one and contempt for the other, because of the false opinion I had of myself and, to confess briefly my own sin too, because of my youthful insolence, and as I now understand and clearly see, the prompting of the devil."[26] Petrarch makes a similar acknowledgment to Luca della Penna as well, while describing his longstanding love of Cicero: "Only the sweetness and melodiousness of the words so engaged me that anything else I either read or heard seemed to me raucous and largely discordant."[27]

In a perceptive study P. Courcelle has noted several specific areas in which Petrarch agrees only in part with Augustine's thought, while at the same time recognizing the saint as his personal guide to sacred texts. If Petrarch responds to the appeal to his conscience and Christian contrition, he stops short of true conversion. He shows himself to be relatively indifferent, at least on the surface, to theological issues and does not fail to place special emphasis on the themes that legitimize the study of the ancients (such as praise bestowed on Platonic philosophy, or the memory of the particular impression provoked by the reading of *Hortensius*).[28] Courcelle also notes that at least in the *Familiares,* "one is first of all surprised how rarely Petrarch mentions or makes use of the Church Fathers."[29] This parsimonious use of Christian authorities seems to fit well with the particular way, at times tendentious and reticent, in which Petrarch uses the *De civitate Dei,* a text that he treats very differently from the *Confessions.* In fact, responding to doubts expressed by Giacomo Colonna, he writes: "But why should I have been torn away from [the poets and philosophers], when I saw Augustine himself holding fast? Otherwise he never would have grounded *De civitate Dei,* not to mention other works, on so many philosophers and poets, never would he have adorned them with so many ornaments from orators and historians."[30] This quotation can be considered typical of Petrarch's approach to *De civitate Dei,* in which, as U. Bosco has observed, he often conceals his reference.[31]

It seems appropriate in the context of this discussion to make some observations about Petrarch's practice (which would become a model for his followers) of concealing citations, quite different in purpose from that practiced by compilers. In compilations a reference is in a certain sense viewed as anonymous and common property, and therefore it is not necessary to acknowledge the authors cited from one text to another. Giovanni Colonna, among others, clarifies such a practice in the introduction to his *Liber de viris illustribus:* "The references that I have inserted into this book belong to other writers, and even the points that I myself make have been taken from others, so that, in imitation of the histories and annals of ancient authors, I can weave a crown for our text from a wide field."[32] Petrarch, on the contrary, does not mention the sources he is compelled to use when lacking a more valid authority, as in the case of Isidore, or others with which he is not in agreement. In short, the source of a quotation, whether it is openly acknowledged or not, implies a value judgment or at least agreement with its content. In fact, Petrarch openly dissents from the *De civitate Dei* on the crucial issue of how to evaluate Rome from an ethical standpoint. In *Familiares* 15.9.4–5 he makes an explicit connection to the widespread opinion of those "for whom Rome is a Babylon, and—it makes me angry to say this—her virtue is shameful, and her glory disreputable," to the authority of *magni duces,* the great leaders of Christian doctrine on whom this judgment was based, first and foremost Augustine, who had defined Rome, "like another . . . Babylon in the West."[33] Petrarch concludes with a remark that would be echoed in the century to come: "What more need I say? Whatever end awaits the city of Rome, its name will live as long as the memory of Greek and Latin literature survives, and therefore envious people will not lack a subject for blame. This is my response to Augustine and indeed to Jerome, too, whom it is not permitted to disparage."[34] This passage is particularly valuable because it demonstrates how his pejorative use of the term "Babylon"—Petrarch's customary title for the curia in Avignon and its related "labyrinth" of theologians and canonists—was a form of retaliation against the theological tradition he deplored, which disparaged ancient Rome and the fascination it continued to have in Petrarch's own day.[35]

In this perspective we can better understand the significance of Petrarch's opposition to the contemporary assessment of Valerius Maximus, which in the cited letter to Giovanni d'Andrea immediately follows his discussion of the Church Fathers. Leaving aside the general nature of this polemic in which Petrarch opposes the dogmatic and compilatory tendencies of the time to a real understanding and evaluation of classical authors, as soon as one recognizes the position of uncontested authority that the culture of the day assigned to the ancient collector of exempla, whose work had been consecrated by the sanction of commentaries and school teaching as a true specimen of the vices and virtues at the level of the highest moral authorities, it becomes obvious that Petrarch's criticism is not confined merely to the text's literary merit. In the words of B. Smalley, a renowned scholar of fourteenth-century erudition and themes of monastic preaching and exegesis, "Valerius Maximus produced a collection of exempla *avant la lettre:* his *Facta et dicta memorabilia* seem to have been written specifically to satisfy the medieval taste." Many other observations and examples could easily be cited to this purpose.[36] Perhaps never more than on this occasion did Petrarch oppose the currents of his age so forcefully. Commenting on the success Valerius Maximus enjoyed as a moralist in fourteenth-century France and Italy, G. Di Stefano writes: "Throughout the entire century only Petrarch's voice was raised loud and sure." He was referring to the aforementioned letter to Giovanni d'Andrea, in which Petrarch writes: "But who would not be amazed that you give precedence among the moralists to Valerius, if it is said in all seriousness and persistently, and not as a joke and a provocation? For if Valerius is ranked first, where, I ask, does Plato come, and Aristotle, and Cicero, and Anneus Seneca, whom in this context indeed some great admirers elevate above all the others?" It is worth noting here that Petrarch demonstrates a certain reservation about Seneca, or, more precisely, about the preeminence he was accorded by authors of scholastic treatises, precisely those "great admirers" he fails to identify as a sign of his low regard.[37]

Despite this eloquent citation, Di Stefano yields to the temptation of attributing to Petrarch himself a pretended "studiorum summa conformitas," that utmost conformity in learning, which, according to *Familiares* 4.2.13, would unite King Robert of Naples to Dionigi of Borgo San Sepolcro, the learned Augustinian and author, among other works, of the most important fourteenth-century commentary on Valerius, identifying him precisely as the writer who "must be ranked among the authors of ethics" (*supponitur ethyce,* as we read in a contemporary note to a manuscript of Valerius's commentary). With the help of various other texts (which together constitute a veritable survey of late medieval encyclopedic and scholastic culture), Dionigi attempts to reinforce and, of course, christianize the classical and canonical collection of exempla.[38] Petrarch's purpose is exactly the opposite. According to him, Valerius is to be ranked among historians,[39] but as a bad historian, a compiler indeed of illustrious authors, "so that you filled a large part of your own work with extracts from the books of Cicero" (*ut qui ex tullianis libris magnam con-flasti operis tui partem*). Perhaps he was thinking, as Petrarch insinuates else-where, "that the books of Cicero, whence where you get all this material of yours, will never be passed down into the hands of posterity."[40] Clearly, such a harsh attack is directed even more at the recent compilations in-spired by Valerius rather than at Valerius himself. What is more significant still is the fact that Petrarch's remarks were directed to issues that most interested the contemporary reader, such as the observance or neglect of religion, omens, oracles, and miraculous interventions[41]—quite the opposite of Cicero's rationalism. That Petrarch was attacking not only the ancients' beliefs reported by Valerius is evident from his skeptical refer-ence to the Eritrean Sybil: "She is believed to have predicted many things about Christ." In the following century Valla's polemic will revive and elaborate just this theme.[42]

Given the radical way Petrarch discredits the established model of the medieval exemplum, and with it the model of official morality of his age, there had to be a modification and, I would say, almost a dislodgement of the very language of ethics. In the same way that Petrarch claims the right to his personal judgment, or, more precisely, a personal relationship with *libri mei peculiares,* his own favorite books, he liberates maxims and examples from the rigidity and conventionality that they had assumed in the doctrine and tradition, and he effects to some degree a conversion from abstract truth to fact, where the anecdote, returned to a context of plausible and verified events, finds its colloquial nature, inspired by a variety of reflections, and where maxims can no longer be isolated from the spirit and dignity of their author, and therefore become to a certain extent relativized.

Admittedly, Petrarch's works are always somewhat elusive and difficult to define. As a result it is easier to establish what they reject than precisely what they affirm.[43] In more general terms it can be said that Petrarch con-tinued to be conditioned by his own intention to react against the cultural currents of his time. Leaving aside his reluctance to subject his works to the judgment of his contemporaries, it is significant that his criticism of Valerius Maximus has remained somewhat concealed to the present day, also because Petrarch adopted him as a model for his own work, the *Re-rum memorandarum libri,* while being careful that his references to the an-cient text were, as noted by Billanovich, "cloaked in rhetoric and anony-mous."[44] In fact, Petrarch's desire to present a sharp counterpart to the basic currents of medieval literature unites the works that were destined to become the summa of his own humanism. The collection of his letters, the *Familiares,* freely inspired by Cicero's example, rejected the institutionalized model of the *ars dictaminis;*[45] the *Rerum memorandarum* appear as a challenge to Valerius Maximus, as an *auctor ethice;* the *De viris illustribus,* a challenge to the tradition of biographies of wise and learned men that, beginning with Jerome, is linked to compilations such as those of Walter Burley and Giovanni Colonna; and last of all, *Africa* represented a challenge to the medieval epic of Alexander.[46]

With the exception of the *Familiares* none of these works was completed. By the time of the posthumous publication of *Africa* and *De viris* (that is, those for which Petrarch had pursued the previous recognition of the *privilegium lauree*), they seemed to the younger generation of lettered men to have already outlived their cultural relevance.[47]

Therefore the pause before Petrarch's inspiring animus was again taken up and developed seems less surprising. Bruni's *Dialogi* are important for the way they reveal how the feeling of the young humanists, his contemporaries, was such that they had to start over again. Indeed, at least for the first two decades of the new century, the activity of humanist circles was rather of a preparatory nature, and only occasionally and gingerly did they attempt new literary forms. For example, consider Bruni's writings and programmatic introductions and his political historiography (in contrast to Petrarch's moralistic one); consider Vergerio's and Barbaro's pedagogical treatises, but above all the letter writing and the basic project of translating works of Greek literature and philosophy that constitutes the first serious challenge to scholastic authority. By the 1420s the situation changes. At the end of the decade appear the first two works with the ambition of introducing a new model for the moral essay: the dialogues *De avaritia,* written by the veteran Poggio Bracciolini, and *De voluptate,* by the neophyte Lorenzo Valla.

In my opinion, neither of these texts, beginning with their titles, can be easily understood without deciphering the significance of their allusions. The remainder of this essay will be devoted to an examination of this matter. As the works are more or less contemporary,[48] I shall take a logical rather than a chronological approach in order to demonstrate how a certain technique intended to evince through the citation of the authorities the differing of cultural levels, and with it of moral and religious traditions as well, is elevated by the younger writer to the rank of a real methodology.

As all his writings make evident, Poggio takes up and popularizes a Petrar-chan brand of *moralis philosophia*. Indeed, in an explicit acknowledgment which for the time and for his own custom was somewhat unusual, Poggio refers to Petrarch as a model of independent life: ". . . because there is the recent example of that most distinguished man Francesco Petrarca. Cou-rageously renouncing all interest in the power and dignities offered him by the pope, and fleeing the threshholds of power . . . he advocated in his words and actions a quiet life."[49] Hence Poggio derives, with his penchant for anecdote, epistolary descriptions, and wit, a particular kind of Stoic moralism that exalts the reward of virtue for itself; but one in which the harshness of Stoic philosophy, with its rigid contraries of virtue and vice, is moderated by an appeal to the "common opinion." This requires differ-ent criteria for evaluating the seriousness of vices, and the admittance of a human tempering of rigid virtue.[50] Seneca, though frequently adopted, is thus filtered through the good sense of Cicero, with the consideration — suggested more by Salutati than by Petrarch — of the necessary approxi-mation in fulfilling moral precepts, so that the educated man — and the frankness here is typical of Poggio — should not be ashamed of himself or of his human inclinations. "I would have liked to have had such strength and vigor to contemplate at least, if not imitate, the wisdom of others; but my capability is such that I must go at a distance and always adore from afar where they have trodden."[51] But where Poggio exceeds the bound-aries of fourteenth-century culture and morality is in his identification of the virtuous with the *docti,* the educated people, and his related aware-ness of a category of learned men united by commonly held predilic-tions outside any institutional dependence, who stand as strongholds of the stable good of "virtue," beyond the variable sway of "fortune." Poggio senses this corporate spirit very strongly: this is by the way a motive — indeed, not the last one — that makes him so loquacious. All his treatises are nothing more than consecutive illustrations, according to the circum-stance, of the assumption stated above and first developed in the context of his early letters.[52] Drawing a comparison with the virtue of the learned man, Poggio denounces one by one the avarice of prelates; the hypoc-risy of friars; the unhappiness and depravity of princes; the varied mis-fortunes of pontificates and kingdoms; the pride of the dominant social castes, such as the Venetian; the factiousness of republican regimes, such as the Florentine; and the misery of human life in general.[53] From this one easily understands the seeds of Poggio's skepticism toward the practical effectiveness—if not the objective validity—of precepts confined within so narrow a sphere of doctrine and reason. Moreover, insofar as virtue is identified with the cult of letters, the profession of moralist tends to be identified with the career of a learned man, which grants him esteem and security in public life. All this in turn contributes to the establishment of genuine utilitarian motives within a Stoical framework. When his friend Niccolò Niccoli reproached him for rejecting a profitable ecclesiastical career, presuming that the explanation lay in his inability to resist sexual passions, Poggio replied indignantly: "I take little interest in the Sirens you mentioned . . . I never abhorred such things, as you know; I am, after all, a man. But it is also true that I have never diverged from what is useful to me. However, it is simply absurd to think that in a matter of such seriousness as resolving how I should lead my life I would base my decision on this most trivial and worthless issue. Do not think me so foolish and so destitute of reason that I would turn away from the course I have set for myself because I was moved by the Sirens' song."[54] The significance of his remarks lies in the connection he makes between practical goals (he was trying, and for the moment without success, to be reinstated in the position he had lost as papal secretary) and the moral choice of leading a life faithful to one's convictions. Poggio would eventually express this idea as his *institutio vitae,* the instruction for his life, which he understood in explicit and prideful lay terms, in comparison to what the corruption of the Church in his day symbolized to him. He would reiterate the same thoughts years later, this time addressing none other than Cardinal Giuliano Cesarini, the president of the Council of Basel and the man who had admonished him for his scandalizing concubinage: "Because you write about the kind of life I should led, [I will reply that] for a long time now I have resolved on a certain course for my life, which I follow, not straying from the established path. I do not want to be a priest, nor do I want any benefices: for I have seen many men, whom I have judged to be good, . . . become misers and forgetful of all virtues once they have joined the priesthood . . . And lest the same thing happen to me, I decided long ago that I will spend whatever remains of my journey far from your order: for with the great shaving of the priests' heads I perceive that not only their hair but also their conscience and virtue is removed."[55]

Poggio's criticism of the contemporary Church does not mean, however, that he did not have recourse to the sacred authorities. Repeating (or imitating?) to some degree the path that Petrarch followed, after an early phase of more rigorous classicism, during his sojourn in England Poggio turned almost contritely to Christian, especially patristic, texts, which he used rather extensively in his subsequent writings.[56] Walser's conclusion, however, that Poggio intended to synthesize classical moral philosophy and Christian wisdom, seems rather hasty and imprecise to me.[57] In the first place, to consider patristic authorities on the same level as classical ones meant ignoring their theological content. Moreover, it does not differ from the methodological approach outlined above, of a free choice of authorities and the consequent relativization of precepts. In brief, it does not alter what was already at the time an irreversible process of secularizing morality. Secondly, Poggio called upon the texts of the Fathers expressly as a way to compensate for the crisis of faith that, in his opinion (and certainly not his alone), resulted from the discredited image of the contemporary Church: "If both the words and deeds of the past did not delight us more than the corrupt examples of the present, faith would undoubtely be lost."[58] In other words, such recourse to the Fathers reinforces Poggio's typically polemical and antihierarchical framework rather than repudiates it. Significant in this regard is his fondness for St. John Chrysostom ("whom I prefer to all authors I have ever read"),[59] especially for his Homilies. Poggio is attracted to him not only for his predominately moralistic rather than theological character but also for his instruction of priestly duties, which could apply to the degenerate clergy of his day. Indeed, Poggio seems to make implied reference to Chrysostom when he proposes a noble concept of sacerdotal duty, a concept that influenced his choice for secular life: "I am not unaware of the seriousness of assuming a cleric's burden nor of how much care is required for one's conscience who lives off benefices."[60]

These observations help to elucidate De avaritia, where for the first time Poggio expresses his individual themes as a homogenous set of ideas; and more importantly, he does so with the intent of presenting them publicly. Without fear of generalization, we may assert that the overriding purpose of this work is anticlerical, as it is openly avowed in more than one passage. An equally important purpose is the arrangement of theological precepts into more suitable ethical categories, less inflexible and more universal. "Avarice," as we have seen, was almost by definition a charge leveled at the clergy, and Poggio had emphasized this specifically in his address in 1417 to the Fathers of the Council of Constance.[61] In the dialogue the opportunity for discussing the matter comes from the interlocutors' criticisms of Fra Bernardino of Siena's preaching, which they explicitly berate not only for its typically demagogical tricks but also more implicitly for the theological content itself.[62]

On the contrary, Poggio strives for a rational form of persuasion, and thus his arguments were to be circumscribed within a narrow and congenial circle ("if we can be of any use . . . if not to others, at least to ourselves").[63] After a thorough examination of arguments against avarice by Christian and pagan authorities ("much has been written by the most learned Christian men, but also by the pagans in both Greek and Latin"), the second interlocutor, Antonio Loschi, presents a defense of avariciousness and in so doing contradicts the traditional theological condemnation of profit, which was Bernardino's principle argument in his "economic" sermons. Loschi does not so much criticize the substance of the theological tradition (as if Poggio were here taking a stand in the doctrinal debate over usury) as point out its irrelevance to the general theme of avarice, taking the opportunity to condemn both monastic asceticism and the notion of morality understood as an inflexible set of rules: "We must not regulate our lives by the standards of philosophy."[64] The ambiguity present in the twofold meaning of "philosophy," in the sense represented by scholastic theology and in the rhetorical context of the humanist moral essay, constitutes the third and last part of the dialogue.[65] Andreas of Constantinople, a Dominican and the Master of the Sacred Palace,[66] is the speaker who, in a context ever more openly anticlerical,[67] cites the sacred authorities of Saints Paul and Augustine, along with John Chrysostom, who equate avarice with idolatry and heresy.[68] Poggio explains more openly in his letters this kind of allusive implications, and precisely in his reply to objections by Niccoli, who was annoyed by Poggio's including "modern" authorities and references to real events in the dialogue: among other things, "the mention of Fra Bernardino is displeasing."[69] As for the reference to Isidore of Seville to which Niccoli had objected, Poggio writes: "You must know that I mentioned Isidore not out of dearth of authorities, but because seemed to me that in order to accuse the avarice of clerics, the writings they read everyday in their own laws and decrets were most fit for the purpose."[70] After Andreas's emphatic peroration, the presentation by Bartolomeo of Montepulciano, drawing on the support of two recently discovered pagan authorities, Lucian and Silius Italicus, serves to reestablish the balance between the Christian and classical authorities by recognizing their congruence: "These are not the voices of one man or another, but of nature and truth itself."[71] Thus, the unity of the dialogue is restored and the discussion concludes with a return to the cultural issues laid out at the beginning. However, as I have said, only by comprehending the controversy implied by the two different kinds of authorities can we understand the significance, and with it the basic similarities of the different opinions that express (from different viewpoints) the real informing motive behind Poggio's "moral philosophy": that is, the vindication of moral independence, not without a degree of retaliation against theological tradition and ecclesiastical discipline.

These intentions become even more apparent in the criticisms adduced by Niccoli, who, as already mentioned, was troubled by the dialogue's extensive use of Christian authorities and by the contemporary setting. A perceptive scholar, Helene Harth, has argued that Poggio proceeded to revise the dialogue in deference to his friend's reproaches.[72] However, I cannot agree with her opinion that his revision represented simply a "literary censorship," dictated by purist biases and not by considerations of prudence or propriety. To exclude, as the corrected version does, the anti-Observants polemic presented at the very beginning of the discussion was actually to conceal the dialogue's real purpose. The political prudence seems even more obvious in the different role given to the theologian Andreas of Constantinople in the revised version. Among other variations, there is the suppression of the embarrassing and intimidating apparition of Andreas in the very middle of the humanists' circle, which falls momentarily silent: "but in your presence we are silent, moved by shame lest you become the censor of our ineptitudes."[73] This is undoubtedly a reference to the disciplinary censures stemming from the sumptuary laws of the Roman curia that had affected Poggio himself in 1426. Poggio had complained of the "secret accusation" of "those critics who are extremely inflexible about other people's lives" (*censores quidam perrigidi vitae alienae*), and had denounced them in *Contra delatores*, advocating in Petrarchan terms freedom for the language used at banquets.[74] In the dialogue, however, Andreas of Constantinople represents a tolerant and "convivial" theologian. This is a proof among others that the revised version cannot be explained only in terms of a classsicist concern. To the point, it is expedient, remembering that in one of his letters Niccoli had reproved Poggio "for his banquets and their luxury."[75] Moreover, this kind of an antisumptuary and antidisciplinary controversy was not an isolated episode. To judge from the preface dedicated to the curial officer Gio-vanni Moroni of Rieti, for example, a similar purpose underlies the ver-sion of Lucian's *Calumnia* by Lapo of Castiglionchio the Younger;[76] and it is interesting to find this work still paired with Poggio's *Contra delatores* in a German translation of 1516.[77]

Taking all this into consideration, the criteria Harth proposed for her edition of *De avaritia* is also perplexing. According to her project (still unrealized) the edition had to be based on the revised version of the dialogue. Yet, as she herself has documented, the first version is more represented than the second in manuscript tradition, and still more im-portantly, it is this version that appears in the collection of the *Dialogi* belonging to the author himself.[78] The most reasonable explanation is that Poggio himself, at a later date, restored the dialogue to its earlier form once the worries that had led him to solicit his friend's advice were no longer an issue. However, leaving these arguments aside, the question remains how the editor must behave in presence of two (or multiple) ver-sions of a work primarily ideological and documentary in nature, modi-fied not only by a stylistic revision but also for conceptual or external motives. This is also the case with Valla's *De voluptate,* which will conclude this discussion.[79]

Since G. Mancini's biography, the origin of Valla's dialogue has been linked to Bruni's translation of the *Ethics to Nicomachus* and to the de-bate it sparked about the notion of the *summum bonum.*[80] It also seems plausible to me that Valla had been influenced by a contemporary rekin-dling of interest in classical moral philosophy, first expressed by Bruni in *Isagogicon moralis disciplinae,* a manifesto of an antischolastic approach to Aristotle, filtered through Ciceronian eclecticism, in an effort to harmo-nize his teaching with Stoic and Epicurean doctrines. There was also at this time a reevaluation of Epicurean philosophy that finds an authorita-tive witness in a letter, perhaps Petrarchan in its inspiration, written by Francesco Filelfo in 1428.[81] More likely to have had an impact on Valla was the rather uncommon tract, *Defensio Epicuri,*[82] written by a humanist from Cremona, Cosma Raimondi. Whatever the source of Valla's inspi-ration, unlike the authors already mentioned, he not only follows philo-sophical teachings but also relies on patristic tradition, as it is declared from the beginning of the dialogue's introduction and reflected even in the title, *De vero bono.* The Father in this instance is Lactantius who, be-sides being mentioned by Valla along with Augustine, titled books 3 and 4 of his *Divinae institutiones,* respectively, "De falsa sapientia" and "De vera sapientia et religione." Therefore, according to his preliminary remarks, Valla intended to align his work with the apologetics of the Fathers, such as Augustine and Lactantius, and not grapple with the philosophers from a religious point of view but use their philosophical arguments for this purpose.[83] Taking Valla's comments literally, the Jesuit scholar Mario Fois maintains that the target of his polemics was the inevitable "Averroists," as well as the rebirth of the classical philosophical schools and the consequent secularization of ethics effected by Bruni and his followers, with the object of reestablishing the primacy of faith.[84]

Fois's argument sounds like one paradox added to another: let us only consider the humanistic frame of the work and what is implied by the celebration of classical eloquence over dialectical argumentation that precedes the speech of the advocate of Epicureanism, the central and longest part of the entire dialogue: "For how much clearer, more dignified, and more splendid are those things discussed by orators, in comparison with those squalid and lifeless matters examined by dialecticians!"[85] The introduction is actually more subtle. An opening passage, suppressed after the first edition, explains the dialogue's original title, *De voluptate,* as a notion that was identical to and included the "true moral good." This in turn was understood also in terms of its religious significance: "If, by chance, one of my friends wondering about this title should ask me what passion compelled me to write about pleasure, he should understand that I preferred to entitle these books *De voluptate* rather than *De vero bono,* which I could have, since what I discuss in this work is the true moral good which, in my opinion, is the same thing as pleasure." Such notion of the good, "which is the true one, the only one, and which we assume to be pleasure," is defined as twofold, "the one in this life, the other in the afterlife"; and subsequent versions of the dialogue open precisely with this distinction.[86] It should be added that the suppression of the introductory proposition appears only to have been a matter of expediency, inasmuch as the concept remains unaltered throughout all the argumentation of the dialogue. Valla insists, in opposition to the most common definition of twofold nature of the *voluptas* that differentiates between the pleasures of the senses and those of the soul, on the essential singleness of the concept, based on people's consensus: "Popular opinion, which speaks of the goods of the soul, the goods of the body, the goods of fortune, is itself witness to the unicity." And more specifically: "I myself, however, do not understand, since the word is one and the same, how we can suppose different things, and indeed, still more because all pleasure is not so much in the body as it is in the soul, which governs the body."[87]

Such an amalgamation of notions, traditionally conceived as diammetrically opposed, can only suppose a common polemical object. Now Valla declares, as noted earlier, that the polemic is against philosophical concepts that are far from the true faith; this is the reason he was induced to align himself with the attacks once conducted by Lactantius and Augustine, even though using arguments drawn from the philosophical schools themselves. However, the argument can be overturned. Once established that pleasure has both sacred and secular ends, the attempt to set the philosophers in contradiction with one another can be implicitly understood as one of exposing the contradictions inherent in theology itself.

Let me at this point make a brief digression. A passage in Salutati's *De laboribus Herculis* depicts the two most ill-famed of ancient philosophical sects, according to popular doctrine. "At that time the people had embraced the principle of utility! Conversely, the entire school of philosophers had taught poverty, maintaining that wealth—a word commonly understood as utility—should be despised. On the other hand, utility had been sanctioned, even followed by all the philosophical heresies. In fact, the Epicureans, and the more shameless sect of the Cynics, not only preached pleasure, but made a profession of it."[88] It should be noted here that in the medieval manner, the correct doctrine (abhorrence for advantage, wealth, and pleasure, etc.) can only be considered in the singular, such as *philosophorum scola,* while popular deviations are in the plural, such as the *hereses* (principally Epicureanism and Cynicism). While Valla exalts pleasure as the utilitarian cause that moves all human acts, in its highest form equal to the exercise of charity, inspired by hope in a happy afterlife, he overturns the accusation of "cynicism"—that is the ethical dogmatism in its extreme form—against the *philosophorum scola,* which is typified in the standard name of "Stoicism" but as a whole comprehends "Aristotelianism," that is, contemporary scholasticism. This complex of doctrinarian teachings is refuted as much by the defender of worldly Epicureanism as by the apologist for celestial beatitude.[89] On the other hand, behind the classical labels of Stoicism and Cynicism it is not difficult to recognize the doctrine of Christian pessimism and the ascetic practices of monastic life. In fact, the defender of Stoicism makes reference to a doctrine that resembles what Paul and Augustine had to say about predestination: "Nevertheless the care and love of virtue has been conceded to very few, as a kindness and a special gift of nature; to most it has been denied by the maliciousness of that same nature, in the same way as in terms of the body we see monstrous, weak and corrupted people. The minds of men that she should have enlightened she had blinded, so they cannot contemplate the light of wisdom."[90] Elsewhere, in regard to "Stoics" and "Cynics," the attack on monasticism becomes quite explicit: "Indeed I firmly believe that there were some men, as there still are today, who, loving negligence and laziness and repelled by having to obtain the necessities, chose to live this wasteful and unrefined life."[91]

In this context Valla characteristically employs famous exempla, such as Cato, Lucretia, and Attilius Regulus, borrowed from *De civitate Dei,* but directly counter to spirit of the original. Whereas Augustine's purpose was to discredit the dignity of Stoic suicide with respect to inner Christian virtues, Valla assumes in another signification both exemplary suicides and the exception to them, Attilius Regulus, who, faithful to his oath, preferred to suffer torture. For Valla, instead, these acts must be related to their utilitarian common motive, such as the protection of his social reputation, the rewards of entitlement from his country, or the avowal of a total political defeat.[92] The same utilitarian motive can be recognized in the heroes of contemplation who are moved—and here again Valla has recourse to his favorite technique of turning upside down traditional assumptions of doctrine, in a kind of philosophical retaliation—by a more or less unconfessed desire for glory.[93] Into this discussion he deliberately introduces a new exemplum from a patristic source well-known to medieval audiences, the legend of how Aristotle, unable to grasp the nature of the Euripus, drowned in its whirlpools, according to the *Oratio IV in Iulianum* by St. Gregory of Nazianzus.[94] In keeping with this pattern of implicitly referring to the diatribes of theologians, we encounter another old acquaintance when Valla deals extensively with poetry and myth. Here, too, the traditional justification of allegory seems turned on its head. The authority of poets is in itself enough to credit the hedonistic and utilitarian motives attributed to the gods: "Who would dare compare himself to the poets, or, worse, put himself above them and reproach their lives and ways of thinking?"[95]

After this brief explanation, the discrepancy between the blatant materialism of the first two books and the Christian doctrine expounded in the third book no longer seems so contradictory, or at least not so embarrassing. What links them is not, in fact, the dialectical contrast of opposing arguments—from which the reader is asked to choose—but rather the denial that a concept of materialism, according to the medieval cliché, necessarily springs from the principle of usefulness (*utilitatis ratio*), which the "Epicurean" interlocutor defends.[96] Such a criterion, epitomized in the notion of "pleasure" encompassing both the motives and ends of human behavior, can be transferred to the higher plane of action that is moved by faith and manifested in the voluntary fervor of "charity," a *voluptas* itself that epitomizes the highest virtues. In this way Valla avoids every form of ethical dogmatism as well as every theological ontologism. Not only that, but to the extent that the proposed criterion of the greatest usefulness finds its methodological equivalent in argumentative principles speciously assimilated to rhetorical ones, and which are actually opposed to the essential points of scholastic argumentation, the medieval system of *auctoritates* breaks down. Here, as he does elsewhere in his works, Valla directs his attack particularly toward those *auctores* and tendencies upon whose grounds medieval culture had attempted to build a theological or Christian synthesis, or in any case, which it had maintained as fundamental in the teachings of the school and in the formulation of its doctrine—from Platonism to Aristotelianism, from Seneca to Boethius.[97]

Let me now recapitulate the outline I have tried to trace in the preceding pages. Petrarch, almost isolating the great ancients from the succeeding patristic tradition, had vindicated their autonomous worth, but always as bearers of values equivalent to those celebrated by the Christian faith, and of whom he could boast, as in the case of the Platonists and Cicero, on the high authority of Augustine. Then Bruni and Poggio, linking up with Petrarch, had more definitely circumscribed the sphere of secular culture, shaping it according to a Ciceronian model of eclectic and relativistic tendencies, but at the same time adding something of their own. Valla, taking up the question at the level of first principles, came to an absolute separation of culture and faith. He conflated culture with a methodology that, whatever the field of application, precluded any straying from the strict terms of empirical reasoning, and limited faith to a pure but undefined adherence to the revealed word. Opposition to the ideal and practical order of medieval culture could not have been more complete.

As can be seen from the cautious and circumspect assessments by Bruni and Marsuppini, not to mention Traversari,[98] when the *De vero bono* first circulated, contemporaries were not so ready to welcome the challenge. With some analogy to Petrarch's fortune, Valla's profound influence would have to wait until the next century before it would be felt. Unlike Petrarch, however, his impact would take the shape of a transposition of methods in the field of philosophical debate and even more so that of religious conflicts. Thus Valla's writings extended their influence far beyond philology, in the domain of philosophic and religious issues as well. That is as if to say, far beyond the limits I established for this essay.

3
Poggio Bracciolini and San Bernardino
The Themes and Motives of a Polemic

This study deals primarily with Poggio Bracciolini and his epistolary and literary works in which he refers, usually in polemical tones, to San Bernardino and to the Observant movement in general. But first of all, it is useful to identify two different but clearly connected factors motivating these writings. In some contexts he essentially limits himself to reiterating the criticism raised in ecclesiastic circles and religious orders by Bernardino's preaching, speaking with his customary independence but also in some way from his privileged standpoint as papal secretary. At other times he expresses more personal opinions as a layman and especially as a spokesman for a secular humanist culture, and nowhere more emphatically than in his dialogue *De avaritia* (1429). In this essay I shall discuss the criticisms that Poggio leveled against Bernardino while the saint was alive, and not the later and more broadly antimonastic polemics in his later dialogue *Contra hypocritas.* This discussion will seek to illuminate Poggio's cultural and ethical perspectives and, consequently, will enter neither into "the world of San Bernardino"—to echo the title of a successful book—nor into the various exegetical problems related to Bernardino's own works. If in the process of this study I must review rather irreverent remarks, I do so in the belief that such polemics are an important indication of the climate of opinion and historical moment when Bernardino's preaching captured the attention of fifteenth-century Italy.

All things considered, Poggio's marginal participation in ecclesiastical disputes may seem of slight importance, however much expressed with his typical frankness and argumentative skill. I refer to the controversies surrounding the worship of the Holy Name of Jesus that Bernardino introduced as a triumphal veneration of Christ's Majesty. This subject has been amply treated and needs no further comment here, nor do the theological and disciplinary issues that fueled the debate. The Holy Name devotion also had an impact on the learned community. The Venetian humanist Francesco Barbaro, for example, who met Bernardino in 1423 while serving as podestà of Treviso, was one of many who adopted the sign of IHS as invocatio in his letters. Later, in 1426, when Bernardino's adversaries (and the Dominicans in particular) accused him of having separated the human from the divine, almost in a new version of Arianism, and particularly of having tried to evade obedience to the pope, the vicar of Christ (a serious issue indeed because of the contemporary censures of the Hussites' free preaching), Martin V responded by summoning Bernardino to Rome. The pope absolved Bernardino, but with the admonition to impose limits temporarily on his popular new form of devotion. This is alluded to in a letter Poggio wrote to Barbaro, congratulating him because "you have made yourself a Christian, having set aside that 'jesuity' which you used to write at the beginning of your letters." Poggio seems to make himself an interpreter of heresy charges ("they were devising a new heretical sect"), and especially charges of religious demagogy that had been made against Bernardino ("this separation is the result of ambition and pomp more than of sanctity and religious feeling").[1] The theological controversy, resolved in the Roman trial, now seems to be reduced to a question of philology. As a learned man, Barbaro rightfully joining the names of Jesus and Christ, "does not separate words that cannot be separated." There was more dignity in the name of Christ, whence the denomination of Christians comes, than Jesus' (*ex quo et Christiani dicimur, quam Iesu*). Given the humanists' custom to refer anonymously to one another in their writings, in all probability these remarks influenced Valla's same argument in the *Collatio Novi Testamenti*. With a grammatical rigor featured as an ideology proper, Valla uses precisely Poggio's words: "The name Christ, by which we are called Christians, is no less venerable than Jesus, after whom we are not named" (*Neque minus venerable nomen est*

Christus, unde Christiani dicimur, quam Iesu, unde non dicimur). Among other things, Valla added with a certain malicious satisfaction that the mistaken confusion of the Greek capital *H* (actually the "eta," or lengthy "e," in the Greek alphabet) with the Latin aspirated *h* (and the respective symbolism of the cross) had bordered on heresy: "so that, while they prefer to correct rather than to follow antiquity, they have fallen into the pit they deserved, and almost into heresy."[2] We see here an early example of the humanistic disdain for symbols and allegories such as Bernardino's investment in the Trigraph. (Such was, so to speak, the dissolving spirit of new philology.)

I agree only partially with A. Morisi, who says such humanist criticism of the superstitious manifestations of popular piety conformed with an "inner, spiritual piety, wholly individualistic, and not especially concerned with specific dogmatic motivations."[3] Morisi's interpretation is influenced by the writings of the Augustinian friar Andrea Biglia, who played an important role in the dispute about the Holy Name and who presented arguments somewhat analogous (perhaps not accidentally) to remarks by Poggio and Valla. Biglia accuses Bernardino of resorting to magic tricks in order to enthrall the imagination of his simple audience. He also claims that by tending to anthropomorphize the image of God, Bernardino loses the wholly Augustinian sense of the infinite distance between Creator and creature, and of the enlightening power of grace that excludes a narrowly prescribed ethics. Biglia's reproaches in some way resemble the remarks in a recent historical essay by G. Miccoli, who concludes that "once that name and symbol were stripped of their elements of Joachimitism, they assumed an autonomy so charged with power, and therefore with reverence and adoration, as to become a symbol endowed with a value in and for itself, so to be proposed to the attention and devotion of faithful," and which was conceived as a correction as well as a substitution to those of a magical nature.[4] But to return to Poggio (with Valla the question is more complex), it would be difficult to recognize genuine theological, not to say religious, motivation for his criticism. As we have seen, Poggio accuses friars of "pomp" and pride mixed with "ignorance," and soon to these accusations he would add another one, directed more generally at the spread of the Observants' preaching, in which he condemns their lust for power disguised in hypocrisy ("obeying no one, and being the masters of everybody").[5] This constitutes the central theme of the short dialogue *Contra hypocritas,* written at the end of the pontificate of Eugenius IV, who had favored and most fully integrated the Observant friars into the ecclesiastical power structure.[6]

Although aligning with, and almost concealing himself behind, theological polemics and established Church authority, the humanist papal secretary viewed the new form of worship introduced by Bernardino as essentially nothing more than a troublesome intrusion in the already sufficiently unsettled events of this world.

Poggio became involved in a controversy of a more personal nature when, in 1429–30, he was accused of taking advantage of his powers as Apostolic secretary to block the construction of an Observant Franciscan monastery near San Giovanni Valdarno, on land bequeathed to Bernardino by the wealthy Florentine, Carlo Ricasoli. Pointing out that Poggio himself owned property in the same area, some modern scholars too have drawn the rather simplistic conclusion that his challenge to Bernardino's claim and his feelings of hostility toward the friars stemmed from self-interest. In reality, immersed as he was in the affairs of the curia, Poggio's position permitted him easy access to the conflicts between the two branches of the Franciscan Minor Order, the Conventuals and Observants (who refused to obey the minister general, Antonio da Massa). In 1431 the pope demanded that the General Chapter in Assisi find a resolution to their quarrels, and he arranged that until such a settlement had been reached no new convents would be founded. However things stood, and whatever the incident may reveal about the privileges of discretion that papal secretaries were thought to enjoy in this period, we can be sure that Poggio was acting in accordance with instructions from superiors.[7] But this does not preclude that Poggio found in the situation a good opportunity to state more fully his own personal impatience with the Observants and the spread of their activity. The episode is also interesting because it provoked an explicit response — the only one to our knowledge — from an authority within the order, Alberto of Sarteano, perhaps the spokesman for Bernardino himself. Alberto, writing to Niccoli, expressed his concern "about the eloquence and authority of Poggio" whose invectives might be heard and believed by "people foreign to religious orders." Alberto's remarks raise the sensitive point of the broader audience for Poggio's works and at least the potential impact on public opinion that his letters enjoyed — precisely what Niccoli had been urged to keep in check. (The issue is an important one because scholarly opinion has traditionally considered Poggio's correspondence only for its literary or biographical value.)[8] Writing to Niccoli, who evidently played the part of spokesman and moderator in the affair, Poggio intensified his accusations of the friars' "hypocrisy" and of their desire to subvert good social order under the cover of their sacred cassock, as he had learned from long experience in the curia: "But I have been deceived so often, and tricked so often by opinion, that I no longer know what to believe or in whom to trust. . . . Many things come to be known in the curia, who remain unknown to those outside it. . . . Here indeed all the vices meet so that (Roman curia) acts like a mirror in which both the actions and mores of many people are perceived."[9] Although his words profess respect for the religious habit, the basic motive for Poggio's attack is a deep-seated skepticism of the effectiveness of that ideal of perfection as followed in the monastic state. Alberto of Sarteano referred to this criticism in a long letter to Poggio, written like a manifesto for public audience. Both in his letter to Niccoli and in his reply to Alberto, the position Poggio adopts is not based on doctrine but on common human experience; it comes not from within the Church but from a layman who claims, on the basis of his own wisdom and experience, his right to have his say: "Let it be known to you that I am one who, although bad, nevertheless shrinks from the conduct of those, who, with the pretence of good, do not deceive others as much as they do themselves. . . . A squalid vestment does not contribute to virtue, but only character and holy living." Whether the convent was built or not was of little importance: "For I have no need of their doctrines or their examples."[10]

Poggio actually made an exception for Bernardino, along with Alberto, who demonstrates in his sermons "the greatest moderation and diligence" and more precisely who "has been many different places and has caused neither error nor agitation among the people."[11] This is an obvious allusion to a temporary renunciation of the cult of the Holy Name ("a thing that seemed to require a little censure:" *quod videbatur in eo paulo reprehendendum*). In such remarks it is difficult to ascertain to what extent motives of obvious caution, irony, and sincerity may be at play, in an ambiguity typical of Poggio that will be illustrated later. What is worth noting, however, is how Poggio affirms in his own way what research has since clarified about Bernardino's cautious tactics, his concern not to offend the established orders, both ecclesiastical and secular, the "narrow boundaries" that circumscribed his political and social activity, such as the fulfillment of unenforced rules or the legitimizing of daily activities as far as they were compatible with the precepts of good Christian living.[12]

It is not my intention to dwell on questions that Bernardino's preaching have raised for historical interpretation—whether it represents the sanctioning of a "pastoral action of utilitarianism and terror" due to discouragement with Church reform and responsible lay participation; or whether it serves as a limit to the secularization of public life, conceived as "a completed and irreversible fact."[13] We could easily read in Poggio's polemics (and some scholars have actually done so) the sign of that secularization Bernardino preached against, while, through an opposite platitude, also recognize a solidarity between the humanists' "civic" concern and Bernardino's social preaching. As the irreconcilability of such general assumptions suggests, the question is actually more complex. Even though his ethical and cultural attitude is soundly different from Bernardino's, Poggio too is driven by respect for the present social order that does not preclude a pessimistic view of contemporary reality and is pointing his own way to a restoration of morality. Poggio's argument, violent to the point of caricature, seems somewhat paradoxical, and it is precisely on this paradox that his dialogue *De avaritia* was constructed. This text has been a subject of controversial interpretations among scholars and may be considered the real ground on which Poggio's and Bernardino's attitudes confronted each other. The dialogue was published in 1429, in the midst of the public disputes I have mentioned at the beginning of this chapter.[14]

According to its literary frame, the dialogue opens with the discussion of the theme of the day: Fra Bernardino's preaching in Rome in 1426. Antonio Loschi, dean of papal secretaries and one of the principal interlocutors, praises him as "a man among whom all those I have heard is, in my opinion, eloquent and learned enough." Loschi was especially struck by Bernardino's ability to arouse the emotions of his audience: "he excels in one thing: by persuading and exciting the people he prevails on their emotions and leads them wherever he wants, moving them to tears and, when it fits, to laughter."[15] Loschi's appraisal deliberately echoes the contemporary apologetic praise of Bernardino's preaching that amplified the friar's explicit boast about renewing traditional preaching styles (the humanist Matteo Vegio would later refer to him as a "Christian Cicero," adding that "he has so much power over men that the greatest orators attest there is nothing stronger").[16] However, what sparks the discussion is actually not Loschi's praise but a challenge to the common opinion. The second interlocutor, Cencio Rustici—a background figure in the dialogue, but one who in several instances actually serves as spokesman for the author himself—acknowledges that Bernardino's concern with amending customs, and especially soothing civil conflicts "which were many and serious," was a beneficial one. However, distancing himself from the common assumptions, he confesses to being profoundly skeptical about the methods and effectiveness of preaching: "But on one point (with your good leave) both [Bernardino] himself and other preachers like him seem to me be wrong. For though they say many things, they adapt their sermons not to our advantage, but rather to their own loquaciousness." Instead of attending to spiritual ills, they try to win the people over and receive their applause. On the basis of some stereotypes they talk about "abstruse and obscure things" that are inaccessible to their audience; or they squander their words on silly women and common riff-raff, "whom you see going away more foolish than before they came." By discussing vices the preachers are actually teaching them; they do not consider the impact of their words, and with all their demagoguery, "few if any of them . . . come away from their sermons actually improved." The foolishness of those people is laughable. When queried about the merit of a sermon they had praised enthusiastically, "they hesitate and fall silent, or confess they don't know."[17]

Such comments are reminiscent of Poggio's *Facetiae* that often satirize the preacher and reveal here as in no other place their innovative cultural significance compared to the traditional genre of exemplum. Scholars have spoken of a "decline" or a "secularization" of the exemplum. By this they mean the erosion of a tradition of edifying morality, as presented in brief apologues, into a more precise narrative adapted to the social climate, until they take the form and wit of a literary tale (those by Bernardino, for example, among others).[18] Even taking into account the popular extensions and vernacular transformations of the genre, Poggio's *facetia*, if judged according to its least rash characteristics, does not fit easily into that definition. Quite the contrary, with its own repertory of themes, identical at times to those used in sermons, it appears to be a genuine alternative to the old genre of exemplum. The intended purpose, in fact, is not didactic but colloquial ("I want to be read . . . by witty and well-educated people"), involving the approval of an enlightened and learned public and, conversely, taking for granted the harsh criticism of those who were devoid, even "in the basest things" (*in rebus infimis*), of such breadth of humanity.[19] In rhetorical terms, Poggio's attempt, destined to enjoy so great a success, can be defined as the application to popular matters of that ethos on which classical oratorical doctrine based the principle of the "delectare" (within the three degrees of persuasion: docere, delectare, movere—to teach, to delight, to move). Quintilian had set ethos against pathos: "According to the teaching of learned men, the emotions are stirred by pathos and calmed by ethos; they are violently aroused by the first, made gentle by the second; at last the first makes commands, the second persuades; the first moves to confusion, the second to kindness"; consequently, Quintilian describes its property as "rather similar to comedy" (*comoediae . . . magis simile*).[20] This explains Poggio's adoption of a comical lexicon in his *Facetiae,* which would become a canonical prerequisite in the literary theorizing of the genre, as in Pontano's treatise *De sermone.*[21] However, of more importance for us now is the fact that the ethos informing the *Facetiae* is the opposite of oratory intended to excite the emotions and instill terror, according to a charge, among others, for which Poggio reproaches Bernardino at the very beginning of his dialogue. His style is also described in the words of Bartolomeo of Montepulciano, who, as we will see, hints ironically at the tenor of Bernardino's preaching when he presents an allegorical image of avarice that "strikes great terror in the minds of men."[22] The *Facetiae* that focus on the figure of the usurer are obviously quite different in tenor from Bernardino's treatment of the theme, which, according to Poggio, created an unintentional comical effect: "Once he spoke about usurers, moving the people to laughter more than to horror at such a great crime."[23] The *Facetia* 91, for example, focuses on the feigned repentance of an old usurer who convinces himself to abandon his job, so that he can preserve his good name and riches after death—clearly a loaded reference to what was then a usual practice: "he professed that he would abandon the practice of usury not out of awareness of his sin, but for fear of having to give up everything he had put aside."[24] The theme of the old usurer is taken up again later (*Facetia* 251), where the old man, "who has destroyed and lost his soul," leaves his trade to his son, only to use his own experience later to advise him secretly. This time the anecdote concludes with a moral: "Things return easily to their own nature."[25] This last *facetia* is somewhat analogous to one of Bernardino's exempla: a usurer who refuses to let a priest pawn a crucifix, protesting that he has reformed his ways ("I gave back [unjust profit] and I amended: therefore I do not lend any more"). But then he hypocritically directs the priest to his son for instructions ("I take pity on you: let you go to my son who is lending").[26] In Poggio's story, the exemplary aim—to stir up a horror of sacrilege and of the unpardonable nature of the sin of usury—is turned into a game of appearances and reality, of opinion and essence. This is the serious side of Poggio's *Facetiae*. Beyond the purely rhetorical context of the literary genre we are led back to the central motive of Poggio's moral discourse: the falsehood that hides behind appearances, the discrepancy between words and deeds, the foolish pretense of shaping reality with words; in short, the denunciation of those "bombastic words and pompous sayings," as Poggio had characterized sermon oratory in another context.[27] The medicine, according to a Stoic terminology borrowed by Cicero, Seneca, and Petrarch, was to be sought elsewhere.

At this point a parenthesis is in order. The metaphor of the doctor, and the Stoic concept of "remedy," which identifies the roots of spiritual ills and indicates the cure, unlike the mere casuistry's precepts of the mendicant preaching ("they run in different directions and wander indiscriminately through various kinds of illnesses, according to where their love of talking takes them, without persisting in anyone's cure")[28] leads back to Petrarch's lesson and his appeal to the inner self—but this is an interiority understood not in a strictly religious sense but in a broadly moral one, insofar as it is conceived from the standpoint of common human weaknesses, that can appeal on a level of autonomous dignity to the testimonies of secular authors. The scheme of *Secretum*, with its subtle interchangeability of penitential motives and moral introspection, of Christian spirituality and secular wisdom, has been sufficiently explored, and there is no need for elaboration here. Rather, what needs emphasizing, especially since it concerns an aspect perhaps not sufficiently appreciated for its moral implications, is the significance Petrarch places on a recurring passage in Seneca about his inclusion of Epicurean maxims within the very core of Stoic doctrine. "What is true is my own" (*Quod verum est, meum est*), wrote Seneca; and Petrarch echoes him, "Whatever is said well by anyone, it is no more something extraneous, but as if were belonging to myself."[29] Considered by scholars especially important to the rhetorical theory of imitation, the maxim is also remarkable for the direct polemical intentions that it implies. In fact, it does not differ in nature from the Petrarchan notion of the *libri mei peculiares*—his own favorite books—which turned upside down the old ecclesiastical concept of an exploitable appropriation of pagan authors, of a "twisting" (*retorquere*) of ancient moral maxims into precepts of Christian ethics.[30] Hence we can better understand Petrarch's polemics "against those who display knowledge which is not their own and pluck off florets" (*contra ostentatores scientie non sue ac flosculorum decerptores*): that is, his opposition to the extrinsic and repetitive genre of the florilegia and collections of moralities and examples.[31] Petrarch's open target, but more generally assumed as the prototype of so many other literary compilations of the time, is Valerius Maximus's collection, *Facta ac dicta memorabilia,* a text almost canonized at the time as a manual of ethics. Once again, Petrarch backs up his argument with a passage from Seneca (this philosopher "hors de l'école," independent from scholastic narrowness, as described by the French scholar Pierre Grimal), almost as a defiance of the vast medieval fortune of Seneca himself through the tradition of various compendia and "tables" of moral sayings. In Seneca's opinion, it was shameful for an experienced man "to pick florets" (*captare flosculos*), that is, to resort to the manuals of commonplaces (or *chrias*) usual in schools, which Petrarch compared to the *deflorationes,* or repertories for contemporary preaching: "to be sure it is fitting (for a man of ripe age) to enjoy the fruit, not the flowers."[32]

These are the same main concepts that Poggio brought down from the rarefied and allusive context of Petrarch's writings into a militantly polemical context, directly contrasting with the traditional metaphor of the garden (or *viridarium*), quoted by Bernardino to describe the fruit he hoped his preaching would produce: "and you pick one flower, and then another, and then another again, and in this way you make yourself a wreath and wear it on your head as you learn what you should learn."[33] Alongside and inseparable from this argument against a preaching exercised through "authorities, reason, and examples" is another more general disagreement with allegorical interpretation. This, too, is grounded on Petrarch's formulations that excluded allegory from moral and historical discourse, "clear sky" compared to the "cloudiness" of poetry,[34] because of which, also with regard to poetry, the allegorical-moral exegesis seemed to him like an optional exercise and an arbitrary one when compared to the poet's actual intentions. The passage from the *Secretum* is well known, where the storm in *Aeneid* 1.52–57 is cited as representing the tumult of anger; but then the author adds, through the authoritative intervention of the Augustine's character, that the interpretation was more ingenious ("spoken aptly and wittily enough") than faithful to Virgil's intentions: "Whether Virgil himself understood it this way, or whether it was the furthest thing from his mind, he wanted to describe a stormy sea with these words, and nothing more."[35] This ambivalence is not significantly different from the more elaborate and subtle context of *Seniles* 4.5, "On certain fictions in Virgil."[36]

The same argumentation is taken up and further developed in Poggio's *De avaritia*. The interlocutor, Bartolomeo of Montepulciano, first entrusted with the detestatio of avarice, in a context ironically allusive to preaching styles, alleges that the image of Virgil's Harpies symbolizes the monstrosity of vice and insatiability of a miser, "who surpasses the deformity of any kind of monster."[37] The irony implicit in the pedantry of his exegesis, as he builds on the proposed *thema* in the style of a sermon, is made explicit in a passage added to the second version of the dialogue. Antonio Loschi, Bartolomeo's refuter, judges this interpretation to be "quite ridiculous and inept . . . and unworthy of a learned man," and in any case no more pertinent to avarice than to any other vice. "And so I have always despised the silly presumption of the authority and wisdom that certain people for their superstitious fancy suppose to be concealed into the poets' tales": what could be more foolish than to think that there were hidden meanings in the tales of Plautus and Terence, "which were invented to delight the ears of the people and which were accustomed to be sold by the aediles?"[38] As has been suggested, in all probability Poggio is making a direct reference to Coluccio Salutati's *De laboribus Herculis* ("which happened to a certain man of our time"), who, in an extensive Virgilian exegesis, alludes to the episode of the Harpies as a metaphor for avarice.[39] Salutati's brief reference (which he took from Servius) is given more extensive treatment in Bartolomeo's discourse, as a way of leading into a parody of the typical procedures of the *ars praedicandi*.[40] Therefore, it seems plausible, as one scholar has suggested, to see a connection between Harpies' imagery and Bernardino's allegorical interpretation of the thema of Psalm 38.12 ("you have made my soul languish like a spider"), where the monstrosity of avarice is represented in the Scriptural image of the spider (in other words, parallel to its equivalent of the Harpies in the poetic fiction).[41] Finally, it is important to note the allusion to comic theater, which is particularly appropriate considering the language of Plautus that is used to describe the exempla of misers (further on Plautus's *Aulu-*

laria is expressly cited), once again with malicious comparisons to Bernardino's repertory of *exempla* ("and he doesn't eat as much as he wants; out of avarice he eats badly and sleeps worse").[42] Stripped of its measure of ethos—to recall what we observed with regard to the *Facetiae*—oratory is transformed from tragedy into comedy: it becomes itself a dramatic performance. In his Oration to the Fathers at the Council of Constance, Poggio had said of preachers that "they are little different from the mimes who once, in the time of our ancestors, used to tell stories on the stage."[43]

The humanistic return to the precepts of classical eloquence is also to be understood in terms of a conscious opposition to the rhetoric of the school, and especially to the *artes praedicandi,* as well as to its various utilitarian applications at the level of popular preaching. We must return again to Petrarch, whose ideological impact on his humanist followers cannot be overemphasized. It is typical that, in his copy of Quintilian's *Oratory Institution,* next to the passage "Imitation alone is not enough, especially because to be content with the inventions of others is a characteristic of the lazy mind," he added his autograph note: *Hinc illud est quod in scholastica disciplina,* this is the very thing that happens in the scholastic method of today.[44] As if continuing and radicalizing this same statement, Valla in *De voluptate* draws a harsh comparison between good and bad rhetoric: "Such is the insistence on the arguments put forward, such the excess of *exempla,* such the repetition of the same things, such the twisting of the discourse which clings, like vines, to everything, that we do not know which is greater, its uselessness or its shamefulness."[45] The reference to the ritual "distinction" and "divisions" within the ecclesiastical sermon, as well as the emblematic representation of the sermon itself as a tree, is here unmistakable.

Poggio had been even more explicit in his Oration to the Fathers of the Council of Constance. The main point of his discourse was to condemn the hollow words pouring forth from the pulpits that could not be verified through a purity of intentions or real examples of life. As previously stated, preachers ascended the pulpit like ancient mimes: "they begin with some maxim—the thema of the sermon—and then go on to weave their orations with the words of others." Like Cato in ancient times, they exhorted their audiences to love virtue and hate vice, while preaching's actual outcome contrasts dramatically with its magniloquence and the solemnity of verbal apparatus: "these things need to be reformed, otherwise confusion will result in everything."[46] Poggio's "Oratio ad patres,"

by the way, provides an important historical evidence of a surely not in-
sulated mistrust of traditional instruments of religious ethical persuasion,
at a crucial point in the Church's crisis. In the oration Poggio has no reform to propose; he limits himself to concrete examples of life, the only
teachings to him that would avoid a real crisis of faith: "If both the words
and deeds of the past did not delight us more than the corrupt examples
of the present, faith would doubtless be lost."[47]

This explains the paradox that made the understanding of *De avaritia* so controversial. According to Poggio, Bernardino's preaching seemed
"useless" and particularly ineffective concerning the major vice of avarice.
This kind of preaching against "avarice" (actually, usury) is the cue and the
motive of the dialogue: "Bernardino never touches on this vice; once he
has spoken about usurers, moving people to laughter more than to horror
of such a crime. But avarice, which encourages usury, he leaves unmen-
tioned."[48] Avarice, insofar as it represents a general ethical category, is previously distinguished from the sin of usury (which is to say, from its most
serious and wicked manifestation at the social level, according to Bernardino's preaching). Poggio makes the distinction not so much to justify de
facto current economic practices as to dissociate the vice from the casuistry of precepts (the "eighteen ways to sin in business," "who is obliged
to return what, and how much," etc.), which he considers unfitting and
inept with regard to the basic theme. Inspired by Seneca, the "preceptor of morals," and moved by his own skepticism of the actual impact
of the precepts on society, the author challenges Bernardino's belief in a
correlation between maxims and moral life; and therefore, leaving aside
the subtleties of scholasticism ("those acute and philosophical things"),
he aims at a circumscribed, or—that is the same—a colloquial sphere of
persuasion: "Whereby let us try to be of some use with our conversation,
if not to others, at least to ourselves."[49]

This divergence in method, leading to a different meaning of morality, is
essential for understanding *De avaritia*. The dialogue is conducted, as the
author himself states, according to the "custom of the Academics," as a debate in utramque partem. The opening condemnation of avarice by Bartolomeo of Montepulciano is followed by a defense of misers by Antonio
Loschi. It concludes with a lengthy peroration delivered by Andreas of
Constantinople, a Christian theologian who is introduced into the dia-

logue to confirm from the highest position of authority the condemnation of such a ruinous and widespread vice, and so to establish a consensus among the participants. As the dialogue unfolds, however, the classical model of Academic debate seems inappropriate: there is no real confrontation of opposing doctrines, and no suspension of judgment, as was typical of the Skeptics; nor is there, as in Cicero, an attempt to come to an eclectic composition. All three of the major discourses are serious and ironic as well, precisely what we are accustomed to find elsewhere in Poggio's writings. Most importantly, as the dialogue unfolds, the author does not follow Cicero's model of philosophical dialogue as much as he follows Seneca's moral exhortations.[50] The variety of opinions, rather than clearly individuated philosophical theses, reflects the sometimes interchangeable subjectivity of different points of view, so that the final impression can only be ambiguous. In the first discourse, Bartolomeo of Montepulciano judges that of the two most reprehensible vices, avarice is worse than lust: the latter is alluring but natural and controllable by reason,[51] while the former is contrary to nature and must be uprooted since it cannot be moderated. Loschi overturns the criterion for judgment. Avarice is the common impetus behind human activity, and "we are all led by greed for riches." Therefore, according to experience, the impulse (cupiditas) is natural, being compatible with social virtues, and indeed is the very stimulus necessary for civic life. Who would do anything if not moved by utility? Who does not put his own aims first in arming himself "against future mishaps and blow of fortune"?[52] Understood on these terms, avarice cannot be evaluated according to doctrine, as the legislators who had avoided establishing any rules regarding it had well understood, maintaining that "something like as seeds of avarice" (*semina quaedam avaritiae*) were congenital.[53]

In a subtle dialectical passage (Loschi had conflated two different concepts, cupiditas and avaritia, defining the second as an excess of the first: "a desire which greatly exceeds measure"),[54] Andreas reestablishes the primacy of philosophy as life's instruction. Avarice is the negation of every virtue, and for this reason cannot be acknowledged by nature. It was condemned not only by philosophers but by the highest apostolic and patristic authorities as the root of all evil, comparable to idolatry and heresy.[55] Therefore, men should cultivate virtue, and not uncertain goods subject to fickle fortune; and they should keep in mind the immortality of the soul and fear the Last Judgment. Beyond the individual authorities, avarice is condemned by truth and the voice of nature itself, according to the unanimous testimonies of wise men. The only salvation for the usurer was to repent and recognize the value of reason.

The emphasis of the concluding peroration, which would seem to overcome every doubt, is nonetheless far from resolving the ambiguities evident in the vacillation of terms and criteria used for judgment: nature and reason, experience and authority. There is no question that Poggio assigns a primary position to reason, and thereby to the instructive value of philosophy, "the leader and teacher of how to live a good life," consistent with his statements more or less freely derived from Stoic philosophy and so often reiterated and consistent with adherence to Christian precepts.[56] The difficulty, however, lies at the level of direct perception, in the problematic congruence between principles and concrete experience, hence in the ambivalence of the concept of "nature" itself. If, on the one hand, as the Stoics believe, the very foundation of human reason relies on nature, on the other hand nature seems to be nothing but the domain of the human instincts, over which men have little control. This is essentially the same dilemma that Poggio proposes elsewhere regarding the concept of "fortune," which he refuses to define in philosophical terms ("leaving aside any search for a definition") and which he recognizes only in the irrationality of its effects ("so that the random affairs of mortals seem to be tossed about according to her will"), without the counterbalance of a "consolation of philosophy"; in other words, without faith in a fixed order in the world beyond the subjective and empirical sphere of experience, or in a direct rapport with divine providence.[57]

The same applies to the theme of avarice. Its definition cannot be based on philosophical certitudes, and so the developing speeches in the dialogue will be distinguished instead by the different degrees of persuasiveness, and therefore on a broadly relativistic plane. Andreas appears to be reaffirming what Bartolomeo has said, assuming a purely repetitive role, though with greater eloquence and authority. However, by not disavowing the reality of the passions—that *cupiditas* which is strongly condemned in the first discourse—he puts himself on the more elevated plane of principles and authority, of lofty exhortation, but for this very reason he does not aim at a prescriptive level.

The dialogue, as has been recognized by scholars, revolves around the concept of *eicere*, the "casting out," the expulsion of the avaricious, the rooting out vice, according to an implicit reference to the fundamental canon *Eiciens Dominus* (D. 88, c.11). The canon reproduced the anonymous commentary on Matthew 21.12, which the *Decretum Gratiani* improperly attributes to John Chrysostom, where the expulsion of the merchants from the temple was credited to divine disapproval of commerce and so became an obligatory point of reference in theological speculation about the legitimacy of profit-based activity.[58]

Scholasticism, and particularly the speculations by the Franciscan Pietro di Giovanni Olivi, extensively used by Bernardino, had tempered the ancient prohibition, legitimizing the figure of the merchant insofar as he was useful to society ("because in commerce many things contribute to the service and benefit of the state"). The threat of divine punishment was understood as applicable to illicit business, to the usurers who were the real source of evil and who therefore ought to be expelled, "since two or three in one great city can corrupt the entire business community."[59] On this basis, Oppel formulated the paradoxical thesis that Poggio's intention, "very conservative indeed," had been aimed at reestablishing, in opposition to Bernardino and Olivi, the pseudo-Chrysostom's rigor. According to him, Loschi would hint ironically at the Franciscan doctrine, while Andreas's concluding discourse confirms pseudo-Chrysostom's severity, in connection with the programs of ecclesiastical reform.[60] Oppel's argument is clearly an artificial one, and Goldbrunner has produced an easy refutation of it. However, I cannot agree with Goldbrunner on another topic. According to him, the references in Poggio's dialogue to Bernardino are nothing more but a contribution to its historical setting, while he ignores the role they have as a key motive in its inner development.[61] The ironic re-echoing of themes from Bernardino's sermons is particularly obvious in Bartolomeo's opening discourse. It is no accident that in the economy of the unfolding dialogue, Bartolomeo's discourse needs the correction of the two subsequent speakers, though from different points of view. For example, when Bartolomeo states that misers should be banished from human society "like a seed-bed of evils,"[62] he is repeating almost literally the pivotal point of Bernardino's preaching on economics: that there ought to be a decree expelling the evil merchant, precisely because he was at the very origin of sin.

Loschi replies that in such a case the cities would be deserted, implying the impossibility of distinguishing the lawful from the unlawful in the real world of profit-based activities and from actions in general aimed at procuring advantage.[63] But also inside Andreas's discourse we can recognize subtle ironical intentions in the rhetorical variations about the basic theme of the "eicere." Mindful of Plato's decree to banish poets from his utopian state, Andreas remarks, "Indeed if it were up to me . . . I would decree all misers be banished from the cities." The banishment then appears to be reduced to a vain hope, to an unrealistic hypothesis. And the irony is transformed into parody by Cencio Rustici's comment, which, in a sense, frames the ancient threatening like an antiquarian table of laws, as if to contemplate its ineffectiveness: "Let the misers no longer be in the cities, let us expel them by public decree whenever they still remain" (*Avari in urbibus ne sunto, qui fuerint publico edicto eiicantur*). More wisely, Cicero in his "Laws," "perhaps complying with the times," limited himself to punishing with a fine.[64]

Another point needs to be made. As already mentioned, Oppel claims to recognize in Loschi's defense of profit "a kind of parody" of Bernardino's presumed "permissiveness," which Oppel badly confuses with Scotist so-called latitudinarianism—the concept of a *magna latitudo*, of a great extension in matters of value and prices—or, in the words of Olivi and Bernardino, with the realization that it was impossible to establish precise quantitive values "by a rule and measurement indivisible into greater or lesser amounts, if not with some approximation, and an appropriate respect for the times, places, and the people."[65] Loschi's rather surprising statement, that no one has ever established a law "against avarice," perhaps refers precisely to this teaching.[66] Nevertheless, as Goldbrunner has perceptively observed, Loschi's basic arguments are posited in direct antithesis ("diametral gegenüber") to scholastic and theological speculations, as is made clear in the debate over Augustine's fundamental authority concerning the notion of the superfluous ("to want more than is enough").[67] Although he is referring to Bernardino and indeed develops his most original points in the course of his polemical confrontation with him, Loschi's discourse owes less to treatises "on merchants" than to Leonardo Bruni's translation and commentary on the *Economics* of pseudo-Aristotle (1420), which begins, like a real cultural manifesto, with a celebration of private wealth as an incentive for exercising virtue.[68] Poggio's ability to combine ideas drawn from different contexts is typical of his humanist prose, "such that . . . one thing will fall from another," as he himself once said.[69]

Recent studies by Soudek and Goldbrunner have clarified the meaning of Bruni's interpretation. Breaking from the systematic approach of scholasticism and showing little interest in defining the relationship between "economics" and "politics," Bruni assigned, in a simplified and empirical popularization of Aristotle's practical philosophy, an independent status to the treatment of *res familiaris*. The result was to offer an ethical justification of wealth for its own sake, a point that succeeded in attracting broad public interest, not to mention the incitement Bruni gave his younger contemporaries to outlining treatises on the topic, beginning with L. B. Alberti's *Libri della famiglia*.[70] Using Loschi as his spokesman, Poggio radicalized these arguments about economic individualism, going so far as to position them as the antithesis of the notion of the common good—the "key element," as it has been defined, of the Franciscans' subtle speculation about commerce ("for the common good," as Bernardino preached, "merchandising should be practiced"). This same central concept had been incorporated into Bartolomeo's discourse, where he defines a miser as someone "unmindful of public welfare" (*oblitus publici commodi*), or as "the public common enemy."[71] The frontal contrast with these assumptions makes the very core of Loschi's intervention: "Some things of this kind are said by philosophers, with more show than truth, about how the common good should come first." The reference becomes even more explicit in the words that follow: "The lives of mortals should not, however, be weighed on the scales of philosophy."[72] It has been suggested that this passage was prompted by Cicero's criticism of the Stoics' captious dialectic, inaccessible to general understanding: a good orator should adapt his speech "not to a goldsmith's scales, but to a kind of popular balance."[73] While the relevance of this comparison cannot be denied—indeed, Cicero's attitude toward ancient Stoic severity is a subject Poggio frequently resumed and utilized—this passage becomes still more meaningful if compared to typical postures in Bernardino's preaching: "How many examples you have, miser! Trust in the one who weighed the world!"; "I went with my scale, weighing Italy."[74] The implicit assimilation of Stoic rigor with theological doctrinarianism becomes transparent in the introduction of the second version of *De avaritia*. In keeping with the restraint to which he was exhorted by his friend Niccoli, Poggio replaced the passages in which he criticizes the preacher explicitly with another one from Cicero's anti-Stoical polemic, pronounced in the name of *humana prudentia,* the human common sense.[75] The meaning of these thoughts is further clarified in the developments of Loschi's speech. From the beginning of time (*ab ipsius mundi ortu*) man has always been moved more by private than by public interest.[76] Thus everyone would agree, "unless we prefer to pronounce pompous words instead of signifying what usually happens"[77] (*nisi malimus magnifica loqui quam consueta*). The juxtaposition of the two adjectives in antithesis, *magnifica-consueta*, once again on the authority of Cicero, and of Petrarch as well, is a valuable indication of the real aim of the discourse. But there is still another motive, perhaps not yet sufficiently recognized, that also makes this passage noteworthy. The evidence of common experience itself negated the Stoic doctrine, later developed by patristic and scholastic theologians, of an original state of innocence and common ownership of goods, the loss of which had furnished a justification for ownership as protection against human cupidity.[78]

These propositions are only partially corrected in Andreas's concluding discourse. It has been seen how he accepts the notion of *cupiditas* in a positive, though a "moderate and temperate," way, perhaps mindful, as a good Dominican theologian, of the "moderate profit" (*lucrum moderatum*) legitimized by Aquinas; whereas in the School tradition, "cupidity" was used only in its negative sense.[79] Moreover, with the exception of a few marginal asides, Andreas's peroration avoids referring to commerce in specific terms. The scriptural and patristic authorities that he cites indicate that the principal target is actually the clergy who fail to observe the canonical rules that regard them most directly. Once again, it is the figure in the background, Cencio Rustici, who expresses the author's intentions: "They read but they do not pay heed to the words of Isidore, who orders them to shun the love of money."[80] In connection with this, Marsh has appropriately observed that the immediate model for Andreas's admonition is not so much the rigorism of pseudo-Chrysostom as it is Petrarch's *Familiares* 6.1 ("Against the high prelates"), which likewise turns on the canonical passage of St. Paul, 1 Timothy 6.10, where cupidity is described as "the root . . . of all evil." Poggio's hostility to the clergy thus become obvious, as appears directly here and in numerous other places as well.[81] The reason for such attitude, however, is not, as Oppel claims, because Poggio adopts two different standards of judgment, one for clerics and another for laymen. "In this way he would be close to schizophrenia," was Goldbrunner's ironic response.[82] But the latter's own argument, that Poggio and his colleagues in the curia were actually part of the clerical order, is still more questionable. The clearest denial comes from Poggio himself, who—though enjoying ecclesiastical benefices in virtue of his minor orders, as was the custom of his time—had explicitly declared his desire to remain a layman, as his own *institutio vitae,* the rule of his life: "For a long time now I have resolved on a certain course of life . . . I do not want to be a priest, I do not want benefices . . . I have decided to live out whatever time remains of my life's journey far away from your order."[83] His attitude is even reflected in his Oration to the Fathers at the Council of Constance, in the apostrophe directed to the clergy, specified as "you" (*vos*), made in his own name, "myself" (*ego*), or of the laity's in general ("we," *nos*).[84] Poggio's profession to make the lay status as his own *institutio vitae* in the heart of the ecclesiastical structure went hand in hand with his preference for secular humanist culture. According to Poggio's testimony itself, this was a choice directly linked to his distrust of a Church that would be able to raise itself as an example of virtuous living, beyond mere oratorical or dogmatic verbal enunciations. Even though Poggio did not renounce his faith as a Christian and remained faithful to the traditional papal order, the clergy's bad example was evidence of the dichotomy between the Church's solemn principles and its actual behavior; in brief, it acted as a warning of the precariousness of the ethical-religious norm in and for itself.

Returning to the *De avaritia,* I have described the dialogue as less a confrontation of opposing theses than a treatment of the same theme in successive degrees of persuasiveness. Indeed, the high principles expressed by Andreas find a complement, almost an attenuation, in the words, though formally in full consensus, pronounced by Bartolomeo at the conclusion of the dialogue, which in reality insinuate a note of skepticism about their efficacy for the human soul: "But it is amazing that although we have so many reminders of excellent men, so much sound advice, so many authoritative and serious maxims placed before our eyes, by which the minds of men ought to be moved, nevertheless there exist those, who, having neglected reason, devote themselves to cupidity as though to a god."[85] As we see, the precept is diluted with a conditional ("ought to be"), the mood which, as grammarians explain, "weakens the actualization of the verb by desire"; by contrast, the relativism is further emphasized by the appeal in broad terms to the voice "of nature and truth"; that is, a voice that has always been heard in the world and that nevertheless has remained the same, so as to discourage any hope that men could actually improve themselves.[86] Poggio is only developing here in a more mature and literary fashion what he had already written in his Oration at

Constance, about the vices of the clergy and the decline of Christianity: "Those many warnings do not help lead us from vices, nor do we seek any help."[87]

For this reason the dialogue ends with no real conclusion if not broadly relativistic, and without a univocal interpretation. Framed as a discussion of the traditional theme of avarice, the dialogue actually insinuates more than a simple doubt about traditional instruments of ethical-religious persuasion. In this connection, Bernardino's successful preaching was for Poggio a stimulus and a polemical target as well. In contrast, exhortations of a vague Senecan and Petrarchan stamp are raised, interwoven with secular wisdom and sacred authorities, though extrapolated from a doctrinal context. The author, acknowledging the weakness of human will, tries hard to adhere to these with a seriousness that conceals neither his motives of uncertainty nor his frank recognition of the utilitarian motives of human behavior that are subject to the control of reason in only a limited and relative degree. Morality is therefore secularized in a crisis of faith in the end and above all in the awareness of the limits of what, in common human experience, congruence of words and deeds can be achieved, or, in a word, can be maintained the measure of the *humanitas*. Without such awareness, religious precepts themselves risk being reduced to mere magniloquence when not degraded into hypocritical dissembling, a much more serious because less controlled vice, and the source of sheer ethical skepticism, if not disbelief.[88]

On this ambiguous note, on this precarious religious and ethical balance typical of Poggio's entire works, I could conclude this discussion.

As has been pointed out, Bernardino's preaching offered Poggio the opportunity to recast in his first substantial work the vigorously polemical themes of a humanistic and secular "moral philosophy" that had been maturing over the course of the first two decades of the century, and to which he had originally contributed with brief texts in oratorical and epistolary form. But the comparison between Bernardino and Poggio, two personalities so different as to seem from incompatible worlds, does not finish here. By chance they were born the same year, 1380. But it was not by chance that the activity and public notoriety of both came relatively late, in the years of the Council of Constance, and especially after its conclusion. In his Oration to the Fathers of the Council, Poggio expressed his distrust of the call for Church reform, unable as he was to discern in the plans of the conciliarists anything more than a self-serving aversion to the papacy (as well as to Italy). Only partial improvements could be hoped for: "let us begin, therefore, by putting the limbs together, then the body can be easily reconstructed."[89] Bernardino became known for his preaching especially after the end of the Schism, and as a herald not of a reform to be realized but a discipline to be reestablished, in a vision no less disillusioned than Poggio's about the evils afflicting Christianity. Even if the pope were a saint, as Bernardino used to say, he could not have achieved this goal and instituted a more worthy clergy: "One is allowed to keep his post because he is friends with the emperor, another because he is friends with the king or some barons, and another because he knows some cardinals or other noblemen or prelates of the Holy Church . . . A general reform of the Church has never been made, but only in its parts . . . All you can do is increase your help to good men."[90] So in his turn, in 1432, Poggio wrote similar words to Cardinal Cesarini, the president and champion of the Council of Basel who opposed the decree by Pope Eugenius IV for its dissolution: "This is not a reform, but the making of something deformed; if you commit abuse contrasting the order of the Pope, you do not bring peace but the sword to the people. Under the veil of a council they are plotting something else." Things usually go contrary to our intentions, even though they may be good: "I know how difficult it is to check anger, hatreds, and desires: He is the Head; if anything he would fail, it is your duty to say what you think, and act in a way that you can avoid harm. A wise man has to be free of guilt . . . It remains for you to be obedient to his injunction. You have acted as you thought would be useful."[91]

In our comparison of Poggio and Bernardino, the antihierarchical individualism and ethical relativism of the first and the disciplinarism of the other, so strict as to seem narrow-minded, reflect in their coming together —as opposite, yet still complementary testimonies—a common perception of a world, symbolized in its highest institution, the Church, that has strayed from its right path, without hope for an early restoration and a rational resolution to its conflicts. In other words, the polemical themes that this study has sought to illustrate through a comparison of two opposite ethical and cultural perspectives acquire meaning if we measure them against the more generalized crisis of institutional certainties that create the climate of those historical circumstances.

With no intention of echoing the celebratory tones of an old historiography—be it the apologetics of the Saint or certain style of glorifying
Renaissance humanism—I should like to limit myself to acknowledging
the genuine value of a controversy that, representing the great institutional crisis of an epoch in terms of a crisis of moral persuasion, reveals
its seriousness, and with that, I would add, its relevance for us today.

4

The Theater of the World
in the Moral and Historical Thought
of Poggio Bracciolini

Although in both style and substance Poggio Bracciolini's writings are seemingly clear and readable, nevertheless he is not an author who lends himself readily to critical evaluation, and as a consequence he cannot easily be assigned an acknowledged role in history. Those familiar with Quattrocento humanism have little difficulty identifying his characteristic voice in the large and varied corpus of his letters, dialogues, and essays. These writings, however, cannot afford a basis for articulating the substance of a doctrine or of a distinctive exegetical contribution like that of a Leonardo Bruni, not to say of a Lorenzo Valla. In this chapter my purpose is not to investigate the manuscript discoveries for which Poggio is so famous, nor his equally significant recovery of the *littera antiqua.* These undertakings that he himself—even before his contemporaries and posterity—exalted as the very symbol of the renaissance of letters are still today attracting serious scholarly attention.[1] What is most important to me is the author's own original work that, despite the monograph by E. Walser (which I will discuss further on), still remains somehow concealed as part or testimony of a broader cultural movement, or is discussed only superficially in descriptive biographical accounts. Literary histories mainly limit themselves to mentioning Poggio among the representative figures of Florentine humanist circles (Bruni, Traversari, Marsuppini, Manetti, etc.), while historical surveys have emphasized single aspects, in most cases extrapolated from their original contexts, of his best-known writings (for example, the positive values of economic activity proposed in *De avaritia* or the claims made for individual virtue in *De nobilitate*, etc.). Literary criticism has focused on his Latin prose, whose liveliness seems to reproduce in some degree the ease of spoken language. On the other hand, we cannot now acknowledge C. G. Gutkind's attempt to trace Poggio's "spiritual development"[2] as a real advance in studies. While contrasting Walser's representation of Poggio's full Christian orthodoxy, Gutkind cannot help but propose the opposite image of an aesthetically centered "Weltanschauung," tinged with Epicurean relativism "devoid of any moral rules" and with an amoral behavior wherever ethical principles came into conflict "with the *voluptas mundi*." The vagueness of such propositions—a typical outcome of certain "Geistesgeschichte" in the early decades of the twentieth century, where the problematic aspects of an individual writer are defined in terms of rigidly juxtaposed theses—has played a part in discouraging anything other than occasional scholarly investigation into so important a field as the moralistic literature of early humanism, and into Poggio in particular—surely one of its most distinguished voices.

Recent scholarship in Quattrocento Italian culture and society has done little to foster the thorough investigation this field demands. It would be inappropriate to detach Poggio from the group and generation of intellectuals with whom he was so directly involved. In a climate charged with controversy and antitraditionalism, this group brought about a decisive cultural shift through a free elaboration of Petrarch's teachings and the continual assimilation of both newly discovered and long-familiar authors of classical Greece and Rome. Of particular significance was the transformation of traditional treatise composition, exegesis, and poetry into oratory, essay writing, historiography, philology, and with that the establishment of the *studia humanitatis* as the mark of a new status for the intellectual. There was, in other words, a real cultural movement taking place, though still confined to very restricted circles. This was not a movement in the sense of having a uniform character but, instead, in the dynamic of mutual exchanges and reciprocity of references from work to work and of a succession of initiatives and proposals, until culminating, almost as an end point, in Lorenzo Valla's methodological radicalism and in the relative dissolution of doctrinal foundations of scholastic disciplines through dialectical and philological examination.[3] A more meticulous reconstruction of this culture and its ideas would undoubtedly provide a more balanced set of interpretive criteria. For several good reasons, however, not the least the dispersion of texts and the imperfect state of textual editing, this remains as yet a *desideratum* for scholarship. Whether a cause or consequence, the present state of monographic research of individual authors is characterized by its dispersive tendency. Rarely have Petrarch studies taken into account the insightful perspective of his daring and often reticent Quattrocento followers (among whom Poggio figures prominently). Hans Baron's interpretation of "Florentine civic humanism," which almost identifies the movement with the figure of Leonardo Bruni, inevitably marginalizes Poggio's restless individualism, despite its unmistakable Tuscan imprint and his ties with Florentine friends. Only occasionally, in studies about such eminent curial humanists as Biondo and Leon Battista Alberti, have connections and exchanges with Poggio's writings been noticed, though both of them worked for many years in the same atmosphere of the Papal court as did Poggio.[4] Finally, in research on Valla, especially recent scholarship on his religious thought, Poggio runs the risk of appearing in the highly improbable clothes of a hard traditionalist on the basis of the old polemics between the two humanists, which instead should be more rightfully understood in the terms of a rivalry between members of the same cultural context. Poggio encounters even less justice in the cautious classification by disciplines and intellectual orientations, such as that proposed by Paul Oskar Kristeller, especially when, as in the rigid approach by J. E. Seigel, rhetorical and philosophical traditions are considered as if they were almost permanently opposed.[5] If oratory is understood as practical wisdom directed toward persuasion, sociability, and impatience with abstractions, no one was more of an "orator" than Poggio; if, on the contrary, rhetoric is understood as scholasticism, as rule of discourse, and as a professional tradition, no one is less a "rhetorician by profession" than he was.

Poggio's want of discipline in rhetoric and, more importantly, in ethics is what has dictated the reservations about him since his own times. Let us consider the unsympathetic portrait sketched by Pius II,[6] as well as Paolo Cortesi's blame—a judgment also later echoed by Erasmus—that although he was endowed with a "certain kind of eloquence" (*quaedam species eloquentiae*) Poggio was lacking in "art" (*artificium*);[7] and finally conclude with Paolo Giovio's bittersweet eulogy that seems to summarize the condemnation of a well-established curial tradition. The charges of slander, excess, and buffoonery are only slightly mitigated by the acknowledgment of Poggio's longstanding papal service.[8] On Poggio, therefore, as well as on his own cultural age, weighs the burden of judgments prompted by an opposing attitude. These criticisms, operative since late-Quattrocento culture, stemmed from general programs, which aimed at redefining the rules of discourse as well as of conduct in accordance with its basic ethical categories (Pontano's treatises, both ethical and rhetorical, are typical in this regard).

Poggio's image, therefore, was deliberately obscured (since his writings were surely more widely disseminated than fifteenth- and sixteenth-century biographical sketches suppose), and modern reconstructions have had to reckon with these early reservations. We can better understand, therefore, how so vague an image of Poggio has persisted in scholarship to this time. However, we must add that interest in Poggio has been revived in recent times by the reprinting of his *Opera omnia;*[9] by L. Martines's research on Poggio's biographical details;[10] by the discussions and analyses of the problematical dialogue, *De avaritia;*[11] by studies on structure of the Quattrocento dialogue,[12] on his letters and on the genre of letter-writing,[13] and on the language and reception of the *Facetiae;*[14] and lastly, by analyses of the *Historiae Florentinae populi.*[15] N. S. Struever's book on the relationship between "rhetoric and historical consciousness" in Florentine humanists includes a long chapter on Poggio.[16] The discussion is admittedly complicated by a sometimes gratuitous recourse to modern categories of rhetoric and epistemology, but it still provides a sensitive treatment of the most fundamental points in Poggio's discourse, representing him as "a pivotal figure in the history of Humanism." Also noteworthy is the perceptive survey by the English historian G. Holmes on the "Florentine Enlightenment" of the first half of the fifteenth century,[17] for its clear awareness of an avant-garde intellectual movement both in Florence and in the Papal curia ("this is a movement with a history and not a collection of individuals best considered separately," p. xvii). Such movement was characterized by a truly broad range of individual solutions, though on the basis of common assumptions. "A movement [as Holmes describes it] of extreme and sudden secularization of ideas under the auspices of the classics, over a broad spectrum of interests" (p. xix), and one that was destined to exhaust itself within the span of a few decades. The historical background against which this movement played out was not so much the political and social conditions in Florence as "the immense institutional crisis" of the Schism and the Councils. This, of course, is the sphere in which Poggio moved, and in several ways he provides evidence for Holmes's narrative (albeit only as a hint or as rapid evaluations according to the nature of the book). Note, for example, the comments on the problematic relationship between "philosophy and religion" (pp. 117 ff.) and on the sometimes hidden motivations of Poggio's persistent anticlericalism, which would eventually stimulate religious radicalism until the time of reform.

Holmes deserves further recognition for attaching importance to the substantial role that Poggio assumed, "rather surprisingly," as a historian of his own time, first in *De varietate fortuna* and later in *Florentine Histories* (p. 164 f.). I can only in part agree, however, with his statement that Poggio was the writer "who came the closest to bridging the gap between humanist and vernacular history." Holmes's surprise is nevertheless justified. An independent historiography on a strictly individual perspective, and on contemporary events the author himself lived through in an age of such conflicts, was a bold undertaking. Leonardo Bruni's previous historiographical model was not meant to present events of contemporary Florentine history but rather their antecedents, while the more elliptical form of the "commentary" was the genre in which he framed his discussions of the most recent past.[18] "History," as opposed to chronicles, was a literary work proper, destined for wide circulation, and thereby implying a public responsibility on the part of the author. A more pertinent comparison to Poggio's contemporary historiography are surely the *Historiae* of Biondo Flavio, conceived at the same time as *De varietate,* in the same curial atmosphere, and emerging, as did Poggio's work, out of the collapse of Pope Martin V's restoration. In Biondo's work, moreover, these ecclesiastical events are incorporated (and fused) into a broader, contemporary political framework.[19] Poggio instead, and probably in deliberate emulation of Biondo's political historiography,[20] broadened his own disenchanted moralistic reflections to the point of converting them into "history," which he represented as the "theater of fortune," where he himself had been direct spectator and where he had previously found incentive for his spirited moral reflections. In other words, Poggio's various writings culminate in a portrait of an age of disorder, represented symbolically in the ancient image (from Seneca, but also from Lucian) of a theatrical performance that disguises the reality, and that in the end frustrates actors' haughtiness, as though to indicate a pronounced crisis of trust in civic and ecclesiastical institutions and, more generally, in traditions, paradigms, and ends. This is the proper perspective from which

Poggio's basic themes should be considered. They should not be assessed on the ground of first principles but rather the empirical realm of their relationship to factual reality, according to the greater or lesser persuasiveness that ancient precepts still retain, and, consequently, of their relativization confronting the broader theater of human events beyond the control of human reason. Simply stated, Poggio's basic call is for an absolute antidoctrinairism as the appropriate standard for evaluating a moral life restricted to the private and individual sphere, as well as the condition for an unfettered observation of reality and for an independent reading of the authors.

The remarks that follow will focus chiefly on the consistency of Poggio's moral discourse, in terms of how he embraces as well as combines, circumscribes, or alters traditional precepts; on his view of history as a field of lively and direct observations, but also, inseparably, as the ground where exemplary values are relativized and emptied; lastly in his polemical and antidoctrinaire recourse to images and emblems of the moralistic-philosophical tradition (Fortune, the theater of the world, the misfortunes of princes). In this way, I hope to be able to explain Poggio's peculiar discourse within the movement of *studia humanitatis,* as well as his consistent will to get a public hearing for his own independent, laical point of view as a representative voice of his own times, not only in Italy, but in Europe as well.

A close reading of Walser's monograph reveals the complexities of Poggio's character, once we set aside the author's axiomatic comments about the humanist's solid religious orthodoxy based on ancient wisdom, in order to purge Poggio of the traditional suspicions of "free-thinking and paganism."[21] Walser's emphasis on the importance of ethical-religious issues is surely a relevant assessment, so that his work remains a necessary point of reference for scholars. But it is precisely in his careful attention to the context of Poggio's work that contradictions become apparent. How to reconcile Poggio's youthful attack of Salutati's "one-sided medieval patristic *Weltanschauung*" with the harmonious synthesis of Christian and ancient wisdom he would later effect?[22] Is he returning to the teachings of his old master, or does he offer a different approach for reading sacred authorities? Moreover, how can his Christianity, which rejects asceticism for a "joy of living" in harmony with the natural world, be reconciled with the harshness of his anticlerical and antimonastic bias? and even further, with his constant quest for inner freedom, like a "lay asceticism modelled on the Church Fathers"?[23] Finally, what kind of relation does exist between Poggio's Christian and ancient "moral philosophy" and his own pessimistic fatalism, his pre-Machiavellian outlook ("a quite clear Realpolitik"), his indiscriminate condemnation of modern and ancient histories ("the intrinsic injustice of a world dominated by violence") in the later *De miseria humanae conditionis,* which, according to Walser, sums up his earlier work?[24]

These interrogations are still valid, of course, but for an answer we must consider the interior working of a moral discourse consistent enough, though with differing tones and emphases, and not search for an evolution of thought that would follow distinct historical phases. (Judging from the writings we know, that is, from the works that he himself intended for publication, Poggio began to write in his mature years, and with his intellectual identity already well established.) Before opening up a broader discussion of his moral discourse it would be worthwhile to explore the elusive contours of his doctrine; his dispute with Salutati seems a good place to begin. The conflict centers on how to evaluate Petrarch's works, which Salutati had praised as higher than the ancients themselves for their excellence in both prose and poetry.[25] The theme is the same as Bruni's *Dialogi ad Petrum Histrum,* where in their dual aspect of arguing against the "three Florentine crowns" (essentially against the apologetic tradition begun by Boccaccio) and then retracting these attacks, they ended by challenging Petrarch's exemplary authority and, consequently, by "opening the way" for the free rising of the *studia humanitatis.*[26] The debate between Salutati and Poggio introduces other issues, however, which the more prudent Bruni had thought better to omit. Discussing Petrarch implied not only a revision of rhetorical canons but also a reconsideration of the nature of eloquence itself, that is, its basis in truth. An opinion similar to Salutati's was voiced by the chancellor of France, Jean de Montreuil. In his eyes, Petrarch represented "the most faithful, catholic and celebrated moral philosopher" (*devotissimus, catholicus ac celeberrimus philosophus moralis*), according to a model of eloquence through which "you gain both certitude and learning" (*certum reddas ac pariter doctum facias*), and in which interlaced citations of both sacred and secular authors were intended "to serve the one and only truth."[27] Such virtuosity in weaving citations of ancient authorities was, for this admirer of

Petrarch and Salutati, a kind of antidote to the doubts (he considered almost heresy) expressed by the Milanese "Epicurean," Ambrogio de' Migli, about the effectiveness of eloquence itself. Migli's criticism was not in line with the traditional Christian condemnation of ancient eloquence but was inspired by Petrarch's denunciation of Cicero's human weakness: "since there are many more . . . wicked human beings than good, and since it is agreed that orators must be good, it follows, therefore, that neither eloquence nor rhetoricians are expedient."[28] The practice of rhetoric was useless, as the canonical teachings of De inventione (1.1) admit, "when it is divorced from the honorable studies of reason and duty" (obmissis rectissimis atque honestissimis studiis rationis et officii). This became for Migli the means by which he thought to undermine the very credibility of oratory. Thus Petrarch was considered in a twofold and almost contradictory way. On the one hand he was hailed as the modern doctor (Salutati describes him as "not only a Christian in his religion, faith, and baptism, but also both a theologian because of his learning and one to be preferred to those pagan philosophers").[29] But from the opposite perspective he was conceived as introducing hints of relativism, through a growing awareness of the incompatibility (or at least the diversity in cultural frame) between an absolute religious norm and the varied wisdom of the gentiles, which for this very reason seemed more eloquent and hence more persuasive. To Salutati this seemed a separation of the indivisible union of eloquence and wisdom, "the two things . . . by which our learning is distinguished," against which he retaliated with an explicit warning to Poggio that he not stray from the teachings of the Church Fathers: "you and that learned friend of yours, as you write, are deferring and giving way too much to antiquity. And to come to my major point, whom do you say are the most learned ancient men, the followers of Christ or the pagans?" For this reason, despite all the possible imperfections in style, Petrarch was to be kept on his pedestal of excellence as an example and a stern warning for the moderns and, because of his Christian foundation, to be preferred "to the Gentiles, Cicero, Varro and to all the Romans, and to Aristotle, Plato and all Greece."[30]

It is certainly not by chance that we know of these criticisms primarily through their confutations, such as that by Jean de Montreuil concerning Ambrogio Migli and Salutati with regard to Poggio.[31] It should be remembered that in the early phases of the studia humanitatis, these new initiates articulated their principles using reticence and allusion, so that many of the writings which they intended to be read within their exclusive circles have since been lost. Poggio's youthful silence is characteristic of this. Likewise, from a psychological point of view, Poggio was the young man who confronted his old teacher, "in an abusive rather than a joking way" (*non scommatibus sed ledoriis*), about the very roots of a revolution in culture destined to create real incompatibilities within a world still culturally unified, where both Salutati and Jean de Montreuil still found their identity.

Such a breach took place primarily in the fields of ethics and rhetoric, or, more precisely, in the relationships between rhetoric, moral doctrine, and religion. Petrarch, of course, provides the indispensable precedent and as a consequence becomes an obligatory point of reference. The polemical themes that the young literati were pursuing actually were drawn from Petrarch himself—a secret Petrarch, so to speak, whose line of thought concealed more radical elements that they then turned against his late-fourteenth-century public image. Of decisive importance had been Petrarch's discovery of Seneca as a philosopher independent of school teaching, whose moral exhortation did not preclude Epicurean maxims as preparatory to a broader ground of moral doctrine, for the Stoic exercise of virtue.[32] For Petrarch, too, moral discourse essentially meant preparation, disposition of the soul according to common human consensus, and not actualization through models of perfection (of hagiography, exemplarity, and doctrine), which are inevitably abstract and thereby ineloquent, which sound in the ear but fail to penetrate the soul. Thus we explain Petrarch's self-indulgence, his subtleties, his irony present in even the stern reflection of the *Secretum,* a text that diverges from its model, Augustine's *Confessions,* in that it offers no conclusions, keeps within the boundaries of a moral rather than a penitential confession, and refuses to be limited by the terms of a doctrinaire teaching.[33] Petrarch's attitude toward theology is analogous to that of Seneca's Epicurus toward Stoic virtue. In this way the wisdom of the gentiles (Seneca, Cicero, and Aristotle) can be evoked along with that of the sacred authorities. Instead of effecting a decisive religious conversion, Augustine's exhortation to cultivate his inner self, which came like a revelation to Petrarch on the summit of Mount Ventoux, led him back to a (Senecan) axiom of human wisdom: "I, who already from the gentile philosophers themselves should have learned that nothing except the soul is admirable."[34] So Petrarch countered the image of Seneca as a master of asceticism, and especially that of Seneca as a Christian, who enjoyed such popularity in the moral doctrine of his century, with the image of the more flexible secular wisdom. In his own day, Seneca had challenged the compilations of "florets" (*flosculi*), and now his words encouraged Petrarch to launch a more general attack "against those who exhibited the wisdom of others and who are collecting florets"; in other words, against the rigidly defined ethical doctrine in the various *florilegia* and collections of *sententiae* and *exempla,* which had been adopted and institutionalized as instruments of moral and religious persuasion.[35] In effect, Petrarch's insight into the inner intentions of major authorities such as Augustine and Seneca succeeded in undermining a firmly established rhetorical tradition and arousing some unsettling doubts about the very discipline of ethics: could moral certitude exist outside a vague and, indeed, hopeful aspiration for virtue? Could models and precepts exist apart from the common rules of human behavior or, in any case, be isolated from the effective testimony of history? How and through what means could the Christian norm in its absoluteness penetrate the human soul and intrinsically regulate its behavior? In essence, was it possible to teach virtue?

As has already been pointed out, rejecting the figure of Petrarch as model and teacher, as Salutati had described him (perhaps as a warning of a boundary not to transgress) was linked to doubts that now found new impetus in the increasing knowledge about the ancient world, particularly as contact with Greek learning solidified, opening up new perspectives and historical-ideological traditions no longer ascribable to a single common discipline. In one of his earliest tracts, which we know only through a fortuitous manuscript transmission, Poggio demonstrates how real this issue was. Praising the Veronese lawyer Ludovico Cattaneo, while avowing his own modesty ("I don't consider myself apt to give my judgment on the excellence of illustrious men"), Poggio adds, "but it is an endowment that nature itself has given to men's minds that they might more easily discern the fault in anything than correct what is wrong, since we see that a thorough knowledge of what is right is an attribute of few minds. It may be for this reason that the Academics were quicker to refute (*ad refellendum*) than to assert."[36]

Poggio's remarks remind us of the young humanists who scandalized the likes of Cino Rinuccini with their jeering attacks on Petrarch's *De viris illustribus.* Referring to its popularity as a sourcebook of exempla, they ridiculed it as a "zibaldone da quaresima"—a collection of Lenten preachings.[37] Precisely because so few people have the natural gift to know what is right, it would be difficult to expect such knowledge from common sense, which is capable only of ascertaining what is wrong. Later Poggio would often repeat a phrase of Seneca's Epicurus: "An awareness of sin is the beginning of deliverance," but always from the perspective of someone who remains at this preliminary stage: "and this brings me some hope of one day putting myself right."[38] His reference to the Skeptics is remarkable as we consider the unaltered relevance of Augustine's *Contra Academicos,* which incidentally is a text that Poggio had transcribed at an earlier point in his career.[39] In successive correspondence and dialogues, Poggio would conform himself someway to the pattern of Seneca and Petrarch, in the sense of believing in philosophy's instruction—as "the guide and teacher of how to lead a good life."[40] However, the infiltrations, so to speak, of Epicureanism and Skepticism, recognizable since his earliest writings, cannot be ignored insofar as they concur to narrow even further the extent of moral persuasion.

In fact, Poggio's entire literary production is infused with negative ethics—precisely *ad refellendum*—in the twofold sense of denouncing the most corrupting vices while also revealing the deceptive appearances of virtue. Another important cultural element needs attention here: his knowledge of Greek authors, which early on had an impact on him, at least from an ideological point of view. Though only briefly, Poggio was a member of Chrysoloras's circle *(cum eo familiarius viximus)*, joining in the gathering's funeral celebrations and, at an early age, beginning a somewhat laborious training in Greek, which he would resume periodically over the years.[41] Thanks to close friendships with Bruni and Rinuccio Aretino he had some access to texts,[42] and he also took part in the controversy surrounding the new theory of translation, *ad sensum,* that challenged the traditional scholastic approach, *ad verbum,* along the lines still vigorously defended on the occasion of Poggio's own later versions of Xenophon and Diodorus Siculus.[43] Most of all, however, he saw in these new studies, in which he participated only marginally, something that distinguished "literate" men even more conclusively from common opinion and those who conformed "to the rule of unlearned people."[44] At times the citation of themes drawn directly from the deposit of Greek wisdom assumes the nature of a coded message,[45] or a provocation, depending on the audience. Hesiod's maxim about the difficult path to virtue was used in just this way. Greek in origin, the proverb had not come down through the tradition of medieval Latin sentences and was unfamiliar to both Salutati and Petrarch.[46] Instead Petrarch, for a similar purpose, once made reference to the Gospels within a context both Augustinian and Stoic: "Truly the life we call blessed is set in a high place: a narrow path, as it is commonly said, leads to it."[47] Poggio, as if making a rhetorical variation in the sentence, introduced his own citation from Hesiod, giving it a programmatic significance. In his Oration at Constance,[48] where it appears for the first time, it is inserted into a context we already know and, with respect to the weakness of human nature, emphasizes the futility of every claim to denounce human vices in general from a virtuous standpoint. Virtue lies far from the human sphere, Poggio writes; it is sheltered "in a high place and within a lofty citadel," which cannot be reached without extreme suffering: "The gods had placed sweat in front of it, says the noble poet Hesiod, as a sign of how hard it is to attain."[49] However indirect Hesiod's citation may be, the source of this passage is unquestionably Greek; and — what most interests us — it recalls the precise context and similar words of a passage in Plato's *Protagoras* that centers on the Sophists' thesis that virtue cannot be taught.[50] Hesiod's sentence was equally popular in the second Sophistic, and Lucian often refers to it ironically in his work.[51] It is conceivable that Poggio, too, could have been familiar with Lucian's pertinent passages when he wrote his Oration. In *De avaritia,* written in 1429, he makes explicit reference to it with regard to the avariciousness shown by Aristotle and many other philosophers, and thus, ironically, to how conduct differs from the teachings about it; and he frequently cites another of Lucian's texts on the theme, the *Menippus,* in his *De infelicitate principum* of 1440.[52] Nevertheless there is already an indication of his familiarity with and use of Lucian in the "Oratio ad Patres reverendissimos." The empty preaching from the pulpit, disguise for the most serious vices prevalent in society, is likened to an ancient pantomime: "For if someone was seen in a performance parading around in royal dress, pronouncing dignified, pompous, arrogant words worthy of a king, ordering about his attendants with sceptre in hand, and if he knew nothing else, he would certainly think he was a king. Strip away the ornaments, take off the elegant clothes, remove the mask: what remains is surely a slave, and very likely the most worthless of them."[53]

Poggio is taking up Petrarch's old polemic against the "wisdom of others" and against sacred knowledge being reduced to collections of *sententiae* ("some people mention them [the Church Fathers] as men of much speech rather than of much learning"),[54] but directing it specifically at the art of preaching ("they begin with a sentence, and then interweave their orations with the words of others")[55] and expanding it into an image of disguise, of deception concealed, in this particular instance, under ecclesiastical robes. We will return to this point later. For now, let us investigate the source of the theater metaphor. In Seneca, for example, the image had been employed to illustrate the usual theme of the deceptive happiness of wealth which, when exposed to the light of reason, is found to be hollow.[56] Poggio would, in fact, take up this theme elsewhere and elaborate it more fully. Still more extensive was John Chrysostom's Christian interpretation of the imagery as a *memento mori*. In his oration *De Lazaro* the reversal of roles in the Last Judgment is represented metaphorically in the action and dénoument of a theatrical performance ("some truly rich, others truly poor"),[57] and it is known how sensitive Poggio was to the ethical-religious persuasiveness of Chrysostom's homiletics. Nevertheless, the interchangeability of king and slave roles—alluded to by Poggio—is a theme specifically from the Cynics. Lucian elaborates it in detail in *Menippus,* in a famous representation of life as a pageant. Fortune assigns the various roles—"and takes someone at random and dresses him as a king, puts a crown on his head, encircles him with corfei and places a diadem on his head; then he dresses another in a slave's costume" etc.— and when the procession has ended, everyone reluctantly gives back his costume, "returning to what he was before birth."[58] The grotesque representation of religious preaching therefore appears to be interwoven with various motifs: where Chrysostom's Christian exhortation ("take off your mask!")[59] blends with themes drawn from the Cynics (the randomness of human roles, the illusiveness of opinions, the uselessness of solemn precepts); and where, on a more general level, the points of reference to the ancient, neglected wisdom of the Greeks validate a claim for a more human, more cautious, and more detached and independent standard of judgment. Thus Hesiod's adage, discussed by Plato for its relativistic implications, and which Lucian had satirized (in, among other places, the *Menippus* itself) as a futile yearning for hard-earned virtue, was repeatedly incorporated into Poggio's polemic against stern censorship (ep. II, 18); against panegyrical rhetoric (ep. III, 23); against the "hypocrisy" of monks (ep. IV, 7); and against the conceit of rank (ep. VIII, 39). Because, as he concluded in a letter to Richard Petworth, "according to the opinion of the ancient Greeks, it is difficult to be good."[60]

Poggio's discourse, particularly his letters, even though circumscribing persuasion into so narrow a circle, never ceases to be moral discourse, an exhortation to virtuous living, not merely satire, polemics, descriptions. Consider, for example, the famous letter he wrote to Niccoli from the baths at Baden, which he positioned quite deliberately at the beginning of his collected correspondence. It opens with a debate about the value of learning Hebrew, which, contrary to his friend's advice (but, as we know, in agreement with Bruni), Poggio considered a language useless "for the learning of wisdom." These comments followed on an earlier debate, no longer extant, in which Poggio had advocated a morality independent of the Bible's theological teachings.[61] His provocative description of the baths, as entertaining as it is, is not an end in itself. Rather, it offers an opportunity for reflection on that unconscious serenity of life, like the "teaching of the Epicurean sect"—an image that resonated with condemnation of the anxieties of his day ("I curse the perversities of our souls . . . while we are terrified of future calamities, we constantly immerse ourselves in calamity and anxiety"). The conclusion echoes Seneca and, once more, the Seneca informed by Epicurean thought: "And so they are enriched by this thought alone: he has lived who has lived well."[62] Distinctly Epicurean themes are found throughout Poggio's writings: the comfort of friendship; pleasure as a viaticum of existence; leanings toward utilitarianism; the ideal of "quiet" as a kind of Lucretian seclusion in one's own *portiuncula,* the little "portion" we are endowed with, away from "the immense and stormy sea" that encircles us; the mockery of the world's miseries.[63] It is in any case an Epicureanism contained within the matrix and a framework, albeit broad, of Senecan thought. Hence, for example, the proverbial theme of Democritus's laugh (but without Heraclitus's tears), which Poggio frequently cited and transformed into various stock phrases: "I laugh at myself," "I laughed at your ineptitude," "we all laughed at the ineptitude and petulance of these words," etc.[64] The source for these statements actually lies in Seneca's *De tranquillitate animi* 15.2: "In this matter we ought to be much more inclined to laugh at the faults of common man, than to deplore them, and rather to imitate Democritus than Eraclitus. For it is more human to laugh at life than to complain about it." Poggio would himself repeat these words, for instance in ep. IV, 16: "As Democritus said, it is better to laugh at the common man's folly than to cry about it."[65]

The evils of the Church and the Council were not exempt from "the common man's folly,"[66] and this leads us to the other programmatic manifesto of Poggio's correspondence, the famous letter to Bruni (viewed by its recipient as an imprudent gesture) about the torturing of Jerome of Prague. Poggio wrote the letter at approximately the same time as the provocative Oration directed to the "Most Reverent Fathers" at Constance.[67] Walser cites the letter as evidence of Poggio's profound religiosity, if his "Epicurean" description of the baths should ever call it into question. Actually the contrast between the two is probably deliberate: whereas in the first case there was a longing for Epicurean "quiet," the second represented a Stoic philosopher fearless in the face of persecution and death, "like a second Cato." Jerome's figure in Poggio's letter is essentially abstracted from the real circumstances at hand, and no judgment is made on the merit of the ecclesiastical indictment. The words he addresses to his accusers are in reality the accusations that Poggio himself directed to the clergy (the unworthiness of their claim to judge their peers, their hypocrisy, avarice, pride, etc.). Different from Poggio's, however, the Stoic's words owe their persuasive force to the way of life he exemplifies ("he demonstrated his life and studies to be full of the sense of duty and virtue"),[68] in contrast to the evidence presented against him, colored by hatred and prejudice, and thus, in terms of its persuasiveness, hardly credible outside of the pure theological controversy: "they were so probable, that except for the argument of faith, little belief could be applied to their testimony."[69] Jerome, in other words, speaks from the high pedestal of virtue, like a modern Cato, making a show of both eloquence and wisdom. But—Poggio remarks—"I fear that all these things granted to him by nature will be the cause of his own ruin."[70] "Omnia praeclara rara"— all good things are hard to be found—he would often repeat according to the ancient proverb;[71] but the "rare" example of Jerome also warned that virtue, because it was modeled on the teaching of the philosophers, was, aside from being difficult, ultimately unadvisable.

In this way the two letters, starting from opposite perspectives, led to similar conclusions, in the sense of the precariousness of any standard of judging that was not merely negative and of a personal crisis of certainty. The unquestionable "Epicurean" (or skeptical, or relativistic) inclinations are limited to tenets compatible with Stoic "reason," and thereby are contained in the terms of Seneca's propedeutica. To overstep this boundary in Poggio's eyes meant compromising religious, not to mention ethical, values. Hence his violent reaction at the appearance of the *De voluptate* by

Lorenzo Valla, who daringly defended a philosophical sect "wiped away and almost buried centuries ago and condemned by all philosophers."[72] Valla's reduction of morality and religion to the dynamic principle of the "useful," in opposition to the philosophers' "uprightness" and the theologians' ontologism, like the consequent development of the relativism and utilitarianism taking shape in Poggio's own thought, was tantamount to the rupture of a precarious equilibrium—but precisely as such it was to be protected. Poggio's reaction to Valla was of the same nature as his attack on Antonio Panormita's *Ermaphroditus* and the provocation it contained: he showed obvious concern that lettered men be governed by a rule of moderation, of "temperance": "this would be most pleasing and useful to you, to your friends and certainly to me."[73] In this context, Leon Battista Alberti's biting moralism, openly referring to Poggio, in its radical pessimism now released from religious restraint, represents an outcome that Poggio had actually feared.[74]

For Poggio, "virtue" signified a residual margin of certainty without the objective consistency of a doctrine or the reassurance of models such as the proverbial Stoic paradigm of the wise man, which could only be cultivated in a subjective and empirical sphere. As Poggio writes in *De infelicitate principum,* summarizing previous remarks in his letters, "I do not seek after the good and wise man according to Stoic teaching, who is yet to be found; I understand good things to be those which are sanctioned by use and by human experience. It is enough that there be in them some virtue; it need not be perfect, but at the very least that there be the semblance and feigned likeness of those virtues toward which the civic life is directed."[75]

We note in this passage something like a contamination between Cicero and Seneca, or more precisely, a reciprocal retort of one author to the other. The Panetian-Ciceronian doctrine of the *officia media* is understood in terms of relaxing a rigid conception of virtue, but not in terms of a practical set of precepts designed for civic life;[76] the goal is always the Senecan ideal of the "tranquillity of the soul," but compatible with a human dimension that serves as a guide in unforeseeable situations, in that "labyrinth" that is life.[77] Hence Poggio's utilitarian (and Ciceronian) maxim of adapting to the times: "For it is right to adapt to the times, which, since they are not always the same, it is proper to change our purposes in keeping with their variety"; "wise men always comply with the times,"[78] etc. The traditional definitions of "virtues," therefore, are vanishing and, in sharp contrast with the Aristotelian concept of the *medietas,* Poggio's insistent plea for a moderation, a *mediocritas,* remains by its very nature undefinable: "We seek to follow that mean, whereby following God, we are not completely enslaved to the world";[79] "for everything . . . there must be a limit to greed"; "I have checked my desire . . . desiring only what is enough." The last of these comments, incidentally, becomes a subject of irony wherever it is formulated as a matter of doctrine, as it is in the Church's teaching on excess (*plus velle quam quod satis est*).[80] In a letter written in old age, this search for indeterminate formulations reaches the point of becoming a paradoxical truism: "If however you put aside something for unforseen circumstances or for the blows of fortune . . . this is not something to be criticized. An attitude of moderation, nevertheless, should be applied as a moderating element to all things."[81]

In another context, and in one of his most meaningful letters, Poggio stresses the importance of "discretion," as a virtue equivalent to the "prudence" of classical philosophy. According to Poggio, discretion should be understood not so much as practical wisdom and a behavioral norm as essentially a caution in assessing the particular and the contingent, in recognition of the unstable and deceptive appearance of virtue: "For, because certain vices seem similar and almost the same as many virtues, if one does not exercize discretion very well . . . he will inevitably run into countless errors."[82]

It has already been pointed out how the terms in which Poggio expresses his ethical ideas differ little from his more specifically religious comments. Indeed, it would be more precise to say that the terms are complementary. There is, of course, a clear difference between the goal of salvation and self-sufficiency of virtue, just as there is a difference between the Christian norm and the rational ideal of the wise man. Nevertheless, on the basis of common experience the two perspectives do converge, since both are directed toward an end equally remote and equally difficult to verify. Consequently, even in specifically religious matters, Poggio clearly distinguishes his own individual point of view from general concerns with precepts and ends. A passage in the Oration at Constance illustrates this particularly well. In Poggio's opinion the preaching of churchmen was incapable of curbing the vices arising everywhere and had even less chance of reestablishing order in the Church. Indeed, how could it, being nothing more than a hypocritical mask for vice? Only the example of life itself was effective: "the journey directed by precept is long, but that by example is short, efficient, and clear." In this way our Savior, who, as Poggio writes elsewhere, "began doing before teaching,"[83] was able to inculcate God's challenging precepts: "Those words seemed to stem from a too harsh divine law: leave your father and mother; sell all your possessions and give them to the poor; take up your cross and follow me; love your enemies, bless those who hate you; suffer injustices, and similar admonishments, stern indeed, which we consider abhorrent to common human sense."

As Poggio explains, these commands seemed so stern "because there were much easier and simpler precepts in pagan law; they were clearly better suited to human nature, and were proven by daily use and sanctioned by law."[84] Poggio—and surely not he alone in his times—felt the alternative as an actual one, as he affirms in conceding to exhortations sent him by Niccoli: "If both the words and deeds of the past were not better for us than the corrupt examples of the present, no doubt that faith would be lost."[85] But were the lofty examples of the apostles really "suitable" to the present, if, as the wise saying went, we should "conform to the times"? In one of the letters upon which Walser bases his assumption of Poggio's Christian philosophy, where Poggio himself seems to abandon his earlier passion for the *studia humanitatis* ("for the principles of these studies are worthless: some are ambiguous, others are false, and all are untruths. The foundation of sacred eloquence is truth, and when it slips away we can hold nothing as virtuous, and we cannot act rightly"),[86] he answers to the question with more doubts than certainty. The knowledge of precepts is not translated into action; a concern like that of Petrarch's *Secretum* (the image of a silent and inaccessible Truth without the "human" mediation of Augustine, a vacillation between sacred and secular authorities, and a tension between desire and actual will) is resolved by Poggio's frank admission: "I have the will but not the strength to carry it out." True, these words recall, though in a slightly modified form, the verse of St. Paul, Romans 7.18: "For the will to do good is within my reach, but I do not find how to carry it out."[87] Poggio's comment, however, does not represent a longing for perfection, or a loathing of sin, but rather a very human admission of weakness. It is in this context that his skeptical view of Christian perfection according to evangelical precept reappears in an even more provocative way: "For I am not one of those perfect ones who are commanded to abandon their mother and father, to sell all their belongings and give them to the poor: that has happened with very few and in an earlier age."[88] Poggio would repeat the statement in a later discussion about the freedom of the soul—"that happened once and in an earlier age"—and another time in an ironic context: "If virtues die with the good and holy men, they perished long ago with Peter and Paul and the other apostles."[89]

The result is a kind of Christian Epicureanism, or more precisely, an Epicurean sense of moderation that will protect Christian living at least from the most serious offenses: "I would be happy if I were one of those of the first rank, who, living sparingly and temperately, began to abstain from those vices which deprive us of the kingdom of God."[90]

The significance of Poggio's statement lies in its veiled reference to the distinction, proposed by Epicurus according to Seneca, between those who know how to attain truth "without the help of others" and those who require assistance, "who would not proceed unless someone led the way, being nevertheless ready to follow him." Such are the two groups, and as Seneca acknowledges, he "does not belong to the first, and would do well if he were received into the second."[91] Poggio, with Seneca's statement in mind, overturns its conclusion. Instead, as for the problematic adherence to such a hard precept (*iubemur,* we are ordered to), as Christian norm is, he proposes a criterion of more modest and free individual inquiry, independent of disciplinary norms and doctrinal frame. Elsewhere he compares an absolute spiritual freedom unattainable without divine vocation ("not because of accomplishments but because they were chosen") with his own less pretentious and more empirical freedom: "I seek that liberty in which I am subjected to the fewest orders: that very freedom which Tullius calls 'living as you like.'"[92] On the other hand, to his own acknowledgment of human weakness ("as one among those who do not possess such spiritual strength") he compares the familiar example of Ambrogio Traversari ("whom I judge to be very happy: he treats everything as dung, so that he might count Christ as his gain").[93] Poggio's direct and, in the context, rather provocative assimilation of Traversari to the Pauline precept makes his praise somewhat suspect. We know that later Poggio would reveal doubts about the "hypocrisy" of the learned Camoldolese; and if there is any truth to the tradition that Traversari was the real target of Leonardo Bruni's oration *Contra hypocritas,* the suspicion must have had its origins at an earlier date in the intellectual circle in Florence. These almost hidden ideological conflicts are the same that appear in Poggio's correspondence, through his studied working with references both to sacred and secular authorities.[94] Actually this point on the harshness of scriptural precept is at the very heart of his attack on hypocrisy "which crushes the whole world with false appearances of goodness,"[95] as he wrote in the Oration at Constance. Aside from its militant attack on monks, these words anticipate one of the central themes of Poggio's moral discourse.

This explains why Poggio deliberately avoids any mention of traditional Christian virtues, and here again his Oration at Constance gives an important indication. In the course of a rhetorical comparison between the precepts found in the Gospels—"the footprints of the apostles and of the other holy fathers"—and the evil actions of modern prelates, a singular duplicity in textual reading appears in one of the earliest manuscript copies, which may probably be ascribed to the author himself: "they disdained worldly power, following humanity (*alias* humility), and you delight in possession and pride" etc.[96] Clearly, *humilitas* would be the appropriate term to contrast with the Christian notion of *elatio*, the pride (as Poggio was to repeat elsewhere: "many of them converted their humility into pride . . . , their charity into hatred").[97] However, it must have seemed inappropriate to Poggio to recommend such a model of Christian virtue that could be so easily, and so hypocritically, converted to its opposite: hence he substituted, in a real break with tradition, the wiser standard of moderation inherent in the ancient notion of *humanitas*. Such was actually the warning he later addressed to high-ranking prelates and even to the Pope: "They [*scil.* Popes] should also be encouraged to be human . . . for humanity is the spice of all virtues. They need to be reminded to think of themselves as human beings . . . even though they are called as 'the holiest and most blessed.' "[98]

Poggio's intention, in short, was not to reiterate everything the ancient texts had said about moral or religious virtues but rather to extract from them, and, I would say, like marginal notes on them, some teachings appropriate to his own experience and that of his times. Thus the discipline of ethics was in the end relativized, but differently from a purely skeptical or sophistic attitude, making way for a more modern and dynamic shifting of values.

First and foremost among them, as a real value in and for itself, I would propose Poggio's colloquial attitude, a feature that almost without exception characterizes the entire corpus of his writings. It is evident in his really Petrarchan attitude toward his favorite books, in his predilection for expository genres such as letters and dialogues, in his bonds of friendship and intellectual fellowship, and lastly in his bold addressing in his correspondence, as if their equal, high-ranking personages. In short, according to the words Poggio himself wrote in a letter of invitation to Niccoli: "By heavens, I would prefer a conversation between us to the papacy itself!"[99]

Underlying all this is Poggio's concept of liberty, basically understood as a moral coherence of life, where various meanings are in turn included, antihierarchical ("for I want to be free, not a public slave,")[100] as well as political (at least in the negative sense of being against tyranny).[101] But above all other concerns is Poggio's predilection for independence of ideas and language, the only means by which we are able to attain truth. That faith is strengthened through differences of opinion is an affirmation attributed to Jerome of Prague;[102] and Poggio repeats it often in his own way: "for by discussing an issue from both sides truth usually emerges."[103] This is the basis of Poggio's broad standard, or claim, of tolerance, affirmed in various stock phrases: "I will say what I think" (*dicam quod sentio*) "let them judge as they like" (*sentiant ut libet*), "the faculty of being able to think what you want is not restricted to anyone in particular" (*cuiusquam est libera sentiendi quod velit facultas*), "but everyone is allowed to say the truth" (*sed vera loqui unicuique licet*), etc.[104]

One of the most characteristic features of Poggio's approach to liberty as interior coherence and intolerance of unnatural and dogmatic discipline is the open vindication of his own lay status. Judging from the image Poggio drew of himself in his epistolary collections, his entire career seems to have taken as its very purpose the dignifying of lay conditions within the framework of ecclesiastical hierarchy and in front of powers of this world. Unlike Bruni, whom Poggio perceived somewhat as a herald for his own studies and career, and who since 1411 had chosen marriage over attractive offers of promotion within the Church hierarchy, Poggio remained suspended for a long time in the ambiguous status of minor orders. The need to escape from this ambiguity—the same ambiguity indeed that surrounded Petrarch his entire life—explains the vigor with which, beginning with his letters from England, he confronted the issue of choosing a status—as a layman or as a cleric—for his life, elevating it to a question of principle, precisely as an "instruction for his life."[105] As usual, there was a variety of more or less interconnected reasons underlying his choice to remain a layman: the intolerable burden of caring for souls, coupled with the very human aversion to judging one's peers; human inadequacy in the face of sacred doctrine, but also the more positive appeal of secular culture; a refusal to be shackled by the chains of discipline, along with a refreshing awareness of life's pleasures ("I am a man inclined to gentleness and friendship").[106] Most decisive of all, however, was his belief in the intrinsic corruptibility of power, especially within the hierarchy of the Church, and thus the very opposite of freedom. Therefore, when announcing to his English friend, the priest Nicholas Bildeston, that he has married, he uses words that, in their somewhat solemn emphasis, border on desecration: "A great change has come over me, and, accordingly, I wanted to call it to your attention . . . You know that up until now I have led my life in an uncertain direction, since I was neither escaping from the world nor seeking to become a priest. However, given that I have always shrunk from the priesthood, and since I was of that age that I had at least to choose a certain plan for my life, I decided to get married."

This overturning of values—the "institutio" of a layman contrasted to that of a cleric—finds even more explicit expression in his more confidential letter to Guarino: "And in the same way as (dramatic) poets make the last act most refined and closest to perfection, so do I in the time that remains dedicate myself to a more perfect life."[107]

I would emphasize this challenge to common opinion, which is a consistent feature in Poggio's writings, as if he wanted to illuminate the prejudices, ambitions, and misunderstandings that weigh upon men's lives and confuse their relations. Among learned men, he told Francesco Barbaro on one occasion, "I am the one whose letters contain nothing ambiguous."[108] At the opposite pole stand the "sybilline oracles," to be understood either as rules of discipline emanating from the occult wisdom of the "satraps," or as protests of a legal or doctrinal nature, or finally as ethical and religious teachings.[109]

Therefore, in its broadest sense, Poggio's moral philosophy, or if one prefers, his own antimoral philosophy, is less a direct attack on specific ideas than on a general approach or method. A good illustration of this is his persistent criticism of the panegyric tradition, as exemplified in his satire on the eulogy for the cardinal vice-chancellor by his curial fellow,

Francesco of Velate. Poggio observes that in the oration the cardinal's virtues "immediately advance, and as if marshalled together into a cohort, burst forth with a great attack." Moreover, his Christian qualities ("he was humble and kind, and to everyone he was pleasantly good-natured and extremely gentle"; *humilis, benignus atque omnibus gratus facilis et humanissimus*) are nothing more than a long series of words. His religious practices "are of the common sort and practised by many people"; while the ceremonies he patronized "can truly be called 'ceremonies,' for since they mean *a carendo*—that is, their etymology is from the verb *carere*, to lack—they lack not only every virtue but even every trace of virtue."[110] Something like it is to be found in his oration for Nicholas V's elevation to the papacy, where his exhortation to "humanity" has already been mentioned. He attacks the art of official panegyric, remarking, "but those, Holy Father, who wrap your honors—that are indeed exquisite—within their orations ought, in my opinion, to be considered vaunters of words and flatterers, even if they might be worthy of you."[111]

Passages similar to these could be drawn from Poggio's other seemingly encomiastic writings, and in particular from a letter of congratulation to the newly appointed bishop Scipione Mainenti. Consistent with his usual emphasis on the "difficulties" of office, Poggio dismisses as inappropriate any discussion of "what befits a bishop, in what his duties and his tasks are, in what his office consists."[112]

Poggio's polemic against the panegyric tradition is really only one aspect of a much larger criticism directed at a philosophy of "precepts," of "duties" (the Ciceronian *officia*). Consider his early comments about Francesco Barbaro's *De re uxoria*, with ironies that would be repeated over time. Poggio observes that the treatise's casuistry of marriage and domestic obligations (in observance of authorities such as Plutarch, Roman law, Augustine, Jerome, Vergerio, and even Guarino) was such as to discourage the desired effect: ". . . after I see how much and how great are the duties wise men require of marriage . . . we can aspire to them more than we can achieve them."[113] Poggio was to reject similar precepts in the context of his own marriage: "These affairs are of a kind that cannot be distilled into doctrine, for they come to be known better by experiencing them rather than by reading about them. . . . For since advice is specific to each circumstance and must originate at that moment in time, it cannot be reduced to a fixed formula, especially in the case of things about which there is no certainty and for which it is difficult to reason."

He emphasized instead affective motivations ("in fact, a wife aware of your worries and desires will rejoice and suffer with you") and even a good physical relationship between husband and wife.[114] His short dialogue *An seni sit uxor ducenda* does more than just undermine the antifeminist tradition based on Saint Jerome's *Adversus Iovinianum,* beginning with its very title.[115] It also functions as an alternative to treatises such as *De re uxoria,* in being a claim that, irrespective of every precept, a happy marriage is possible in old age, and at the same time furnishes additional support for an independent and secular way of life.

Similar to his ideas on marriage, but even more striking, are Poggio's reactions to the educational guidelines the bishop of Modena sent him at the birth of his son. Such concerns, he writes to the bishop, were "not superfluous, to be sure, . . . but neither were they suitable for a child of his age or his circumstance." An infant's life, he argues, cannot be governed by fixed rules, for "with nature as their guide, each age of human life delights in its own specific pursuits." Every stage of life has its own rights, and a child's is to sharpen his wits with games. If this license is denied "it is sure to make him more foolish and more dull." But even in more advanced years it is necessary to adopt an attitude of moderation toward precepts, "lest . . . harm be done if they are neglected, or, although diligence should be used, prove themselves useless." Nor should much faith be placed in their ability to change character, for "it is God who allots to each one as He desires."[116] In short, the stern warnings—"the testimony of the most holy and most learned men"—seem ridiculous ("I laughed a little at your concern"), not only because they are untimely but also because at the opportune moment they will inevitably be forgotten: "but when they could perhaps be of some assistance, they are buried in oblivion and of no use at all."

Harsher still was Poggio's mockery of the claim Filelfo makes in his *Commentationes Florentinae de exilio* that "I have undertaken to treat and explicate all matters of moral philosophy up to the very point that you called the highest good." Despite the difference in the two contexts, Poggio reacts no differently here than he does to the bishop's precepts. Echoing Filelfo, he remarks, "It is a madman who says he can treat all matters of moral philosophy in his books; an enormous promise, indeed, difficult for both Cicero and Aristotle and much more so for the shameless brawling wrangler Filelfo!"[117]

The material was rich in political implications: the moral doctrine extolled by Filelfo was part of a dialogue attacking the Medici party, among whose supporters the author placed Poggio himself; the "infamy" of the present would be clarified against the background of the principles of good. But aside from its contingent motivation, the controversy bears on our subject in other ways. Poggio's criticism of the ambitious philosophy of the *officia,* and thus to an even greater extent of a philosophy of "ends," becomes eventually an attack on officialdom and institutionalism. Filelfo's mistake was to let himself get caught up rashly in political struggles—struggles in which he tried now to involve even Poggio—and disguising his foolishness with a philosophical coating.[118] On another occasion Poggio had written: "The lives of mortals should not be weighed on the scales of philosophy."[119] Political situations should be assessed not according to what could or should happen but rather what usually happened: "I have not investigated what could happen—because many things could happen that never do—but rather what up until now has usually happened."[120] Moral discourse broadens in this negative sense into a discourse of politics and history, and personal experience is projected against the irrational background of the theater of the world.

In fact, Poggio's works, and above all his will to give them a public literary form, were totally involved with specific events. It is by no means accidental that the real starting point of his literary career coincides with the Council of Constance, precisely during the greatest crisis of the medieval papacy; or that his first fully developed ideas on fortune and virtue (and on the slender limits to which virtuous living is confined) were related to the laborious settlement of the papacy and its domains, as well as the rekindling of the wars in Italy;[121] or, lastly, that in his first work of some breadth, the dialogue *De avaritia*—the work that shifted the then almost fifty-year-old Poggio onto the public stage[122]—he reacted with skepticism to the efforts of Saint Bernardino and the Observant friars to promote a renewal of morality and discipline.[123] The political and historical writings that followed, the *De infelicitate principum* (together with *De nobilitate,* 1440) and *De varietate fortunae* (1442–43 and 1448) had direct precedents in some of his letters: the ones to Niccoli, where he discusses Florence's internal struggles and risky war policy;[124] and the others to Cardinal Giuliano Cesarini concerning the vicissitudes of the Church, oppressed by the contemporary and equally subversive events of the internal rebellion by the Colonna family at the death of Martin V and the convocation of the Council of Basel.[125] In this situation involving both Poggio's *patriae* any reassuring sense of continuity with the past seemed to have vanished: Florence was on the brink of collapse, and its war with Lucca, driven by private ambitions, threatened to lead to an uncontrollable situation: "Such are the times that drive, such are the movements of affairs being prepared, that as I see it, each one would regret the state of his fortune."[126] In the past the ship of the Church had weathered every storm, but now it was without its traditional political support, and two great princes (obviously the emperor and the king of France) were conspiring to bring about its ruin: "But now where can you suggest it take refuge, so that it does not dash itself against a rock? It is as if a common madness has come over us."[127] The Holy Spirit the fathers invoked in the Council—"if it is anywhere really with us"—seemed to have changed nature: "to such an extent that charity and love seem to have been converted into hatred and discord." Fate would decide the outcome.[128] In the end he was anxious for the common destiny of Italy, which lay not only in the papacy's stability but also in a resolution of Florence's conflict with Milan: "I, however, would prefer anything to starting a new war with the duke, whose outcome will be difficult to predict; and trust me, with his [*scil.* duke of Milan] ruin will come our own. . . . Commit this to memory: unless war is avoided, within four years you will see Italy restored to the barbarians and much handed over as plunder."[129]

These were precisely the circumstances in which Poggio began to plan his *De varietate fortunae,* completed more than ten years later. In the same way that he had been accustomed to collect excerpts from his readings as a *vademecum* of his own moral reflections,[130] he announced to Cardinal Cesarini that he was taking historical notes: "as if I were gathering together into memoirs for these times the vicissitudes of fortune, so that what I am thinking doesn't slip from my memory."[131]

Poggio's reflections on political history were thus closely tied to events in his contemporary world. In his own way Poggio shared the critical concerns, common to other historians of the day (primarily Bruni and Biondo), about the reliability of the historical accounts, according to the principle of *autopsia,* that is, trust in facts "perceived by the eyes" compared to "those heard by the ears," which are subject to exaggeration and legend.[132] Furthermore, in regard to more remote traditions, for example, in a letter about the imperial coronation, Poggio was intent on making it clear that the election of the emperor by the pope, insofar as distinct from the Carolingian tradition of imperial coronations, had in his opinion not started before the pontificate of Gregory VII: "I will say nothing about this gap in historical accounts," he insists, "lest I should confirm something that has not been established for certain."[133] Moreover, Poggio was in agreement with Biondo that modern events were awaiting literary "illustration" capable of rescuing them from obscurity and giving them a dignity comparable to the events extolled by ancient writers, as he explains at the opening of the letter about Sigismund's coronation.[134] However, one aspect distinguishes Poggio's approach from Bruni's Florentine historiography and Biondo's history of Italy in a preliminary way: his extending his consideration to European and even exotic events. Among the examples quoted to be rescued from oblivion, for example, he mentions the magnificent deeds of Tamburlain, a man who "never experienced misfortune," a point he will develop later in the *De varietate*. Poggio's, incidentally, is one of the earliest references in European literature to the myth of the great conquistador that would culminate in Marlowe's Elizabethan tragedy.[135]

Up to this point the example of Tamburlain would seem a matter of positive historical interest, and in fact it is used as an example in a letter of encouragement to Leonello d'Este. But intrinsic to this choice of a contemporary focus and the related one of a broader geographical perspective is also a strong element of relativism, and consequently of historiographical ambiguity. In fact Poggio's historical standpoint is not that of stable values (such as Florentine liberty, the Roman state, contemporary civilization); it is instead of the shifting course of individual events, precisely "the theater of fortune," within whose undefined bounds accepted values are weakened or even invalidated, so that even those sanctioned by tradition are called into question. The principle of the *autopsia* is introduced in *De varietate fortunae* not so much as a way to gauge the accuracy of an account as it is a means to invalidate the credibility of illustrious traditions and popular elaborations: "For I do not know why what we hear with our ears is always held to be more complete than that which we see with our eyes. Since rumor lies all too often, I believe the eyes decide what is truth. Moreover, certain ancient things are held to be more worthy of veneration, and we always recommend the past out of weariness for the present."

Hence his invalidation of ancient authority: "But are you so foolish as to believe that everything antiquity produced are magnificent deeds, just as they are recounted, and not greatly amplified by the many flourishes and ornaments of a skillful author?"[136] Poggio's skepticism about the past, however, is balanced by his tone of doubt in evaluating the present. The comparison he draws, for example, between Sigismund's coronation and imperial triumphs is permeated with ambiguity ("I am enjoying a twofold pleasure, since I perceive on the one side things which delight the eye, being quite unusual with respect to our experience; and, on the other, bearing in mind these ancient deeds which we admire in our readings"). The narrative unfolds, in other words, as a game of appearances and reality to such an extent that Poggio uses the same vocabulary to describe the imperial majesty of the emperor that he had used to describe the regal looks of the simple actor: "There was a kindness and majesty in his expression, so that those who did not know . . . believed he was really the king of all others kings."[137] Valerius Maximus, the model for exemplary history (and for traditions of court historiography, such as that promoted by Alfonso of Aragon), appears to Poggio "the most flattering of all the flattering authors."[138] The work he himself chose to dedicate to the Aragonese king was the version of Xenophon's *Cyropaedia,* not a history at all but rather a novel concerning the education of the perfect ruler, who, just like the Stoic wise man, "is nowhere to be found."[139] Along the same lines, and pursuing an interest in the legendary and the exotic that was unusual in his intellectual circle, Poggio translated one of the oldest sources of legends and tales, Diodorus Siculus's "archaeology" of ancient peoples (or, according to Poggio's title, *Historiae priscae*).[140] Together with his reportage of Niccolò de' Conti's voyages,[141] it served to underscore how easy it was in human affairs to exchange in turn illusion and reality, the singular and the common, the history and the lies. Viewed from this detached Epicurean perspective, the political activity of Poggio's own age seemed to him like "empty little stories."[142] On the other hand, "the game of human affairs" was described as an everlasting source of surprise and fear: "But I have called to mind former events, because they are so recent, marvelling at the change in human affairs and the vicissitudes of fortune . . . Who could not be frightened at such a game of human weakness?"[143] *Sbigottire*—to be bewildered—would be a typical Machiavellian expression on this very purpose.

Historical investigation proper is thus restricted to direct and detached observation. The contemporary perspective that Poggio offers, however, where outcomes cannot be defined and where comforting traditions

(Florentine liberty, the majesty of the Church, peace in Italy) had waned, also serves as a criterion for evaluating, or, more accurately, for devaluing the past, to the extent that one might derive from its morally relativistic outlook a principle of historiographical skepticism.

———⊶⊷———

At this point it would be useful to return to the metaphor of the theater of fortune that introduces *De varietate fortunae* and reappears throughout the work, just as it does in the preceding and closely related dialogue, *De infelicitate principum*. The powerful of the world, represented as masked actors raised high by fortune, "perform like a show the spectacle of her favors"; but fortune herself sees to their unmasking: "for when the pedestal was pulled away on which she had placed them up high to be conspicuous, like mimes on a stage dressed in other's clothes, she brought them down, ridiculous, and scorned." One example of the fallen is Braccio of Montone, "who, on the highest level of the theater . . . was taken as some kind of masked king"; later, however, he is stripped of all his decorations, in less than an hour's time.[144] Not even the popes, or at least the most recent ones, were immune to fortune's power:

> Indeed in the case of the popes themselves, except for a very few . . . to what else can you owe their position other than to the wonderful power of fortune? When they are of lowly birth, like Egyptian kings, sometimes coming from the lowest class of men, they are by no means more outstanding than other people, . . . and our age looks up to these men, elevated to such a height that I too am often persuaded to wonder whether so prominent a power is governed in accordance with God's providence and will, or is driven disorderly by fate and chance."[145]

Even worthy deeds are vulnerable to fortune's power, Poggio points out: consider, for example, the sudden disintegration of Giangaleazzo Visconti's state, "a man worthy to have belonged to ancient times"; his story alone is enough to suggest that "nothing about human affairs can be established for certain, and where fortune stands in the way, the plans we make are of little use."[146] From this comes the complementary image of the tragedy: "It is well-known that the lives of princes are full of calamity, and many episodes could be staged, as if in a theater, to illustrate their unhappiness."[147]

It is possible to recognize here a combination of different themes: the

Stoic idea of the deceptive pleasure of riches (Seneca's *personata felicitas*),[148] linked more or less to the concept of fortune and, as in Lucian, to her arbitrary assignment of roles; the problematic relationship between fortune and providence, between fortune and wisdom as in the Stoic tradition, in Boethius, and then in various medieval treatises and symbolism; and finally, the concept of tragedy as the tales of unfortunate famous men, a definition passed down from Isidore of Seville which then merged with the widespread reception of Seneca's tragedies during the fourteenth century. However, Poggio does not assimilate these themes in a conventional or passive way as might be suggested at first glance. In a lengthy debate in *De varietate* (which will be treated more thoroughly further on), he rejects any definition of fortune from a philosophical point of view, and instead he limits himself to reassert its power exclusively on the basis of the common human perception. Modern scholars studying the idea of "fortune" have been puzzled about how to define Poggio's position. He seemed to one of them to waver continuously "between a deeply rooted faith in God, a fatalistic astrological superstition, and a belief that fortune, independent of God, had power over earthly affairs." As a result, he would stand in opposition to the confident Renaissance belief, as in Machiavelli or Pontano, that human prudence (or virtue) could overcome chance events.[149] This standard of interpretation now seems to me difficult to accept. What distinguishes Poggio's position is not, in fact, the degree to which he aligns himself with tradition, be it ancient, patristic, or medieval, but rather his clear-cut refusal to recognize any conceptual relationship outside the realm of empirical experience. If the definition of virtue according to Stoic teaching is precarious ("it restricts good men to excessively narrow limits"),[150] all the more reason fortune's definition will be fundamentally negative in character, such as that broad area that eludes the restricted and equally undefined sphere of reason and liberty — an area Poggio identifies chiefly with the arena where the powerful act: "among princes so rare is fortune's conjunction with virtue, . . . that they are thought to be shut off from such happiness."[151]

Once one denies any relationship between virtue and fortune (or, as in Poggio's words, any "society"), the image of them as antagonists, too, fades away. This antagonism was exemplified in Seneca's classical example of Cato, fighting with Fortune in the arena of life like a gladiator who, unlike the "pairs" of gladiators in the circus, tests his strength with obstacles set before him by Providence and God: "Behold! the worthy performance, where God is intently watching his creation. That is a pair (of wrestlers) worthy of God!"[152] This image would be developed later in Christian terms: according to Augustine, the Church replaced the ancient spectacle by substituting the great mysteries, so the Christian would not be left without a spectacle: "(Whoever) did contemplate human miracles, let him turn to the admirable works of God."[153] The "admirable spectacle" was that of faith infused by God, of the triumphal sanctity, and of the expected reward.[154] By both transcending and sustaining the ancient metaphor of "playing one's part"—in the sense of fulfilling one's assigned role in life—Augustine meant to represent the overcoming of worldly temptations: "Let us play out our parts," he encourages, "for the role of human life is a life full of temptation."[155] The twofold metaphor had in some sense become institutionalized in the medieval tradition: both in its "mystical" sense, of the theater of the present world where men of the Church were held up to everbody's mockery ("For the sake of God we are made a spectacle in this world to angels and to men"); and, afterward, in the triumphant sense of the priest battling victoriously in the liturgy of the mass ("Thus in his actions our cleric represents Christ's fight for the Christian people in the theater of the Church").[156] Poggio was well aware of these meanings. For example, in a letter to Cosimo de' Medici consoling him on his exile, Poggio urges him to take shelter in the stronghold of reason, "namely in the vast theater of virtue and good conscience."[157] Elsewhere in his aforementioned satire on ecclesiastical panegyric, he makes rather ambiguous reference to the various kinds of Christian asceticism, writing ". . . if you should praise them, you would excite great tragedies."[158] Therefore his leaning toward limiting or even overthrowing themes received by tradition is still more evident in his writings. The exemplary nature of the Church, though not completely disregarded, is nonetheless ambiguously relegated "to a previous age"; and the accomplishment of the *humanae vitae mimus* is defined not in terms of a Christian sanctification, as a priest or a monk, but as the matrimonial seal to Poggio's own vocation as a layman ("I am dedicated to a more perfect life"). Reciprocally, the "spectacle" does not symbolize an exemplary event but a generalized representation of human foolishness or weakness—meaning the spectacle directed by fortune, from whom not even the Church in its visible, and thereby political, role can escape: "But in fact while powerful men, puffed up by its favors, grow exceedingly scornful of virtue, . . . once they have entered the theater of fortune, they present performances of these favors to the populace. But fortune exercising her right, first casts down those whom she had once favored, and then reveals their folly."[159]

Once exemplarity had faded away, the prospect of fortune and of man become interchangeable; so that, as one scholar has perceptively observed about Poggio: "Fortune becomes a term for the inordinate complexity of events which impinge on the human will; Fortune is not a cosmic necessity, but a transparent shell focusing attention on the incoherence of the phenomena themselves."[160] In other words fortune becomes, as Poggio writes, a symbol of the disorder in the world, "such that the affairs of mortals seem to turn at its will, without any order directing them."[161] The "game" of fortune is simply the whimsical nature of individual events and, in more general terms, a playing of human weakness (*ad huiuscemodi ludum imbecillitatis nostrae*); so her "game" blends with Democritus's mockery, that of the disillusioned observer. Therefore, Boethius is silently set aside, as well as the various testimonies of his fortune in the Middle Ages, where the symbolic wheel image had been established against a background of transcendent rationality. Although the image was very popular in Poggio's time,[162] it appears in his writings in only vague and deliberately indirect references: "It is believed that there is a certain greater and more ordering force turning and upsetting human affairs according to its fancy, holding nothing apart from it stable or safe."[163] When rational certainty is lacking, its opposite obviously is also deprived of any meaning: in the words of Alain de Lille, "This alone [fortune] is true because it is always shown to be false / this alone stands firm because it always wanders in motion."[164] Poggio also acknowledges this topos somewhat indirectly, amidst refuting the intellectualistic conceptions of Aristotelian and Thomistic physics (a subject to which we will return): "For when I think to myself what these whom I have just mentioned and moreover what others believe, to what an extent they make fortune . . . powerful, it seems not to be some accident or without purpose, but something firm and stable and long premeditated in many ways." Nevertheless, when an ideal of rationality is given (as in Boethius, or, for example, in Petrarch's *De remediis*), Poggio suggests, the concept of fortune itself should fade away: "Thus does men's madness assign authority to fortune and make it into something fearful."[165]

Neither do we find in Poggio's work the popular image of the "world upside down," even though he does make passing reference to the tradition of foolish kings: "whom we have seen before described as foolish asses; and just as the animal is slow, stupid, insipid, lazy, . . . so people fittingly represent the human body with the head of an ass, whenever fortune adds generosity and benefit to foolishness." The transformation of king into ass at the turning of the wheel was actually an iconographic theme. Saint Bernardino commented on it in a sermon on the scriptural theme of the downfall of kingdoms: "Have you ever seen how the wheel of Fortune works, and its changeable nature? . . . Whoever punishes will himself later be punished," etc.[166] However, Poggio's representation is not of the world as it should or could be, paradoxically and polemically portrayed in his topsy-turvy image; instead, he is concerned with how things happen (*sed quid hactenus fieri consuevit*).[167] To borrow the title from one of Voltaire's novels, Poggio's was an image of "the world as it goes."

In this sense, the problem of a relationship between fortune and providence could only be set through vague and doubtful formulations. Either out of scruple or caution, Poggio limited himself to reporting the patristic prohibition of appealing even to the name of fortune: "let us add another [definition] that is not disparaging to our theologians, who assume that fortune is nothing more than the hint of the divine will which ordered or consented to do something."[168] He is obviously less convinced by the second half of the proposition: ". . . so that whatever is believed to proceed from fortune is brought about by the arrangement of God most high for a specific reason, which holds command over human affairs." Not by chance at the same time he was writing *De varietate*—almost as if to tone down the theological statements—he was translating Lucian's *Iuppiter confutatus,* "in which that most learned man seemed to joke with Jove himself about fate and providence."[169] Whatever its nature and causes ("setting aside any concern with definitions"),[170] fortune is evident in the course of events themselves. The treatment of such events, therefore, did not consist of a doctrinal exposition but precisely a "history" from which could be drawn practical advice for personal prudence: "by which, protected and fortified in advance we may be able to break the thrust of its weapons."[171]

Therefore, the subject is "the theater of fortune," and not, it should be emphasized, the Platonic or Neoplatonic vision of "the theater of the world," which presupposes the existence of a rationally ordered cosmos; nor, in terms of the theatrical metaphor, is Poggio conveying the idea of an author, a redistribution of roles, and an edifying resolution.[172] Clearly, such as he depicts it, the tragedy of the princes will continue without end ("Many acts can be played out as if in a theater in order to represent their unhappiness"). And above all, their disastrous outcome does not stem as much from their wicked conduct as it does from the inherent nature of monarchical rule: "such is its nature that it even makes good men bad in its practice and custom."[173]

Seneca's tragedies were especially authoritative on this very point. As described by a modern scholar, they express a "genuine hatred of power and regal grandeur, which Seneca demonstrated as indissolubly linked to crime and exposed to hatred;"[174] and Poggio reads and annotates them in his own copy, clearly alien to the moralizing concern of the authoritative fourteenth-century commentary by N. Trevet.[175] By combining a hint from Boethius ("What else does the clamor of tragedies bring but Fortune, turning round happy kingdoms with her indiscriminate power?"),[176] with Isidore's definition ("Authors of tragedies are those who used to sing of the ancient deeds and crimes of wicked kings in sorrowful song as their audience looked on"),[177] the prehumanist tradition had used the unfortunate affairs of kings as the subject of tragedy by antonomasia. Naturally, there was a didactic purpose: the *regula iuris,* the right rule, would endure as a solid guarantee of well-being, in conformity with the concluding exhortation of A. Mussato's *Ecerinis: Fidite, iusti,*[178] be confident, just men! The theme of the unhappy king combined in various ways with that of Fortune, in which the turning wheel completed the cycle of the rise and fall of kingdoms, and which punished the human pride of those whom she herself had exalted too much.[179] The image was assumed as a theme of political satire, and from the fourteenth century on, high prelates and popes, together with secular authorities, were particularly popular targets in iconographic and poetic representations.[180]

The fundamental text that fuses these themes and organizes them into a historical narrative is Boccaccio's *De casibus illustrium virorum,* a work designed as both a warning and a criticism for kings and popes. Considering its widespread success in Europe, as well as the expansions of the work's adaptations by Laurent de Premierfait in French and John Lydgate in English, *De casibus* represents a necessary point of reference for princely precepts in an age of crisis. It was a kind of "mirror for princes" turned upside down, in which the actual vicissitudes of dynasties and the established orders in society were reflected. From this perspective, even Poggio's work could be considered a variation, albeit a substantial one, on a theme widely diffused in his time.[181] It is worth asking, therefore, whether he consciously intended to associate himself with the contemporary European literature of the *Cas des nobles hommes,* or the *Fall of Princes,* and most importantly, if there is evidence of Poggio's direct knowledge of Boccaccio's work as well as the development of themes originally treated by him. It would not be out of place to examine Boccaccio's vigorous attack against the corruption of authority, barely masked behind the vision of a crowd of "unfortunate men," within the traditional framework of universal history. Boccaccio's intention is surely didactic, aiming "to teach princes wisdom and moderation by showing them the outcome of mishaps provoked by egotism, pride and intemperate ambition."[182] Nevertheless, he has little faith in the results, and in contrast to Premierfait and Lydgate after him, he refuses to dedicate "such excellent work" to the "Pope or the Emperor or to any prince," addressing himself instead to his confidential friend, Mainardo Cavalcanti.[183] Princes were accustomed to trusting evil counselors. Forgetting that power was rooted in popular suffrage, they established their honor "with the sweat of the people." Civic customs had degenerated from the good ancient examples, and those of the present-day papacy were best not discussed.[184] Rational illustrations of fortune's power and the instability of human affairs are shown to be insufficiently persuasive. Unable to deal with the mysteries of God, Boccaccio would turn more humbly—as he affirms in his dispute with fortune—"to your bosom which is loaded with all the affairs of men . . . , from which outstanding poets and famous historians have taken neverfailing material for singing and writing." In other words, Boccaccio rejects philosophical traditions and Boethian symbolism, to nourish his argument with examples taken from history and myth.[185] Instruction will come from facts, not from words, at least for those who will allow themselves to be gently corrected; and Fortune, transformed from a menacing into a kind figure, agrees with him: after all, her continuous threats had not produced any better results.[186]

The vanishing in Poggio of the symbolism of fortune within a historical narrative and a militant polemic, therefore, had a conspicuous precedent, one of which he was certainly aware. In fact, in both *De varietate fortunae* and *De infelicitate principum* he makes more or less indirect references to Boccaccio. In the latter work he describes him as "a man of genius, though inferior in his learning, whose many published books survive for the instruction of those who hear and read them." Poggio's comments are made in connection with the turns of fortune that Boccaccio experienced at the Neapolitan court and his subsequent withdrawal to

Florence, "having spurned the halls of princes"—one of the themes, in fact, of the *De casibus*.[187] *De varietate* contains an obvious allusion to the title of the *De casibus*, although Poggio outdoes Boccaccio's universalist framework: "Time would run out on me if I wished to survey all the examples of famous men (*illustrium virorum*), in which the licentiousness of fortune is found: for the books are filled with stories of that kind, which antiquity has entrusted to the memory of posterity."[188] Thus, unlike Boccaccio's only incidental discussion of recent historical issues,[189] and his polemic carried out through positive and negative *exempla* of universal history, Poggio overcame any remaining reluctance and confronted the contemporary world, "so that at least by writing I can comprehend this age."[190] Furthermore, unlike Boccaccio with his Christian ideal of "humility," not to mention his tenacious attachment to the civic world, Poggio means to address the princes of his time directly, perhaps with the intention of emulating the French and English translations that were expressly directed to princes and gentlemen of the court.[191] In fact, *De infelicitate* was addressed to, among others, Humphrey of Gloucester, the man to whom *The Fall of Princes* was dedicated,[192] and it also found its way by various means to the courts of France and Castile;[193] and in addition, before finally selecting Nicholas V as the recipient of his completed and expanded *De varietate fortunae,* he had planned to dedicate it to a secular monarch, in all likelihood Charles VII of France.[194]

By focusing on the contemporary world, and by demonstrating a nearly defiant attitude toward modern rulers, Poggio was shattering another more substantial barrier, which even Boccaccio with all his animosity had been careful to respect as a boundary not to be transgressed. Citing John XII—like the twin of the contemporary and equally disliked John XXII[195]—as a warning example of the profanation of the papacy, Boccaccio confessed he was tempted "to describe the papacy of my age fallen into wantonness and indolence and heavy arrogance."[196] Nevertheless, he had obeyed the scriptural warning, according to Psalm 104.5, "Do not touch my Christs," and which the French translator expanded for additional clarity: "qui . . . commande que len ne touche ne de fait de parolle les prestres ne les roys, pource que ilz sont oingtz et consacrez."[197] For Poggio, following once again in the footsteps of Seneca and Petrarch,[198] sacredness was nothing but an empty name derisively to the popes' titles: "for when they are called 'the holiest and most blessed' . . . it seems reasonable that all popes . . . could rightly be called happy."[199]

Equally meaningless was the traditional distinction, confirmed by the insistent appeal to the bygone authority of John of Salisbury, between legitimate king and tyrant: "I know nothing about those whom you call tyrants: we know this for certain, that some of those kings were better and exercised power over their subjects more justly. For they are distinguished not by their name but by their deeds."[200] Genuine concern for the public good was something even more rare than the Stoic wise man who was nowhere to be found. Without illusions of a mythical Golden Age only instinct and nature's rule were to be acknowledged: "For the forces of Nature exercise their power on us even when we resist"; "in itself and in its licentiousness principality is evil."[201] Christianity had not lessened the wickedness of power in any substantial way ("and Christian kings, too . . . , I maintain, want for happiness.") Not even David, the Biblical model of kingship, was free of guilt, so that we feel discouraged from explaining "those most hidden purposes of the All High."[202] Moreover, the difference between public happiness and private was only relative: far from finding a refuge from the blows of fortune on a solid foundation of virtue (such as Boccaccio's "humility"), compared to the powerful, private citizens have less power to do harm ("those, who are constrained by laws, can only do minor harm"). It would be much better to seek comfort in study, "if it is ever permitted to enjoy a more peaceful condition."[203]

The interest awakened by these ideas, and for which the *De varietate fortunae* would have provided so ample a corollary, in a mixture of attraction and repulsion, is of remarkable historical significance not limited to Italian humanist culture. Although we have only fragmentary and indirect notice of it, it is hinted at in Poggio's persistent attempts to gain recognition for his work in the court of France and to a greater extent in that of England, once familiar to him. From the letters he sent to Richard Petworth, his old friend from the chancery of Cardinal Henry of Beaufort, the king's chancellor, and especially from polemical references to certain "little arguments, disputes, useless even to those who engage in them"—to which he opposed the maxims of the *De infelicitate* "useful for living well"—it seems possible to assume that discussion was under way.[204] The ups and downs of fortune were an actual theme indeed, as the lengthy poem by Lydgate illustrates. The insistence with which he endows traditional precepts with Boccaccio's impassioned invectives betrays the general concern for preserving the established order and fundamental constraints of society. In the same way, the contemporary poet Thomas

Hocleeve (1370–1450) popularized an exposition on the theme of *De regimine principum* in vernacular verse, constructing it as a response to what seemed to him a very urgent question: "Consydering how changeable a thyng/ That office is, for so shall ye it fynd."[205] At a later date, Thomas Basin, the historian of Charles VII and Louis IX of France, and Poggio's friend during Eugenius IV's stay in Florence, used both *De casibus* and *De infelicitate* as illustrations of the inevitable upheavals in kingdoms ("the dangers of enemies, of tricks, of rebellions, of betrayals, of exiles, of sedition and the like . . . are either never or very rarely absent from them").[206]

Precisely because they were so closely intertwined with the actual events of his age, the paradoxical statements in Poggio's writings could not pass unnoticed while challenging established beliefs. Such was the realization of the perceptive Alonso Garcia of Cartagena, bishop of Burgos and an eminent figure at the court of King John II of Castile. Alonso is known to have been the major promoter and one of the authors of a vernacular translation and commentary on Seneca, which, as an "institutio principis Christiani," was designed to educate the sovereign and his court.[207] Among other things, he translated the fourteenth-century *Tabulatio Senece* by L. Mannelli, under the title "Tratado del amor, . . . de los casos de la Fortuna, . . . de la crueltad, . . . de los mudamientos, del amor y amistad" etc. In the prefaces to his versions, Alonso made a point of upholding the traditional belief that pagan philosophy should be subordinated to Christian doctrine. What needed to be avoided in particular was an appeal to the concept of fortune, which he instead identified as divine providence, and with it, the disturbing image of blind causality that emerges from Seneca's verse, "Fortune rules human affairs with no order . . .," the very image, as we have already seen, that Poggio had so strongly emphasized.[208] It comes as no surprise that Alonso was puzzled to find in Poggio's work a Seneca so completely at odds with canonical interpretation, and so unilaterally developed with respect to the Senecan doctrine itself. Unfortunately, except from what can be deduced from the tone of Poggio's reply, nothing is known of the extensive letter that Alonso wrote to the Italian humanist in the spring of 1443. Its discovery would possibly help to illuminate the ethical and cultural dilemmas of the entire age, similar in importance to Alonso's well-known and thoughtful reaction to Bruni's version of the Aristotelian *Ethics to Nicomachus*.[209] The point of conflict, nonetheless, is still quite evident. As Poggio writes in response, "Your letters cover many serious and wisely written issues;

if I wanted to respond to them all individually, I would have to compose a rather lengthy booklet. . . . As for your exhortation that I write you something about the glory of rulers, in order that they may be more enthusiastic about ruling well, I shall perhaps do it if my soul has leisure and serenity."[210]

Therefore, Alonso had requested that Poggio—with all the strength of his renowned eloquence—oppose to the *casos de la fortuna, mudamientos*—the mishaps, the changes of fortune—and cruelty the positive principle of "love and friendship," in the guise of his own book of good precepts (*Libro de amonestamientos y doctrinas*), or a further elaboration of Seneca's *De clementia,* traditionally held to be a guide for kings in their exercise of Christian charity.[211] As we already know, Poggio disagrees: "Whoever holds power seems to have such deaf ears that my words can do little for them in the future. 'Everyone is carried away by his own pleasure.' And although very often wise words and maxims are put forward, their lives nevertheless stay far from these wise precepts."[212]

Likewise he answered the bishop of Como, who, identifying the central theme of the *De infelicitate,* had objected that not all princes were unhappy, only the evil ones.[213]

Unlike the case of *De infelicitate principum,* we have direct evidence of a reaction to Poggio's political ideas in connection with the contemporary and equally provocative dialogue *De nobilitate.* In spite of the apparently more traditional theme of equalizing nobility with virtue, Poggio's treatment does as much to undermine the canonical statements of tradition as does his discussion of princely rule. The concept of nobility, in contrast to the theological ethics debated in Dante (to which Poggio refers implicitly)[214] is judged not pertinent to a moral treatment: "no virtue exists called nobility."[215] Bartolo of Sassoferrato's "civic nobility" (the *nobiles bullati,* as Poggio ironically calls them, because coming from princely privilege) shares the irrationality of the principality itself, "without any consideration to virtue."[216] The variety of customs and opinions about nobility among various nations confirms the inanity of expecting to derive a concept from it "in accordance with a common standard" (*ex certa norma*): "There is general agreement about the name; about the substance, however, no one agrees."[217] Nobility is, thus, nothing at all, but its alternative is the pure autarchy of the Stoic wise man, who, as it is well known, cannot be found, if he exists at all ("few seek that nobility of the Stoics, still fewer achieve it").[218] According to the argument Lorenzo de'

Medici makes to Niccoli (who in the dialogue represents the strictly Stoic perspective), virtue must "enter the city" in order to develop; that is, it needs fortune's blessings (the *patria,* good birth, wealth, etc.), which is to say, a social standing. In other words, if the meaning of nobility becomes completely relativized when compared to the idea of virtue, so does the very notion of virtue itself; and it is on this note of uncertainty that the dialogue concludes: "Those who possess a sharper talent for disputation will judge whose is the truer opinion."[219] P. O. Kristeller has correctly observed that Poggio "does not succeed in explaining or defining what constitutes virtue, and as a result, his discussion on a philosophical level remains superficial."[220] But it should be emphasized that this "superficiality" was still another refusal on Poggio's part to understand human affairs "according to the standard of philosophy," thereby bringing about a real dissolution of ethical and, to an even greater extent, metaphysical categories. Poggio's ideas, as has been said, disconcerted his contemporaries, creating a bewilderment that found one of its most eloquent expressions in the reaction of a group of educated Venetian gentlemen who had the philosopher and lawyer Lauro Quirini as their spokesman. The indignation over the reputation of "factiousness" attributed to Venetian nobility ("like a certain faction distinct from the rest of the people")[221] was but one reason for him to deplore Poggio's sacrilegious tract "against the nobility"[222] According to Quirini, in demonstrating the varied and uncertain rule of opinion, Poggio had complicated matters to such an extent that he could neither "resolve or explain the question according to the tenets of reason"; as presented, it promised to be an "insoluble enigma."[223] Only by appealing to good juridical, philosophical, natural, and metaphysical reasoning—and thereby to a conclusive ordering of the world and social hierarchy—could the question be properly dealt with; and this is precisely what Quirini attempted to do in his retaliatory tract, *De nobilitate.* "For the concept of nobility is more important than what could be discussed by students of eloquence," Quirini claimed; whereas Poggio declared he would resolutely await such "sybilline oracles."[224]

All the more reason the vast performance of the "theater of fortune," summarizing the variety of opinions and the illusoriness of ends, must have displeased the man to whom it was dedicated, Nicholas V, just at the time, thanks to an orchestrated propaganda campaign, he was portraying himself as the providential restorer of ecclesiastical order and Christian peace. In fact, in a panegyric written in 1451, quite likely on commission, the question is faced "whether the office and government of states are carried out by fortune and random accident, or by divine plan and power": the pope's accomplishments were the most effective refutation of such a mistaken opinion.[225] "For how can one who is subject to other powers administer to magistracies and kingdoms, and accomplish most weighty matters?" (Whereas, it will be recalled, Poggio, beginning with his dedication, had described the pope's temporal powers as "subject to the rule of fortune.") The author continues: neither is it necessary to attend to fortune; "a mind instructed in good arts will listen to itself . . . , it follows good and excellent things, provided it does not retreat from moderation, constancy, maturity, and prudence." Moderation, in contrast to Poggio's mere cautionary meaning, is defined here according to the classical concept of "prudence," as upright behavior, and from a perspective wholly dominated by a belief in providential designs and the holy mission of the pope.[226]

Still another author, far removed from Pope Nicholas's time and even more from his spirit, expressed similar objections: Giovanni Pontano. At the crux of Poggio's thorough discussion about the concept of fortune, which he probably drafted initially as an introduction to his "history" *De varietate fortunae,*[227] was his refutation of the ideas of Aristotle and St. Thomas, the only ones, he states, who have treated the concept philosophically, "and whose authority is approved by all" (p. 27). Aristotle's brief treatment of the principle of causality in *Physics* 2.4–6 had defined chance occurrences as those that stray outside the determined and necessary causal order, or at least outside the usual order of recurring phenomena. These were, therefore, exceptions and subject to an indeterminate causal force (St. Thomas referred to them as "causes by accident" [*causas per accidens*], and Poggio as the "accidental cause" [*causam accidentem*] of things that happened "outside a plan" [*praeter propositum*]).[228] In other words, in the Aristotelian view of a world directed toward its end and capable of being "penetrated by intelligibility,"[229] chance represented a lesser, marginal occurrence, to be understood in a negative sense, insofar as it operated outside the necessary or more typical order of causes, and as such was "not a subject of science." In an expanded analysis of Aristotelian doctrine, St. Thomas had introduced the concept of a concurrence of two causes; something which Poggio may have misunderstood—perhaps by combining the idea with other aspects of Thomistic theory—as a concurrence of heavenly dispositions: "By virtue of a heavenly disposition inclining us towards it without our awareness."[230] Whatever the case, like Stoic moral doctrine in its own ambit, the Aristotelian and Thomistic perspectives seemed to Poggio to have too narrowly restricted (*nimis angustis . . . finibus*) the vast area of influence commonly considered fortune's: "For there is certainly something else beyond these philosophers' definition, which is commonly called fortune, exercising its powers far and wide beyond the limits they create, about which we can more quickly produce doubts than we can express a definite idea."[231] Human history, Poggio believed, cannot be understood as part of a presumed order in the natural world, any more than it can be considered within the boundaries of ethical doctrine. Nature itself—if this is the meaning his reportage of Niccolò de' Conti's voyages, appended to the *De varietate* as the final chapter of the dialogue—conceals more unforseen events than those revealed in our philosophy.

Returning to Pontano, in his treatise *De fortuna* (and no less in the corresponding work, *De prudentia*) he intends to reaffirm the precarious balance of moral and physical worlds essentially on the basis of a rhetorically amplified Aristotelian doctrine.[232] In light of this, it would seem that although scholars have generally failed to recognize in this work any direct link or implicit debate with the statements put forward by Poggio, these connections can indeed be documented with a sufficient degree of reliability. Just like Poggio's work, *De fortuna* begins with a summary of ideas about fortune as a way to ascertain its existence on the basis of common consensus, as an introduction to a more strictly philosophical examination: "The term Fortune has spread to such an extent that even learned men consent to its use. . . . About fortune men conjecture what its power is, and how many things either good or bad were attributed to it." Compare this with Poggio's words:

> Much . . . have I heard and read about this fortune and its power
> in works of historians, poets, orators; much more by men speaking
> who say all human affairs are subjected to fortune . . . , which they
> hope will be favorable to them, and curse it when it goes against
> them . . . to such a degree that the opinion develops that it will
> lavish wealth and power on them; it is not only a popular belief, but
> believed also by the most learned and wise men.[233]

This remark was probably suggested to Poggio by Aristotle's brief summary of the various ideas about chance (*Physics* 2.196 a-b, 4), which St.

Thomas had thus summarized: "He makes an account of those things which are said about fortune. First, what ancient philosophers have said about fortune; second, what is said by the common man about fortune."[234] However, Poggio undoubtedly has also in mind the famous passage in Pliny's *Naturalis historia* 2.5.22, about the cult of the goddess Fortune: "Indeed by the whole world and everywhere . . . fortune alone is called upon by all (*omnium vocibus Fortuna sola invocatur*), she alone is denounced (*arguitur*) and worshipped with imprecations" (*cum conviciis colitur*); and then Poggio pauses on the point where Pliny actually discusses beliefs in astral determinism (perhaps because Poggio had assimilated these ideas with his more general notion of fortune): "This idea began to take hold, and a crowd of equally learned and ignorant men ran in its direction" (*Sedere coepit sententia haec, pariterque et eruditum vulgus et rude in eam cursu vadit*, § 23). Poggio's *De varietate* runs along very similar lines: "For the words of very learned men and the common consent of all (*omnium consensus*) compel me to concede that it is something rather divine. . . . For all learned and unlearned alike (*omnes docti atque indocti pariter*) agree that it is fortune" (p. 26), and further on he also refers to the opposing definition, "which our theologians should not dislike," asserting that fortune was nothing more than "the hint of the divine will (*divinae nutum voluntatis*), . . . ordering that things happen in such a way, that what is believed to be the work of fortune is the arrangement of God Almighty, according to a definite plan" (p. 31). A combination of these two passages from Poggio, sometimes literally paraphrased, seems to me the most definite sign of Pontano's dependence on him:

> For people (*populi gentesque*) both learned and unlearned alike agree (*docti pariter indoctique consentiunt*) that this is a cause, although very pious men most dedicated to the divine majesty call power and will of God himself what others are accustomed to call fortune (*Dei nutum voluntatemque esse dicunt*, etc.: f. 266r).

Hence the following can be logically deduced: first, that Pontano went through Poggio to the passage of Pliny I cited, about the consensus "indeed by the whole world and everywhere" (*toto quippe mundo et omnibus locis*) (expressed by Pontano as *populi gentesque*, which is not found in Poggio); secondly, that he has nevertheless literally retained Poggio's free paraphrasing (*docti pariter indoctique*), though incongruent with the Plinian context; and lastly, that the borrowing is made still more evident by the further incongruence with regard to Poggio, where the reference was to the common belief in the existence of fortune, and not to the philosophical question posed in Pontano's chapter in question: "Whether fortune can be defined as a cause" (*An fortuna ipsa sit aliqua causa:* f. 266r), for which, strictly speaking, it would seem nonsense to appeal to a consensus of the unlearned.

It is possible, according to a technique common at the time, that the implicit citations referred to above were intended to signal their origin to the knowledgeable reader. Anyway, we can reliably identify the points where Pontano enters into debate with Poggio's text, a work that was doubtless very familiar to him. I said that Poggio denied the notion of accidental causes, unwilling to acknowledge a stable world order as a counterpart; the only thing that could be known for certain was, indeed, fortune, not accidental "but rather anything fixed and stable, and in most cases already pre-established since a long time."[235] Quite the contrary, Pontano emphasizes the opposition between natural order and fortune. This latter, he writes, "is inconstant, disordered, variable, sudden. But in contrast, what is more orderly, more constant, more certain than nature itself?"[236] Poggio, moreover, was unwilling to admit that the chance outcomes of voluntary actions could be defined as "beyond intention": according to a way of thinking both dynamic and anti-intellectualist, fortune and intention were one and the same. Alexander the Great would have scoffed at his teacher Aristotle had he learned that his own adventurous conquests had been carried out "beyond intention"; just as would the merchant who finds a run of unexpectedly favorable prices in a distant market, and who indeed is not inconsistent in his aim of becoming rich, "since they all, once they have adopted a strong resolution, have accomplished nothing without a hope, nothing beyond expectation."[237] Pontano, moreover, maintains the opposition of intellect and fortune, the former relative to what is intelligible, the latter to external matters. Since choices come from the intellect, "how can it be denied that prudence is guide and teacher of all human actions? . . . Therefore fortune is the opposite of intelligence, which is teacher of prudence."[238] Thus for Pontano, no differently than for Aristotle, fortune constitutes an exception to natural order, and yet an exception not external to it; and contrary to Poggio's warning, he suggests a problematic definition, or, better to say, proposes a variation on Aristotelian teaching: "Whereas fortune is a mode of nature" (*Quare fortuna sit natura quaedam*). Fortune, in fact, "is a kind of natural energy" (*naturae impetum esse cuiusdam*), inspiring the rare species of the "fortunate," in a way that recalls the divine inspiration given to the Sybils and the poets.[239] Thus in some sense within this definition, drawn from and expanding on an Aristotelian and Thomistic context, Poggio's own anti-intellectualist and dynamic concepts are in some way recovered, which in *De varietate fortunae* he had exemplified with figures like Alexander the Great, Tamburlain, and Braccio of Montone, not to mention the autobiographical hints at Poggio's own youthful experiences. Once again, however, Pontano's firm faith in an ordered world indirectly permits him, unlike Poggio, to have a positive view of fortune's natural and creative force, to the extent that he defends fortune against whoever accuses it, as an element of nature itself: "A defence of both fortune and nature against their own accusers."[240]

We can explain why Pontano's *De fortuna* has been the subject of contradictory interpretations. According to one scholar it provides a "new perspective" on previously unexplored territory; to another, it seems "a curious return to the scholastic debate."[241] The preceding analysis has tried to show how the treatise is characterized by its firm grounding in Aristotle's *ratio naturalis,* and also—and perhaps more—by a reaction to Poggio's philosophically destructive, anti-intellectualistic pessimism. Poggio's arguments are thereby concealed in Pontano's discussion and brought back to the positive reasons and values of classical philosophy, reinforced with the balanced analysis of Aquinas.

The *De fortuna* is not the only work in which Poggio's provocative ideas are covertly amended. There are other near-contemporary authors who referred to him, such as Cristoforo Landino, who in his *De vera nobilitate,* following Poggio's lead, reproposes Dante's idea of nobility as the capacity for human perfection, attainable through the practice of public duties (the Ciceronian *officia*), which according to him stood precisely for "true nobility."[242] While Poggio, as will be recalled, had overturned Dante's propositions, understanding nobility not as a "seed that includes all the other branches," but rather "like a certain splendor emanating from virtue which brings glory to those who possess it." This way it was a kind of promise, a commitment, an omen, which thereby deferred the attainment of "true nobility" to an indefinite time in the future: "and whether they follow the example of their parents, or whether they liken themselves to the example of others, they will attain true nobility."[243] The notion of nobility as the fullness of individual virtue did not traditionally exclude—and Poggio himself alludes to this in the passage here cited—the value of hereditary nobility. On this basis Landino, ever faithful to Dante, tempers Poggio's anti-institutional polemic and takes up again, though much more moderately, the debate over Bartolo of Sassaferato's teachings on "civic nobility," and finally can make an honorable peace with the Venetians:

> And so, as I finally bring this discussion to a close, I do not say that Venetian nobles are noble because these citizens originate from the ranks of the ancient Senate of the city; but rather, because most of them live in such a way and excel in such skills, that they can according to their own custom rightly be called nobles.[244]

As has already been pointed out, Poggio' s most important works were shaped by the times in which they were written. This was an age particularly marked by upheaval and change: from the Council of Constance and the papacy of Martin V, to the turmoil under his successor Eugenius IV, to the Council of Basel, up to the institutional crisis in Florence and the wars in Italy. Against this backdrop, Poggio had opposed his own individual quest for peace and intellectual freedom, which found their chief support in the institutional position of apostolic secretary, which he recovered in 1423; then the privilege of fiscal immunity in Florence, which Cosimo de' Medici had helped him to obtain in 1434; and, surely as a consequence of this kind of social assurance, his marriage to a Florentine noblewoman shortly afterward. There were factors that all together helped to sanction his choice of the secular life and that guaranteed a certain status for himself and his descendants in the insidious environment of civic society.[245] Instead of fulfilling Poggio's expectations, however, the gradual process of pacification and adjustment of the established hierarchies in the following years left him disoriented and as though he had outlived his time. The election of Nicholas V and the triumphal aura surrounding him can be assumed to be the first indication of this different atmosphere. Poggio not only reacted against the palingenetic ideology of the new pope, but he even went so far as to express some doubts about the vaunted providential pacification of the Church ("We must acknowledge all such benefits as coming from knowledge, learning, and literature only").[246] Relying on his own experience of human affairs he judged that it was untimely for the pope to make himself the promoter of peace in Italy,[247] and he even made known, albeit covertly, his personal disapproval of Nicholas's building projects (". . . goodness shines forth by itself . . . I would hope . . . : without the need for the triumphal trappings").[248] It should be remembered that De varietate, together with his version of Diodorus Siculus, were the last works Poggio dedicated to Tommaso of Sarzana, the old friend and patron of his studies; and the Contra hypocritas, though taking part in the general polemical climate toward the recently concluded papacy of Eugenius IV, is in strident contrast with the atmosphere that soon after led to the canonization of Saint Bernardino.[249] But above all the De miseria humanae conditionis, inspired by the fall of Constantinople, actually targets the papacy itself most directly, as well as its secular partner, the Roman Empire: "let me sharpen my pen to attack many people, and even the popes themselves, where perhaps I'll have much to say."[250] He even goes so far as to deliberately dedicate this final dialogue to an enemy of the Church, such as Sigismondo Pandolfo Malatesta ("that I suppose will please somebody else"), whose protection he invokes in a later insertion into the text: "But you, Sigismond, I implore and entreat . . . to take under your care by your authority this our disputation, in case any perhaps with ill will and spite should try to attack it."[251] Poggio's polemic merges with his criticism of the "corruption" brought into the office of apostolic secretary under Nicholas V and later Calixtus III, and thereby more broadly with the organization of studies patronized by the pope, which made room for, among others, Poggio's great enemy, Lorenzo Valla. As the generation his old friends was dying out ("I speak with the dead,")[252] his ideal of a free confidential discourse was giving way to a more rigorous discipline sponsored from on high, and his polemic with Valla seems to summarize both regret and retaliation for a liberty and a privilege which now his rival was almost symbolically taking away from him.[253] Although by now often repetitive, his writings in old age are characterized by a bitter and at times strident tone of attack ("It is difficult at this time not to write satire"):[254] an attitude that would earn him the posthumous reputation, for example by way of Erasmus, of "Poggius the wrangler," persecutor of good men.[255]

Poggio's relations with his hometown, Florence, were no better. His attitude toward the ideals of civic life, as already mentioned, was one of detachment, and on more than one occasion he had made a particular point of distancing himself from a municipal vision, such as in his eulogy of Giangaleazzo Visconti, later repeated in his *Florentine Histories*.[256] Although a native of the village of Terranuova, he had a cosmopolitan spirit as well, so Poggio had remained nonpartisan when Francesco Guidi of Battifolle, Count of Poppi and the ancient lord of Terranuova was deposed and the Casentino area came under Florentine control. The episode had sparked celebrative chronicles and outpourings of propaganda among the Florentines ("I am that fair and beautiful flower / who holds a large part of Neptune and Thetis/and with my decrees / I rule in their land / and under my power I rule and hold almost all of Tuscany").[257] On the contrary, for Poggio the fateful event provided an opportunity to review the history of the Guidi family, who had been governing their territories "according to right rule" for three hundred years. Poggio showed particular interest in the vicissitudes of the last two descendants of the Guidi line, and rather than directly charge them with treason, he explains their politically risky balance between Florence and the Visconti, which caused their downfall: "I should accuse Fortune, except that some people impute this fault more to ambition than to fortune." In lamenting the sad destiny of the Guidi family, Poggio gives vent in erudite language to a villager's persistent and affectionate attachment to the ancient lords, even in a land long ago liberated from signorial rule, such as "Terranuova, our homeland."[258]

When considering Florence's internal affairs, Poggio combines an aristocratic disdain toward the popular government—"always quick to choose the worse option"[259]—with a more general dislike of the town's burdensome conditions, "the most annoying of all and full of cares and sweat."[260] At the same time he reveals a distrust of the *ottimati*, "who prefer private concerns to public welfare."[261] These ambivalent sentiments inspire Poggio's *Disceptatio convivalis* on laws and medicine in which, among his skeptical comments on the objectivity of legal norms, he observes that, "the more powerful and prominent citizens transgress the tenor of laws," remarking moreover that cities' governments surely would not ask the opinions of jurists about waging wars of conquest.[262] In fact Poggio had condemned several times Florence's military aggressiveness and the resulting dissipation of the public treasury, adding his voice to a large chorus of popular outcry. As early as 1423, he had deplored Florence's involvement in renewed wars with the Visconti duchy, pointing out that it would not happen "without an outpouring of our money,"[263] emphasizing at every opportunity his love of peace. For this reason, the reflections introducing his *Florentne Histories* appear ambiguous. They seem to reiterate themes typical in apologies for civic life, such as the vast financial capabilities Florence had demonstrated in the wars of the previous century, just recently concluded with the Peace of Lodi: "It indeed must seem a cause for wonder that there was so much money to supply the inexhaustible expenses of so many wars, since for so many consecutive years in which wars were fought, liberty was defended not by our own but by mercenary forces"; and he adds that "not only our soldiers, but also foreign peoples and kings were urged to help us, giving them a great amount of money."[264] Poggio is making particular reference to the large sums Florence invested in the expeditions led by Jean d'Armagnac (1391) and above all by Robert of Bavaria (1401) during the wars against Giangaleazzo Visconti, events recorded in Bruni's as well as in Poggio's own historical narratives. The moments of glory were by now past, while over the present a veil of reticence, if not of open criticism, is drawn, such as that regarding money being both badly collected and badly spent. It is typical that the *Historiae* are less than a celebration of the ruling Medici regime; indeed, not a single word is spent about its rise to power. Moreover, even more explicitly than Bruni's model, Poggio does not treat only the just, defensive wars, but also — to quote from his own preface — "the wars in which at times the Florentine people withstood the offenses, at times initiated them."[265] Insofar as it is principally a history of military vicissitudes, the *Florentine Histories* are far from being a patriotic apology. For Poggio, they represented a kind of updating of the *De varietate fortunae*, without any triumphal outcomes, and with the implicit, detached warning to use wise moderation. The work was drafted as Poggio was nominated to be chancellor of the Florentine republic, a position he accepted with some hesitation,[266] and his doubts were fully confirmed on various accounts. Florence now seemed foreign to him ("it seems to me that I have come into my fatherland not as a citizen but rather a kind of guest and new inhabitant,")[267] and the mores of the city seemed to have little to recommend.[268] Most of all, according to Vespasiano da Bisticci, some of the most influential citizens conceived a dislike for him and were urging his removal from office.[269] Poggio's aims had been primarily to confirm his own privilege for his children, so as to guarantee them a firmer position in public life. The outcome dashed his hopes and expectations, and the revocation of his fiscal privilege through the bills of 27 May and 28 September 1457, following the developments in the more general public debate that seriously challenged the very safety of the Medici regime, had made him rudely aware of the situation. Independently of the political situation, for Poggio it meant the crumbling of the last existing pillar of his own social guarantee, which he thought he needed to protect his own liberty and by extension that of his descendants. In a state of exasperation he paradoxically went so far as to question his own loyalty to the ruling regime, making it responsible for the "breach of faith."[270] And like the anti-Medici partisans, such as Girolamo Machiavelli, the head of the opposition, who in the public debate of the "Pratica" referred to the Venetian administration as an example of civic fairness ("as the Venetians do," he pointed out) and called for the restoration of a republican and just government ("so that justice might be administered and that we might live justly"),[271] Poggio proposes in one of his final writings a polemical contrast between the factiousness of his own land and the idealized model of Venice, the only possible refuge for justice and peace.[272]

Poggio's career is thus concluded in that (at least potential) involvement with factionalism that throughout his life he had sought to escape. Works like *De miseria humanae conditionis,* and the subsequent pair of pamphlets, *Contra fidei violatores* and *In laudem reipublicae Venetorum,* were but an admission that his ever consistent pursuit of a *portiuncula* of peace and liberty could only be attained in a utopia. Instead of the refuge of reason, Poggio was leaving as a legacy to his sons the uncertainties of fortune. As far as we know from the movements of the copyist who transcribed the manuscript, his controversial praise of Venice must have circulated within the anti-Medici party of Dietisalvi Neroni,[273] with which Poggio's only untonsured son, Jacopo, was affiliated. In 1466, in fact, Jacopo suffered, along with banishment, a heavy fine of a thousand florins, the prelude to the family's financial ruin and his later involvement in the Pazzi conspiracy.[274]

In all likelihood these are the events referred to in Jacopo's *Contra detractores,* a little tract addressed to Lorenzo de' Medici. Jacopo had modeled the title and content of his writing on his father's *Contra delatores,* which Poggio had written as a response to the accusations of licentious behavior brought against him in the Roman curia.[275] However, while comparing the two albeit similar tracts, it is worth noting Jacopo's loss of his father's trust in individual liberty. Citing examples of learned and virtuous men, victims of slander, he observes: "None of these things would happen to us, if only the princes and whoever holds the government, and according to whose will we live and whose whims decide our safety and all our affairs, were just, restrained and prudent" (he excludes from consideration the populace, which show no reason in their judgment and who are always enemies of honorable men, "being driven, like wild beasts, only by their appetite").[276] But the hypothesis was far from reality, and Jacopo emphasizes his pessimistic outlook with the image, once dear to Poggio, of the mask, of the game of fortune: "Whence we see many men who have achieved by fortune's jest the emblems of virtue without a shadow of it, while men most glorious and most saintly have been held of less account and cast away. Indeed, if that men would show off for appraisal after their mask had been set aside, their dullness would easily be recognized."[277]

This same Jacopo would go afterward into the service of the Riario and Salviati families, joined with the Pazzi in the conspiracy against Lorenzo de' Medici; and thus—as Poggio would have said it—trespassing beyond "the gates of reason," he would behave at the mercy of fortune, according to the whims of his new masters, with the ill-fated results only too well known. Jacopo's spirit was still faithful to his father's; but he lacked that capacity for a somewhat libertarian independence—truly a requirement for literary production and for an unmasked moral reflection—with which Poggio once ended one of his letters in the manner of an epigraph: "As is our custom, we will not be unwilling to be summoned to banquets, where in spite of those fault-finders, we will continue to talk freely," *ob istorum reprehensorum contumeliam libere colloquemur.*[278]

5

An Analysis of Lorenzo Valla's *De voluptate*
His Sojourn in Pavia and the Composition of the Dialogue

"Laurentius Valla patricius romanus" declares the frontispiece of some early editions of his works.[1] The Roman epithet was suggested by Lorenzo Valla's own boast that he was the new Camillus, determined to rescue Latin language from barbarians. Although born in Rome in 1407, Valla was, in fact, of solid Lombard stock: both his father and mother were descended from the landed nobility of Piacenza (a social class which often in that epoch contributed members to the ranks of intellectuals).[2] Careers in law had led the de Valle and the Scrivani (the mother's family of Lorenzo) into the sphere of the Roman curia, but they never lost their close ties and attachment to the region of their origin, as the intermarrying itself demonstrates.

Valla's ambition from an early age was to follow in the footsteps of his uncle, Melchior Scrivani, papal secretary from 1426, conforming to the pattern typical of curial officers to perpetuate (like small dynasties) acquired privileges. However, given the increasingly humanistic character of the college of papal secretaries, Valla was also motivated by intellectual ambition. Beginning with Leonardo Bruni, the position of secretary had been occupied by a series of humanists, including Antonio Loschi, Cencio Rustici, and Poggio Bracciolini, the same figures, incidentally, who appear in the first version and Roman setting of Valla's dialogue, the *De voluptate*.[3]

This was the ambience in which Valla produced his first work, the lost *Comparatio Ciceronis Quintilianique*. Perhaps in the traditional connection between rhetorical teaching and chancery's practice, surely emulating Antonio Loschi, the senior among papal secretaries, whose *Inquisitio artis super XI orationes Ciceronis* (1395) was one of the fundamental texts of the new "Ciceronianism" shaping rhetorical teaching in northern Italian universities (Pavia and Padua in particular), Valla thus intended to compete with the schooltexts of Lombard milieu, following his own taste for competition, which would characterize his entire career. In this regard the work and influence of Gasparino Barzizza comes especially to mind. Recent scholarship has increasingly put Barzizza at the center of Lombard cultural endeavors, according to analogous concerns, but maintaining its own character against the parallel Florentine experiences, both well represented in the Roman curia.[4]

Rejected by the humanist curial establishment, perhaps for this attack on Loschi's Ciceronianism, Valla won the patronage of that other influential and yet restless and provocative figure, Antonio Beccadelli (better known as "the Panormita"), the author of a scandalous collection of erotic poems, the *Ermaphroditus,* who was in Rome in 1428. The following year, when Panormita was awarded a prestigious and well-paying position at the court of the Visconti in Milan, Valla, with Panormita's recommendation, and having established a patronage obligation with him, went in turn to Lombardy, settling first in Piacenza, but with his sights on the chair of rhetoric at Pavia.[5]

Rhetorical teaching was in a critical state owing to the decline of Barzizza, now old and nearing death, who was concluding his long career in Milan. In 1428–29 the university records report that "the teaching of rhetoric is now in abeyance" (*ista lectura Rhetorice stat in suspenso*), while in 1429–30 the position was occupied by Tommaso Seneca of Camerino, another of Panormita's protégés. The following year Panormita himself obtained a lectureship with the support of the duke, aiming thereby to transfer to the Studio the charge of paying his exorbitant salary of four hundred florins as court poet.[6] In 1431 Valla actually got his official position at the university, thanks to Panormita's sponsorship (he describes himself as *familiaris Panormitae* in a letter to Antonio of Rho). His appointment was probably secured by an agreement between Panormita himself (who, because of local resistance, had been unable to obtain the official nomination in the records of the Studio), and a member of the faculty of law, easily identifiable as the influential Catone Sacco, "our lawyer," as Panormita was used to refer to him. (Valla's appointment was recorded in unorthodox terms: "inscribed on the roster proposed by the rector of jurists," although he actually taught in the faculty of medicine and arts).[7]

The reasons for the subsequent break between Valla and his patron remain obscure in the drawn-out disputes that followed. Valla's desire to free himself from such an intrusive guardianship was certainly one ("I have been released as though from some kind of a seige," he wrote in the letter to Antonio of Rho referred to above), especially after Panormita's own *maecenas,* Francesco Barbavara, had fallen into disgrace with the duke and left him stripped of support at the Milanese court. In June of 1432 Valla thus transferred his allegiance to the rival party. His new patron was the ducal secretary, Pier Candido Decembrio, who had as his spokesman the eccentric figure of Antonio of Rho—humanist, Franciscan, and heir to Barzizza's chair in Milan.[8]

The events outlined represent the framework for the dialogue *De voluptate,* as Valla titled the first edition published in 1431. Notwithstanding the fact that its setting and characters belong for the most part to the circle of humanists in the Roman curia and the purported year is 1427 to judge from the dialogue's fictitious action, there is no doubt that Valla conceived and composed the work during the years of his sojourn in Piacenza and frequent visits to Milan and Pavia. For one thing, Valla explicitly establishes the events as having taken place "three years ago." The setting, moreover, seems intentionally fictional, given that the Roman sojourns of Bruni and Panormita, to which reference is made, occurred at different times (in 1426 and 1428 respectively). Furthermore, as far as we know, the third principal interlocutor, the Florentine humanist Niccolò Niccoli, actually came in Rome only in 1424.[9] The date is also supported by evidence within the text itself, most of all by the implicit but clear references to Poggio's dialogue, *De avaritia,* which was not in circulation until 1429.[10]

These deductions also have a significant bearing on the interpretation of the dialogue, as will become evident later on. It will suffice now to point out what Valla's intentions actually were. While summarizing his Roman experience, on the one hand, he aimed to consecrate his connection (or, better to say, the one he wished to establish) with the humanist elite of the time, particularly represented by the Florentines Bruni and Niccoli; and on the other hand, to give a literary form to his fellowship with Panormita, who, in effect, had patronized the work and who, as the defender of pleasure, was assigned the central and most extensive role in the debate.[11] Alongside these particular aims, however, was Valla's desire to establish his own presence in a rapidly expanding cultural movement, contributing his own voice to cultural endeavors, and proposing new and unthought-of conclusions. First, I refer to Valla's choice of the dialogue genre on philosophical and literary matters: a genre revived by Bruni and which Poggio had in turn adapted to ethical issues. Valla's antischolastic polemic, moreover, was in line with antischolastic criticisms that had started with Bruni's own Latin translation of the *Nichomachean Ethics* (1417). In response to attacks against his rendering of the Aristotelian concept of "the good" (*tagathòn*) with the Ciceronian locution "the highest good" (*summum bonum*), Bruni in his tract *Isagogicon moralis disciplinae* (c. 1424) had outlined a rather eclectic concordance of Aristotelian, Stoic, and Epicurean moral teachings, therefore implicitly leaving out Platonic and theological doctrines.[12] Finally, on the basis of Cicero and even more of Quintilian, Valla emphasized the praise of eloquence and its excellence over scholastic dialectic, making of this claim one of the most emphatic premises of the dialogue: "For how much clearer, more dignified and more splendid are those things discussed by orators, compared to those squalid and bloodless matters examined by dialecticians!"[13]

There is evidence that while composing the work Valla was still hoping to make a reentry into the Roman ambience, probably at a time coinciding with the election of the new pope, Eugenius IV (on 7 March 1431), Valla's old schoolmate and in the same year restorer of the *Studium Urbis,* whom he deliberately mentioned in the dialogue.[14] Nevertheless, his glorification of oratory and of its ability to compete with dialectics, not to mention the vast learning it embraced (and the dialogue itself illustrates this), suggests that Valla also wrote it with the aim of being named to a chair at the university, a goal, as we have seen, he was to achieve shortly thereafter.

The publication of the dialogue did not fail to arouse interest in humanist circles, as is evident from Antonio of Rho's inquiry in June of 1432 about "that book of yours which many of us have heard and many claim is divine in its eloquence, teaching, and art."[15] The second edition followed Valla's break with Panormita, whose role in the dialogue was assigned another and more innocuous poet, Maffeo Vegio.[16] This and other substitutions were aimed as well at winning favor with the intellectual community in Milan and Pavia. The part of the Stoic, the defender of *honestas,* uprightness, is played by Catone Sacco, the powerful jurist who probably had used his influence to secure Valla a teaching position and who had then joined forces with Panormita's enemies. The part of the Christian interlocutor is taken by Antonio of Rho, while the moderator of the debate is Guarino of Verona, another famous humanist who had been active as a mediator and catalyst in Lombard humanism and with whom Valla sought later to ingratiate himself.[17] Other background figures are further proof of Valla's interest in including important members of the sociopolitical and academic worlds in his dialogue. Clerics like Antonio Berneri, the vicar of the archbishop of Milan, and Giuseppe Brivio, a canon of the cathedral, lent an air of legitimacy to the author's most daring statements by virtue of their tolerant attitudes, according to a procedure Valla borrowed from Poggio.[18] The appearance of Giovanni Marchi, a well-known doctor, was probably meant to please the faculty of medicine to which Valla had been formally appointed. The ducal secretary, Francesco Piccinino (replaced in a later version by Pier Candido Decembrio), represented the court, while the young Antonio Bossi, a member of a noble Milanese family with which Valla had established a friendly connection, served to consecrate, in the role of his student, Valla's recently acquired honor of "magister."[19]

The higher authorities represented in this version of the dialogue required Valla to exercise greater caution in its formal presentation. The scandalous and provocative title *De voluptate* was replaced with the more dissimulating and at the same time more ambitious *De vero bono,* the title it would retain throughout the complicated process of publication. By way of conclusion to this introductory section, we need only note that by the time the second edition of the dialogue began to circulate, Valla had been forced to resign from his teaching post in Pavia as a result of a quarrel with the jurists and was in search of another position.[20]

Before turning to discuss the interpretation, a brief summary of the dialogue is in order.[21] As previously stated, it consists of the discourses of three principal interlocutors: in order the Stoic, the Epicurean, and the Christian. The first defends the strenuous ideal of the *honestum* (uprightness), the only good, which embraces the highest virtues: justice, fortitude, and temperance.[22] The ideal is so arduous, however, that only a few men exceptionally gifted by nature are capable of attaining it. The greater part of humanity is prone to error and beset by vices, which in turn are twice the number of virtues, according to Aristotle's teaching that a virtue is a mean between two extremes. Nature herself, more like a wicked stepmother than a mother, has thus condemned mankind to unhappiness.[23]

The Epicurean interlocutor responds to these preemptory assertions with a discourse that runs through much of the first book and through all of the second. The ideal of *honestas,* uprightness, repugnant to basic human nature, is contrasted with that of *voluptas,* pleasure, an instinct which nature lavished on both humans and animals. Everything that nature creates must of necessity be good, and consequently the uprightness advocated by the Stoics is shown to be unsubstantial, as the foolish behavior of Cynic philosophers (hardly distinguishable from the Stoics) confirms. Pleasure of body is undistinguishable from that of mind and is basically identified with the pursuit of the useful, the purpose of all human actions.[24] The pleasures of each of the senses and bodily well-being are then reviewed (health and beauty, the pleasures of hearing, taste, and smell);[25] and after these the pleasures of the soul, including "the four so-called virtues," prudence, continence, justice, and modesty, insofar as they are directed to advantage.[26]

Self-preservation is man's fundamental responsibility, which makes the ideal of virginity seem foolish. Philosophers waste their time thinking up arguments about duty, while the poets more wisely attribute the passions and the search for pleasure to the gods.[27]

Book 2 develops more fully the theme of utilitarianism and a criticism of the system of virtues.[28] Virtue is conceived of as an act (*actio virtutis*),[29] the quality of which is relative to specific circumstance, on the principle of seeking the greatest individual and collective benefit.[30]

The contemplative life and the safety of the soul are discussed in similar terms. Happiness, according to Aristotle, is the ultimate goal, but, in a departure from Aristotle, happiness is conceived within the unitary, indivisible, and all-encompassing concept of "pleasure." Both Plato and Aristotle had made the mistake of separating pleasure of the senses and pleasure of the mind.[31]

Likewise meaningless is the contemplative ideal, based on the static notion of God as pure intellect. Contemplation is improvement in understanding, that is, a kind of activity. It would be absurd, therefore, for human beings to model themselves on an image of the gods whose very substance, precisely because it lies outside the realm of human experience, remains unintelligible. The strains of contemplation, and thus of thinking, are themselves directed to some benefit or pleasure, such as the pursuit of glory. If, however, they are perceived as ends in themselves, they bring nothing but anguish and desperation, the very point illustrated in the legend that Aristotle, unable to understand the nature of the Euripus, threw himself into its whirlpools.[32]

The postulate of *vita beata,* the happiness in this life, attainable through tranquillity of the soul, should be understood simply as the care we take in order to avoid vices and the related troubles they inflict the soul, and not as the ascetic practices of the Stoics and their more modern disciples, often a hypocritical mask concealing more serious vices.[33]

The wise Epicurean, considering it foolish "to give up what is certain for what is not so," will enjoy the pleasures of this life, fully recognizing the principle of utility as the very source of arts and civilization.[34]

Book 3, in which the Christian is called upon to judge the preceding philosophical dispute, is no less wide-ranging and subtle than the first two. A preface by the author explains how, in response to the previous contenders, the third interlocutor "decides in favor of the Epicureans and against the Stoics, and then moves on to uphold the Christian cause of true pleasure and true good," and how he concludes with a speech "about paradise, where the seat of true good resides."[35]

As is fitting for a theologian, the Christian begins by distancing himself from the opinions of the two previous interlocutors. While each of them had presented good arguments, they should be understood differently (*aliter accipiendum*) from what had been said.[36]

However, more than the Epicurean, the longer discussion concerns the Stoic, whose position was founded on the Aristotelian notion that there are more vices than there are virtues. The theory of virtue as a happy mean (*medietas*) is countered with the argument, already put forth by the Epicurean, that virtue is an act that must be evaluated according to the specific situation.[37] The real issue, therefore, is to try to determine one by one "which vice best contrasts with which virtue," since the mean should not necessarily always be considered good.[38] "All things can happen either rightly or wrongly," whence comes the difficulty in judging human action (*tanta . . . in iudicandis hominum actis ambiguitas*).[39]

It cannot be denied that more wicked than good people exist in the world, but the cause of this lies with individuals, not with nature.[40] Nevertheless, everyone aspires to the good, and so the problem lies in determining the nature of such good. The ideal of uprightness can be accepted only insofar as it tends to distinguish what "touches human dignity" with respect to mere natural appetite but not, however, basing it on the dichotomy between what is desirable and what should be chosen.[41]

A fault common to both speakers has been their speaking like ancient philosophers. The Epicurean, for example, disregarding Christian doctrine, upholds the principle, "capable of corrupting souls," that the soul dies with the body, while the Christian, aware of the soul's divine nature, will not limit himself "to comparing act with act" but compares "substance with substance."[42]

If the Epicurean can be suspected of having spoken with Socratic irony, the Stoic, with undeniable seriousness, without making any reference to the Christian religion has implied it could be "shaped artificially out of the philosophers' precepts."[43] Such inferences did injury not to nature indeed, which is nothing at all, but to God the creator.

There exists no virtue outside faith, operating on the hope of reward and the inspiration of charity, "the mistress of all virtues."[44] Unless there is hope for some reward, every virtue becomes a suffering, as stated more than once in the Sacred Scriptures. In this "the *vita beata* hailed by philosophers" does really consist![45] The verdict therefore favors the Epicureans who abstained from the Stoic's false promise, comparable to the Pharisees, the pretended guardians of God's law, while the Epicureans are likened to the Sadducees.[46]

Christian uprightness, although "hard, bitter, and difficult," will be desirable not for itself or for its earthly advantages but as a step (*gradum facit*) toward the beatitude the soul will enjoy when reunited with its Creator. What is beatitude, after all, but pleasure, according to the words of the Sacred Scriptures themselves?[47] Therefore pleasure is desirable in itself, in its twofold nature, earthly and heavenly, "the one the mother of vices, the other of the virtues." In this life, however, exists a kind of laudable pleasure (*probabilis quaedam voluptas*) that, in its highest form, "comes from the hope of future happiness," in the knowledge of what is right and in the foreshadowing of promised glory.[48]

How, then, can God be made responsible for the rewards and punishments in this life, where the just are sometimes punished and the evil rewarded? Philosophers have labored in vain over this question, as did Boethius, who, echoing Plato and ascribing greater honor to philosophy than to religion, equated virtue with happiness, thereby confusing actions (vices and virtues) with qualities (happiness, unhappiness): "things that are very different from one another, even in the effect that they produce."[49]

Consequently it will be fruitless to complain about fortune or God; He will be praised not as the beatitude but as the source of it.[50] It follows that God will be loved not "for His own sake" (*propter se*) but for the beatitude that comes from Him, "not as the final, but as the efficient cause." To say otherwise would be to speak more "according to the practice of philosophers than theologians," who are faithful to the simple dictates of Scripture. 'Being' in itself is neither good nor evil; goodness (or evil) comes from the quality that joins something to that being and concerns the receiver (the eye, for example) as much as what is received (in this instance, light). The union of the two produces pleasure, which will be considered the end; the pleasure generated by love of God will be the ultimate end: "Love is nothing but this delight, or pleasure, or happiness, or charity, which is the ultimate end and the reason because all things happen."[51]

The discourse is concluded with a kind of fictional sermon. Setting aside the traditional theme about despising this world, appropriate for "unlearned and ill-mannered men" but unnecessary in the context of his audience (since generous souls "do not fear laws" and are not frightened by the threat of torments, "but rather are attracted by rewards"), the Christian speaker chooses instead to foreshadow the delights of paradise.[52]

God created the world for man, indeed, for all of human society; moreover, he has shown his concern, in spite of the evil committed on earth. Finally, he has expressed his promise for a higher happiness, albeit through "enigmas and allegories" that would be useless to try to explain.[53] "However," the speaker adds, "it would be worthwhile if we tried to imagine it."[54]

The imagination is more easily drawn to the time when bodies will be resurrected and the pleasures of this world will be enjoyed in a more refined and perfect form, difficult to imagine. Beauty will exist without lust, and rulers without the anxieties and the yearnings associated with governing. The pleasures of the spirit will be even greater, and all knowledge will be fulfilled and satisfied. Finally, the heavenly Jerusalem awaits the blessed, where, as described in the Apocalypse, they will be welcomed in an imaginary triumph that culminates in a vision of the Saints, the Virgin Mary, and Christ.[55]

With a few closing remarks, the speakers are brought back to earth. Guarino, prudently abstaining from passing judgment on the speech of the Stoic, Cato, presents a kind of epilogue. He extols the persuasive eloquence of Vegio and Antonio of Rho, praising the first for his oratorical turns and the second for his more elevated poetical tones. They are, he suggests, comparable to the two daughters of Pandion, the swallow and the nightingale.

⸺⸺⸻⸻

From the moment of its appearance, Valla's dialogue has been a source of puzzlement and has given rise to contrasting interpretations. For example, at the turn of the sixteenth century, Pietro Marino Aleandro, second-cousin to the more famous Girolamo, and Cardinal Domenico Grimani's future secretary, recommended that the work be published as a new kind of learned Christian edification. Philip Melanchthon formed a very different opinion of the dialogue, classifying it among those texts that "overturn laws, religions, and arts," and therefore siding with the Catholic Inquisition that had included the work in the Roman Index of 1559 and continued to consider it "suspect" until its release in Leo XIII's reform in 1900.[56]

It would be of little use to review other and more recent interpretations or the tenacious ideological premises that often underlie them. The difficulty was mostly perpetuated by the subtle ambiguity of Valla's preface. The point of the dialogue, so he states, is to discuss the issue of the true and false good in a way that contends with pagan philosophers and their modern disciples, who presume to leave Christianity out of consideration, without which there can be "nothing virtuous or right." In such a statement, Valla aligns himself with the Christian apologetics of Lactantius and Augustine, but with the difference that, setting aside the issue of religion, he would fight the philosophers with their own philosophical arguments—piercing them with their own sword.[57] Valla's words were taken literally by M. Fois, a Jesuit scholar, author of the sizable monograph *Il pensiero cristiano di Lorenzo Valla*. According to Fois, Valla focused his dispute on the secularization of ethics brought about by Bruni and circles of humanists, not to mention Averroist philosophers.[58] More recently, other scholars have turned their attention to the methodological and disciplinary aspects of the work. The American J. E. Seigel and the German H. B. Gerl identified in Valla's antiphilosophical stance a desire to assert the superiority of rhetorical argumentation, in keeping with the objective he developed more fully later in the so-called *Dialecticae disputationes*.[59] Considering the work from a historical-philosophical standpoint, Gerl more ambitiously identifies in the dialogue the foundation for a "new" philosophy of "common sense," based on the classical sources of Cicero and Quintilian and designed to oppose every abstract "rationalism" that failed to take into account the unity of "object" (*res*) and "word" (*verbum*). The risk of a purely utilitarian empiricism would be overthrown by the intervention of the Christian speaker, a poetic metaphor that actually indicates the objective reality, "das notwendige Sosein."[60]

I will not linger over the artificial character of such a proposal; rather, it is worth noting how the idea of objectivity, achieved through a deeper understanding of common sense, contrasts strikingly with the subsequent interpretation proposed by the English scholar L. A. Panizza.[61] Guided by recent works on Renaissance traditions of ancient skepticism (Popkin, Schmitt), Panizza has shrewdly noted Valla's debt to the *Divinae institutiones,* in which Lactantius exploits the academic method of "a debate on both sides" to undermine the "false wisdom" of the pagan wise men, "so that the philosophers by their own weapons above all . . . would be crushed by us" (*ut philosophi suis armis potissimum . . . opprimerentur a nobis*)—the very metaphor Valla would later take up in his own work.[62] Thus the dialogue represents, according to Panizza, a renewal of "Christian oratorical skepticism," developed along the lines of the ironic Socratic method, which, acknowledged by Valla himself, would pervade the Epicurean discourse. In short, Valla aimed at a reform of ethics by reforming eloquence; a new Carneades, he would expose the false synthesis of Christianity and Stoic ethics; a new Socrates, he would pretend his adversaries were ignorant of Lactantius, Saint Jerome, Saint Augustine, and the Scriptures, whose tacit presence, on the contrary, bestows significance to the dialogue.[63]

There is no doubt that recognition of the dialogue's implicit references is essential for its interpretation. But it seems equally clear that a unilateral insistence on Lactantius as the source and on Skepticism as the methodological inspiration for the dialogue almost paints Valla as a Socratic Erasmus, a characterization indeed that little suits him. Valla, in fact, is so little a Skeptic that in his introductory remarks he warns that "all the books that follow" are "designed to refute and overthrow the race of Stoics," both from an Epicurean and from a Christian standpoint.[64] Thus the pro and con debate is merely specious, the outcome having been decided from the beginning. The real problem lies in specifying exactly what is meant by "Stoicism," charged with being a "false good" from the very beginning of the exordium. Consequently, the question inseparably concerns both method and ideology. Interpretations that focus exclusively on methodology (or, more accurately, on the pedagogical or apologetic devices), concentrating respectively on the two *Institutiones* so familiar to Valla—Quintilian's *oratoria* and Lactantius's *divinae* (the second of which, incidentally, rejected the "oratorical profession" as useless)—end by annulling each other, not without a malicious intention on the part of Valla himself.[65]

It is worth returning, therefore, to Valla's preface, and more specifically to those passages, then suppressed in following versions, that explain the original (and then likewise abandoned) title, *De voluptate*: "If, by chance, one of my friends . . . wondering about this title . . . should ask me what passion seized me to write about pleasure . . . he should understand that I . . . preferred to entitle these books *De voluptate* . . . rather than *De vero bono*, which I could have, since what I discuss in this work is the 'true good' which, I believe, is the same thing as 'pleasure.' " According to such introduction, the work assumed the character of a deliberate paradox, even more provocative in that it elevates the pleasure—the negative value by antonomasia, as defined by centuries of philosophical and religious rejection—to the level of the highest human end, not only in a philosophical but also in a religious sense. This should be the "true good," capable of establishing a connection between human beings and the divine: "which I call the true one, the only one, in a word that I call pleasure"; in terms of its twofold meaning ("one in this life, another in the next").[66] Precisely with this distinction the revised version begins, this time under the title—which previously, as we have seen, Valla presented as alternative— *De vero bono*. Valla's deliberate ambiguity is apparent as he conceals, at least in the words of the introduction, what is essentially the leading concept of the unfolding development. I mean (it bears repeating) the uniqueness of the *voluptas*, not as much in the concept as in its "name," albeit in its distinction of degree in relation to present or future life, to utilitarian action, or to the meritorious one, moved by the certainty of a heavenly reward and inspired by the love of God.

These are the conclusions reached by M. De Panizza Lorch, editor of the dialogue, who argues that Valla's opening statement, which he later suppresses, nevertheless remains "the key idea of the work."[67] Her analysis exempts me from providing further evidence, but I would like to add that only in one instance does Valla appear to depart from this concept. Responding in the *Defensio* to charges brought against him in the inquisitorial trial of 1444, he cites in his defense his own supposed statement: "There is a double pleasure: one is right, the other on the contrary is wicked" (*Voluptas duplex est, altera quidem recta, altera vero prava*). As the editor of the text, G. Zippel, observes, this statement is not to be found in any of the versions of the dialogue we actually know; it might be perhaps the copy of book 3, which Valla had sent earlier to Pope Eugenius IV for his own recommendation.[68] For these reasons, I disagree with De Panizza Lorch, who denies that Valla suppressed the original title out of tactical prudence, especially when we have evidence of the reactions, along a continuity of censuring arguments, from contemporary and subsequent authors.

The humanist Carlo Marsuppini, one of the first to receive a copy of the dialogue, wrote to Valla that he would approve the work, provided that he recognize the Platonic distinction of the two Venuses, "Uraniam et Pandemon," the celestial and the popular one, on the basis of which "this above all must be maintained, that there are two distinct pleasures."[69] Later, in the 1470s, the Sienese humanist Agostino Dati in his *Sermo de voluptate* (which, incidentally, was based on the same authors referred to by Valla: Augustine and Lactantius, Aristotle and Cicero) openly censures Valla's formulation: "You cannot believe it appropriate to embrace by a single word [i.e., pleasure] two things so different from each other. It would be as if someone called virtue either good or bad, while some things are good, and others quite bad."[70] Finally, Josse Bade d'Assch (Badius Ascensius), editor of the first version of the dialogue, observed in the prefatory letter to the theologian and grand inquisitor of France, Guillaume Petit, that the third book seemed to him quite different from the impiety, worse than Epicurean, of the preceding two. Of consequence, Badius chose the arbitrary title *De voluptate ac de vero bono,* as if the dialogue dealt with two antithetical and distinct concepts; and this was the title also adopted in the *Opera omnia* of 1540, the vulgate edition of Valla's writings.[71]

The uniqueness of *voluptas,* in that it refers to the senses as much as to the soul, is further proved by Valla on the basis of a passage from Cicero's *De finibus* (2.4.13): "no word can be found in Latin which better expresses the Greek *edoné* than *voluptas.* To all people everywhere this word . . . means two things: happiness of the soul through pleasing excitement and delightfulness in the body."[72] We should not therefore infer that the concerns of the future author of the *Elegantiae latinae linguae* are here of a strict philological order, aimed at reestablishing the original "true" meaning of the Latin expression. Actually, Valla was fully aware that in extrapolating this passage he was altering its Ciceronian context. According to Cicero, in effect it was possible, optionally ("si vis," § 14), to extend the concept of *voluptas* to *laetitia,* the joy of the soul, in spite of what the Stoics said to the contrary, but not the opposite, since no one would apply the terms *laetitia* or *gaudium* to the senses: "non dicitur laetitia nec gaudium in corpore." With this reasoning Cicero refuted the Epicurean doctrine of a "catastematic" pleasure (or *in stabilitate,* according to its Latin expression, that is, a "firm habit of pleasure"). In a subsequent passage, Valla, in explicit disagreement with Plato and Aristotle, stresses still further his own departure from classical philosophy: "I myself, however, do not understand, since the word is one and the same, how we can understand from it different things, and indeed, still more because all pleasure is felt not so much in the body as it is in the soul, which governs the body; that, in my opinion is what Epicurus meant."[73]

From this emerges Valla's ambivalence toward Cicero, who, particularly in the first two books of *De finibus,* offers the gamut of arguments for and against Epicurus.[74] If, on the one hand, Valla borrows, up to a point, the concern "for reestablishing the unity of language and a certain logic among various philosophical systems" (A. Michel), basing it on notions commonly accessible to all, and if he praises the antidogmatic stance taken by Cicero, "not bound to any doctrine";[75] on the other hand, he shows toward him, even more than a competitive spirit, an antagonistic one.

This is evident, to repeat once again, from the words of the preface, and here I would like to point out the phrase he uses to qualify the *voluptas:* "molle quodam et non invidiosum nomen"—a pleasing name that does not excite envy. The phrase, in fact, represents a deliberate reversal of the deprecatory epithets that Cicero had used in his attack on Epicureanism: "a voluptuous, delicate, soft discipline," "an envious, infamous, suspicious term."[76] The same pattern of reversals continues throughout the dialogue. For example, immediately following the cited passage, Cicero adds: "For why is it necessary to summon pleasure into the council of virtues, as if I should call a prostitute into an assembly of matrons?" To which Valla, echoing, replies: "You have a true and brief definition of the virtues. Among them pleasure will not be, as that very insulting race of men prates, a prostitute among good matrons, but rather, a mistress among her servants."[77]

I have already observed how Valla avoids referring to Epicureanism in the exact meaning of the "brave, continent, and severe" discipline defended by Torquatus in the first book of De finibus. The reappraisal of Epicureanism as a contemplative philosophy liberating the soul from troubles, which had been the trend from Petrarch to Zabarella to, most recently, Philelphus, remained irrelevant to him.[78] Rather than an Epicurean doctrine, we could say that Valla developed a kind of anti-anti-Epicureanism, interpreting in a positive sense the charges that had been leveled against Epicurus and his teachers, the Cyrenaics, from Cicero onward. The insatiability of pleasure of the senses, which Cicero describes as "pleasure in motion" (voluptas in motu) in opposition to the Epicurean illusion of reaching a firm habit of pleasure, is thus translated into the dynamic concept of "pleasure" as the basic motive to which can be reduced all human actions, which had been so wrongly classified in the traditional system of the virtues. Thus in a sense it was Cicero himself who suggested that the notion of voluptas be extended to include that of utilitas, the usefulness. Like a seal put at the conclusion of the dialogue's first and second books, Valla explicitly invalidates the philosophy of the De officiis: "Philosophers' inquiries on duties, indeed, are the best proof of what I mean, considering how tortuous and confused they are, differing in opinion each other."[79] And later in connection with the doctrine on licit gain, he writes: "Nevertheless they [i.e., Stoic philosophers] have appropriated what was not theirs, saying that the useful derives from the upright, while at the same time they also gave to our own philosophy the name of those 'duties' which properly belonged to their own opposing faction."[80] On this subject it is worth remembering the pages he devotes to satirizing the ideal of communis utilitas, the common good hailed by philosophers and jurists, as it was exemplified by the heroes who died for their homeland.[81]

In a more general way, the entire rhetorical-philosophical method of exposition, typical of Cicero, is to be invalidated: "I would have preferred, however, that he [i.e., M. Tullius] had chosen to treat those issues not as a philosopher, but rather as an orator."[82] Whereas Cicero—to borrow once again the words of Michel—sets out to create a broadly eclectic and probabilistic discussion, "to let the systems engage each other in dialogue," in an ideal of "philosophical ecumenicism,"[83] Valla points at "philosophers," generally speaking, as the main target of his controversy. Thus, to keep within Cicero's terminology, once the objective foundation of honestas is eliminated, Valla is free to convert the "nomen utilitatis," that is the most comprehensive definition of the principle of usefulness, into an absolute, and thus nothing prevents its assimilation into the very concept of "pleasure." Furthermore, if Cicero's inventory of "decorous behavior"—which, in various ways, conforms to the ideal of uprightness—results in "the application of the rhetorical categories of *inventio* and *dispositio* to moral reflection" (M. Testard),[84] Valla's discourse, inversely, though dressed in brilliant and ostentatious rhetorical devices, will rely on a philosophical foundation of his own. It is this philosophy that allows for the establishment of a unitary logic, capable of deriving from the single term "pleasure" a vast spectrum of semantic meanings including, as we have seen, and once again in disagreement with Cicero, the very notion of "utility." Finally, Valla's discussion of terminology ("de nomine"), unlike Cicero, becomes decisive for the substance itself of the discourse ("de re").[85]

Really a nominalist, which is to say a "modern," in his antitraditional intent to pursue dynamically all the logical implications of a term, Valla focuses on something else, and something higher than the teachings of ancient philosophy alone. His criticism of philosophers, as Valla himself pointed out and which has already been noted in connection with Lactantius, takes as its model the Christian polemic against ancient wisdom. In addition to Lactantius, Valla mentions Saint Augustine and even goes so far—and not without a good dose of irreverence—as to use the very words from the preface of *De civitate Dei* to describe his own work: "a truly great and difficult work, and I don't know if in any time there was another one so audacious."[86] More intrinsically, Valla borrows Augustine's criticisms of the self-sufficiency of Stoic virtue, of the inhuman rigidity of such a doctrine, and of the moral value of the exempla of famous suicides (Lucretia and Cato). On the other hand, from the same source he derives his insistent appeal to Pauline fideism, the celebration of charity as the highest of all virtues, the pleasurable contemplation of the blessings given by God as hope for those to come; in a word, the Christian eudaemonism, which inspires the dialogue's concluding section. This has been recognized by scholars, to mention only the extensive treatment by Fois and Trinkaus.[87]

What has not been noted, however, is that Valla's attitude is no less ambivalent toward Augustine than toward Cicero. Nor is a specific historical justification lacking, recognized by scholars in the fideistic outcome of Ciceronian skepticism, and in particular how it was developed by the

Church Fathers, especially by Augustine.[88] Moreover, Augustine, albeit in the transcendent context of the "Christian doctrine," was perhaps the principal author in the transmission to the Middle Ages of that core of ancient ethical and pedagogical doctrine that is Cicero's classification of virtues in the *De inventione,* and which he quoted literally in his *Diversae quaestiones.*[89] This Ciceronean abstract, in its definition of "habit" (*habitus*) as a "constant and absolute perfection in anything" (*constantem et absolutam aliqua in re perfectionem*), of *honestum* as "what is sought for its own sake" (*quod propter se petitur*), and finally, in its classification of the four principle (or "cardinal") virtues, contains the very synthesis of the teachings that Valla intends to confute.[90]

Was Valla, therefore, more Augustinian than Augustine himself, as some modern interpretations would seem to imply? Actually, as has already been noted, the doctrine of the love of God, in whom all other virtues are recapitulated and unified, presupposes Augustine's belief in the Creator's absolute transcendence with respect to creature: only by God will man be directed to the right, and only in God will he find appeasement. Herein lies the distinction, destined to become fundamental to Christian tradition, between the mere use of a good (and, therefore, of a virtue) and the delight taken in the only true good of the divine essence, the difference between "uti" and "frui" — a distinction, according to H. I. Marrou, which embodies "the entirety of Augustinian ethics."[91] For Valla, instead, *fruitio* in the aforementioned sense of "love of something good in and for itself" (*propter se*) was nothing other than a new proposition of the ancient notion of *honestas;* a point indeed that was not incorrect in strictly formal terms, if one considers that Augustine's tripartite scheme of things to be enjoyed, to be used, and to be both used and enjoyed is consonant with Cicero's scheme in the *Academica,* about the ends of "uprightness" (*honestatem*), of "pleasure" (*voluptatem*), or of both (*aut utrumque*).[92]

For Valla, the issue once again revolves around the basic concept of an all-inclusive notion of "pleasure." Having established it as the principle that embraces both sacred and secular aims — even though distinguishable by degrees — Valla's purpose of putting the philosophers in contradiction with one another has the implicit meaning of emphasizing the contradictions inherent in theology itself. As it will appear obvious, the most direct target of his criticisms is precisely the aforementioned distinction between *uti* and *frui,* or, in other words, the strict utilitarian subordination of every earthly end to the single true end of the enjoyment, or "frui-tion," of God. In Valla, the two terms are assimilated, and the hedonistic-utilitarian principle, used in a secular context, is extended by analogy into the sacred one and given authoritative sanction, in the context of the dialogical debate, by the Christian speaker himself.[93]

Ontology is thus expunged from religious-ethical reasoning. As a result, Valla (and in his stead, it is worth repeating, his Christian interlocutor) insists on the concept that we do not love God "for himself" but rather as the "efficient cause" of our love.[94] It is precisely on this subject that his anti-Augustinian discussion, until now kept on an implicit level, is brought out into the open, or nearly so. I refer particularly to his later self-defense in the *Retractatio,* where in a tendentious aim to identify *voluptas* with the Augustinian concept of *fruitio,* Valla adds, "he himself [i.e., Augustine] shows that was no difference between *frui* and *amare,* stating elsewhere: '*frui* means to be connected by love (*inherere amore*) to anything for itself (*propter se*).' But 'to adhere with love' (*adherere amore*), is the same thing as 'to love' (*amare*); he said 'for itself' (*propter se*) according to the custom of philosophers (*ex consuetudine philosophorum*), not because of the nature of the thing, as I have elsewhere shown."[95] "Ex consuetudine philosophorum": here is one of the most direct evidences of Valla's direct attack at the very roots of theological ontology (concealed in—or more accurately still, amalgamated with—the term "philosophy"), and not simply, as it is usually stated, against the speculative developments of Aristotelian scholasticism, or even less so against the logical subtleties of late scholasticism.

There is still another and stronger evidence of Valla's direct and controversial reference to Augustine. Preparing to pronounce judgment on the dispute between the Stoic and the Epicurean, his own Christian interlocutor recalls a passage in the Acts of the Apostles where Saint Paul is invited by Epicurean and Stoic philosophers to debate before the Areopagus, almost as a kind of scriptural dignifying "of the two most noble philosophical schools."[96] Augustine had commented on this passage in one of his *Sermones* where, in accordance with the concept of the absolute subordination of human wisdom to the gift of divine grace, he sketches this dialogue: "What now, let us interrogate these three standing before us, the Epicurean, the Stoic, and the Christian, one by one. Tell me, Epicurean, what is it that makes us happy? He replies: bodily pleasure. Speak, Stoic: virtue of the soul. Speak, Christian: the gift of God."[97] Did Valla have this passage in mind when writing *De voluptate*? Without precise textual proofs, some brief considerations will suffice. The three figures of the Epicurean, the Stoic, and the Christian, inserted by Augustine into a context that transcends ancient ethics and at the same time interiorizes and personalizes abstract philosophical concepts—and which, therefore, tends to assume the form of a dialogue—are the same as those who appear in Valla's dialogue. It is, then, an appealing and not at all improbable supposition that Augustine's sermon suggested the very scheme for Valla's composition. At any rate it gives us a valuable opportunity to compare the context of Valla's work with Augustinian teachings, which, as we have seen, are widely present in it.

In the series of discourses, Valla's variation from Augustine is of fundamental importance. In the order of dignity, the roles of the Epicurean and the Stoic are inverted, with the result that the latter, introduced somewhat in the way that Cicero brings the Epicurean Torquatus into his *De finibus,* comes to represent the common target of both confutations by the subsequent interlocutors. Far more than a simple expository device moved Valla to make such a change. As has been remarked, the Augustinian confutation of Stoicism is founded on the doctrine of grace, "the gift of God." Now, it is the implicit echo of this same doctrine that in Valla's dialogue inspires the pessimistic tone of the Stoic interlocutor, quite differing from the optimistic rationalism of the ancient doctrine:

> But nevertheless the care and love of virtue has been conceded to very few, as a kindness and a special gift of nature; to most it has been denied by the maliciousness of nature herself, in the same way, as in terms of the body we see monstrous, weak and corrupted people. The minds of men which she should have enlightened she has blinded, so they cannot contemplate the light of wisdom.[98]

Even this passage is not without its allusion, and a somewhat malicious one, to ancient philosophy. In keeping with Valla's favorite technique of ideological reversals and pretended doctrinal assumptions, it is made up of objections that the Skeptic Cotta raises to the Stoic Balbus's concept of providence in Cicero's *De natura deorum.*[99] If indeed, Cotta observes, using at times the very words of Valla's "Stoic" interlocutor, "even though the divine mind and will has accorded favor to men by giving them reason," in reality, it has helped only a very few: "it provides only for those whom it has endowed with good reason, whom we see are very few, if there are any at all." Nor does the objection put forward by the Stoics, that "many of them utilize this benefit wrongly," have any value, since the wrong comes from the gods themselves: "if only the gods had never given to men that wretched shrewdness! Insofar as few use it well, and they themselves are often crushed by those who use it badly, and innumerable people use it wickedly, it would seem that this gift of divine reason and prudence has been given not for good purposes, but rather for deceit."[100]

The peremptory comments of Valla's "Stoic" interlocutor are therefore relatively close to the objections the Skeptics and Epicureans had raised against the ancient belief in a rational providence. Nevertheless, some substantial variations in Valla—the "gift and blessing" not of "reason" but rather of "love," and the antithesis of blinding and enlightening (*excaecare-illuminare*)—refer unequivocally to Christian, and specifically scriptural concepts. We can recognize in fact the juxtaposition of different passages from Saint Paul. I refer in particular to the Christian doctrines of the election and of the illumination of the soul, having its foundation in the basic Romans 11.6–7, among the principal allegations in Augustine's anti-Pelagius polemic: "But if it is by grace, it is no longer on the basis of works: otherwise grace would no longer be grace. What then? Israel did not obtain what it sought; the elect, however, obtained it; the rest were blinded."

But in connection with the theme of illumination, also echoed in Valla, and one of those inspiring Pelagius's teaching, note Ephesians 1.17–18: "That God . . . may give to you a spirit of wisdom and revelation in the knowledge of him: so that, once the eyes of your heart have been illuminated, you might know what hope of his calling there is for you."[101]

The "Stoic" interlocutor, however, alludes to another text, well-known and widely circulated at the time the dialogue was written: Guglielmus Peraldus's institutional *Summa de vitiis et virtutibus* (thirteenth century). I refer in particular to the representation of "Envy" in the biblical figure of the great priest Eli (1 Kings 3.2–3)—a pattern for the allegorical imagery of this vice. With eyes darkened by age, Eli did not see the lantern in the temple "before it was extinguished" and as a result did not perceive God calling Samuel, his young minister. Like Eli, envious people actually bar the vision of good works of their fellow men, "like candles shining forth the light of good example." Whence the definition of envy: "that most unhappy vice, because it blinds while it ought to enlighten."[102]

Here, by the way, we can realize further on, in the clarity of contrast, the characterization of "pleasure" in the preface of *De voluptate* as "non invidiosum," that is, a good that in its very nature does not arouse envy. But the most important issue is another. The malevolent "nature" of the so-called Stoic vision, which obscures what it ought to enlighten, just like envy among human beings, implies through the evidence of its scriptural allusions a radical shift of the theological perspective into an anthropological one. This is quite the same perspective that, in Valla's next dialogue, *De libero arbitrio,* will inspire Tarquinius Sextus's accusation of Jove's iniquity. (Jove represents the divine will, distinct from Apollo, the divine intellect: that is, in an anthropological perspective the divine psychology cannot be conceived in any other terms than human, in the two distinct faculties to which predestination and foreknowledge in order correspond.) In this accusation, according to Leibniz, who reworked and elaborated the apologue, Valla seems to "condemn Providence, as represented by Jove, whom he nearly makes the author of sin."[103] In *De libero arbitrio* Valla concludes with an absolute philosophical agnosticism, supporting his criticism of theological speculations with Pauline fideism, or, better to say, with a specious and negative allegation of it. (This is actually the extent of Valla's pretended "Paulinism," which is not without the intention of turning against the theological teachings of Paul himself).[104] Likewise in *De voluptate* the Epicurean and Christian interlocutors will serve, from their respective (at least nominally) philosophical and religious viewpoints, to avoid the dilemma of defining the good and the evil, by jointly eliminating the doctrinal and ontological aspect, both the *honestas* of the philosophers and the *fruitio* of the theologians, insofar as theologians assumed Augustine's dualistic ontology. Valla's preannounced method of "turning someone's sword against himself" is thus applied, in the guise of a "philosophical" debate, in a context not only patristic but scriptural as well, while maintaining as its major reference point, even if partially disguised, Augustine's basic teachings.

At this point let us discuss another strictly Augustinian theme, perhaps more marginal but certainly not of secondary interest. I refer to the recognition of human nature's corruption in, to use Marrou's expression, "the multiform perversity of children." The "Stoic" interlocutor characterizes it in this way: "we can see from the earliest years of life that children descend to the vices of gluttony, jokes, and luxury, rather than raising themselves to moral dignity and virtue: they hate punishment and love flattery; they flee rules and follow after lasciviousness."

Augustine's argument is taken up again and corrected, not by the Epicurean speaker but by the Christian. While making implicit reference to the basic Augustinian principle, "beati prorsus omnes esse volumus," we all indeed are willing to be happy, the Christian refuses to make the distinction between intention and choice of good, translating it thus: "It is enough that human will is inclined to the good." It should not, therefore, be considered a vice "if children desire the bodily good which is all they understand," and a good education should be provided instead.[105]

───── ✺ ─────

The significance of such direct criticism of authorities fundamental to the Christian tradition demands an explanation. Can Valla's criticisms be reconciled with his proclaimed apologetic aim, or should his defensive stance be understood as a deliberate obscuring, a cover for irreligious purposes?

A slight digression will be useful here. I have already mentioned how the spirit of antagonism with which Valla confronts the tradition of anti-Epicureanism differs from contemporary trends to restore dignity to Epicurus's philosophy and thereby to reconcile it with the major teachings of classical philosophy. Valla was not entirely original on this point, however. There exists, in fact, a short epistolary tract by Cosma Raimondi, a humanist from Cremona, which, according to the title in one manuscript, represents a *Defensio Epicuri contra Stoicos, Academicos et Peripateticos*.[106] The vindication of Epicurus and the principle of "*voluptas*" is therefore turned primarily against Cicero's teachings in *De finibus* but also against the more recent doctrine proposed in Leonardo Bruni's *Isagogicon moralis disciplinae* (where Aristotelianism was given the preference).[107]

According to the opinion of one scholar, "a vindication of hedonism and Epicurus like that of Raimondi's in *Quattrocento* humanism is only found in the by far more important work of Lorenzo Valla"; and another has added that "there is no doubt that Raimondi's solution, as well as a good number of his main themes, are the same as those found in *De vero bono.*"[108] The analogies are in fact quite obvious: the claim of pleasure as self-preservation, the celebration of the senses, the condemnation of the ascetic life, etc. These coincidences go beyond the simple thematic character. In his polemic on Stoic virtue, referring directly to *De finibus* 2.20.65, Raimondi cites the *exemplum* of Attilius Regulus, "whom they glorify and celebrate so greatly in all their books." Raimondi, instead, considers it absurd to claim that Regulus was actually happy—and not extremely miserable, indeed—while being subjected to torture.[109] But the allusion can be extended implicitly to Augustine, who in the *De civitate Dei* 1.15 also cites the "very noble example" of Regulus, as a symbol of the value of sacrifice, and one to whom true Christian virtue would guarantee beatitude. The same criticism of the *exemplum* of Regulus and of the relative authorities ("as some great authors record") also appears extensively in Valla's work.[110] Perhaps the most important aspect of Raimondi's tract, however, is his "Epicurean" (which is to say naturalistic) overturning of Stoic teaching about the providentiality of nature and of man in his physical structure and rational privilege. This was just a theme developed by Cicero in *De natura deorum* and later given a more conspicuously anthropocentric and crypto-Christian shape by Lactantius in his *De opificio Dei*.[111] Raimondi, in fact, uses in his writing a real mosaic of implicit references from both classical treatises, the pagan and the Christian, while pointing out his own opposite conclusions, as in the following passage:

> Where else should I begin to examine these matters but from that one nature, prince and creator of all things, whose judgment must be thought to be the most truthful always in every matter? Since therefore she has fashioned man, and refined him in such a way as if by applying her skill on all sides, so that he seems made for no other thing but to be able to possess and delight in every pleasure.[112]

In responding to Lactantius's anti-Epicurean trust in Providence with his own Epicurean trust in nature, Raimondi relies on the passage from Cicero's *De natura deorum,* where there is a celebration of the senses, and which Lactantius had omitted in his detailed description of the human body in *De opificio.* "Nature"—Raimondi writes—"gave man many various, distinct, necessary senses, so that since there are many kinds of pleasure he could partake of them all."[113] This approach is very similar to Valla's, who in turn refers, this time openly, to *De opificio* ("Just as Lactantius . . . clearly shows in the book he entitled 'De Opificio' "), giving Lactantius's conception of Christian providence an Epicurean—that is, naturalistic—meaning and twisting the anti-Epicurean polemic against so-called Stoic pessimism.[114]

Such similarities in method, content, and sources can hardly be coincidental. Raimondi's sphere of activity was Lombardy where, like Valla, he cultivated ties to court society through family connections. He wrote his tract sometime between 1426 (according to an allusion to one of Poggio's letters that year) and 1429, when he went into exile in Avignon (the letter being directed to the Italian Ambrogio Tignosi—a university student?—in answer to a previous discussion on Epicureanism, presupposes Raimondi was still living in the Lombard milieu). Finally, evidence has been found in two letters that Raimondi wrote to Vegio in 1429 that he knew Panormita, or at least tried to solicit favors from him, once Panormita had become powerful at court.[115]

We should now reconsider the accusation that Bartolomeo Facio (at the prompting of Panormita) made years later in his invective against Valla, accusing him of having recast in the *De voluptate* a writing he attributes to his uncle, Melchior Scrivani: "just like a drone devouring the labors of the bees, you collected it furtively into your beehive, having changed certain words only."[116] We can suppose therefore that the character in Valla's dialogue originally given to Panormita was in reality meant to provide an expansion of Raimondi's *Defensio Epicuri;* or perhaps, if we want to go even further, that it was Panormita himself, notably inclined toward a show of "Epicurean" hedonism both in his morals and in his writings, who handed on Raimondi's tract to Valla, furnishing him with the starting point for his own more thorough approach to the subject.

There is, nevertheless, an essential difference between Valla and Raimondi. The latter, a student of Gasparino Barzizza and a scholar of Cicero himself, was the one who encouraged Antonio of Rho to write a work on the "elegance" of the Latin language: a work that suggested to Valla the project of his own *Elegantiae latinae linguae*.[117] At the same time, however, Raimondi professed to be both philosopher and astrologer: in other words, a disciple of radical Aristotelian naturalism, a strong tradition in the medical faculty at Pavia. The basic points of such a doctrine, as illustrated in the teachings of the celebrated Biagio Pelacani (whose immediate successors included, among others, his own son), were the eternity of the world, the astrological explanation of positive religions, and the mortality of the individual soul.[118] In 1396 Pelacani had been forced by the Bishop of Pavia to retract his views, but nevertheless his ideas continued to be widely circulated. At least this is what Catone Sacco declares in his *Origines,* a little tract some scholars have associated with Valla's criticisms of Aristotle. Sacco's purpose, in fact, was much more limited: on the basis of Isidore of Seville's homonimous work, he aimed to refute the conception of the world's eternity by going back through the beginning of all things to the origin of the world itself. His preface states: "Let us say a few words about this ridiculous opinion and authority which is celebrated in all the schools: the Philosopher, they said, stated that the world is eternal, because without any argument from reason his authority has as much worth in the eyes of the Aristotelians, as we read with respect to Pythagoras."[119]

Just as the "philosophers" were blamed by Sacco, Raimondi makes no mystery of his opposition to Christian beliefs. In a letter about the recent deeds of Joan of Arc, he suggests he knows how to find a *physica ratio*, that is, an astrological explanation, for her miracles; and in an elegy addressed to Niccolò Arcimboldi a little before he committed suicide in 1436, Raimondi confesses to doubting in the soul's afterlife: "But I am not certain if there will be a future after the end of my days."[120] Raimondi's defense of Epicurus was, by his own admission, nothing more than a digression, or a corollary to his arduous philosophical-astrological studies. Though hailed in the terms of ancient moral philosophy, Epicureanism for Raimondi ends up by being assimilated, according to the medieval tradition, with assumptions of materialistic Aristotelian naturalism.[121]

It is precisely on this point that Valla distances himself from Raimondi. The reason for the difference between the Epicurean and the Christian interlocutors does not consist in the common and parallel hedonistic-utilitarian premises but in the denial by Valla that such a theory necessarily implies the materialistic conclusions of classic Epicureanism, as well as its patristic and medieval tradition. At the same time, however, Valla goes further than Raimondi—perhaps at the prompting of Raimondi himself—by criticizing theological traditions from within, beginning with their origins in the Church Fathers. In this sense there is some truth in Valla's claim to present himself as defender of the Christian republic. Faith can be defended from philosophical unbelief on condition that religious belief is ready to renounce its claim to be "philosophy" itself, which is to say, to decline its theological doctrinairism. An absolute ontology, insofar as it is placed beyond the reach of human comprehension, was as contrary to faith conceived in terms of mere persuasion as was absolute negation. It was vain to inquire into God's justice, the nature of evil, and the definition of good in order to avoid formulation of doctrines obviously repugnant to common human sense, such as the predestination of the elected few. The absurdity of ascetic practice was self-revealing, not to mention the vain pride that inspired it.

In other words, Valla could appropriate and radicalize Raimondi's "Epicureanism" by shifting the boundaries of the discussion from *summum bonum,* the highest good, to *verum bonum,* the "true" good, and thus from the domain of philosophical doctrinairism to that most encompassing of the argument, an approach he would soon deepen in the appropriate context of the *Repastinatio dialecticae et philosophiae.* Here the more traditional opposition between *honestum* and *voluptas* is turned into the formal one of *habitus,* habit, and *affectus,* the emotions, where the extremely simplified categorical coordinates of *actio* (the act), and *qualitas* (quality) constitute the only dynamic framework for reality, in its infinite gradations between the two polar extremes, as far as the ethical reasoning is concerned, of the soul of man and that of beast, of *fortitudo* (fortitude), and *imbecillitas* (feebleness). Once it is denied the legitimacy itself of metaphysical elaborations, *a fortiori* if in the case of the theological ones, faith was reduced to a mere "act": "an act of trust," as it was so well defined by J. Chomarat.[122]

We might debate the sincerity of Valla's fideism, once it is pruned of the often captious emphasis of certain pronouncements. Similarly we should curtail the contrary emphasis on naturalistic optimism, relating it to the rhetorical division of roles in the dialogue. Actually Valla can be called neither an optimist nor a pessimist. What rather distinguishes him, beyond the richness of rhetorical developments, is above all his argumentive rigor, as well as his deep and passionate concern with intellectual inquiry. But this is not the point in question. It has sometimes been stated that in the later Renaissance, beginning especially with Marsilio Ficino (the reference is of course to the *Theologia platonica*), philosophy and theology, kept rigorously separate in medieval and scholastic traditions, were unified for the first time. A corollary of this separation was the theory of the so-called double truth, the philosophical and the theological, behind which a scholar like Cosma Raimondi still concealed himself.[123] Now this philosophical-theological unification is already realized by Valla, though in a sense diametrically opposed to Ficino's, as a negative unification. And, such as later in Ficino, who had also started with an Epicurean experience (by the way, in a much more genuine sense than Valla), the assimilation of religion into philosophy (or vice versa) involved highly controversial philosophical-religious issues. An exhaustion of confidence in positive tradition is obvious in both authors, in the anti-Platonism of Valla as well as the Neo-Platonism of Ficino. To mention but one of his salient passages, Valla in the *Elegantiae* declares that the Latin term *persuasio* is a better definition for *Christiana religio* than "faith": "For *fides* in its proper Latin sense is a "proof" (*probatio*). . . . But the Christian religion relies not on proof, but on persuasion, which is preferable to proof. . . . Whoever is persuaded is entirely appeased, and requires no further proof."[124]

It will seem now less paradoxical that Luther would later set Valla against Erasmus on the question of free will.[125] The rigorously theocentric conception of the one and the no less rigorously anthropological vision of the other did, in fact, have as a point in common the exclusion of the mediation of the saints, that is, of the testimonies of positive tradition. Valla's polemical and at times antagonistic relationship with tradition was actually the real motive that sparked the charge by the Inquisition. (Following his debate with the Franciscan preacher, Antonio of Bitonto, over the presumed apostolic origins of the Creed, Valla had expected the college of jurists in Naples to take it upon themselves to autonomously sanction the correction he had suggested for a controversial passage in the *Decretum Gratiani,* thereby inviting doctoral colleges throughout Italy to pronounce judgment on dubious points of canonist tradition: in the background, of course, were the programmatic statements of Valla's recent tract on the Donation of Constantine.)[126] It was then that Valla was summoned by the tribunal of Inquisition, where exception was taken particularly to the propositions of *De voluptate,* which among the other counts of indictment are clearly the predominant ones.[127]

It seems probable that the trial was more a matter of intimidation than a real desire to provoke the counterproductive action of a public condemnation. It is also true that the bold and at the same time original and subtle nature of Valla's argumentation, and especially the prevailing negative aspect of his conclusions, were not constructed so as to find, then or later, any direct followers; so that modern scholars sometimes are able to recognize only by chance and indirectly the evidence of his circulation and influence.[128] We should not, however, forget the almost organized effort to neutralize Valla's theses. This can be seen, for example, in the great success of Bartolomeo Facio's *De vitae felicitate,* in both manuscript and printed editions. Composed at the Neapolitan court in an environment hostile to Valla, Facio's work assigns Panormita a role diametrically opposed to the one he had been given in *De voluptate.* And many years later, while imprisoned in Castel Sant'Angelo, in 1468–69, Bartolomeo Platina, almost as though to make amends, wrote a dialogue as a corrective to Valla's, whose theses he overturned beginning from the very title, *De falso et vero bono.*[129] A direct witnessing, moreover, comes from Valla himself, who acknowledged openly the existence of such a hostile atmosphere. At the height of his career during the papacy of Nicholas V, he perceived how narrowly restricted were the boundaries imposed on the diffusion of his own work. And so he wrote to Niccolò Perotti, secretary of his last protector, Cardinal Bessarion, using words quite uncommon for him: "For among all people whom do I hold more dear than you? . . . because I designate you the only or the principal defender of my works after I am dead. . . . For others either cannot or do not want."[130]

—⊂∞⊃—

At the time of the composition of *De voluptate* in Pavia in the early 1430s, it must have appeared only a remote possibility that it would provoke Church intervention and be censured. It cannot be overemphasized what a formidable impact the contemporary state of conflict between princes and Church and between Pope and Council had on what clearly was an unorthodox literary production and unorthodox intellectual behavior. In Lombardy, ruled by Filippo Maria Visconti, and later in Naples, under the reign of Alfonso, Valla felt himself under the direct protection of the prince, or in any case of the court. It is not a coincidence that the Church's first explicit reaction to Valla's writings appeared after Alfonso had made peace with Eugenius IV (14 June 1443); or that Valla felt opportunities for his work to be limited under the papacy of Nicholas V, once the twenty-year conflict opened by the Council of Basel had ended, and political relations on the Italian peninsula had begun to improve.

In particular in Pavia, either as a manifestation of the ducal policy in ecclesiastical affairs, or out of specific concerns for the administration of the Studio, the traditional two or three chairs of theology (which were distributed among the mendicant orders and the Augustinians) were reduced to one by ducal decree in 1430. The provision, in any case, testifies at an institutional level that very decline in trust toward ecclesiastical orders, of which sharp satires, such as the poem *Regissol* by M. Vegio, bear in their own way further witness.[131]

On the other hand, Valla could recall with some satisfaction that despite the instigations by his adversaries, he had been defended by the "rector of philosophers," that is to say, the faculty of arts and medicine, which evidently had not felt injured by him.[132] Valla in effect had to defend himself not from the theologians but rather from the far more powerful corporation of jurists, and documents recently appear have brought to light the dramatic circumstances of the conflict.[133]

We have already had occasion to mention Valla's attack on Bartolo, written in the form of a satirical letter about the treatise *De insigniis et armis,* which had been originally addressed to Catone Sacco, while the version we know appears with the name of Pier Candido Decembrio (perhaps because Sacco, a preeminent jurist of the Studio, had refused to appear to publicly endorse the tract).

Valla's polemical writing has traditionally been compared to M. Vegio's nearly contemporary preface to his large compilation, *De verborum significatione.* In fact, the expressions Vegio uses to criticize the "later interpreters, Bartolo and others" appear, not surprisingly, to come from Valla.[134] But a recent scholar, M. Speroni, after remarking on the work's "substantial affinity with Valla's arguments," had to admit later, after comparing Vegio's actual text with the juridical debates in Valla's *Elegantiae,* that the methodologies of the two texts are completely different: one "accepts (jurists') definitions as they are given," while the other "subjects the same ancient jurists to critical examination, defending the independence of the science of philology from every authority."[135] This is not my main point, however. Speroni also notes that in contrast to Valla's attack simply on Bartolo's authority, the target of Vegio's polemic is Tribonian, the compiler of the *Corpus iuris* and the one responsible for mutilating the legacy of ancient jurisprudence, thereby creating the "contradictions," which made interpretation necessary.[136] Tribonian is, in fact, the ostensible target, clearly aiming at the author of the order to intervene in the corpus of ancient law—who was, of course, Justinian. Vegio, in other words, had used the name of an officer as a substitute for the prince, who evidently could not be directly accused. It is for this reason that scholars such as Maffei and Speroni have noticed in Vegio a foreshadowing of the French school of humanistic jurisprudence (the so-called Cults), and, I must add, of their anti-absolutist bias and defense of legal traditions against sovereign interference, as exemplified in Justinian's Digest.

This is obviously not the case with Valla. His relationship to Vegio seems to anticipate *in nuce* the position he would later assume on a much grander scale, in the face of sixteenth-century humanist jurisprudence: the ambivalent position of an author both inspiring new learning and at the same time being considered not without suspicion, with whom was good not to mingle.[137] Moreover, the fact that in the famous preface to book 3 of the *Elegantiae* Valla does not hestitate to mention Justinian ("if only the books of ancient jurisprudence were whole! Surely then there would not be those men, who in spite of Justinian's prohibition, succeeded in interpreting the law")[138] is itself an indication of the difference between the two authors. Valla's main target was the systematic approach to legal exegesis; and Justinian, rather than being pointed out as beginning the process that made interpretation of the law necessary compared with the preexisting more direct legal tradition, was deemed not powerful enough to stem it.

P. Vaccari once suggested, in a time bygone, that Valla's juridical polemic was motivated by the "scientific" concern with coming back to the sources of law, in reaction to the trends toward practicality that dominated the school at Pavia in the wake of Baldus's teaching.[139] Vaccari's argument is clearly rooted in a positivist outlook, and so Valla for him is little more than a symbolic character of Romanist learning. Yet, if approached from a different angle, this interpretation still contains an element of truth that deserves further consideration. Baldus's principle of *ratio naturalis,* the rationale inherent in natural law, and so by extension in every legal rule, was apt to legitimatize the revision and uniformizing of statutes promoted by the Visconti, as well as to allow for a mediation in the face of multiple conflicting legislations. Moreover, the identification of equity with *naturalis iustitia,* the law of nature, a point that Baldus emphasizes, had the effect of safeguarding a principle of absoluteness in the empiricism of individual interpretations, as well as in political directives of the interpretation itself. This kind of synthesis of empiricism and rationality, of interpretative elasticity and ethical and juridical norms, is evident in the widely circulated manual *Practica Papiensis* (1414), written by Giovan Pietro de' Ferraris and studied by Vaccari himself.[140] With some reminiscence of the criticism formulated by the humanists, Ferraris bewares of "subtle reasoning" (*cavillationes*) and excessive recourse to Roman law (or *ius commune*), which he summarizes into basic principles. Moreover, he appeals to the value of "examples," that is, concrete situations; and together with Baldus he acknowledges the absoluteness of prince's authority. At the same time, however, he also shows a strong and contextual concern for the violations of *ius elicitum,* the law in its written form (he refers in particular to the ducal rescripts). Hence comes the value Ferrari assigns to the doctrinal "opinions" in the realm of traditional jurisprudence; and, more generally, as a remedy against the spread of iniquity, he appeals to the moral teachings of Cicero and Seneca, which he recommends as a major topic of teaching.

Against such a background—once more by force of contrast—we have a better understanding of the meaning of Valla's ethical-juridical approach in his controversy against the science of law; and above all we can establish an ideological connection between his criticism of the jurists' exegesis and the philosophical assumptions of *De voluptate.*

For Valla, the invalidation of judicial commentary according to his own methodical outlines was no more than a corollary to the more generalized utilitarianism, which in the dialogue is given such an extensive development. Laws, he maintains, have no other end than to be of the greatest usefulness: what other explanation should we find for allowing reward or inflicting punishment "than to deal with what is useful and not useful, and not at all with what is right?"[141] This was the only way, instead of an abstract notion of justice, to curb the power of rulers. In other words, in place of the empiricism of contemporary jurisprudence, and somehow in competition with it, Valla proposed a frank recognition of utility in and for itself, which by definition requires no rationale for its legitimization.

Nothing illustrates this point better than Valla's interpretation of Carneades's famous debate for and against justice. The question had originally been discussed by Cicero in his *De republica,* then later revived by Quintilian, and explored in still greater depth by Lactantius. The latter had argued that Cicero's equation of "natural justice" with "civil justice" could not be corroborated except by appealing to the superior justice of God, and to the higher Christian virtue, mercy.[142] Quite differently, Valla, in keeping with the general thesis of his dialogue and contesting the theological vision of Lactantius, stresses the instinctual and emotional character of mercy, differentiating it from virtues, which instead derive from unnatural *honestas* ("nature has given us mercy together with the other animals, as she did anger, hope, sorrow, joy, but not virtues").[143]

Quintilian, on the other hand, faithful to his own belief in the goodness, by definition, of his ideal orator, wrote, addressing the issue, "But maliciousness, itself opposite of virtue, reveals what virtue is, and equity becomes more evident from the contemplation of iniquity."[144] Unlike Lactantius's case, Valla's objection to Quintilian this time is direct. If Carneades—he writes—free of the rules established by the Skeptics' dispute, "had been able to proclaim what is more true, I have no doubt that he would have approved the party of utility."[145]

Such a subversive substitution of *utilitas* for *aequitas* triggers two fundamental consequences: (1) the implicit separation of rhetoric from jurisprudence, as *ars boni et aequi,* in reference to Quintilian's text; in the same way, it is worth remembering, that rhetoric is separated from ethics, in reference to Ciceronian writings; (2) the repudiation (which is like a concealed premise of it) of the idea of a superior principle from which "civil justice" proceeds: in other words, the concept of natural law, based as it was on Cicero and on the Digest, that had informed medieval jurisprudence, to the point of strictly identifying with the principles of equity. This point was especially stressed in the definitive juridical exegesis by Baldus, which now seems to us as rigid in its formulation as it is fragile in its actual historical setting.

A fundamental chapter of Valla's *Elegantiae* summarizes these concepts in their mutual connection. With the intention of distinguishing *iura* (the general principles of law) from *leges* (the particular legal collections), and destroying as a result the ideal unity of Justinian's *corpus,* Valla proceeds by denying the traditional tripartite division of "natural law," the "law of nations," and "civil law," "since it is ridiculous to speak about a natural law, which nature would have taught all animals." Nature consists in instinct, "and who therefore has said that harming, despoiling, and killing weaker animals is to be recognized as a law?" *Ius civile,* in turn, was nothing but a collection of its own various constituent parts, "as much laws, as *plebiscita, senatus consulta,* decrees of the princes, and *responsa* of lawyers." It follows that the orator, who presents the law to the people, is superior to the jurist who interprets it, "as if he were his secretary." Once having established the distinction between a law, in the abstract sense of the term, and the effective enforcement of the law (*vim legis*), Valla invalidates precisely the criteria of the "modern" jurists, who, while developing their commentaries on separate paragraphs of legal collections, "each time speak about a law as if it were new, judging that there is not a single law from one legislator, but rather an infinite number of laws coming from an infinite number of interpreters."[146] In this way the various individual points of Valla's argument come together to create a coherent articulation of utilitarianism, relativism, and skeptical attitude toward natural law, which, unlike the predominantly political concern that would characterize similar views by Machiavelli or Guicciardini, was grounded on a direct incursion into the first principles of ethics. And as a clear evidence of Valla's foresight, it would not be until the time of Thomas Hobbes that such a general approach would reappear, then to join variously with modern currents of utilitarian thought.

My exposition has carried us far from Pavia, but, before concluding I would like to return there in order to sum up issues laid out at the beginning of this discussion.

Having competed with the Ciceronianism of Gasparino Barzizza from the beginning of his career, Valla arrived in Pavia at a moment of crisis and transformation of his school, which was just as sensitive as Valla to the influence of Florentine humanism and to its preeminent representative, Leonardo Bruni. In this framework of rapid renovation of scholarly traditions, Valla was able to move ahead on the projects he had already begun. The *Elegantiae,* it should be remembered, grew out of a suggestion by Cosma Raimondi — a figure surely worth reconsidering, even though his life remains somewhat obscure. The *De voluptate,* too, though fundamentally linked to Bruni's Aristotelian translations and the moral essays by Poggio and Bruni himself, in all likelihood found in Raimondi its most direct suggestion, and so an incitement of more radical conclusions.

The culture of Lombardy, however, in both its centers of Milan and Pavia, gravitated toward university and scholastic institutions, and a figure such as Panormita, whose support came essentially from the court, stood out as the jarring exception who, as we then see, imposed the reestablishment of the rule. Such scholarship was naturally faithful to the tested forms of grammatical and rhetorical commentary, lexical collections, and encyclopaedias in its institutional aim of a transformation through continuity. It was in this environment that Valla exercised all his revolutionary potential. The *De voluptate* was not only a sign of ideological dissidence (almost a kind of early libertinism), as it was the case of Raimondi, but included the seeds of a much broader overturning of methods. It was a denial of the basic, multidisciplinary ethical education, just as the *Elegantiae* signified a radical substitution for traditional grammar and lexicography; and the *Repastinatio* invalidated on a broader theoretical level the unitary principle underlying encyclopedic collections; and finally the attack on Bartolo (probably written on the occasion of Vegio's discussion of the humanistic-juridical lexicography) assailed the linguistic and exegetical foundations of legal commentary. The apparent connections between Valla's anti-Aristotelian bias and Catone Sacco's Isodorean *Origines,* as well as, to a greater extent, his rancorous competition with Antonio of Rho (concerning the latter's *De imitatione eloquentiae*), which would continue with important interventions by Vegio and Tortelli,[147] show how equivocal in nature were such cultural relationships, giving further evidence that Valla's violent expulsion from the University of Pavia was not simply the result of a chance controversy with the jurists.

After Valla had surrendered the chair, and following the brief interval when he was succeeded by his own disciple, Antonio Astesano, the position was held steadily from 1435 (and rewarded with an increasingly generous salary) by Baldassare Rasini. He was a rhetorician and jurist ("the most distinguished doctor of civil law and very renowned orator," according to his laudatory epithets), who had been recommended to the post, according to a civic tradition of the Studio, by the communal government of Pavia. Finally, and most importantly, from at least 1439 onward, Rasini's teaching was incorporated into the faculty of jurists.[148]

A special glory of Rasini was his taste for that kind of flowery, or—as we might also call it—late-gothic eloquence, the same which Valla so mocked in *De voluptate,* with particular respect to religious sermons:

> so great is the insistence in inculcating its arguments, so great the redundancy of its examples, so great the repetition of the same ideas, such the tangle of the speech, which like vines cling to everything it touches, that I cannot say whether it is more useless or foul.[149]

And so when Valla, and soon after him his own friend-enemy Panormita, moved from Lombardy to their next common destination at the court of Alfonso of Aragon, the reckless behavior of the one and the provocatory outbursts of the other contributed to a closing up, so to speak, of scholastic ranks in the Studium of Pavia.[150] The rivalry with the increasingly humanistic culture of the Milanese ducal court and its adjoining school of eloquence was, as a consequence, intensified, producing a gap that only late in Sforzas' times ducal policy would attempt to fill.

Notes

—⚬⚬⚬—

Introduction

1   In regard to Pier Candido Decembrio, I refer in particular to the essay "Tra uma-
    nesimo e Concili: L'epistolario di Francesco Pizolpasso," published as chap. 3 in *Uma-
    nesimo e secolarizzazione,* pp. 77–135, which is not included in this translation.

2   "Qui murum oppugnat capite se ipsum laedit"; "omnibus auctoritatibus est ante-
    ferenda." Cf. n. 1 above.

3   Cf. *Umanesimo e secolarizzazione,* chap. 2, "La coscienza del latino: Postscriptum," pp.
    55–75, not included in this volume.

4   Cf. n. 1 above.

5   Cf. R. Fubini, "L'umanista: ritorno di un paradigma? Saggio per un profilo storico
    da Petrarca ad Erasmo," *Archivo storico italiano* 147 (1989): 435–508 (also, with additions,
    in R. Fubini, *L'umanesimo italiano e i suoi storici: Origini rinascimentali—critica moderna,*
    [Milan, 2001], pp. 15–72).

1. Consciousness of the Latin Language among the Humanists

1   For example, E. Norden, *Die antike Kunstprosa* (Leipzig, 1898), p. 770, deals with the
    humanistic struggle against medieval Latin and the struggle against the vernacu-
    lar as if they were two different episodes, the one positive and the other negative.
    But in reality the two controversies were at first indistinguishable; on the contrary,
    the arguments against vernacular were only a marginal part of the whole contro-
    versy against tradition. On this subject, see also P. O. Kristeller, *L'origine e lo sviluppo
    della prosa volgare italiana,* in Kristeller, *Studies in Renaissance Thought and Letters* (Rome,
    1956), pp. 473–93.

2   Cf. M. Puppo, "Introduzione" to *Discussioni linguistiche del Settecento* (Turin, 1957),
    and also A. Monteverdi, "Lodovico Antonio Muratori e gli studi intorno all'origine

della lingua italiana," in *Atti e Memorie dell'Accademia dell'Arcadia,* ser. 3, 1 (1950). For arguments in favor of a revision of the disdain of "scientific" modern linguistics versus previous empirical attempts, cf. G. Nencioni, "Quicquid nostri praedecessores," ibid., 2 (1950).

3   Cf. Biondo Flavio, *De verbis romanae locutionis,* in *Scritti inediti e rari di Biondo Flavio,* ed. B. Nogara (Rome, 1927), pp. 115–30; Leonardo Bruni, ep. VI, 10 (7 May 1435), *Epistolarum libri VIII,* ed. L. Mehus (Florence, 1741), pp. 62–65 (cf. also F. P. Luiso, *Studi sull'Epistolario di Leonardo Bruni,* ed. L. Gualdo Rosa [Rome, 1980], p. 123 f.). These and other texts in question are later published in a critical edition by M. Tavoni, *Latino, grammatica e volgare: Storia di una questione umanistica* (Padua, 1984). A discussion of this contribution can be found in *Umanesimo e secolarizzazione,* chap. 2: "La coscienza del latino: Postscriptum," pp. 55–75. For a historical survey of the question, see G. Tiraboschi, *Storia della letteratura italiana,* vol. 3 (Milan, 1823), pp. v ff.; A. Fuchs, *Die romanische Sprache in ihrem Verhältnisse zum Lateinischem* (Halle, 1849), pp. 44 f.; G. Gröber, "Geschichte der romanischen Philologie: I Zeitraum," *Grundriss der romanischen Philologie,* vol. 1, part 1, § 1 (Strassburg, 1888), pp. 9–13; G. Mancini, *Vita di Leon Battista Alberti* (Florence, 1882), p. 218 ff.; G. Mancini, *Vita di Lorenzo Valla* (Florence, 1891), pp. 283 ff.; R. Sabbadini, *La scuola e gli studi di Guarino Veronese* (Catania, 1886), pp. 148 ff.; *Epistolario di Guarino Veronese,* ed. R. Sabbadini, vol. 3 (Venice, 1919), pp. 408–19; G. Mignini, "L'epistola di Flavio Biondo 'De romana locutione,'" *Il Propugnature* 3 (1890): 133–44; P. Rajna, "Origine della lingua italiana," in A. D'Ancona and O. Bacci, eds., *Manuale della letteratura italiana,* vol. 1 (Florence, 1902), p. 17 f.; E. Walser, *Poggius Florentinus* (Leipzig, 1914), pp. 259 ff.; U. T. Holmes, "The Vulgar Latin Question and the Origin of Roman Tongues: Notes for a Chapter of the History of Romance Philology Prior to 1849," *Studies in Philology* 25 (1928): 51–61; V. Rossi, *Il Quattrocento,* 3rd ed. (Milan, 1938), pp. 110 ff.; F. Strauss, *Vulgärlatein und Vulgärsprache in Zusammenhang der Sprachenfrage im XVI Jahrhundert* (Marburg, 1938), pp. 29–45; M. Vitale, "Le origini del volgare nelle discussioni dei filologi del '400," *Lingua nostra* 14 (1953): 64–69; M. Vitale, *La questione della lingua* (Palermo, 1960), pp. 9–21; H. Baron, *The Crisis of the Early Italian Renaissance* (Princeton, 1955), pp. 297–312, 412–15 (and also 2d ed. in one volume [Princeton, 1966], pp. 339–53, 533 f.); H. W. Klein, *Latein und Volgare in Italien* (Munich, 1957), pp. 50–60; C. Grayson, *A Renaissance Controversy: Latin or Italian?* (Oxford, 1960), pp. 7–12. Most recently the question has been broadly reconsidered by A. Mazzocco, *Linguistic Theories in Dante and the Humanists: Studies of Language and Intellectual History in Late Medieval and Early Renaissance Italy* (Leiden, 1993).

4   Biondo, *De verbis,* p. 116 (Tavoni, p. 198, § 3): "materno ne an passim apud rudem indoctamque multitudinem aetate nostra vulgato idiomate, an grammaticae artis usu, quod Latinam appellamus, Romani orare fuerint soliti."

5   Ibid.: "Magna est apud doctos aetatis nostrae homines altercatio et cui saepenumero interfui contentio. . . ."

6   H. Schuchardt, *Der Vokalismus des Vulgärlateins* (Leipzig, 1866), p. 44. This opinion was repeated, for instance, by Rossi, *Il Quattrocento,* p. 112.

7   Cf., for instance, Guarino, ep. 34 (of 1415), *Epistolario,* vol. 1, p. 8, where, criticizing the old epistolary style—woven with "vocabula externa et abusiva"—by the Tre-

cento rhetorician Pietro da Moglio, he points to the example of Cicero: "Ab quo tam aperta, tam clara, tam familiaris usurpata est dicendi consuetudo, ut praeter concinnam et aptissimam verborum et sententiarum compositionem, vulgaria omnia ferme et in medio posita communi quodam usu atque 'in hominum ore atque sermone versentur'" (Guarino's citation is from Cicero's speech "Pro Roscio," VI). On the other hand, it is significant that the reasoning advanced by Loschi in the dispute (it did not seem to him "satis simile veri esse literatum populo sermonem ab illis — *sc.* Romanis — factum esse, earum potissime rerum quas sua aut reipublicae aut amicorum causa probari persuaderique cupivissent": Biondo, *De verbis*, p. 117) appears to refer to the rhetorical theory of the three styles, while in the introduction to his own comment on the orations by Cicero (cf. Q. Asconii Pediani, *Commentarii eruditissimi in aliquot insigniores M. T. Ciceronis orationes . . . His adiecti sunt A. Luschi Vicentini in XI Ciceronis orationes commentarii* [Paris, 1536], pp. 130 ff.) recalling the ancient discussion on whether eloquence is acquired by nature or by art, ends up with a fair compromise between the two, provided that the following principle was safe: "altior res est eloquentia et a vulgari sermone remotior, quia licet plerumque in ambiguis communibusque versetur, ea tamen proprio quodam ac certo instituto continetur, suis temperatur legibus, suo fine dirigitur, quem semper attinget cum voluerit orator."

8   Cf. Biondo, *De verbis*, p. 117: "vulgare quoddam et plebeium, ut posteriora habuerunt saecula, Romanis fuisse loquendi genus a litteris remotum."

9   Cf. Mignini, "L'epistola," p. 139; see also Vitale, "Le origini," p. 65.

10 Cf. "Invettiva contro a certi calunniatori di Dante e di messer Francesco Petrarca e di messer Giovanni Boccacci, i nomi de' quali per onestà si taciono . . . ," in A. Lanza, *Polemiche e berte letterarie nella Firenze del primo Quattrocento* (Rome, 1971), p. 262, with clear reference to the circle of Niccoli and Bruni: "che per parere litteratissimi apresso el vulgo gridano a piaza quanti dittonghi avevano gli antichi, e perché oggi non se ne usano se non due; e qual grammatica sia migliore, o quella del tempo del comico Terenzio o dell'eroico Vergilio ripulita; e quanti piedi usano gli antichi nel versificare, e perché oggi non s'usa l'anapesto di quatro brievi. E in tali fantasticherie il loro tempo trapassano, lasciando il più utile della gramatica . . . : delle parti dell'orazione, l'ortografia, la distinzione, la temologia [that is, etymology] de' vocaboli, la concordanza delle parti dell'orazione, l'ortografia, il pulito e proprio parlare litterale, niente istudiano di sapere." In other words, for the adversaries of Rinuccini, "grammar" is nothing but an equivalent to this or that moment and form of Latin literary style.

11 Biondo, *De verbis*, p. 117 (Tavoni, p. 198 § 11): "quod (*sc.* bellum) ea gerere modestia institui, ut nec te impudenter abs me lacessitum, nec me maiorum sententiae acquiescendo durum pervicacemque videri velim."

12 Poggius Bracciolini, "Disceptatio convivialis tertia: Utrum priscis Romanis latina lingua omnibus communis fuerit . . . ," *Opera* (Basel, 1538) (*Opera omnia,* ed. R. Fubini, vol. 1 [Turin, 1964]), p. 52 (Tavoni, p. 239 § 8): "Reiicio hoc totum disputationis genus, a quo audivi multa seu multorum dicta et sententias contra Leonardi opinionem investigasse. Ego enim, ut verum fatear, hac in re minime curiosus fui."

13 In this regard Dante's *Vita nuova* 25.3 ff., should also be cited: "Anticamente non erano dicitori d'amore in lingua volgare, anzi erano dicitori d'amore certi poeti in lingua

latina; tra noi dico, avvegna che forse che tra altra gente addivenisse e addivegna ancora, sì come in Grecia, non volgari ma litterati poeti queste cose trattavano. E non è molto numero di anni passati, che apparirono prima questi poeti volgari . . . E la cagione perché alquanto grossi ebbero favore di saper dire, è che furo li primi che dissero in lingua di sì. E lo primo che cominciò a dire sì come poeta volgare, si mosse perché volle fare intendere le parole a una donna, a la quale era malagevole l'intendere li versi latini. E questo è contro color che rimano sopra altra matera che amorosa, conciosia cosa che cotale modo di parlare fosse dal principio trovato per dire d'amore."

14 *De vulgari eloquentia* 1.9.1 (ed. P. V. Mengaldo [Padua, 1968], p. 13 f.): "Nos autem nunc oportet quam habemus rationem periclitari, cum inquirere intendamus de hiis in quibus nullius auctoritate fulcimur, hoc est de unius eiusdemque a principio ydiomatis variatione secuta."

15 Cf., for example, Strauss, *Vulgärlatein und Vulgärsprache*, p. 31: "Dante hat also folgenden Vorstellung: schon in der Antike gab es neben der 'grammatica' eine Volksprache . . . Die Volksprache entwickelte sich nun aus inneren Gründen . . . weiter und präsentiert sich heute in Italien als Italienisch, in Frankreich als Französisch u.s.w. . . . Wenn etwa Cicero schrieb, dan geschah es in der klassischen Sprache der 'grammatica,' hiel er aber seine Rede auf dem Forum, dann was dass Volksprache."

16 Whether Italian more than any other language has its basis in Latin ("initi grammatice," according to *De vulgari eloquentia* 1.10.2), or whether the compilers of the "grammar" were able to collect the most characteristic locutions of old Italian speech (for instance, "accepisse *sic*," ibid. 1.10.1). Hence, by the way, it appears the precarious and, I should say, instrumental character of this concept of the Latin "grammar" as an entirely conventional construction. (Subsequent to this essay C. Grayson wrote "'Nobilor est vulgaris': Latin and Vernacular in Dante's Thought," *Centenary Essays on Dante by Members of the Oxford Dante Society* [Oxford, 1965], pp. 61 ff., in which he proposed, contrary to the traditional emendation to the original manuscript text, *videtur*, to restore the plural form: "quia magis *videntur* initi grammatice, que comunis est," in the sense that the dignity of Italian is based on the fact "that its *familiares et domestici*, like Cino and Dante . . . relies mostly on Latin," etc. This proposal was then accepted by P. V. Mengaldo, the last editor of the *De vulgari eloquentia*, p. lxiii. In this way already in book 1 Dante's linguistic consideration merges into the stylistic.) Furthermore it should be noted that medieval grammarians who are cited in commentaries by scholars (for example by A. Marigo) as possible "sources" of Dante meant the "invention" of grammar as the determination of logical nexuses of speech that are universally valid, having been incorporated into the body of privileged languages (the "grammatical languages"), but that would be easily applicable to any other language (for instance French, as Peter Elie appears to hope: cf. Ch. Turot, "Notices et extraits de divers manuscrits latins pour servir à l'histoire des doctrines grammaticales au Moyen Age, *Notices et extratis* . . . , 23, 2 [Paris, 1868], p. 126: "quod fieri posset facile si tantum nomina et figure illius (*sc.* artis) secundum illam linguam invenirentur"). In this regard G. Vinay, "Ricerche sul 'De vulgari Eloquentia,'" *Giornale storico della letteratura italiana* 136 (1959): 246 ff., points out the diversity

in Dantesque conception, which would deal with the real coining of an artificial language.

17 Cf. *De vulgari eloquentia* 2.4.3: "Differunt tamen a magnis poetis, hoc est regularibus, quia magni sermone et arte regulari poetati sunt, hii vero casu . . . Idcirco accidit ut, quantum illos proximius imitemur, tantum rectius poetemur. Unde nos, doctrine operi intendentes, doctrinatas eorum poetrias emulari oportet." Cp. the analogous, even though more generic, statement by Antonio da Tempo, *Summa artis rythmice* (of 1332), G. Grion ed. (Bologna, 1869), p. 71: "Non potest aliquis esse bonus rithmator vulgaris nisi saltem grammaticalibus studiis sit imbutus."

18 Cf. *De vulgari eloquentia* 1.12.6: "Et dicimus quod, si vulgarem Sicilianum accipere volumus secundum quod prodit a terrigenis mediocribus, ex ore quorum iudicium eligendum videtur," etc. (that is, not from the poets of Frederick II).

19 Ibid., 1.16.7: "Inter quos omnes unum audivimus nitentem divertere a materno et ad vulgare curiale intendere, videlicet Ildobrandinum Paduanum." Cp. the observations on the subject by Leo Spitzer, "Muttersprache und Muttererziehung," *Essays in Historical Semantic* (New York, 1948), pp. 16 ff.

20 Cf. G. Vinay, "Il De Vulgari Eloquentia," *Annali della Pubblica Istruzione* 6 (1960): 685. Cf. also on the subject, S. Pellegrini, " 'De vulgari eloquentia,' I, 1, capp. 10–19," *Studi mediolatini e volgari* 7 (1960): 155–63.

21 Cf. Antonio da Tempo, *Summa,* p. 174: "Lingua tusca magis apta est ad literam sive literaturam quam alia lingua, et ideo magis est communis et intelligibilis."

22 Cf. Giovanni Gherardi da Prato, *Il Paradiso degli Alberti,* ed. A. Lanza (Rome, 1975), p. 216 (4.26–27): "Io dico che in meno parole in alcuno tempo non udî tanto pienamente sadisfare in tanta profonda e alta matera, e in me pensato arei impossibile con tanta brevità quello bene e perlucido, come detto è, poter dire. E ormai chiaro veggio e conosco che l'edioma fiorentino è sì rilimato e copioso che ogni profonda matera si puote chiarissimamente con esso dire, ragionarne e disputarne."

23 On this subject, cf. the accurate analysis by Klein, *Latein und Volgare,* pp. 33 ff.

24 Cf. G. Boccaccio, *Commento alla Divina Commedia e altri scritti intorno a Dante,* ed. D. Guerri (Bari, 1918), p. 115.

25 "Vita di Dante," *Commento alla Divina Commedia,* p. 24.

26 Cf. epistle to Jacopo Pizzinga (of 1372), in Boccaccio, *Opere latine minori,* A. F. Massera ed. (Bari, 1928), p. 195: "Vidimus . . . eos (*sc.* Phebus and the Muses) in maternum cogere cantum ausum, non plebeio et rusticano, ut nonnulli voluere, confecit, quin imo artificioso schemate sensu letiorem fecit quam cortice."

27 Cf. the recent edition: Boccaccio, *De casibus virorum illustrium,* ed. P. G. Ricci and V. Zaccaria (Milan, 1983) (Boccaccio, "Tutte le opere," ed. V. Branca, vol. 9), p. 244 (chap. 3, 10): "presens autem evum, spreta veterum solertia, non dicam a grammaticalibus regulis, sed a nutricum uberibus evellit infantulos, ut eos non in scholis sed in fornicibus trudat."

28 Ibid., p. 534 (chap. 6, 11).

29 Ibid., p. 546 (chap. 6, 13): Huius (*sc.* humane locutionis) cum due sint species, ea scilicet quam a nutrice suscipimis . . . , et reliqua quam ab arte politam, exhornatam . . . pauci provectique volentes assumimus," etc.

30 Ibid., "Non enim semper cibum servis poscituri sumus, aut de ruralibus cum vil-
lico locuturi . . . Non decens est hominum Creatori aut mentis arcanum incom-
posite reserare, aut in eius laudes verbis absque modulatione cantare," etc. We recall
in this regard the anonymous annotation (of 1291) by a scribe (cited by Kristeller,
"L'origine," p. 450) about the inadequacy of the vernacular in expressing "spiritual
things." Except that, where for Boccaccio it is a question of convenience, the scribe
is concerned with a technical consideration of the capacity of the language: "Non si
possono propriamente esprimere (sc. le cose spirituali) per paravole volgari come si
esprimono per latino e per grammatica, per la penuria dei vocaboli volgari."

31 Ibid., p. 171 (chap. 6, 1): "Negasse tulliana incude fabricatum eloquium longe magis
quam rude possit, stultissimum est, sed nec rude caruit effectu quandoque." This
is a dialogue between Fortune and the writer, about the 'humility' of style and its
effectiveness.

32 Cf. "Vita di Dante," p. 53 (chap. 26): "per fare utilità più comune a' suoi cittadini e
agli altri italiani."

33 Ibid.: "fide potius quam eloquentia suadentis inspecta."

34 Cf., for example, A. Buck, "Italienische Dichtungslehren vom Mittelalter bis
zum Ausgang der Renaissance," Beihefte zur Zeitschrift für Romanische Philologie 94
(1952): 57: "Eine theoretische Rechtfertigung für den Gebrauch des Italienischen als
Literatursprache konnte allerdings für den Vater des Humanismus nicht in Betracht
kommen."

35 Cf. Familiares 1.1.6: "Quod genus apud Siculos, ut fama est, non multis ante secu-
lis renatum, brevi per omnem Italiam ac longius manavit, apud Grecorum olim ac
Latinorum vetustissimos celebratum; siquidem et Athicos et Romanos vulgares rith-
mico tantum carmine uti solitos accepimus." Petrarch is referring here to Servius, Ad
Georgicas 2.382: "Nec non Ausonii . . . : hoc est etiam Romani haec sacra celebrant et
canunt: nam hoc est 'versubus incomptis ludunt,' id est carminibus saturnio metro
compositis, quod ad rythmum solum vulgares consuerunt." Petrarch's remark seems
to be a response to Dante's concept cited above (n. 13) on the invention of vernacular
lyric as love's poetry: "dal principio trovata per dire d'amore."

36 On the Petrarchesque myth of his conversion to Latin, see the observations by
G. Barberi Squarotti, "Le poetiche del '300 in Italia," Momenti e problemi di storia
dell'estetica (Milan, 1958), vol. 1, pp. 300 ff.

37 Cf., for example, Familiares 24.4, where Petrarch makes Cicero participate in his own
disdain for the neglect and dispersion of his works, and again for the deplorable "condition of the Roman commonwealth" (reipublice status); but he remains silent, unlike
the century that would follow, about the corruption of the language, unrecognizable
by a Tullius redivivus (see below, n. 122).

38 Familiares 13.5.16: "Quiquid infra est, iam profecto nullum orationis gradum tenet,
sed verborum potius plebeia quedam et agrestis et servilis effusio est; et quanquam
mille annorum observatione continua inoleverit, dignitatem tamen, quam naturali-
ter non habet, ex tempore non habebit."

39 Ibid.: "quem ipsi stilum nominant, non est stilus."

40 Cf. especially Seniles 2.1 (according to the Italian translation of Lettere senili di Francesco

Petrarca, volgarizzate da G. Fracassetti [Florence, 1869], vol. 1, p. 94): "I am anxious after all to hear just once our detractors speak and write something in Latin, and not just for the nooks and crannies, for silly women and woolshops, who circulate their sentences in uncouth vernacular. They philosophize in the schools, they decide in the courtrooms only through such jargon . . . and names long ago illustrious and famous are defaced as they like."

41 *Familiares* 1.7.17: "Quid sene ridiculosius in talibus occupato?"

42 *Familiares* 16.14.2.

43 *Familiares* 1.8.5.

44 Cf. *Epistolario,* ed. F. Novati (Rome, 1891–1911), vol. 3, p. 79 (ep. IX, 9, of 1395): "tenet gradum suum insuperata vetustas et in campo remanet signis immobilibus atque fixis." On Salutati cf. in general R. G. Witt, *Hercules at the Crossroads: The Life, Works, and Thought of Coluccio Salutati* (Durham, N.C., 1983).

45 Ibid., vol. 2, p. 474 (ep. VIII, 22, of 1393): ". . . qui, cum sibimet constare non possit, sed de sede facile moveatur, incertum et inconstans, sibi penitus inconsentiens, antiquitati solide priscique temporis usui, imo rationi, nec potest nec debet . . . comparari."

46 Ibid., vol. 1, p. 77 (ep. II, 9, of 1369): ". . . quia, seu imbecillitate nature, seu difficultate scientie, seu infructuositate laboris, seu—quod mage reor—alio animos cupidatate flectente, nimis etate nostra eloquentie studia negliguntur, et iam reges et principes non latine, sed gallice vel suis vulgaribus scribunt. Nec contendo quod illud genus loquendi non possit etiam eleganter artificio quodam regi, sed indignor potius quod minor labor esse videatur maternam sequi dicendo rudem inscitiam quam scolasticam disciplinam."

47 Ibid.: "veritas soliditasque sermonis." Cf. also ibid., vol. 1, p. 79 (ep. II, 10): "quanto hominibus ceteris antecellit qui, quod et a ratione maxime proficiscitur, eloquentie splendore refulget . . ."

48 Ibid., vol. 1, p. 77, cit.: "modernorum lubricatio"; "religiosorum rithmica sonoritas."

49 Ibid., vol. 2, p. 413 (ep. VII, 9, of 1393): "Audi Gallicos . . . Nonne quodammodo videntur his pronominibus *ego* et *tu* in singulari numero carere cum vulgarem suum expromunt, quo latinitatem extinguere moliuntur?" This passage is interesting because it illustrates the extent to which rhetorical degeneration and linguistic usage proper to the vernaculars that were distancing themselves from Latin were meant to be connected to each other as a part of the same historical process. The particular mention of French (which Salutati already hinted at; cp. vol. 1, p. 76) may perhaps be explained as a political reference, to the kingdom that boasted undue pretensions of hegemony over Christian Europe.

50 Cf. respectively, ibid., p. 415; and vol. 2, p. 439 (ep. VII, 16, of 1393): "In hac materia aliud est quod homines faciunt et aliud quod debere se facere convincuntur." "Sed mentem paulisper remove a sensibus, immo, ut rectius loquar, ab hac consuetudine quam sensibus percepisti. Redi cogitans, imo proficiscere, si potes, animo ad illa tempora quibus nulle gentes, nulli prorsus homines . . . dummodo foret unus, aliter quam verbis simgularibus utebantur."

51 On Coluccio's different criteria in the usage of classics, and of patristic and medieval

texts, see B. L. Ullman, "Coluccio Salutati e i classici latini," *Il mondo antico nel Rinascimento,* Atti del V Convegno internazionale di studi sul Rinascimento (Florence, 1956), p. 47: "Si vede una differenza enorme fra gli autori classici e gli scrittorri patristici e medievali nell'uso di Coluccio. Non meno di dieci copie di Agostino possedute da Coluccio ci restano, ma una sola è postillata copiosamente. E' facile indovinare quale: il *De civitate Dei,* ove si trovano tante allusioni alla letteratura e ad altre cose antiche"; but in general cf. Ullman's *The Humanism of Coluccio Salutati* (Padua, 1962). Furthermore, as a pertinent text by Salutati, see *Epistolario,* vol. 2, p. 145 (ep. IV, 4, of 1385): "Quid igitur quasi nauseante stomacho novas queris epulas quo possis tam splendidarum mensarum convivio saturari? Crede michi, nichil novum fingimus, sed quasi sarcinatores de ditissime vetustatis fragmentis vestis, quas ut novas edimus, resarcimus. Diu dictum est: 'nil intentatum reliquere poete' [cf. Horatius, *Ars poetica,* 285], et si forte quid relictum fuerat, sequentia tum secula rapuerunt."

52 Cf. *Epistolario,* vol. 3, p. 80 (ep. IX, 9, of 1395): "Floruit proculdubio seculum illud priscum omni studio literarum, et adeo in eloquentia valuit, quod non potuerit imitatrix quanvis et studiosa posteritas illam dicendi maiestatem et culmen eloquentie conservare . . . Fuerunt pauci tamen per tempora, qui adeo viderentur inter coevos emergere, quod ad illam attingere sublimitatem ab imperitioribus putarentur." Salutati had been urged by Cardinal Bartolomeo Oliari to collect his letters, and he shielded himself by claiming his own unworthiness in respect to the perfection of models and in consideration of the decadence that followed. We have Oliari's letter; cp. A. Campana, "Lettera del cardinale padovano (Bartolomeo Oliari) a Coluccio Salutati," in *Medieval and Renaissance Studies in Honor of Berthold Louis Ullman,* ed. C. Henderson Jr. (Rome, 1964), vol. 2, pp. 237–54.

53 As the disapproval of the *vos* form, or his thoughts about epistolary art, which are the particular occasion for the more general assumptions in the epistle to Oliari cited above.

54 Cf. *Epistolario,* vol. 1, p. 338 (ep. IV, 20, of 1379): "Quantum flumen a pelago differt, tanto carmina prosis credito fore minore." Benvenuto di Imola (cited in Novati's commentary) reacted to this opinion: "facilius est scribere prosaice quam metrice, sive quis scribat literaliter sive vulgariter." Cf. also, for example, Filippo Villani, "Vita Francisci Petrarchae," in *Le vite di Dante, Petrarca e Boccaccio,* ed. A. Solerti (Milan, 1904), p. 278, where, while enumerating the praises of the poet, he first introduces (also in the chronological sense) the poetic coronation and adds: "cumque apicem poesis accuratissima diligentia tetigisset, eloquentie, que soluto sermone eniteret, tanta claruit maiestate, ut prisce facundie scriptores stilo eminentissimo vel excederet vel equaret." Here too the ideal priority of poetry over eloquence is assumed. For some additional points, see my review of V. Zaccaria, "Le epistole e i carmi di Antonio Loschi," *Rivista storica italiana* 88 (1976): 809 f.

55 *Epistolario,* vol. 3, p. 607 (ep. XIII, 3, of 1402): "Verborum autem ornatus, quem aliqui solam rhetoricam esse putant, circa multa versatur et infinitis conficitur observationibus." The passage is part of a letter to Lodovico degli Alidosi, as a propaedeutic to literary disciplines, in which the arduous nature of eloquence is emphasized: "eloquentia rarior sapientia est, difficiliorem eam esse sapientia non inconvenienter possumus arbitrari."

56 Cf. ibid., vol. 2, p. 350 (ep. VII, 22, of 1392): "Hec doceat pleno quo fonte et origine nobis / rerum signa fluant et que totiformia vocum / corpora coniungant varientque elementa noteque / quaque sumul coeant ratione et federe verba."

57 Ibid., vol. 3, p. 158 (ep. IX, 24), in regard to whether it should be written as *cunctus* or *cuntus*. Salutati concludes by proposing a playful etymology: "potest dicere descendere a *cunctor*, idest moror, quoniam omnia scire vel digerere morosum est."

58 Cf., for example, ibid., vol. 2, p. 308 (ep. VII, 13), in regard to the length of the syllable *nu* of *nutrio*: "et si negatur illa derivatio [that is, "nutu erudio" by the *Catholicon*], que potius videtur esse ad placitum inventa quam aliqua ratione detorta, imo longe magis etymologia quam compositio vel derivatio dici debet, secundum regulam relinquitur inter breves."

59 Ibid., vol. 2, p. 188 (ep. VI, 14): "Vult omnium etatum consuetudo et hominum eruditorum usus 'quem penes arbitrium est et ius et norma loquendi'" (cf. Horatius, *Ars poetica*, 71–72). The topic is the issue of whether *Evangelium* should be written with one or two *u*'s: "Quod sic [that is, with only one *u*] debere fieri vult auctor libri *Catholicon*, vult et Brito in libello *De difficilibus vocabulis Biblie*, vult omnium etatum consuetudo . . ." etc.

60 Ibid., vol. 3, p. 611 (ep. XIII, 3): "Tenenda proprietas, que maxime provenit ex origine . . . et appropriatio, quam usus gignit, nullatenus ignoranda." In addition to the possibility of assigning modern meanings to words, it is also possible to coin new ones, which is part of the baggage of rules for whoever is learning a language. Cp. in this regard vol. 3, p. 130 (ep. IX, 16, of 1396), to Jacopo Angeli of Scarperia on studying Greek: "ut cognoscas et in promptu teneas dictiones quid dicant quidve consignificent . . . percipiarisque canones omnium declinationum et compositionum, quibus significative voces vel arte vel usu coniunguntur et generantur, quo facile possis non solum inventa cognoscere, sed etiam per temet tum vocabula cudere, tum si fuerit commodum combinare."

61 I of course do not affirm the originality of Salutati's grammatical precepts (such as "ab amplificatione consuetudinis non recedas"); and even less do I wish to enter directly into the argument of his contribution to grammatical awareness and methods. Rather it is important for us to point out the characteristic value of such assumptions in the framework of his overall cultural orientation. Cf. in this regard vol. 2, p. 200 (ep. IV, 18), interesting for the comparison that can be made to the position Valla would later take on the same subject (see below, n. 127). Salutati here explains the meaning of the term *persona* in the writings of Valerius Maximus: "Licet ego 'persona' communiori acceptione significet 'naturam individue rationalis substantie' [that is according to the definition of Boethius], quam Greci *hypostasin* spetiali vocabulo dicunt, ibi tamen denotat *habitum*, quo alius ab illo, qui vere subest, representatur."

62 Cf. in particular ibid., vol. 4, pp. 126 ff. (ep. XIV, 13, of 1406 to Poggio Bracciolini, whom he scolds for too little attention to Petrarchesque eloquence), from which the following considerations are paraphrased.

63 Ibid., p. 134: "superlativus excessus unius, non plurium esse potest."

64 It would not be appropriate to define the concept alluded to here, except with a large grain of salt, as "progress"; rather it would be better understood as a historical rela-

tivism that mitigates the principle of authority: "Scio quod in his scientiis [that is, the philosophical ones], ne processus conveniat esse in infinitum, opus est quod unum aliquem habeamus qui locum sublimiorem obtineat, et quem nobis velut fixum aliquid proponamus. Talem habemus nostris his temporibus Aristotelem Abderitem; prius autem reputabatur ab omnibus Plato . . . Qui Platonem recipit, omnes damnat qui Platoni multis ante temporibus, magna licet cum gloria, processerunt. Cur tu et alii, quibus antiquitas ita placet, propter Platonem vel Aristotelem derogatis? . . . Parum est quod in his laudatur quod possint dicere suum esse; vix enim dicere potuerunt: hoc recens est . . . ; et etas nostra quid loquitur, quid disputat, quid addiscit nisi vetera queve illi, quibus tantum tribuis, a prioribus accepere?" Thus this apparent concept of progress ends up with a relativistic "nihil sub sole novum." On medieval formulations of the issue, cf. S. Spörl, "Das Alte und das Neue im Mittelalter," *Historisches Jahrbuch* 4 (1930): 297 ff.; W. Freund, *Modernus und andere Zeitbegriffe des Mittelalters* (Cologne, 1957); and, more recently, *Antiqui und Moderni: Traditionsbewußtein im späten Mittelalter*, ed. A. Zimmermann (Berlin, 1974) (Miscellanea mediavalia, vol. 9).

65 *Epistolario*, vol. 4, p. 138: "Satis eloquens in eo quod scit quilibet esse debet, nisi penitus desipiat et ignarus sit."

66 Ibid., p. 142: "Facundia, quanquam differentia varietur, facundia, id est eloquentia est."

67 Ibid., vol. 4, p. 148 (ep. xiv, 21, of 1406, to Leonardo Bruni): "sed antiquitatem sic semper censui imitandam, quod pura non prodeat, sed aliquid semper secum afferat novitatis"; "vincant vel saltem redoleant vetustatem"; "sed aliud est referre, aliud imitari."

68 Ibid.: "latine quidem constat et ex toto non ipsam refugit vetustatem."

69 Cf. Leonardo Bruni, "Dialogi ad Petrum Histrum," in *Prosatori latini del Quattrocento*, ed. E. Garin (Milan, 1952), p. 54: "Ego quidem, Coluci, in hac faece temporum atque in hac tanta librorum desideratione, quam quis facultatem disputandi assequi possit, non video. Nam quae bona ars, quae doctrina reperiri potest in hoc tempore, quae non aut loco mota sit, aut omnino profiligata?" Bruni's *Dialogues* can now be read in two recent editions with critical comments: *Dialogi ad Petrum Paulum Histrum*, critical edition by S. U. Baldassarri (Florence, 1994); and L. Bruni, *Opere letterarie e politiche*, ed. P. Viti (Turin, 1996), pp. 74–143, with the Latin and Italian texts. See also the English translation in *The Humanism of Leonardo Bruni: Selected Texts*, ed. G. Griffith, J. Hankins, and D. Thompson (New York, 1987), pp. 63–84. On the issue of dating and interpreting Bruni's writing, see also my essay "All'uscita dalla Scolastica medievale: Salutati, Bruni, e i 'Dialogi ad Petrum Histrum,'" *Archivio storico italiano* 51 (1992): 1065–1103 (also in Fubini, *L'umanesimo italiano e i suoi storici*, pp. 75–103).

70 Cf. Bruni's *Epistolae*, ep. I, 14, Mehus ed., vol. 1, p. 29: "Cum enim arbitrium, ius, norma loquendi penes usum consistat [cf. above, n. 59], quis efficacius quam doctissimi et expertissimi homines et in dicendo maxime comprobati possunt de hoc usu testimonium perhibere? Indoctorum enim corruptela non usus loquendi appellandus est, sed abusio . . . Quod si nullam rationem invenerimus cur ita diceretur, tamen usus excellentium virorum pro ratione esset habendus." Cf. also Luiso, *Studi*, p. 22.

71 Ibid.: "a vulgari consuetudine loquendi mentem avocare."

72 Cf., for example, Bruni's ep. viii, 2 (Mehus ed., vol. 2, pp. 107 f.), where Bruni still

defends the spelling form *michi,* relying on the custom, and in particular on the usage of his teacher Salutati.

73 On this issue, cf. especially "Vita di Francesco Petrarca," in L. Bruni, *Humanistisch-philosophische Schriften,* ed. H. Baron (Leipzig, 1928), pp. 63–67; and now in *Opere letterarie,* pp. 553–60; *The Humanism of L. Bruni,* pp. 95–100.

74 Cf. ep. VI, 10 (Mehus ed., vol. 2, p. 62), where Bruni indicates as an exclusive matter of consideration the period from Terentius to Cicero in Rome: "Pressius quoque, si placet, ista curcumscribamus, ut certo tempore locoque diffiniantur. Nam qui 'apud veteres' dicit nec tempus nec locum satis certum designat. Sit igitur quaestio utrum Romae per Terentii poetae et M. Tullii tempora vulgus ita loquebatur, ut loquuntur hi quos nunc latine litterateque loqui dicimus, vel alius fuerit vulgi, alius litteratorum." See Tavoni, p. 216, §§ 3–4.

75 Ibid., p. 63. Bruni refers to the duality of the synonymous forms *Bellum* and *Duellum;* furthermore he adds: "Varro 'villam' a 'veho' dictam putat; adducit vero coniecturam quod rustici pro 'villa' 'vella' dicunt, pro 'vectura' quoque 'vellatura.'" Cf. M. T. Varro, *De re rustica,* 1.2.14.

76 But it should also be remarked that Bruni's arguments (which I refer to first, according to the needs of my exposition) are devised as a reply, or precise retort, to the specific statements by Biondo, to the point of openly switching the cards on the table, so that we are prevented from taking it in too literal a sense. For example, Biondo speaks about a natural grammar, and Bruni responds by introducing the differences between Latin and the vernacular, and the difficulty of learning Latin grammar; the one recalls how Latin orators express themselves correctly by instinct, and then speaks of how the Latin language became corrupted, and the other, changing point of view, introduces the argument: "Nam et habet vulgaris sermo commendationem suam, ut apud Dantem poetam et alios quosdam emendate loquentes apparet" (p. 65). In addition it is worth noting that *latinity* is understood by Bruni also as a sign of distinction of a high social and political dignity: orators could also speak Latin (*litterate*) in the presence of the public; but this term meant both the gentlemen and the crowd: "neque enim appellatione populi turba solum et infimae sortis homines, sed nobiles et ignobiles significabantur . . . Non ad pistores et lanistas, sed multo magis ad eos qui in reipublicae gubernatione versabantur, et quorum intererat quid populus decerneret, orator loquebatur" (p. 63; Tavoni, p. 217, §§ 12–13). This is a characteristic expression of the aristocratic republicanism of the Florentine Chancellor, and perhaps this is also valid for the political implications of his thesis on the language.

77 Biondo, *De verbis,* p. 125 (Tavoni, p. 209, § 72): "Memineris velim verborum non characterum, locutionis non compositionis, corticis non medullae artis disputationem a me institutam esse."

78 That is, *latinitas* as an equivalent of "melior stilus" and as a system of grammatical rules.

79 Ibid., p. 123 (Tavoni, p. 206, § 58): "vulgare aetatis nostrae loquendi genus, cuius gloriam inter Florentinos esse concesserim."

80 Ibid., p. 126 (Tavoni, p. 210, § 78): "vicinitatem similitudinemque vulgari et latino sermoni permaximam."

81 Ibid., p. 118 (Tavoni, p. 200, § 20): "Nulli debet videri dubium quin, si altera lingua

quam si placet velim appelles vulgarem, dictum fuisset quod postea in hanc latinam numerositatem orationis est positum, M. Cicero, Quinitilianus, Q. Asconius Pedianus et alii plurimi, quibus oratorum quaeque minima referre cura fuit, hanc etiam orationis diversitatem aliqualiter innuissent: quod nostra et patrum nostrorum aetate factitatum vidimus de Florentini Dantis *Comoediis,* de luculentis Bocachii fabulis . . . , quae cum grammitico astricto regulis sermone scripta videmus, in latinitatem dicimus esse conversa." Biondo is alluding to the essays on Latin translations of the *Divine Comedy,* such as that of the monk Matteo Ronto (cf. Rossi, *Il Quattrocento,* p. 109), and to the various translations of some tales of the *Decameron,* by Petrarch, Bruni, and others. Biondo's argument would then have been repeated often (in the sense that another language would also have had another name) but no longer with the happy relevance of the passage above.

82 Cf. ibid., p. 123 (Tavoni, p. 206, § 58): "Magni interesse audivisti quos quisque domi audiat, quibuscum loquatur [cf. Cicero, *Brutus* 58.210–211]. Opinor non negabis in vulgari aetatis nostrae loquendi genere . . . multo facundiores esse qui honesto nati loco, ab urbanis educati parentibus et civilibus innutriti sint officiis, quam caeteram ignavae aut rusticanae multitudinis turbam: cumque eisdem verbis sermonem utrique conficiant, suaviloquentia unum placere multitudini, incondito garritu alterum displicere." It is significant that while Cicero places the accent on the transmission of an uncorrupted linguistic tradition, Biondo insists instead on the tones of the language as a sign of social distinction. This is indeed a sentiment typical of the Renaissance rather than of Roman antiquity. Cf. on this issue R. A. Hall Jr., "Linguistic Theory in the Italian Renaissance," *Language* 12 (1936): 96–108 (which refers however to the discussions of the sixteenth century). As a remote precedent I can cite the "sociological" medieval interpretation of the theory of the three styles, referred respectively to the social classes of the *curiales,* the *civiles,* and the *rurales;* cf. E. Faral, *Les arts poétiques du XIIe et XIIIe siècles* (Paris, 1924), pp. 86 ff.

83 Cf. A. Pagliaro, "I 'primissima signa' nella dottrina linguistica di Dante," *Nuovi saggi di critica semantica* (Messina, 1956), p. 234.

84 For the above-mentioned reasons, the real meaning of the pertinent passages by Cicero is understood in a somewhat rigid and schematic manner, and therefore, at least in part, misunderstood. Cf. on the question of the duplicity of forms *Duellum* and *Bellum* (p. 120): "[Cicero] licentiam in ea re multitudinis ostendit de qua statim plurima intulit eum habentia sensum, ut ornate nedum litteraliter dicere, si volumus, trito loquendi usu populo concedamus, scientiam, ut de seipso dicit, nobis reservemus." Cicero, instead, *Orator* 48.160, had written: "Aliquando, idque sero, cum extorta mihi veritas esset, usum loquendi populo concessi, scientiam mihi reservavi." Where, that is, Cicero declares that he is going to abandon the "science" ("ut nusquam nisi in vocali aspiratione uterentur") for the euphony of popular usage, Biondo interprets this passage as a contrast between "licentia" and "scientia," which was— the latter—necessary anyway (if I interpret the passage correctly, as it is not entirely clear, as edited by Nogara and accepted by Tavoni, p. 202, § 34).

85 Biondo, *De verbis,* p. 123 (Tavoni, p. 204, § 45): "Quem Romani primam loquendi consuetudinem communem habuerunt dictionem, bonarum artium studiis excolentes nonnulli reddiderunt meliorem."

86 Ibid., p. 126 (Tavoni, p. 210 § 81): "Quidquid leporis, quidquid suavitatis, quidquid energiae poemati inerat, translatione ipsa corruptum evanuisset, et tanquam in minus sincerum vas acescere coepisset." Another argument that Biondo adopted (p. 128) to confirm the institutional reality of Latin was the survival, like archeological relics, of Latin inflections and terminology in the spoken dialects in central and south Italy and in Rome itself, particularly noticeable to an observer from northern Italy. These inflections did not correspond to orthodox grammatical construction but nevertheless appeared to him to conceal the elegance of the Latin phrase and insert themselves in an opportune context in accord with that regularity that is mainly innate in every speech, no matter how coarse it may be: "Quamquam omnibus ubique apud Italos corruptissima etiam vulgaritate loquentibus idiomatis natura insitum videmus, ut nemo tam rusticus, nemo tam rudis tamque ingenio hebes sit, qui modo loqui possit, quin aliqua ex parte tempora, casus modosque et numeros noverit dicendo variare, prout narrandae rei tempus ratioque videbuntur postulare" (Tavoni, p. 213, § 100). This observation seemed to C. Trabalza, *Storia della grammatica italiana* (Milan, 1908), p. 16, to be a sufficiently important point to open the way to the study of Italian grammar. But in the context it has no programmatic value: rather it is brought up for the purpose of distinguishing the two levels, the grammatical-normative and the empirical-institutional, so that Biondo's remark presupposes the constant term of reference of the antonomastic grammar, that is: Latin grammar. Likewise the observation of the Latin imprint on living spoken dialects is part of a concern that is archeological rather than linguistic history in the proper sense: he is talking about fragments that have survived even though incomplete and that are recognizable, according to Cicero's suggestions, more in women than in men: "Viros tamen ibi [in Rome] a cursu loquendi pristino quam mulieres magis deflexisse ideo crediderim, quia minorem ipsae cum externis rarioremque sermonis consuetudinem habent" (p. 128).

87 Ibid., p. 127 (Tavoni, p. 212, § 93): "Nec didicisse, nec naturae aut bonae consuetudinis munere regulas indoctam multitudinem scivisse, quibus grammaticam orationem omni ex parte congruam faceret, neque etiam tam longe a variationibus inclinationibusque et reliqua grammaticae orationis compostione illius latinitatem abfuisse, quin litterata, qualem mediocriter aetate nostra docti habent, oratio et videretur et esset."

88 Ibid., p. 129 (Tavoni, p. 214, § 107). The notion of a "mixed language" goes back at least as far as Isidore of Seville (*Etymologiae* 9.3.7); and references to the influence of barbaric languages on modern spoken languages can be found in Dante, *De vulgari eloquentia* 1.15.4. On the other hand, the equivalency of "barbarity" with linguistic mistakes and departures from correct Latin was an obvious and old notion (cf. D. Hay, "Italy and Barbaric Europe," in *Italian Renaissance Studies,* ed. E. F. Jacob [London, 1960], pp. 54–58). What is new, however, is the identification of barbarization as a historic cutoff point. This corresponds strictly to the thesis later formulated by Biondo himself, of the "decline" (*inclinatio*) of the empire as datable from the first barbarian incursion into Rome.

89 Ibid., p. 129 (Tavoni, p. 214 f., § 110): "Postea vero quam urbs a Gothis Vandalisque capta inhabitarique coepta est, non unus aut duo infuscati, sed omnes sermone barbarico inquinati ac poenitus sordidati fuerunt; sensimque factum est ut pro Romana

latinitate adulterinam hanc barbarica mixtam loquelam habeamus vulgarem." Baron, *The Crisis* (1955), p. 304, writes in this regard: "Biondo in addition to much critical penetration and superior learning, displayed the typical classicist's disdain of a language alienated from ancient standards." But the statement should be completed by recalling that for Biondo, as well as for Guarino, who expressed himself in the same terms, the *volgare* meant also and especially the personal experience of native northern Italian dialects, and that they were referring in any case to the various domains of the Italian dialects, and not to the literary language. The "disdain" does not imply therefore a literary judgment but is applicable to an actual situation, inasmuch as it was related to the ancient existence of a unitary language of culture.

90 Cf. Francisci Philelphi, *Epistolarum libri XXXVII* (Venice, 1502), ff. 61v–62v (Tavoni, pp. 274–280): ". . . de huius nostrae tempestatis lingua, quam alii Ethruscam, alii vulgarem vocant, nonnulli sermonis materni aut illitterati nomine appellant; . . . latinam linguam vulgarem fuisse, non litteralem."

91 Ibid., ff. 259v–262r (Tavoni, pp. 281–96).

92 That the need for a further historical understanding of Latin was already felt is witnessed by the proposal by Biondo himself, amazing for its time even though it was not followed up, to the Benedictine monk Girolamo Aliotti in 1445, to write a history of Latin in the Middle Ages up to the recent revival: "ut declinationem linguae latinae, postquam fluere in deterius coepit eiusque propagationem a paucis retro annis, tamquam ab inferis excitatam adgrediar scribere" (cf. H. Aliottus O.S.B., *Epistulae et Opuscula*, ed. G. M. Scarmaglii (Aretii, 1769), vol. 1, p. 148). This passage was pointed out by A. Willmans, *Göttingische gelehrten Anzeigen*, vol. 2 (1879), p. 491. We can link this episode with the interest in the history of language still displayed by Biondo in his *Italia illustrata* (*Opera* [Basel, 1559], p. 374), where, referring to the "Marchia Tarvisina," he went back to the tract *De verbis Romanae locutionis*, in order to correct his previous opinion on the corruption by the Goths and Vandals; now, having seen the laws of the Lombards (*visis Langobardorum legibus*), he thought that the essential changes should have been charged to this latter people.

93 Cf. Guarino, *Epistolario,* vol. 2, pp. 503 ff., to Leonello d'Este, of 1449 (Tavoni, pp. 228–38); Franciscus Floridus Sabinus, "Lectionum succissivarum," chap. 2, 1, *Opera* (Basel, 1540), pp. 185 ff.

94 Accolti is obviously influenced by Biondo in claiming modern traditions as deserving of being elevated to historical dignity; cf. B. Accolti, *Dialogus de praestantia virorum sui aevi . . .* , ed. Galletti (Florence, 1847), p. 112; on this subject, see my essay, "Leonardo Bruni e la discussa recezione dell'opera: Giannozzo Manetti e i 'Dialogus' di Benedetto Accolti," in Fubini, *L'umanesimo italiano e i suoi storici,* pp. 104–29.

95 Ibid.: "et hi perpauci numero erant, qui ex oratorum communi grege longius emersi multum operis praestabant, et qui editas orationes suas posteritati reliquerunt."

96 Ibid.: "reliquos cives dum de rebus magnis consulebant, non absimiles eloquio nostro fuisse reor."

97 Ibid.: "Nec multifacio qua quis lingua, materna scilicet an latina, proloquatur, modo graviter ornate copioseque pronuntiet."

98 Angelo Decembrio, *Politia literaria* (Basel, 1562), p. 37: "Qui modus ordoque servandus in curanda poliendoque bibliotheca."

99 *Politia literaria,* p. 37: the mention of Apuleius, whose style, "varius, incompositus rigidusque," was judged unsuitable for a Latin author, is the starting point for turning the discussion to the vernacular. Decembrio maintains that the Latin style cannot be reduced to the vernacular, and therefore he condemns the courtly fashion of the vulgarizations to the benefit of the princes and unlearned men. According to Decembrio, this praxis corresponds to the erroneous conviction of being able to confer grace and eloquence on popular speech, and that such fashion can only result in "making some poor vernacular works from good Latin authors" (*ex latinis bonis vulgares non bonos reddidisse*), with reference to the Italian translations of the classics.

100 Ibid.: "namque a quo veterum unquam audivimus opus materno sermone compositum?" In regard to the difficulty of understanding Latin as a language that extended over the area of the empire, we may recall that "Ioannis Iscerensis" (that is, more precisely, Serra), "praeclarum ex Aragonia virum," mentioned by Valla, "Recriminationes in Facium," *Opera* (Basel, 1540), p. 463 (but see now *Antidotum in Facium,* ed. M. Regoliosi [Padua, 1981], p. 13): "cum iste conaretur multos aetatis nostrae scriptores praeponere Senecae in notitia atque usu linguae latinae, neque hunc latino ore locutum vellet."

101 Ibid.: "si scriptorum plurimam in stylo differentiam advertimus, sequereturque magis nullos ludi magistros vel praeceptores apud veteres extitisse, quorum sapenumero mentionem ab iisdem fieri videmus, cum domestico sermone inter plebemque versando id quotidiano usu facile consequi potuissent."

102 Cf. *Politia literaria,* p. 40 (Tavoni, p. 227, § 179): "Alius quippe eis locus assignandus est cum Gualfredis Gualteriisque similibus, cum Cassiodoris et Isidoris palatini styli lampade . . . corruscantibus."

103 It seems likely to me that this image of the library comes from Petrarch *Seniles* 2.10: "Nugellas meas vulgares non patienter modo nec lete, non dubito, cupideque atque aliqua vel extrema bibliothece tue parte dignabere."

104 Filelfo, *Epistolarum,* f. 61v (Tavoni, p. 275, § 9): "Litteralis (sermo) limatior est fortasse et proprius magis quam maternus, non alius tamen omninoque diversus quo ad dictionum varietatem, declinationem, enunciationem, desinentiam." In this regard, he introduces the example of the word *parentes,* which in the "literal" Latin means "parents," while in vulgar Latin (as witnessed by St. Jerome) it means "relatives"; or the Greek example *agathòn andra,* which "bonum virum significat apud doctos"; while Greek people "pro viro stulto vulgi consuetudine accipiunt." Furthermore, the poets spoke their own language, with the exception of the dramatic authors, "qui toti erant populares," "alia quadam lingua multis in locis loqui existimati sunt"; while the comedy, "ea non grammatice, sed latine referebant," since the grammatical language (the *literatura*) "plerisque in locis obscurior est, et latinitas omnibus nota" (f. 62r; Tavoni, p. 277, § 21).

105 *Epistolario di Guarino veronese,* ep. 813, to Leonello d'Este, 27 July 1449, vol. 2, p. 505: "quamque nequaquam latinam proptera vocabimus."

106 Cf. *Etymologiae* 9.1.3: "Tres sunt linguae sacrae, Hebraea, Graeca et Latina, quae toto orbe maxime excelluerunt"; and ibid., 1.3.5: "Literae latinae et graecae ab Hebraeis videntur exortae." In Guarino, however, the notion of the "sacred languages" is omitted, and the privilege becomes, so to speak, secularized (as, I do believe, under the

influence of Valla): "Cum multae multiplicesque linguae sint, e quibus tres principatum semper tenuisse videbar, Hebraicam, Graecam et huius filiam Latinam" etc. The close relationship established by Guarino between Latin and Greek, through generalizing and modifying his Isidorian guideline, is also noteworthy. Still from Isidore (*Etymologiae* 9.3.6–7) Guarino draws the outline of the four historical-mythical ages of the Latin language: the "prisca" (using vernacular words, but in 'literate' form); the "latina" (typical of the ancient Italic peoples, "grammatical," but by custom and not by reason); the "romana" ("idest 'robustam' appellaverim: in ea tot effloruere poetae, oratores, historici"); and finally the "mixta" ("quam potius corruptionem linguae quis dixerit").

107 Cf. *Epistolario,* vol. 2, p. 582 (ep. 862, of 1452): "Deus, nostram miseratus imperitiam, Manuelem Chrysoloram misit ad nos . . . Is, delatus Florentiam . . . , ex ea urbe coepit, sicut Triptolemus alter, litterarum fruges per nostrorum ingenia dispertiri et nostrates ad colendum animare, unde germinantia late semina brevi fructus mirificos edidere . . . Longa ita desuetudine infuscatus ante latinus sermo et inquinata dictio Chrysolorinis fuerat pharmacis expurganda et admoto lumine illustranda." Cf. also ibid., vol. 1, p. 54 (of 1416), for the idea of Greece and Byzantium as the core of European civilization: "orbis terrarum Europa, Europae Graecia, Greciae regina urbs Byzantii est."

108 Cf. *Facetiae,* Poggio, *Opera,* p. 420.

109 Poggio Bracciolini, "Disceptatio convivalis tertia," *Opera,* p. 53 s. (Tavoni, pp. 240, §§ 12–16; 246): "Quaero a vobis quam linguam appelletis latinam, eam quam grammaticam vocamus, a quibus ortum habuisse putetis. Nempe opinor illam quae Latini populi utebantur et ab eis ortam, illaque eos fuisse usos qui dicebantur Latini, e quibus nomen sortita est . . . in usu fuisse communi necesse est. Nam sicut linguam dicimus Gallicam, Hispanam, Germanam, Italam, qua Galli, Hispani, Germani, Itali loquuntur . . . Latina insuper lingua ex verbis constat, quibus eum sermonem conficiebant Latini . . . 'Omnes prope praeclare locutos, quorum sermone assuefacti, quae erant ne cupientes quidem potuerunt loqui nisi latine.'" Poggio's quotation is from Cicero *De oratore* 3.10.39.

110 Ibid., p. 53: "multa me Romae audisse inter loquendem vocabula quae antea ignorabam." At the mention of Latin terms that Poggio heard from the Roman populace (for example "lupus tyberinus," which a fish peddlar explained to the ignorant author meant "sturgeon"), there follows the acknowledgment of traces of Latin that have survived in Spanish and Rumanian. Walser, p. 261, in this regard points out: "While Poggio draws from vernacular words their own Latin etymology, he really gives birth to Romance philology." However, more than an overstatement, this is incorrect: it is not etymological, albeit embryonic research, into the living body of a language; it is instead somewhat of an empirical lexical archeology, just as I already noted with regard to Biondo (n. 86 above); or, in other words, a search for a more or less extensive survival of Latin lexical relics beneath any later superimposition ("in tanta diversarum . . . gentium colluvione . . . veluti reliquias veteris linguae").

111 Ibid., p. 55: "docti ratione iudicabant quod alii usu assequebantur."

112 Ibid., pp. 53, 59 (Tavoni, p. 250, § 83): "qui pure, simpliciter, incorrupte loquebantur, palmam eloquentiae ferebant."

113 Cf. "In Pogium dialogus secundus" (of 1453), L. Valla, *Opera* (Basel, 1540) (*Opera omnia,* ed. E. Garin, vol. 1 [Turin, 1962], pp. 379–90; Tavoni, pp. 260–73), dedicated to a punctual confutation of Poggio's "Disceptatio convivalis."

114 Ibid., p. 384 (Tavoni, p. 265, § 38): "Vides ut latine loqui est oratorum et eruditorum, et plus etiam quam grammatice? Ideoque 'latine loqui' inter virtutes rhetoricae ponitur, ut grammatica sit locutionis, latinitas elucutionis."

115 *Institutio oratoria* 1.5.23: "aliud latine, aliud grammaice loqui."

116 "In Pogium," p. 387 (Tavoni, p. 270, §§ 65–66): "(Quintilianus) non ratione nititur sed exemplo . . . 'nec lex loquendi sed observatio, ut ipsam analogiam nulla res alia fecerit quam consuetudo.' Cum dico 'analogiam' quicquid paene est in grammatica complector . . . Vides ut vix reddi ratio possit grammaticae, quam tu vis totam constare ratione." Cf. against this passage Poggio, "Disceptatio," p. 55 (Tavoni, p. 243, § 38): "Quibus constat omnes latine sed non omnes grammatice loqui solitos; cum latinam linguam omnibus tribuat (*sc.* Quintilian), grammaticam, hoc est loquendi doctrinam, litterarum peritis."

117 Ibid., p. 385 (Tavoni, p. 266, § 44): "cur dicas emendatius non video. Alius alio ornatius, sublimius, eloquentius fateor, sed non latinius, si omnium Romanorum sic erat communis lingua latina, ut nunc est civitatum sua cuiusque vernacula."

118 Cf. especially Valla's *Antidota in Pogium, Opera,* p. 295: "Certe quae nunc lingua in usu Romanis est, latina appellanda est, etsi multum degeneravit ab illa prisca. Non enim credibile est aliam quandam, nescio unde, venisse linguam et illam veterem deiecisse et in exilium relegasse"; and also "Dialogus," p. 388, and passim.

119 "Dialogus," p. 388 (Tavoni, p. 273, § 85): "Quae natio, si quondam more literatorum loquebatur [as it is confirmed by plurals ending in -*s*: "quo nullum maius indicium est gentem illam olim grammatice locutam"], cur nec ipsa inflectionem . . . casuum . . . nec participia quaedam atque gerundia supinaque, nec derivandi nisi in paucis usum, nec alia plurima quae grammatica praecipit custodivit? Unde articulos quos lingua latina non habet adscivit, quemadmodum et Roma et Italia et Gallia?" Through establishing, at least as a wish, a comparison between the old and the new language on a grammatical and morphological basis, Valla undoubtedly anticipated modern scholarly methods in far greater measure than, for example, Poggio. To use Walser's words, he marks the beginnings of the "romanische Philologie."

120 This is particularly noticeable in book 6 of the *Elegantiae,* dedicated to essays in semantic interpretation, through correcting definitions especially by grammarians and jurists, in order to be of use to students in showing not only proper usage but also errors in interpretation: "quo prodessem aliquid linguam discere volentibus non modo ex nostris praeceptis, sed ex aliorum quoque erratis." According to Valla, every term has its own fundamental meaning from which it is wrong to depart. See, for example, *Elegantiae* 6.12: "*Laetum* Servio placet multa significare: 'foecundum,' 'pingue,' 'gravidum,' 'pulchrum,' 'viride' et multa alia. Sed ipse rationem reddam, cur in varios sensus abutamur, cum unum natura significet. 'Laetum' id appellamus quod aspectu gaudium promit" etc.; cp. also *Elegantiae* 6.36, on the distinction between *munus* and *donum,* contrary to the opinion of jurists; or the confutation of Boethius on the distinction between *persona* and *substantia,* in 6.34: "In Deo personam ponimus . . . cum nullum aliud vocabulum quadrat." In this sense the work of the emendator may be

equated to that of the inventor: "Itaque eum qui emendat non inferiorem existimari debemus quam ipsum illum inventorem, nec minorem ab illo quam ab hoc percipi fructum" (preface to book 6).

121   "Dialogus," p. 487 (Tavoni, p. 272, § 82): "Quales (*sc.* tardiori ingenio) si non sumus sed veteribus pares, unde fit ut vulgus . . . non possit ullo pacto conservare, imo consequi et imitari sonum literatorum vocum . . . ?" Cf. also the preface to book 1 of the *Elegantiae* (*Prosatori latini*, p. 598): "et multae quidem sunt prudentium hominum variaeque sententiae unde hoc rei acciderit, quarum ipse nullam nec improbo nec probo, nihil sane pronuntiare ausus; non magis quam cur illae artes, quae proximae ad liberales accedunt, tamdiu tantoque opere degeneraverint . . . aut brevi tempore excitentur ac reviviscant."

122   Cf. *Antidota in Pogium* 1. cit.: "Certe quae nunc lingua in usu Romanis est, latina appellanda est, etsi multum degeneravit ab illa prisca . . . Cum videmus idem contigisse in lingua grammatice loquentium, quam tu latinam vocas, quae adeo ab illa veteri differt, ut vix eam Cicero si a mortuis redeat queat intelligere."

123   Cf., for example, *Elegantiae* 2.17, on the reasons for the confusion of the conjunction *aut* with the interrogative *an:* where Valla wonders whether confusion stems from the analogy with Greek ("quod caput huius erroris est"), or with the vernacular ("quod reperiunt apud nos in interrogando *aut*").

124   Cf., for example, *Elegantiae* 1.22, on the verbs in *-sco:* "Grammatici uno ore universi aiunt illa verba in *-sco* significare inchoationem; . . . idiomate quoque italico atque hispano (quod ex italico oriundum est) adstipulante, apud quod paene latina voce haec verba pronuntiantur, et certe in hunc quem ego dico sensum, quale est hoc: *ogni dì magrisco,* hoc est 'omni die magrisco,' per quod incrementum assiduum atque continuum derivatur, non inchoatio." It would seem, as Sabbadini points out in *Epistolario di Guarino,* vol. 3, p. 410, that Valla maintains that Spanish derived from Italian. But this statement is contradicted in the passage cited above (n. 109) from the "Dialogus," where traces of Latin grammar are found in the very structure of the Spanish tongue, and in any case this very notion is hinted at in the parenthesis: "apud quos latine paene voce . . ." etc. Therefore *Italicus,* this latter time, is to be understood in a broader sense as a synonym for "Latin," and the meaning should be: "Spanish, having the same italic roots," etc.

125   Cf., for example, *Elegantiae* 6.44: "Neque recte iureconsulti excipiunt 'stuprum' a nupta, cum etiam in quotidiano sic sermone loquamur."

126   Cf. *Elegantiae,* preface to book 3 (*Prosatori latini*, p. 610): "ut linguam latinam dedocerent . . . , nihil aliud docentes quam gothice dicere." Here for the first time in humanism the notion of "gothic" as a disparaging qualification of a cultural age is pronounced, undoubtedly referring to and discussing Biondo's thesis of the vernacular as a product of barbaric corruption ("quemadmodum aliqui puntant"). See E. S. De Beer, "Gothic: Origin and Diffusion of the Term," *Journal of the Warburg and Courtauld Institutes* 9 (1948): 143–62; and also n. 89 above.

127   Cf. *Elegantiae* 6.34: "Tales qualitates statuo in Deo, et has dico esse 'personas,' quae ab eo abesse non possunt, et 'qualitatem' significare, non 'substantiam,' ut Boethius voluit, qui nos barbare loqui docuit. Hinc forsitan adductum vulgus ut sic loquatur:

'tres personas me expectant,' 'hic est bona persona,' qui sermo antea fuit inauditus, et hodie nemo nisi imperitus omnino sic loquiitur." See also above, n. 82.

128 Cf. the edition by L. Vahlen, *Sitzungsberichte der k. Akademie der Wissenschaften,* vol. 62 (Vienna, 1869), pp. 93–98 (*Opera omnia,* vol. 2, pp. 281–86); but see the new critical edition with Italian translation and a rich commentary both philological and historical: Lorenzo Valla, *Orazione per l'inaugurazione dell'anno accademico, 1455–1456,* Atti di un seminario di filologia umanistica a cura di S. Rizzo (Rome, 1994), pp. 190–216.

129 Ibid., p. 282; Rizzo ed., p. 194): "Namque ita natura comparatum est, ut nihil admodum proficere atque excrescere queat, quod non a pluribus componitur, elaboratur, excolitur, praecipue aemulantibus invicem et de laude certantibus."

130 Ibid.: "ab Apostolica Sede effectum esse ne illae (*scil.* scientiae) extinguerentur."

131 *Elegantiae* 3. praef.: "Ita per quotidianam lectionem *Digestorum* et semper aliqua ex parte incolumis atque in honore fuit lingua Romana, et brevi tempore dignitatem atque amplitudinem recuperabit."

132 Cf. Lorenzo il Magnifico, "Commento sopra alcuno dei suoi sonetti" (1484), *Opere,* ed. A. Simioni, vol. 1 (Bari, 1939), p. 32; Andrea Alciato, "Praetermissarum liber I" (1518), *Opera* (Basel, 1582), col. 265 ff.; Pietro Bembo, "Prose della volgar lingua" (1525), *Prose e rime,* ed. C. Dionisotti (Turin, 1960), pp. 80–89; Francesco Florido Sabino, *Opera,* p. 185 (see above, n. 93); on the author, cf. the bibliography by R. Abbondanza, "La giurisprudenza medievale nel giudizio dell'umanista F. Florido Sabino," *Il Mulino* 2 (1953): 654 ff.; Lodovico Castelvetro, "Giunta al libro I delle Prose del Bembo" (of 1563), together with *Corretione d'alcune cose del Dialogo delle lingue* (Basel, 1572), pp. 144 ff.; Celso Cittadini, "Trattato della vera origine e del processo e nome della nostra lingua" (of 1601), *Opere,* ed. G. Gigli (Rome, 1721). Among fifteenth-century authors the name of Filelfo is the one most often cited; the dispute is well known in particular by Castelvetro.

133 Cf. Claudio Tolomei, *Il Cesano* (Venice, 1556), pp. 47, 65.

134 As an antecedent, albeit indirect, to the dispute on what name to give the vernacular, the discussion between Poggio and Valla may be cited, as to whether the language should be called "Latin" or "Roman": that is, whether it should be defined as the language peculiar to Latin people, or as the one propagated and made noble by the Romans (cf. above, n. 108).

135 For the conception of language, so to speak, as a self-sufficient organism, see for example Castelvetro, *Giunta,* p. 148: he denies that Italians must learn Latin in order to improve the Italian language ("per la perfetione dell'italiano"), just as Romans in their own times did not study Greek for perfecting Latin; they studied Latin only in order to understand the literary works.

136 Cittadini, relying on the opinion of the learned of the eighteenth century, is still sometimes mentioned as the first to have set up the theory of popular Latin, from which the Italian tongue has its roots, rather than in literary Latin. But in fact, as some scholars have also observed, for his most innovative ideas Cittadini depends strictly on the authority of other writers, in particular on Tolomei (from whom on other occasions he plagiarized; cf. F. Sensi, *Archivio glottologico italiano,* vol. 12 [1890–92], pp. 441 ff.). See, for example, the comparison with the newly furnished house on

old walls (*Trattato*, p. 64; Tolomei, *Il Cesano*, p. 55); or the phonetic transformations he notes; or most of all the basic idea of the continuity of ways of speech and terms used by the people in the period when the commune of Rome still flowered, which were rejected by literary authors and orators and that are now no other than the present vulgar tongue ("modi del dire et voci usate dal volgo al tempo ancora che fioriva il Comune di Roma, li quali erano rifiutati dagli scrittori e da' dicitori nobili . . . Laonde . . . al presente linguaggio è rimasto il nome antico; cioè volgare, sì come convenevolissimo, poi che la lingua antica del volgo s'è conservata tra noi"); and by consequence the statement of a gradual transformation of language within the framework of Latinity itself (according to previous remarks by Castelvetro). Therefore, rather than a pioneer, Cittadini should be defined as a late representative of the vast linguistic-grammatical speculation of the sixteenth century. One need only read the *Trattato* attentively to realize that a really autonomous thought is lacking. For example, after having sternly assumed the substantial identity of the ancient and the modern vulgar speech ("only varied somewhat in the accidents"), he returns to the idea of contamination by barbaric and foreign languages, and of Italian as a new language (because of the evident influence of Tolomei; cf. *Trattato*, pp. 86 ff.). Moreover, after having defined literary Latin as a mere artificial construction, marginal to natural speech and bringing "violence" to it (p. 61), he ascribes linguistic corruption to the failure of a grammatical discipline. Finally, it is worth noting that Cittadini's treatise was conceived as a response to the by now obsolete question of the right name to be given the vulgar speech—which according to Cittadini should only be defined as such ———— and that it ends with a celebration of the excellence attained in both the parallel modes of expression, the Latin and the vernacular, and particularly of contemporary classicizing skill and of the Latin schools run by the religious orders.

2. Humanist Intentions and Patristic References

1   Cf. Bruni, *Humanistisch-philosophische Schriften*, pp. 99 f.: "Id fecimus, quod auctoritate tanti viri ignaviam ac perversitatem eorum cupiebamus refringere, qui studia humanitatis vituperant atque ab his omnino abhorrendum censent." With these words, Bruni, at the very beginning of the Quattrocento, aimed to sanction his own project of translating and publishing Greek texts, and in this light having recourse to patristic authority—which actually granted "to the pagan writers a value that did not go beyond the purely propedeutic" (H. von Campenhausen, *I Padri greci* [Brescia, 1967], p. 110)—seems obviously a specious argument. Bruni's introduction, in fact, does not even make reference to the main argument of the tract, the "choice," that is, to work in a context of ancient authors, "accepting from them only what is useful," and at the same time recognizing "what must be left aside" (cp. the edition by F. Boulenger [Paris, 1935], p. 42). Bruni's pugnacious preface, which is maintained in a Florentine vernacular translation of the middle-fifteenth century, does not appear in any other printed editions, and notably not in the one edited by G. Budé around 1505, which was of considerable importance for Northern Humanism (cf. Boulenger, p. 32; and

[P. Stromboli], "La orazione di San Basilio Magno, 'Degli studi liberali e de' nobili costumi,' volgarizzata da Antonio Ridolfi nel secolo XV," in *Per nozze Ridolfi Borgnini* [Florence, 1899], p. 13). Bruni's intention cannot therefore be assimilated to that of the Christian humanists, who adopted the translation, on which cf. L. Schucan, *Das Nachleben von Basilius Magnus' "Ad Adolecentes": Ein Beitrag zur Geschichte des christlichen Humanismus* (Geneva, 1973).

2 "qualem beatus Augustinus triumphantem videre desideravit." I will simply make reference here to my own entry, "Biondo Flavio," *Dizionario Biografico degli Italiani,* vol. 10 (1968), p. 552. At this point, I will not identify the specific passage that Biondo probably had in mind. It is nevertheless certain, by Biondo's own admission, that it does not refer to an argument nor to a specific passage by Augustine (cf. *Roma triumphans* [Basel, 1531], p. 212: "quam [formam triumphi] inspexisse Aurelium Augustinum optasse refertur"). Based on an examination of the index in Migne for Augustine's complete works, the term is found only, and rarely, in Christian metaphors (for example, *Sermones,* 163, 9, in Migne, P.L. XXXVIII, col. 892: "Triumphantis autem verba quae erunt? Verba certantis dum domus in ultimo aedificatur"); in contrast, see the ironic observation in *De civitate Dei,* 4.17: "Nam si Victoria dea est, cur non deus est et triumphus, et Victoriae iungitur vel maritus vel frater vel filius?"

3 Cf. Poggio Bracciolini, *Dialogus an seni sit uxor ducenda,* [ed. T. Tonelli] (Florence, 1823) (*Opera omnia,* vol. 2, pp. 673 ff.). The reference is to Jerome, *Adversus Iovinianum* 1.47 (P.L. XXIII, col. 276), in which the "aureolus Theophrasti liber De nuptiis" is cited. The same series of ancient wise men—"Socrati, Platoni, Aristoteli, Theophrasto et, e nostris, Catoni illo prisco, M. Tullio, Varroni, Senecae"—appears in the context of Poggio's text, but with a meaning opposite of the original one.

4 Aside from the most famous inquiries into terms like "persuadere" (5.30), or "persona" (6.34), there are some valuable indications in G. Martellotti, "Latinità del Petrarca," *Studi Petrarcheschi* 7 (1961): 219–30 (and now, G. Martellotti, *Scritti petrarcheschi,* ed. M. Feo and S. Rizzo [Padua, 1983], pp. 289–301): Martellotti precisely relies on Valla's discussions in order to determine the extent to which Petrarch was aware of the boundaries between classical and medieval usage: "Quando il Valla si ferma a condannare un costrutto perché non latino, ci dà con ciò stesso una testimonianza indiretta dell'uso dei suoi tempi; e citando Prisciano, come egli fa spesso con intento polemico, ci addita anche l'autorità grammaticale a cui tale uso si appoggiava" (p. 225).

5 Even recently scholars have insisted on the scholastic origin of the term "humanist." Among others, P. O. Kristeller has articulated with remarkable clarity the conception of humanism as a specific cycle of scholarly disciplines, destined as such to become institutionalized in the context and terminology of schools (cf. *La tradizione classica nel pensiero del Rinascimento* [Florence, 1965], pp. 8 ff., 145 f.). Nevertheless, just as a name is not necessarily the consequence of a reality, so the ideals that animate a cultural movement cannot be reduced to one of their specific and late pedagogical organizations. The view that maintains that there was a break of continuity between humanism and the traditional schools is also documented by G. Billanovich, "Auctorista, humanista, orator," *Rivista di cultura classica e medievale* 7 (1965): 143–63, according

to whom "gli allievi dei retori del nostro secondo Quattrocento . . . dovettero cercare un nome per questi loro maestri, e lo inventarono derivandolo dagli ormai proverbiali 'studia humanitatis' e 'studia humaniora'" (p. 157): terms which had come into being precisely because they had been adopted by figures outside of the schools, such as, apart from Petrarch, Salutati, and his pupils, Bruni and Poggio. But it would not even be correct to make the claim that the culture of the humanists had its origins in the professional training of the chanceries, in which the humanists were employed, both because the chancery and the school were never two completely distinct institutions, and because when viewed in a broader perspective, humanism from Petrarch onward was, from a strictly rhetorical standpoint, a reaction to the tradition of the *ars dictaminis,* which had not yet been completely eliminated from the ordinary chancery practices of the Quattrocento. What matters most of all is the humanists' anti-institutional bias, which, inspired by Petrarch, constituted the real spirit of early humanism, or, if we prefer, the sign of an intellectual solidarity apart from the contingencies of employment and from specific professions. Symptomatic of this was the reciprocal cooptation of humanists into offices, on the basis of that "horum ingenuorum studiorum coniunctio ac societas," which Lapo da Castiglionchio junior had invoked in a letter to P. C. Decembrio of 1437 (cf. F. P. Luiso, "Studi sull'epistolario e le traduzioni di L. da Castiglionchio iuniore," *Studi italiani di filologia classica* 7 [1899]: 256). Finally, it is important to note that in the catalogues of libraries and programs of teaching, the "studia humanitatis" were often kept distinct from the specific disciplines that they incorporated—grammar, rhetoric, poetry, etc. (cf., for example, Hartman Schedel's library, which lists in succession sections comprising "libri grammaticales in utraque lingua, . . . libri rethoricae, . . . in morali philosophia," and last of all, the sections concerning classical and humanistic works, "in arte humanitatis libri"; cf. *Mittelalterliche Bibliothecskatalogue Deutschlands und der Schwiez,* vol. 3, fascicle 3 [Munich, 1939], pp. 807–12); and also, that this position of privilege was still defended in pedagogical treatises of the late Cinquecento (cf. P. F. Grendler, "The Concept of Humanist in Cinquecento Italy," in *Renaissance Studies in Honor of H. Baron,* ed. A. Molho and J. A. Tedeschi [Florence, 1971], pp. 447–63).

6 Cf. Alberti's Prohemium to "Liber Intercenalium decimus," *Intercenali inedite,* ed. E. Garin (Florence, 1965), pp. 91 f.: "Quod si maledicendo tandem exerceri iuvat, omne putabam imperitorum vulgus non modicam neque parum accomodatam esse materiam, in quam omni obloquendi impunitate et licentia, quasi legitimo bello indicto, liceat abuti; siquidem non inter divites et pauperes, non inter potentes atque imbecilles, non inter dominos atque servos, quanta inter doctos atque indoctos inimicitia extat, natura duce."

7 Cf. É. Gilson, *La philosophie au Moyen Âge, . . .* (Paris, 1952), pp. 737 f. He continues: "Pétrarque avait ramené les Lettres latines sous le patronage d'Augustin, Bruni introduit à son tour les Lettres grecques sous le patronage de Basile": clearly, the real point in question here is the very nature of the patronage at issue, and on this subject see my observations in this essay, both above and below.

8 Cf. *Humanistisch-philosophischen Schriften,* p. 100: "Quod iis contigit fere qui ea tarditate ingenii sunt, ut nihil altum neque egregium valeant intueri, qui cum ad nullam

partem humanitatis aspirari ipsi possint, nec alios quidem id debere facere arbitran-
tur"; and Salutati, *Epistolario,* vol. 4, pt. 1, pp. 205–40.

9   Cf. "De studiis et litteris liber ad dominam Baptistam de Malatestis," *Humanistisch-philosophische Schriften,* pp. 17 f., where the poets are defended from the accusations of immorality: "Quod si quando amores describunt, ut Phoebi et Daphnis Vulcanique et Veneris, quis usque adeo hebes est, ut non fictas res et aliud pro alio significantes intelligat?" The moralist does not want to meddle in similar things: "At Plato et Aristoteles legebant! Quibus si te aut gravitate morum aut intelligentia rerum ante-ponis, nullo modo feram. An tu te aliquid discernere putas quod illi non viderint? 'Christianus—inquit—sum.' At illi forsan suo more vixerunt? Quasi vero honestas gravitasque morum non tunc eadem fuerit quae nunc est! Aut quasi non haec ipsa vel etiam deteriora in sacris reperiantur libris! An non ibi Samsonis amores paene insani . . . , an non haec poetica, an non flagitiosa? Taceo filiarum Lothi scelus in-fandum et Sodomitarum execrandam obscoenitatem . . . At etiam Davidis amorem in Bersabe et scelus in Uriam et tam numerosum concubinarum gregem quorsum spectare dicemus? An, quia haec mala sunt et flagitiosa et obscoena propterea negabi-mus sacros libros esse legendos? . . . Equidem, si quando Didonis Aeneaeque amores apud Virgilium lego, ingenium poetae admirari soleo, rem autem ipsam, quia fictam esse scio, nequaquam attendere . . . At enim, cum illa in sacris lego, quia vera fuisse scio, saepe inflector." Gilson has a good understanding of the irony of this passage, *La philosophie,* p. 737. It should be added that one must not be deceived by residual allegorical argument ("aliud pro alio significantes"), introduced solely for polemical purposes; in connection with this, see Poggio's discussion on Virgil's allegory of the Harpies, and my comments below, chap. 3, nn. 39–40.

10 I am referring here to the Salutati who recorded myths and expounded on allegories, as well as the one who extolled Petrarch as the new "classic" and as a model for Chris-tian morality (the major text that deals with this issue, alongside Bruni's *Dialogi,* is Salutati's letter to Poggio, 17 December 1405, *Epistolario,* vol. 4, pt. 1, pp. 126–145).

11 Cf. A. Solerti, ed., *Le vite di Dante, Petrarca, e Boccaccio* (Milan, n.d. [1904], p. 98 (and *Humanistisch-philosophische Schriften,* pp. 50 f.). The same statement can be found in the *Vita di messer Francesco Petrarca,* where there is no mention, among other things, of Petrarch's passion for Laura, a particular preoccupation for Boccaccio in his *De vita et moribus Francisci Petrarchi,* and understood in an allegorical sense. It had been evoked by Petrarch himself in a more realistic approach in his autobiographical epistle *Pos-teritati,* taken up in the biography written by P. P. Vergerio, as well as for different pur-poses in Bruni's own (cf. Solerti, *Le vite,* pp. 241, 262 f., 288–92). On the other hand, as is well known, Bruni inserts a digression on the rebirth of letters, which involves a critical limitation of Petrarch's own works, unthinkable in the earlier biographies (cf. E. Carrara, "L'epistola 'Posteritati' e la leggenda petrarchesca," *Studi petrarcheschi e altri scritti* [Turin, 1959], pp. 3–79; H. Baron, *The Crisis,* pp. 263–68; and also below, nn. 13–14).

12 Cf. *Vita di Dante,* p. 105: "Ab effectu vocavere 'poesim' seu 'poetes,' quod latine so-nat 'exquisita locutio,' et qui composuere 'poete' vocati sunt." Cf. also E. Gilson, "Poésie et vérité dans la Geneologia de Boccace," *Studi sul Boccaccio* 2 (1964): 277. As

noted, Boccaccio in this instance depended on Petrarch, who in *Familiares* 10.4.4 had introduced the quotation from Isidore's *Etymologiae* 8.7.1–3, in accordance with the distorted reading of "poetes": "Id sane non vulgari forma sed artificiosa quadam et exquisita et nova fieri oportuit, que, quoniam greco sermone 'poetes' dicta est, eos quoque qui utebantur poetas dixerunt" (cf. U. Bosco, "Il Petrarcha e l'Umanesimo filologico," *Saggi sul Rinascimento italiano* [Florence, 1970], p. 179; G. Martellotti, "La difesa della poesia del Boccaccio e un giudizio su Lucano," *Studi sul Boccaccio* 4 [1967]: 269 [and now, G. Martellotti, *Dante, Boccaccio, e altri scrittori dall'Umanesimo al Romanticismo,* with a preface by U. Bosco (Florence, 1983), pp. 165–83]). But Bruni discusses the concept directly, in the way it is taken up from Boccaccio in the "Trattatello in laude di Dante" (Solerti, *Le vite,* p. 241).

13 Cf. "Dialogi ad Petrum Histrum," *Prosatori Latini,* p. 94: "studia humanitatis, quae iam extincta erant repararit, et nobis quemadmodum discere possemus viam aperuerit"; and also Baron, *The Crisis,* pp. 265 f.

14 Cf. *Dialogi,* p. 82, where N. Niccoli records that "Franciscum . . . Petrarcham tanti semper feci, ut usque in Patavium profectus sim, ut ex proprio exemplari libros suos transcriberem"; and also p. 90: "solebam crebro convenire eos homines quibus ille, dum viveret, familiarissime utebatur, a quibus mores illius poetae sic didici, quasi ipse vidissem." It seems particularly significant that Salutati's pupils for the occasion followed the same path that he had laid out when, at the poet's death, he substituted for Boccaccio, winning the esteem of Lombardo della Seta as the coeditor, or, one could better say, guarantor of the publication of Petrarch's posthumous legacy. Cf. Salutati's letter to Lombardo, 25 January 1376, *Epistolario,* vol. 1, pp. 229–41; and also N. Festa, preface to *Africa* (Florence, 1926), pp. xli–lii; G. Billanovich, *Petrarca letterato* . . . (Rome, 1947), pp. 321 f., 324 f.; G. Martellotti, "Introduction," *De viris illustribus,* vol. 1 (Florence, 1964), pp. l f.

15 The recent and not so recent studies on Petrarch, from Foresti to Wilkins, from Rossi to Bosco, and from Billanovich to Martellotti, whose focus is to reconstruct accurately Petrarch's biography and the cultural and historical context of his works, have tended quite naturally to set aside the old problem, to borrow De Nolhac's expression, concerning "le rôle de Petrarque dans la Renaissance," or more precisely, concerning his role in connection with the rapid and decisive developments of Quattrocento humanism. If a consideration of Petrarch's works remains essential for the understanding of such a redirection of culture, in some sense the reverse may be true—that by looking at him from the perspective of the Quattrocento, we are able to point out aspects of Petrarch himself that otherwise are neglected or undervalued. In this respect, H. Baron's admirable studies deserve particular mention. Aligning himself with Martellotti's essay, Baron tried to reconstruct the ideological significance of the poet's psychological and cultural vacillations, as well as their actual line of development, and to determine their relationship to the shape of humanism in later years (cf. H. Baron, "On the Evolution of Petrarch's Thought: Reflections on the State of Petrarch Studies," *Bibliotheque d'Humanisme e Renaissance* 24 (1962); "Petrarch's *Secretum:* Was It Revised and Why?" ibid. 25 (1963); and *From Petrarch to Leonardo Bruni: Studies in Humanistic and Political Literature* [Chicago, 1968], pp. 7–101). The con-

clusion the author reaches in a later study, however, seems to me rather surprising, if not contradictory ("Petrarch: His Inner Struggle and the Humanistic Discovery of Man's Nature," *Florilegium Historiale: Essays Presented to W. K. Ferguson*, ed. J. G. Rowe and W. H. Stockdale [Toronto, 1971], pp. 19–51), according to which, "the work of Petrarch in his youth, although a unique prelude to things to come, did not lead directly to the Renaissance ideas of the Quattrocento, and . . . his own final view of life represents one of the great semi-medieval syntheses characteristic of the Trecento" (p. 46). Quite on the contrary, if we want to explain the later impact of Petrarch's work, in all its innovating capacity, we must recognize some constants in it, as the very core of these developments. On the other hand, by postulating Petrarch's retreat to "semi-medieval" ideas, in which the views of his youth are recast and effaced, we are forced to admit the rather implausible conclusion that there was a resurgence of the same experiences in a more propitious context, as if by spontaneous generation or chronological determinism. The purpose of this present essay, which incidentally owes a considerable amount to Baron's many penetrating observations both here and elsewhere, is to outline a more organic line of development.

16   In connection with this, I need only mention the autobiographical epistle "to the posterity" (*Posteritati*), in which Petrarch remembers that he has abandoned his legal studies "when he lost his father" ("mox ut me parentum cura destituit"), probably with some basis in historical truth but also undoubtedly with the intention of molding the episode into a programmatic statement. The words that follow are noteworthy because, as it has been observed, they contain the seed "of what was to be called 'legal humanism' ": ". . . non quia legum michi non placeret auctoritas, que absque dubio magna est et ratione antiquitatis plena, qua delector; sed quia earum usus nequitia hominum depravatur" (ed. P. G. Ricci, in *Prose*, ed. G. Martellotti [Milan, 1955], p. 10; cf. D. Maffei, *Gli inizi dell'umanesimo giuridico* [Milan, 1956], p. 36). Petrarch's contempt, under the cover of moralistic blame, is actually directed at the scholastic method of modern commentators. There is also an element of truth, if only as a symbol of a cultural directive, in the episode recalled in *Seniles* 16.1, according to which Ser Petracco, in answer to his son's pleas, had permitted him to pair his legal studies with the study of Cicero and Virgil: "et Virgilium dextra tenens, laeva Rhetoricam Ciceronis, utramque flenti mihi subridens ipse porrexit: 'Et habe tibi hunc—inquit—pro solatio quodam raro animi; hunc pro adminiculo civilis studii' " (*Opera*, vol. 2, p. 1047). The anecdote is also interesting in that, as he does in other passages in the *Posteritati*, Petrarch probably intends to provide a counterpart to the portrait that Boccaccio had dedicated to him, which presents father and son as antagonists, with the prosaic Ser Petracco on one side, and on the other the "Pyeridum corus" that has taken the young poet into its protection—an obvious imitation of Ovid. In other words, Petrarch places next to Virgil in his own cultural canon a Cicero who is no longer subordinated to the legal profession. It is of some interest that the two versions of this anecdote were juxtaposed in the later biographies of Petrarch; cf. F. Villani's biography, in Solerti, *Le vite*, p. 277; and Carrara, "L'epistola," pp. 13 f.

17   Cf. R. Weiss, *Il primo secolo dell'Umanesimo* (Rome, 1949), pp. 15–51; and A. Avena,

"Guglielmo da Pastrengo e gli inizi dell'Umanesimo a Verona," *Atti e mem. Accad. d'agricoltura, sc. lett. e arti di Verona*, ser. 4, 7 (82) (1907), pp. 256 ff. (See also Guglielmo da Pastrengo, *De viris illustribus et De originibus*, ed. G. Bottari [Padua, 1991].)

18 Cf. Bosco, "Il Petrarca," p. 179 (and De Nolhac, *Pétrarque et l'Humanisme*, 2d ed. [Paris, 1907], pp. 209 f.); but see Petrarch's own *Seniles* 2.1, p. 834, where, in connection with the different ages of human life, he appeals to various authors, "inter quos Isidorus, quo autore raro utor." Even in the famous *Familiares* 10.4.5, in which he appeals extensively to Isidore in support of his defense of poetry, he justifies this choice as the most convenient for the ecclesiastical education of its recipient, his brother Gherardo. Having mentioned Varro and Suetonius, he in fact adds: "tertium non adderem nisi quia is, ut reor, familiarior est tibi. Horum igitur et Ysidorus, breviter licet et ipso teste Tranquillo meminit Ethymologiarum libro octavo," etc.

19 Cf. "Prohemium," *De viris illistribus*, pp. 3 f.: "Qua in re temerariam et inutilem diligentiam eorum fugiendam putavi, qui omnium historicorum verba relegentes, nequid omnino pretermisisse videantur, dum unus alteri adversatur, omnem historie sue textum nebulosis ambagibus et inenodabilibus laqueis involverunt. Ego neque pacificator historicorum, neque collector omnium, sed eorum imitator quibus vel verisimilitudo certior vel autoritas maior est." His comparison to the contemporary genre of biography is still more explicit in *Invective contra medicum*, ed. P. G. Ricci (Rome, 1950), p. 45: ". . . scribo de viris illustribus . . . Nichil ibi de medicis nec de poetis quidem aut philosophis agitur, sed de his tantum qui bellicis virtutibus aut magno reipublice studio floruerunt, et preclaram rerum gestarum gloriam consecuti sunt."

20 Cf. H. Cochin, *Un amico di F. Petraca: Le lettere del Nelli al Petrarca* (Florence, 1901), p. 55 (E. H. Wilkins, *Petrarch's Correspondence* [Padua, 1960], p. 124, dates the letter 4 January 1352): "Tu enim michi in celo es, non dico pro Deo, sed pro ducatu ad Deum." See also Gilson, *La philosophie*, p. 723: "Pétrarque n'a pas d'abord connu la scolastique . . . ; il s'est formé en dehors d'elle, exactement comme si elle n'avait jamais existé. Il la menaçait pourtant du seul fait qu'il était Pétrarque. Retrouver au XIV siècle la culture préconisée au XII siècle par Jean de Salisbury, c'était tourner le dos à la culture scolastique du XIII siècle, et plus la gloire littéraire de Pétrarque croissait avec les années, plus il devenait inévitable qu'on le sût." Following this line of thought is the more recent work of P. P. Gerosa, *Umanesimo cristiano del Petrarca: Influenza agostiniana, attinenze medievali* (Turin, 1966).

21 The title given by Petrarch, which follows the explanation cited above, sounds like "concertatio cum famoso quodam viro," whereas the specification "quod iste vir famosus est Iohannes Andree" is taken from a later gloss in a branch of the manuscript tradition (cf. *Familiares* 1, p. 188). Here, too, as in his other polemical writings, to the extent that he uses symbolic types to indicate representatives of contemporary cultural trends, Petrarch deliberately avoids mentioning the name of his opposition, which is made to come through in an indirect or allusive way (this is what, in a somewhat philosophizing discussion of Petrarch as satirist, A. Tripet, *Pétrarque et la connaissance de soi* [Geneva, 1967], p. 58, defined as "altérité quasi emblématique"). There was a famous model for Petrarch's strategy: the passage in the *Confessions* in which

Augustine, while remembering how profitable he had found Ciceronian Hortensius, discredits the rhetorical culture of Cicero: "perveneram in librum cuiusdam Ciceronis, cuius linguam fere omnes mirantur, pectus non ita" (3.4.1). Petrarch, in some sense overturning the patristic argument, attacks those of his own day who depreciated antiquity: "Contra medicum quendam"; against the ignorance "multorum," "contra quendam magni status hominem," etc; he leaves "sine nomine" the invectives against the curia; and descends into an argument "cum famoso quodam viro." On Giovanni d'Andrea (1270–1348), the leading professor of canon law at Bologna and Padua, a man in the confidence of the popes, and a typical representative of the encyclopedic culture of the late Middle Ages, cf. the entry by S. Stelling-Michaud, in *Dictionnaire de droit canonique,* vol. 6 (1954), cols. 89–92. Petrarch's letter can probably be dated between 1345 and 1346, according to R. Sabbadini, *Le scoperte dei codici latini e greci ne' secoli XIV e XV, Nuove ricerche* (Florence, 1914), p. 158.

22 Cf. R. Sabbadini, "Giovanni Colonna biografo e bibliografo del secolo XV," *Atti della R. Accademia delle sc. di Torino* 46 (1910–11), p. 38. As Sabbadini has already pointed out, *Le scoperte,* pp. 159 ff., Petrarch is referring to Giovanni d'Andrea's *Ieronimianus,* a vast compilation that included the biography, list of works, noteworthy passages, and testimonies of the saint, and that was published precisely in 1346. In keeping with the contemporary taste for systematic compilations that gathered together into a single volume various *florilegia,* collections, and biographies of individual sacred and doctrinal authorities (a taste which Pope Clement VI in particular was encouraging, "talium compendiorum avidissimo," as Petrarch put it rather unkindly, *Familiares* 8.6.2), Giovanni d'Andrea's undertaking stimulated, or anyway was worked out in mutual connection with, the great alphabetical corpus of Augustine's teachings, the *Milleloquium veritatis S. Augustini,* compiled by the Augustinian hermit Bartolomeo Carusi of Urbino, who was also the author in sequence of a *Milleloquium* of St. Ambrose (cf. Sabbadini, *Le scoperte,* pp. 159–64; U. Mariani, *Petrarca e gli Agostiniani* [Rome, 1949], pp. 49–52; B. M. Peebles, "The Verse Embellishments of the 'Milleloquium Sancti Augustini,' " *Traditio* 10 [1954]: 555–56; R. Arbesmann, *Der Augustinereremitenorden und der Beginn des humanistischen Bewegung* [Würzburg, 1965], pp. 38–55). As is known, Bartolomeo asked Petrarch for a few verses in a kind of epigraph for his own work, verses that, indeed sent and handed down with the work, nevertheless betrayed Petrarch's reservations in its regard: ". . . Hinc sibi posteritas stillas studiosa salubres / Hauriat, *hinc lectos componat in ordine flores*" (cf. Peebles, pp. 557 f.; italics mine). Petrarch, moreover, made his reservation explicit in the letter to Bartolomeo that accompanied his verses, the *Familiares* 8.6.1, already cited, in which he describes the work as "rem maioris opere quam glorie." These are, no doubt, the "flosculorum decerptores" alleged by Petrarch as his general target in the epistle to Giovanni d'Andrea (see Bartolomeo's dedication of the Milleloquium to Clement VI, in which he states that "mihi facile non fuisse multa volumina revolvendo flores eligere," in Arbesmann, p. 45; this was similar to Giovanni d'Andrea's declared intention: "aliqua prenotanda ad mores salubria rethoricis et prelocutoribus," in Sabbadini, *Le scoperte,* p. 160). Nor was this attack destined to be an isolated one. A transparent reference to the Milleloquia literature (on which cf. P. Lehmann, "Mittelalterliche Bücher-

titel," in *Erforschung des Mittelalters,* vol. 5 [Stuttgart, 1962], p. 47), and specifically to the work of Bartolomeo da Urbino, with the treatise on Jerome that the layman Giovanni d'Andrea had attached to it, can be found in *Seniles* 5.2 (to Boccaccio, 28 August 1364, *Opera,* p. 880): "Quid de alio nunc hominum monstro loquar, qui religiosi habitu, moribus atque animo profani, Ambrosium, Augustinum, Hieronymum *multiloquos magis quam multiscios appellant?* Nescio unde novi veniunt theologi, qui iam doctoribus non parcunt, nec mox Apostolis ipsique parcent Evangelio, ora denique ipsum in Christum temeraria laxantur, nisi ipse cuius agitur res occurrat atque indomitis animantibus frenum stringat" (italics mine). The question was not so much one of a comparison between Jerome and Augustine as it was a vindication on Petrarch's part for his own personal reading of the *Confessions* in contrast to the Scholastics' doctrinaire approach to the Fathers of the Church, according to the systematic methods, which the religious orders were working out at this time. Cf. on this issue chap. 3, n. 31 below.

23 Cf. P. De Labriolle, *Histoire de la littérature latine chrétienne,* 3d ed. (Paris, 1947), pp. 537 f.: "Il s'agissait, dans la pensée de Jérôme, de dresser pour les écrivains chrétiens un catalogue qui rappellerait, sous une forme beaucoup plus brève, le *De viris illustribus* de Suétone. . . . C'était un procédé courant parmi ls païens de railler la médiocrité intellectuelle des catholiques. Quel meilleur moyen pour demontrer leur erreur ou leur mauvaise foi, que de recenser les écrivains dont s'honorait la littérature chrétienne?"

24 Cf. *Rerum memorandarum,* bk. 1, chap. 19: "sed quot preclaros vetustatis auctores, tot posteritatis pudores ac delicta commemoro." On this point, see É. Gilson, "Notes sur une frontière contestée . . . III, In confinio duorum populorum," *Archives d'histoire doctrinale et littéraire au Moyen Age* 33 (1958): 81–88.

25 *Familiares* 2.9.9: "Nunquam enim in somniis ad tribunal eterni iudicis tractus accesserat Augustinus meus sicut Ieronymus tuus, nunquam exprobrari sibi Ciceronianum nomen audierat, quod cum audisset Ieronymus fidemque dedisset quod nunquam amplius libros gentilium attingeret, quam diligenter ab omnibus, sed a Cicerone presertim abstinuerit, nosti"; "Augustinum et eius libros quadam benivolentia complexum, re autem vera a poetis et philosophis non avelli." The epistle, which Petrarch titled "Responsio ad quandam iocosam epystolam Iacobi de Columna Lomberiensis episcopi," is generally dated by scholars to 21 December 1336 (cf. Wilkins, *Petrarch's Correspondence,* p. 51). I cannot agree with Gilson, *La philosophie,* pp. 122 f., who believes Petrarch's affirmation that the dispute was all in good fun ("Comme son ami Giovanni [*sic*] Colonna le plaisantait de prétendre aimer Augustin, lui qui ne pouvait se détacher de Cicéron ni de Virgile, Pétrarque eut cette excellente riposte: 'Pourquoi m'en détacherais-je quand je vois Augustin lui même s'y attacher?'"); whereas it has all the signs of being a rhetorical understatement, in order to conceal the seriousness of a real disciplinary warning. The discussion with Colonna is also recalled in the aforementioned *Familiares* 4.15.3, to Giovanni d'Andrea: ". . . licet de hac re inter amicum tuum clare memorie Lomberiensem episcopum et me crebro disceptatum esse meminerim illo per vestigia tua semper uno ore Ieronimum, me vero Augustinum inter scriptores catholicos preferente."

26 *Seniles* 8.6: *Opera,* p. 928: "Illum librum mihi aditum fuisse ad omnes sacras litteras,

quas ut humiles et incomptas ac saecularibus impares et nimio illarum amore et contemptu harum et opinione de me falsa atque . . . insolentia iuvenili et demonico, ut intelligo clareque video nunc, suggestu, diu tumidus adolescens fugi."

27 *Seniles* 16.1, *Opera*, p. 948: "Sola me verborum dulcedo et sonoritas detinebat, ut quicquid aliud vel legerem vel audirem raucum mihi longeque dissonum videretur." An analogous idea is found in the introduction to the *Secretum*, where Truth introduces Petrarch to Augustine: "Nam et iste tui semper nominis amantissimus fuit: habet autem hoc omnis doctrina, quod multo facilius in auditorum animum ab amato preceptore transfunditur" (*Prose*, ed. Carrara, p. 24). The famous passage cited above has led to the question of the "evolution" of Petrarch's thought, concerning which, as has already been noted, Baron has offered some reconsiderations. Without a doubt, it would be completely arbitrary to underestimate the significance of Petrarch's own autobiographical statements. But it is equally important that the two moments he describes—the discovery of ancient values and the aspiration that came with it for the emulation and attainment of literary glory, and, successively, his return with Augustine's guidance to the Christian authors and as a consequence his own leaning toward religious ethics—were together the antecedents that find their stratifications or, alternatively, their polarities in the context of the literary works that are known to us, where the themes prevail alternatively in a varied and studied pattern but in such a way that it is simply not possible to describe them in terms of an "evolution." Consider that Petrarch's polemic found in the letter to Giovanni d'Andrea, and in various passages in the *Rerum memorandarum,* is more or less contemporary with his reflections in the *Secretum;* that the harshest suggestions of his attack on theology, such as those in the *Seniles* 2.1 and 5.2, to Boccaccio, were written in old age; and finally, that if in his *Senilis* to Donato Albanzani (10 June 1367) he urges the study of sacred literature, in a subsequent one to Luca della Penna (March, c. 1374) he recalls with pleasure his longstanding love for Cicero, once again in opposition to the dictamen of public chanceries. Moreover, the treatises on religious ethics are conceived by Petrarch according to their very titles as relating to subjective situations (either Petrarch's own situation or that of the dedicatee). So an argument easily shifts into its opposite, rhetorically contrasting with it. Thus, if the *De secreto conflictu curarum mearum* had to be followed by "De secreta pace animi," so too, after Petrarch had abandoned his solitary existence in Vaucluse and discovered that the recipient of his *De vita solitaria,* Philippe de Cabassoles, was to be appointed a cardinal, he determined on a whim to integrate the text with "totidem Vitae activae libros" (cf. *Seniles* 11.3 to Fr. Bruni, 5 October 1368, in *Opera*, p. 978). In his insistence on the subjectivity of his experiences and in their correlation with developments in rhetoric, his treatises tend to express values that are more relative than they are absolute. In fact, and this seems the most important point, Petrarch never approaches Christian and Patristic texts in order to agree with them completely but rather as if to measure himself against them, and as a result reserving space for a parallel appreciation of pagan authors. This is the very theme of scholarly debate on the interpretation of the *Secretum.* But there is another less acknowledged passage in *Seniles* 2.1 (in *Opera,* pp. 833 f.), which may represent the real key for interpretation of this issue. In con-

nection with the criticisms—which undoubtedly were brought by theologians—concerning an excerpt in *Africa* that describes the lament of the dying Mago, which had seemed to be an undue transfer of peculiarly Christian sentiments to a pagan, Petrarch thus writes: "Quid enim, per Christum obsecro, quid christianum ibi et non potius humanum omniumque gentium commune? Quid enim nisi dolor ac gemitus et poenitentia in extremis? De qua quid Cicero ipse scripserit audivisti; quamquam quid uno teste res agitur, de qua quisque sibi totusque adeo terrarum orbis uno ore respondeat? . . . Nullus ibi fidei articulus, nullum Ecclesiae sacramentum, denique nihil evangelicum, nihil omnino quod non in caput hominis multa experti iamque ad finem experientiae festinantis secundum naturale ingenium atque insitam rationem possit ascendere. . . . Potest errorem ac peccatum suum recognoscere et perinde erubescere ac dolere homo etiam non christianus, fructu quidem impari, poenitentia autem pari. . . . Quamvis ergo cui et qualiter confitendum sit nemo nisi christianus noverit, tamen peccati notitia et conscientiae stimulus, poenitentia et confessio communia sunt omnium ratione pollentium, et si verba respicimus, quid minus est quod amans ille Terentianus, paulo ante loquebatur, quam quod ipse David in Psalmo illo notissimo et illiciti sui amoris et sceleris: 'Quoniam iniquitatem meam ego agnosco et peccatum meum contra me est semper' [Psalm 50.5]?" In other words, although incited by the words of Augustine, Petrarch does not cease to be "in confinio duorum populorum constitutus": where the ambiguity lies in the uncertain boundary between the sphere of ethics and the sphere of religion, between introspection—"secundum naturale ingenium atque insitam rationem"—and confession, in the penitential sense of the word. It was a dualism that had its foundations not within the framework of doctrine but rather in a twofold and unhierarchical ordering of authorities: "Sed parum mihi videntur correctores mei seu haec pauca quae diximus, seu philosophica illa multorum, ante alios Platonica et Ciceroniana, relegisse, quibus si nomen desit authoris, ab Ambrosio sive Augustino scripta iuraveris, de Deo, de anima, de miseriis et erroribus hominum, de contemptu vitae huius et desiderio alterius" (*Seniles* 2.1).

28 Cf. P. Courcelle, "Pétrarque entre Saint Augustin et les Augustins du XIV siècle," *Studi petrarcheschi* 7 (1961): 51–71. A more extensive version of the study had been published in *Rivista di cultura classica e medievale* 1 (1959); and it is taken up again with some omissions and additions, Courcelle, *Les Confessions de Saint Augustin dans la tradition littéraire: Antécédents et postérité* (Paris, 1963), pp. 329–51.

29 Ibid., p. 51.

30 *Familiares* 2.9.8: "Quid autem inde divellerer [*sc.* a poetis et philosophis], ubi ipsum Augustinum inherentem video? Quod nisi ita esset, nunquam libros De civitate Dei, ut reliqua sileam, tanta philosophorum et poetarum calce fundaret, nunquam tantis oratorum et historicorum coloribus exornaret."

31 Cf. Bosco, "Il Petrarca," p. 179 (about the esteem in which Cicero held Varro, according to the veiled quotation from the *De civitate*). Bosco's observation can be extended to other texts, such as the *Rerum memorandarum;* cf. 1.14 (p. 14), about the preeminence that Scipio and Caesar should be recognized as having over Varro, in an implicit debate with *De civitate Dei,* 6.2; and also, with reference to the evaluation of Varro and

later Sallust, ibid., 1.15.17, etc. An explicit reference is made when Petrarch wants to corroborate an opinion of particular importance, philosophical rather than historical and literary, as is the case in particular in Augustine's panegyric on Plato (but it is after the quotations from ancient authors, as an open exception to his methodical approach, "nequid aliunde quam ex secularibus literis sumptum intersererem," 1.25, and in general 16–24, also important for its opposition to scholastic Aristotelianism).

32 Cf. Sabbadini, "G. Colonna," p. 838: "Hec quoque ipsa que huic libello inserui aliena sunt et eciam que loquor ab aliis accepi, ut antiquorum scriptorum ystorias veteres annalesque replicans possim quasi de ingenti prato opusculi nostri coronam intexere."

33 Familiares 15.9.4–5: "apud quos Babilon Roma, et, ut ita stomacer, feda virtus, infamis est gloria"; "veluti alteram . . . in occidente Babiloniam." The epistle is titled "Disceptatio super quibusdam que contra urbis Rome gloriam dicta videntur a multis" and is dated by scholars 24–30 April 1352; cf. Familiares 3, pp. 157–63; see further on § 5, p. 158: "Vellem quod sequitur tacuisset: 'veluti alteram,' inquit, 'in occidente Babiloniam' [De civitate Dei 28.22]." Cf. also Sine nomine, ep. 10 (ed. U. Dotti [Bari, 1974], p. 109).

34 Familiares 15.9.14, p. 160: "Quid multa? Quisquis urbem Romam eventus exceperit, nomen vivet quandiu Grecarum aut Latinarum memoria literarum ulla supererit, nec unquam deerit invidis materia tabescendi. Augustino sane ac Ieronimo, quos contemnere fas non est, hoc modo responsum sit."

35 Cf. the summary given by R. Di Sabatino, "Le epistole metriche a Benedetto XII e Clemente VI," Studi petrarcheshi 6 (1956): 43–54. Against K. Burdach and P. Piur's thesis (echoed more recently by H. Helbling, Saeculum Humanum: Ansätze zu einem Versuch über spätmittelalterliches Geschichtsdenkens [Naples, 1958]), which assimilates or at least aligns with millennarian expectations, Petrarch was actually moved more by a cultural and moralistic than an ecclesiological concern. His polemical writing on the occasion of Urban V's return to Rome is particularly significant. On this occasion his attack against the French cardinals, culminating in the Invectiva contra eum qui maledixit Italie, slips into an explicit criticism of scholastic theology at the Sorbonne (cf. Prose, ed. P. G. Ricci, p. 800: "Non scripsit Tullius Phisicam; addo ego: nec Ethicam; non scripsit Varro Methaphisicam; addo ego: nec Problemata. Sumus enim non greci, non barbari, sed itali et latini," etc.). On the other hand, Urban's call to Petrarch that he cooperate with the renovatio Ecclesiae, which he himself had so strongly pursued, flows, in the face of this violent polemic, into an open appeal for discipline. This, at least, is what we can infer from the letter that Petrarch received from C. Salutati, who was at the time the assistant to the papal secretary, Francesco Bruni, Rome, 3 April 1369, Epistolario, vol. 1, pp. 80–84. Accusing him of ingratitude for having failed to come to Rome, Salutati adds: "expectas forsitan, quod suo ipse iure potest, illum tibi precipere aut iterum te pulsare ut venias? tota, si hoc est, erras via: scit bene posse precipere potens cum se orat. . . . Inauditum etenim est tantum principem, qui non fama a carminibus expectat, summo etiam poete tantum tribuisse quantum hic suis litteris tribuivit. Cessit quandoque armata gloria ianue litterarum; celeste autem fastigium nunquam. Cave igitur ne superbus reputeris," etc. (p. 83). Such severe comments are certainly not those of a modest apprentice, which

is what Salutati was at the time, and one, moreover, who was particularly interested in winning Petrarch's approval. If it is difficult to dissent from P. Piur's claim, *Petrarcas Buch "Ohne Namen" und die papstlichen Kurie* (Halle, 1925), pp. 137 ff., that Petrarch is far from any idea of a religious rebellion against the Church, there nevertheless remains the problem of his position with respect to the institution and tradition of the Church itself from a cultural standpoint, and thus from an ethical and disciplinary one as well.

36 Cf. B. Smalley, *English Friars and Antiquity in the Early Fourteenth Century* (Oxford, 1960), pp. 87 f.; and also J. Th. Welter, *L'exemplum dans la littérature religieuse et didactique du moyen âge* (Paris, 1927); S. Battaglia, "L'esempio medievale," *Filologia romanza* 6 (1959): pp. 60 ff. (also Battaglia, *La coscienza letteraria del Medioevo* [Naples, 1965]). But see in particular the introduction to a late fourteenth-century commentary to Valerius: "Causa efficiens fuit Valerius, Maximus dictus ex cognomine, . . . non per excellentiam maximus, ut dicit frater Simon de Hesdinio ordinis sancti Iohannis Iherosolimitani magistri in theologia, qui presentem textum de latino transtulit in gallicum. Secundum eundem fratrem Symonem, Valerius fuit doctor maxime moralis, et Lucas de Penna legum doctor, domini Gregorii pape XI secretarius, qui presentem textum commentavit, dicit eum fuisse virum nedum maxime, sed summe peritie et eloquentie" (cf. T. Kaeppeli, "Luca Mannelli [+ 1362] e la sua 'Tabulatio et expositio Senecae,'" *Archivum fratrum Praedicatorum* 18 [1948]: 250; the commentary, in imitation of the canonical one by Dionigi, is attributed to a certain Luca, who was sometimes wrongly identified with Mannelli). The aforesaid Mannelli, a Dominican theologian and writing on commission by Pope Clement VI, made extensive use of Valerius in order to complement his *Tabularium Senece;* moreover, in the miniature of the frontispiece of his *Compendium moralis philosophie* the picture of Valerius appears beside that of Seneca and Aristotle as the greatest ancient authorities and deserving a place alongside the Christians, St. Thomas Aquinas, St. Ambrose, St. Augustine (Kaeppeli, p. 244). The same statement is found in one of Salutati's early letters to the lawyer Luigi Gianfigliazzi, Stignano, 26 December 1365, *Epistolario,* vol. 1, p. 10: ". . . scito me hunc Valerium semper non tam excerptorem hystorie, quam moralium preceptorem uberem, acutum et lepidum iudicasse, cuius siquidem oratio tota clarissimorum virorum exemplis, aut virtutis precepta latenter insinuans, ad honestatem lectorem hortetur et formet, aut a vitiis omnino deterreat; aut si eius dicta altiori mente librentur non iam Annei Senece quis documenta pretulerit: satis enim abundeque ad omnem vite partem solus ipse suffecerit."

37 Cf. G. Di Stefano, "Dionigi di Borgo San Sepolcro amico del Petrarca e maestro del Boccaccio," *Atti dell'Accademia delle scienze di Torino: Classe di scienze morali, storiche e filologiche* 96 (1961–62) disp. 1, p. 301; and *Familiares* 4.15.6: "At quod sequitur, te inter morales Valerium preferre, quis non stupeat, si tam serio perseveranterque dictum est et non iocandi tentandique animo? Si enim Valerius primus est, quotus, queso, Plato est, quotus Aristoteles, quotus Cicero, quotus Anneus Seneca, quem in hac re magni quidam extimatores omnibus pretulerunt?"

38 Cf. Di Stefano, "Dionigi," p. 274: "L'accenno del Petrarca ad una 'studiorum summa conformitas' in una lettera all'amico ormai a Napoli, insieme all'accenno al 'curis

solamen,' ci sembra che assuma il sapore di una certa confessione autobiografica dei trascorsi rapporti tra lo stesso Petrarca ed il dotto ed influente agostiniano." *Familiares* 4.2, to which Di Stefano is referring, is actually an encomium of King Robert ("Congratulatio super eo quod ad Robertum isset summum regem et philosophum"), joined together with a moral disquisition: "quid clarorum virorum conversatio prosit ad quietem animi." Here, if we can infer anything about the relationship between the poet and its recipient, there is an implicit condemnation of the court of Avignon, from which Dionigi came, and which evidently, in contrast to the Neapolitan one, did little to help the tranquillity of the soul; and, secondly, a certain distance taken, by turning to a man of religion, "sacre pagine professorem," from issues of theology (as can be seen from a comparison with the first draft of the letter [the so-called version gamma], where we read the following sentence, which Petrarch then eliminated in his definitive version ["version alpha"]: "Cum enim non habeamus hic manentem civitatem quandiu peregrinamur a celesti Ierusalem, quid aliud dicendi sumus quam viatores et exules?" in *Familiares* 1, pp. 199 f.). This, in fact, is the passage in its entirety, where, among other things, "studia" actually has the meaning of "feelings" or "moral inclinations": "Ad hunc itaque regem . . . vocatus ivisti; quod ut ille iuberet et ut tu pareres, quid aliud quam studiorum summa conformitas fecit?" (*Familiares* 4.2, p. 164). For the classification of Valerius among "morals," Di Stefano quotes the explanation at the beginning of the commentary in cod. Vatican latin 1924, f. 1 r: "Liber iste supponitur ethyce" (ibid., p. 287). Concerning the culture reflected therein, cf. Sabbadini, *Le scoperte,* vol. 2, pp. 36–44; but above all Arbesmann, *Der Augustinereremitenorden,* pp. 28 ff.: "Das erstaunlich lange und eindrucksvolle Verzeichnis umfasst neben klassischen auch patristischen und mittelalterlichen Autoren," etc.

39   Cf. the list of "Libri mei peculiares" in De Nolhac, *Pétrarque,* vol. 2, p. 294 (and B. L. Ullman, "Petrarch's Favorite Books," in *Studies in the Italian Renaissance* [Rome, 1955], p. 122), where Valerius is classified under the heading "ystorica."

40   "Ciceronis libros, unde ista sumebas, in manus posterorum nequaquam perventuros." Cf. *Rerum memorandarum* 4.97; 4.29, pp. 258, 210.

41   In connection with this, it is particularly interesting to draw a comparison between Petrarch's text and the *De modernis gestis* written by the Veronese grammarian Marzagaia, as a kind of appendix to Valerius Maximus—where he introduces a section on the "moderns" too, quite likely on the example of Petrarch's—written in behalf of the aristocratic circles at the end of the Trecento (cf. the edition and introduction by C. Cipolla, *Antiche cronache veronesi,* vol. 1 [Venice, 1890]; and cf. now R. Avesani, "Verona nel Quattrocento: La civilta delle lettere," in *Verona e il suo territorio,* vol. 4, 2 [Verona, 1984], pp. 28–30). In contrast, however, with Petrarch's *Rerum memorandarum,* Marzagaia's work, at least programmatically, uses the organization of the ancient model as a pattern for its new material; in this way the points that he considers worthy of further development are made evident. Following are the titles relating to the first section on religion, and in parentheses their agreement with or divergence from the corresponding titles in Valerius: *De religione observata* [Val.: *De religione*]; *De religione neglecta* [= Val.]; *De miraculis* [Val.: *De ominibus*]; *De prodigiis* [= Val.]; *Qui*

consilio vatum vel astrorum cognoverint discrimina sive vitaverunt sive non [not in Val.]; *De fatatis* [not in Val.]. It is also noteworthy that the letter cited above from Salutati to L. Gianfigliazzi concerns the exegesis of a passage in the same section (whether death inflicted by God on his unfaithful priests was to be considered a punishment; Valerius Maximus, I, 1, 7).

42 Cf. *Rerum memorandum* 4.30, p. 213: "multa que de Christo predixisse creditur." Throughout the chapter in question, "De sibillis," Petrarch explains the authors' tradition objectively but here and there lets his own skepticism come through: he tends, in fact, to recognize in such oracles "aliquam iniquissimorum spirituum . . . fallaciam, ni viderem doctores nostros divino spiritu afflatos Sibillis credere, et presertim Erithree," who had foretold the coming of Christ; but he is equally disposed to listening to "Ciceronem, ex adverso divinationis hoc genus, quamvis paulo reverentius quam cetera, refellentem tamen." It is interesting, on the other hand, that in the *De otio religioso,* where he goes over patristic and medieval traditions programmatically, Petrarch dwells on the "vaticinia" of the Eritrean sybil, following Augustine, *De civitate Dei* 28.23 (cf. *De otio,* ed. G. Rotondi, [Vatican City, 1958], pp. 27 f.; and also Ch. Trinkaus, "Humanist Treatises on the Status of the Religious: Petrarch, Salutati, Valla," *Studies in the Renaissance,* vol. 9 [1964], p. 14). On Valla, see especially the *De falso credita et ementia Constantini donatione,* chap. 23, par. 71, p. 39 [cf. ed. W. Setz (Weimar, 1979), pp. 141 f.]), where in a violently polemical context a contemptuous reference is made to the Tiburtine sybil, who had predicted the birth of the Virgin to Octavian, "ex auctoritate Innocenti tertii." Finally, it is worth noting that Valla, in a deliberately polemical strategy of positioning the portents of hagiography beside those of the Roman tradition, drew his examples from Valerius Maximus (§ 72 [ed. Setz, p. 145]), to which he compares the more critical Livy (ibid., 24.75, ed. Setz, pp. 148 f.).

43 It must not be overlooked here that this elusiveness reflects Petrarch's own concern to avoid the judgment of his contemporaries. His attitude is well illustrated in a letter he writes to Boccaccio on 10 June 1357, announcing his own autobiography: "Ne tantorum voces hominum contempsisse dicerer, libellum de vitae meae cursu contexui, ubi si res meas, non dicam irreprehensibiles aut laudabiles, sed tolerabiles excusabilesque miravero, et illi amico et aliis miratoribus meis, sive amatoribus, sive temptatoribus, sive ex professo carpentibus, puto responsum erit" (cf. E. H. Wilkins and G. Billanovich, "The Miscellaneous Letters of Petrarch," *Speculum* 37 (1962): 227; and also Wilkins, "On the Evolution of Petrarch's Letter to Posterity," *Speculum* 39 [1964]: 305).

44 Cf. *Rerum memorandum,* p. cxxxix.

45 Cf. Billanovich, *Petrarca letterato,* pp. 4 ff.; and also, in particular, *Familiares* 13.5.17 (to Fr. Nelli, 9 August 1352, concerning his refusal to take up a position in the papal chancery): "Certe quo me uti iubent et quem ipsi stilum nominant, non est stilus." To think only of the tradition of the dictamen, developed and theorized as the style of the curial chancery, the principal object in scholastic rhetorical education, a documentary expression of the institutional culture of the Middle Ages and as a result a standard against which even individual compositions were to be measured, we can

understand the significance of Petrarch's provocation (see H. Wieruszowski's clear presentation of this point, "Rhetoric and the Classics in Italian Education of the Thirteenth Century" [1967], in *Politics and Culture in Medieval Spain and Italy* [Rome, 1971], pp. 589–627).

46 Cf. especially G. Martellotti, "La Collatio inter Scipionem, Alexandrum, Hannibalem et Pyrrum: Un inedito del Petrarca nella Biblioteca della University of Pennsylvania," Ch. Henderson, ed., *Classical, Medieval and Renaissance Studies in Honor of B. L. Ullman,* vol. 2 (Rome, 1964), pp. 152 ff.; and also Martellotti, "Linee di sviluppo dell'umanesimo petrarchesco," *Studi petrarcheschi* 2 (1949): 56 [now, respectively, in *Scritti petrarcheschi,* pp. 321–46; pp. 115 f.]; Baron, *The Crisis,* p. 30. In this way, Petrarch synthesizes the comparison in the *De viris,* p. 294: "et pugnavit (Scipio) non in Asia cum imbelli barbarie, sed in Hispania atque Africa cum illis, qui victores gentium Romanos vicerant."

47 For the *Africa,* cf. Billanovich, *Petrarca letterato,* pp. 383–86; and also, in particular, Bruni's *Dialogi ad Petrum Histrum,* p. 72: "Atqui nihil unquam tanta professione praedicatum est, quanta Franciscus Petrarcha Africam suam praedicavit. . . . Quid autem postea? Ex tanta professione nonne natus est ridiculus mus? . . . Quanti igitur hunc poetam facere debemus, qui, quod maximum suorum operum esse profitetur atque in quo vires suas omnes intendit, id omnes consentiant potius eius famae nocere quam prodesse?" The argument is not taken up again in the "palinode" of *Dialogue II.* On *De viris,* cf. Cino Rinuccini's *Invectiva contro a certi calumniatori di Dante e di messer Francesco Petrarca,* where the attack on Petrarch's historiographical moralism is outspoken: "E de' libri del coronato poeta messer Francesco Petrarca si beffano, dicendo che quel De viris illustribus è un zibaldone da quaresima" (cf. now A. Lanza, *Polemiche e berte letterarie,* p. 264); cf. also *De viris,* pp. li f.; Baron, *The Crisis,* pp. 287, 521.

48 The *De avaritia* was composed before April 1429, and the revised edition was circulated in January 1430 (cf. Harth, "N. Niccoli," pp. 30 f., 39). Valla finished his first version in Piacenza, about the summer of 1431 (cf. *De vero falsoque bono,* ed. M. De Panizza Lorch [Bari, 1970], p. xxxii). On the composition of the work, cf. chap. 5 in this volume.

49 Cf. the letter to Fr. Pizolpasso, 5 August 1424, *Epistolae,* vol. 1, p. 129 [and now *Lettere,* vol. 2, p. 39]: ". . . quia recens est exemplum preaestantissimi viri Francisci Petrarcae, qui magno animo spernens atque abiciens omnem curam opum ac dignitatum, quae tunc ei a pontifice offerebantur, fugiensque potentiorum limina . . . vitam quietam . . . et dicto et facto comprobavit." From what I have seen, this explicit mention of Petrarch is the only one in the entire collection of Poggio's letters and is referring to the "libellum *De vita solitaria.*" (According to the indices in Harth's edition, Petrarch is actually mentioned again on a few rare occasions, but nowhere else is there a mention of his writings; cf. *Lettere,* vol. 1, pp. 141 f., 143, concerning his acquisition of the "opera Petrarche"; vol. 3, p. 355: Petrarch is mentioned among examples of people who are self-taught.)

50 In the revised version, the *De avaritia* starts with a criticism of the harshness of Stoicism, which, in its rigid opposition of vice to virtue, disregards the "communis prudentia" of man, which evaluates the seriousness of individual vices according

to different standards of judgment (cf. Harth, "N. Niccoli," p. 44). But cf. chap. 3, n. 75 below.

51   "Cf. the letter to Antonio da Pistoia, c. 1424, *Opera omnia,* vol. 4, p. 592: "Vellem ut in me tantum esset roboris ac nervorum, ut mihi, si et non imitari, saltem contemplari eorum sapientiam daretur; sed tamen, quoad erit facultas, ibo procul et longe vestigia semper adorabo." The origins and developments of such themes merit further investigation. On the subject, see C. Salutati's letter to Petrarch, Rome, 2 January 1369, *Epistolario,* vol. 1, p. 73: "Scio enim quod et Arpinas noster affirmat, illam veram atque exactam virtutem quam verbis facilius dicimus quam re consequamur adhuc nemini contigisse; satis est si quantum attingere potest humanitas pertingamus." According to Novati, this is a loose reference to the *De officiis,* 1.15.46: "Quoniam autem vivitur non cum perfectis hominibus pleneque sapientibus, sed cum his in quibus praeclare agitur si sunt simulacra virtutis, etiam hoc intelligendum puto, neminem omnino esse negligendum in quo aliqua significatio virtutis appareat, colendum autem esse ita quemque maxime ut quisque maxime virtutibus his lenioribus erit ornatus, modestia, temperantia, hac ipsa de qua multa iam dicta sunt iustitia. Nam fortis animus et magnus in homine non perfecto nec sapiente ferventior plerumque est, illae virtutes bonum virum videntur potius attingere." The argument is the same one Salutati used in counseling a friend against entering the monastic profession, except that in this instance it has been transferred into a theological context; cf. the letter to Pellegrino Zambeccari (Florence, 23 April 1398, *Epistolario,* vol. 3, p. 307: "Et ut aliquando concludam, sit licet melior contemplatio, divinior atque sublimior, permiscenda tamen est actioni; nec semper in illo speculationis culmine persistendum.").

52   Cf. in particular the letter to Antonio Loschi, 20 June 1424, ed. Tonelli, vol. 1, pp. 117 f. [ed. Harth, vol. 2, p. 9]: "Aliud enim quiddam nobis videntur polliceri haec humanitatis studia, quam aliis aliae artium facultates: haec enim nostra, semota procul ab omni spe quaestus, nulla cupiditatum irritamenta repromittunt nobis, sed earum contemptum et verae virtutis viam," etc. See also the letters to Pietro Donato, 23 July 1424, ibid., pp. 120–26; to Richard Petworth, 18 October 1425, pp. 139–43 [ed. Harth, vol. 2, pp. 14–18, 34–37]. On the argument, cf. in general Walser, pp. 122–24.

53   The allusion here is, of course, to the title and central themes of Poggio's various dialogues, treatises, and polemical writings, which are respectively: *De avaritia, Contra hypocritas, De infelicitate principum, De varietate fortunae, De nobilitate, Invectiva in fidei violatores, De miseria humanae conditionis.* It is worth noting that Poggio chooses as his titles themes that had been common in medieval treatises, but he develops them in a secular sense (as is obvious in the *De miseria,* but also in the original combination of motives of that kind of "De nugis" of the powerful that is the *De infelicitate principum,* a real overturning of the traditional "Specula"). The most interesting case is perhaps represented by the *De varietate fortunae,* a new kind of moralizing historiography whose title recalls the elegiac poem inspired by Boethius, Enrico of Settimello's *De diversitate fortunae et Philosophiae consolatione* (cf. P. Courcelle, *La Consolation de Philosophie dans la tradition littérarie: Antécédents et postérité de Boèce* [Paris, 1967], pp. 56–58; 136 f.). Actually in Poggio's "History" there is no providential design and transcendent eternity to oppose changeable fortune, but a human ideal of rationality and

interior independence, and, moreover, that the sphere of things subjected to fortune extends to include, among other political institutions, the Church itself, understood if not in terms of its inspiring principles then certainly in its temporal form.

54 Cf. the letter to Niccoli, London, 30 November 1421, ed. Tonelli, vol. 1, p. 50 [ed. Harth, vol. 1, p. 259]: "De sirenis vero quod mentionem facis, non magnopere curo . . . Ista, ut scis, nunquam abhorrui, homo enim sum. Sed nunquam praeterea ab utilitate mea diverti . . . Quod autem in re tam gravi, prout est consilium capere de instituenda vita, ex levissima ac deterrima causa sumpserim occasionem deliberandi, ridiculum est opinari. Non existimes me ita dementem atque ita rationis expertem, ut motus sirenarum cantu ab instituta navigatione deflectam."

55 Cf. letter to Cardinal Giuliano Cesarini, Rome, 10 July 1432, *Opera omnia,* vol. 4, p. 492 [ed. Harth, vol. 2, p. 145]: "Quod autem de instituendo vitae genere scribis, ego iamdudum decrevi certum vitae cursum, quo et proficiscor non devians ab itinere constituto. Nolo esse sacerdos, nolo beneficia: vidi enim plurimos, quos bonos viros censebam . . . post susceptum sacerdotium et avaros esse et nulli deditos virtuti. . . . Quod ne mihi quoque accidat veritus, decrevi procul a vestro ordine consumere hoc quicquid superest temporis peregrinationis meae: ex hac enim magna capitis sacerdotum rasura conspicio non solum pilos abradi, sed etiam conscientiam et virtutem." On Poggio's correspondence with the Cardinal, cf. Walser, pp. 151–53.

56 Cf. the letter to Niccoli, London, 12 February 1421, p. 63 [ed. Harth, vol. 1, p. 36]: "Libri sacri, quos legi et quotidie lego, refrixerunt studium pristinum humanitatis, cui deditus fui, ut nosti, a pueritia. Nam horum studiorum principia inania sunt, partim ambigua, partim falsa, omnia ad vanitatem. Sacri vero eloquii principium est veritas, qua amissa nihil rectius tenere, nihil operari possumus." Cf. also Walser, pp. 78–82.

57 Cf. Walser, pp. 81, 83: "After his return to Italy the unhappy conditions that had brought on or favored anyway his religious crisis were mitigated; but this triple concern [that is, the office of the priesthood, the difference between the current practice and ideal patristics, and the secular Christian's faith in God] remained to provide the solid foundation of his entire moral philosophy. . . . Here [in England] he laid the foundation of his future moral philosophy. From his treatise on avarice to his last writing on the misery of the human condition, his works all show a close connection of the Fathers of the Church with knowledge of the ancients: as was typical of Humanism from the time of Petrarch and Salutati."

58 Cf. the letter to Niccoli, London 13 June 1420, ed. Tonelli, vol. 1, p. 33 [ed. Harth, vol. 1, p. 11]: "Optima vitae instituta ad verborum ostentationem transtulerunt, et quod neque religione neque moribus neque vitae sanctimonia merentur, tumore et fastu superstitioneque assequi volunt, et, ut rectissime scribis, nisi nos praeteritorum et dicta et facta magis iuvarent quam praesentium perdita exempla, fides proculdubio perditum iret."

59 Ibid., p. 35 [ed. Harth, vol. 1, p. 12].

60 Cf. the letter to Niccoli, London 15 June 1422, ed. Tonelli, vol. 1, p. 82 [ed. Harth, vol. 1, p. 58]: "Non ignoro quam grave sit subire onus clerici et quanta cura oporteat eos torqueri, si qua sit conscientia, qui ex beneficio vivunt." Poggio's quotation is

not explicit (the only instance in which he mentions Chrysostomos in particular is in reference to the speech he gave at his departure from Constantinople, ibid., p. 35 [ed. Harth, p. 12]; but the reference to the treatise *De sacerdotio,* which emphasizes the "grandi doti morali che per esso si richiedono" (M. Simonetti, *La letteratura cristiana antica* [Florence, 1969], p. 311), seems plausible.

61 Cf. Fubini, "Un' orazione," pp. 26 f.; the text is edited and commented in *Umanesimo e secolarizzazione,* chap. 7, "L'orazione di Poggio Bracciolini a Costanza sui vizi del clero," pp. 303–38. I cite here according to the numeration of lines in the edited text.

62 On this matter, see chap. 3 below.

63 Cf. *De avaritia,* p. 5: "Quare tentemus et ipsi, si quid possumus prodesse hoc sermone nostro, etsi non caeteris, vel saltem nobis."

64 Ibid., p. 16: "Qui enim sunt isti qui publicum quaerant bonum, seposito privato emolumento? . . . Dicuntur nunnulla a philosophis de praeponenda utilitate communi magis speciose quam vere. Sed vita mortalium non est exigenda nobis ad stateram philosophiae. Consuetum est et communi usu concessum atque ab ipsius orbis ortu factitatum, ut magis afficiamur propriis quam communibus rebus." Concerning his skepticism about the traditional Christian condemnation of profit, cf. pp. 12 f.: "Beatus Augustinus . . . in libro De libero arbitio [bk. 3, 17, 48, in Migne, P.L., XXXII col. 1294] aliquanto levius quam tu scripsit avaritiam esse plus velle quam quod satis est. Hoc si verum sit, fateamur oportet avaros nos esse natura: nam quod omnes appetunt, id a natura emanare putandum est eaque suadente fieri. At vero neminem reperias, quin cupiat plus quam sit satis, nullum quin velit multum sibi superesse. Ergo naturalis res est avaritia . . . : si unusquisque neglexerit operari quiquid excedat usum suum, necesse erit, ut omittam reliqua, nos omnes agrum colere. Nullus enim seret, nisi quantum sibi et familiae suae fuerit satis futurum. Vide quanta rerum omnium sequatur confusio, si nihil habere velimus, praeterquam sit nobis satis." The passage, together with the attack on monastic "hypocrisy" that accompanies it, has been rightly considered among the most significant in the *De avaritia;* but precisely because it is often isolated from its context, its significance is sometimes misunderstood. It was important to Poggio to make ethical principles independent in themselves, freed from the casuistry of their applications (as has been noted, theologians like St. Bernardino were anything but unaware of the reality of economic relations: among other things some of his admissions about the necessity of industry and businesses for the civic community — on which cf. C. Bec, *Les marchans écrivains à Florence, 1375–1434* (Paris and The Hague, 1967), p. 267 — are somewhat similar to Poggio's own arguments. But Poggio, as has been said, aims to liberate moralistic discourse from the consequentiality of theological doctrine.

65 Cf. *De avaritia,* pp. 17 f. Cf. chap. 3, n. 73 below.

66 On the character of the Dominican theologian Andreas Chrysoberges, a former member, along with his brothers Maxim and Theodor, of the philo-Latin circle inspired by Demetrios Cydon, student at Pavia and participant in the Council of Constance, afterward member of Martin V's curia, used especially in the negotiations for a union with the Greek Church, cf. R. Loenertz, "Le domenicains byzantins Théodore et Andre Chrysobergès et les negociacions pour l'union des églises grècque

et latine de 1415–1430," *Archivum fratrum Praedicatorum* 9 (1939): 5–61: H. G. Beck, *Kirche und theologische Literatur im byzantinischen Reich* (Munich, 1959), pp. 742 f. Even in reality he figured among Poggio's familiars; cf. the letter to Niccoli, 11 February 1430, ed. Tonelli, vol. I, p. 308 [ed. Harth, vol. 1, p. 101], concerning the festivities for his fiftieth birthday: "Optassem ut nostro huic natalitio adfuisses . . . inter viros mihi amicissimos . . . : nam Antonium Luscum, Andream Constantinopolitanum, Cincium, Ludovicum Ortanum Rinuciumque habuisses convivii socios." The familiarity between the humanist and the Byzantine theologian probably goes back to an ancient custom begun in the time of Emmanuel Chrysoloras, who had ties with the brothers Chrysoberges and who moved with them to Italy, adhering to the Latin Church.

67 In connection with the accusations made by Loschi against kings, which are pointed out by Andreas ("Illud vero quod a te [*sc.* Antonio] multis verbis est explicatum, non plerosque sed omnes—quo verbo nulli excipiuntur—auri cupiditate adductos avarita teneri, refellant hi duo quorum mores . . . sint ab eius vitii labe sepositi"), Cencio Rustici intervenes scornfully: "Atqui, inquit, cum 'omnes' Antonius dixit, de sacerdotibus voluit intelligi, quibus iamdudum hoc est commune malum et moribus consuetum." Ever since the corruption of Judah, this vice "perseveravit . . . ad nostram aetatem, adeoque in eis insedit, ut rarum sit reperire sacerdotem cupiditatis expertem"; so confirmed Augustine in ancient times [*Contra epistolam Parmeniani*, bk. 3, par. 8, Migne, P.L., XLIII, col. 89, concerning the corruption in the Church at Carthage], and more recently Petrarch, who—undoubtedly in reference to the *Sine nomine*—"recte . . . avaram [-um, ed.] Babiloniam nuncupavit: vidit quam insita esset huic generi hominum avaritita, quam infinita cupiditas, quanta libido quaestus" (p. 22). Andreas seems not to recognize the interruption ("Omittamus haec, Andreas inquit, neque enim locus est nunc neque institutum deplorandi mores nostros, quos in multos scio posse fieri meliores"); but the more general maxims that he cites from the sacred authorities have no different meaning, except that there is a somewhat greater degree of confidence in their persuasive force.

68 Ibid., p. 29: "Augustinus comparat illos haereticis [cf. *Contra epistulam Parmeniani* 3.8]; ab Apostolo pro idolatris habentur [cf. ibid.; and also Colossians 3.5]; a Chrysostomo turpiores immundissimis porcis dicuntur [cf. *Homilia in Matt. XIX*, in P.G., LVIII, col. 608]," etc. It is worth noting that Chrysostomos' condemnation, here taken up in a rigoristic sense, is instead tempered by St. Bernardino: "Chrisostomus ibi exagerative locutus est, pro eo quod pauci sunt mercatores qui debitam mensuram iusticiae intendant in suis mercationibus et observent" ("Tractatus S. Bernardini de Senis in contractibus et usuris," quoted by Bec, *Les marchands*, p. 267). But cf. chap. 3 below.

69 Cf. the letter to Niccoli, 10 June 1429, ed. Harth, vol. 1, p. 116: "Nam quod mentio fratris Bernardini displicet eaque in dialogum introductio, id ego non feci ad eum laudandum, sed ad exagitandum paulisper hos molestos latratores ac rabulas foraneos."

70 Ibid., "Mentionem Isidori factam scias non inopia auctoritatum, sed quia in culpanda avarita sacerdotum ii potissime apti videbantur, quos illi dignificant quosque in suis legibus et decretis quotidie legunt"; cf. *De avaritia*, p. 22: "Legunt sed non servant

verba Isodori, qui iubet eos fugere amorem pecuniae, quasi cunctorum criminum materiam: surdis enim narratur fabula."

71 Ibid., p. 31: "Tunc Bartholomaeus: Adiicias licet—inquit—his verbis et quae ab Luciano tuo in eandem sententiam ponuntur, et quae ab Silio Italico poeta nobili. Quorum Lucianus: "O stulti—inquit—quid estis circa terrena solliciti? Quiescite aliquando, nam moriendum est vobis. . . . Nemo cum moritur auferet secum quicquam, sed nudus atque inops ad inferos transibit' [cf. *Mortuorum dialogi,* bk. 1, dialogue 3]. Silius vero, cum defunctum in bello divitem avarum dixisset, hos edidit versus: "Occumbis, generose Volunx, nec clausa reposcis pondera thesauris patriae [*sic*] nec regia quondam / praefulgens ebore . . . / Nudum Tartarea portabit navita cymba' [cf. *Punica* 5, verses 261–67]. Hic Andreas: Et haec ab istis et multa praeterea a pluribus scribuntur; sed hae non unius aut alterius voces, sed naturae et ipsius veritatis, ad quas si homines exhiberent animum, proculdubio substinerent paulisper, nec ita proni coecique in cupiditatum pelagus deferrentur." It is interesting that in the revised version Poggio suppresses the reference, thereby toning down the parallelism between the two orders of authority and the implicit argument that the modern clergy drew helpful precepts from the natural wisdom of the ancients. Cf. the new version in Harth, "N. Niccoli," p. 46: "Tum Bartholomaeus: Plurima in hanc sententiam— inquit—scripta praeclare monumentis litterarum viri sapientissimi tradiderunt. Ad quae si homines adhiberent aures animumque intenderent, proculdubio subsisterent paulisper nec ita proni coecique in cupiditatum pelagus deferrentur."

72 Cf. Harth, "N. Niccoli," pp. 43–50.

73 *De avaritia,* p. 6: "Te vero praesente tacemus, pudore commoti ne fias nostrarum censor ineptiarum."

74 Cf. in particular the letter from Poggio to A. Loschi, 1426, *Opera omnia,* vol. 4, pp. 595–600; it contains a rivendication of "licentiam convivorum . . . vitae communicandae gratia, qui unus habetur vivendi fructus dulcissimus," on the authority of the great ancients, who ignored the censures in real life: "Quantum latrarent canes isti, si quis e nobis symposium Platonis representasset. . . . Non legerunt, opinor, Catonem illum Censorinum ad multam noctem proferentem sodalium epulas. . . . Minime vero te latet quantam Macrobius quoque licentiam dederit convivii" etc. (p. 559). The reference to the episode in the *De avaritia* is made transparent, among other ways, by Loschi's embarassment and his words of justification (the letter had been addressed to him): "Quamquam si quid insulsius aut ineptius diceretur, habenda esset nobis venia, Bartholomaeo autem tribuendum, qui vinum patrium subministravit in coena; sed ipse sui errati poenam luet." Bartolomeo of Montepulciano, a guest of the speakers in the dialogue, in reality conceals Poggio himself, who had been censured as an organizer of banquets: "me vero inprimis notarunt tanquam paulo dissolutiorem" (letter cit., pp. 598 f.). In the dialogue, however, Andreas reassures: "Hoc . . . tunc recte diceretur, Antoni, si essetis quales legi in Simposio Platonis, oscitantes, ebrii, somnolenti. Sed video vos admodum sobrios: quare perge, Bartholomaee, et me velis esse participem tuae sententiae" (ibid.). On the banquet theme in Petrarch, cf. *Familiares* 18.10, to Fr. Nelli, "Varroniana lex convivii"; and H. Cochin, *Un amico,* p. 67. On the connection between Loschi's letter and the *Contra delatores,*

the short tract, written in the form of a letter, which was also directed to Loschi, on 15 February 1426, cf. the introductory notes in *Opera,* vol. 2, p. 708; vol. 4, pp. 595 f.

75 Cf. the letter to Niccoli, 14 September 1426, ed. Tonelli, vol. 1, p. 186 [ed. Harth, vol. 1, p. 171]: "Et primum . . . me reprehendis de conviviis et eorum sumptu . . . Tu, si ego amicos et hospites meos voco ad convivium, reprehendere non potes: est id quidem et antiquum et usitatum, neque vitio dari unquam vel audivi vel legi."

76 Cf. Lapo's dedication to Giovanni Morroni of Rieti, a cleric of the Apostolic Chamber (1436), E. Rotondi, *Lapo da Castiglionchio e il suo epistolario* (University of Florence, Facoltà di Magistero, tesi di laurea, anno accademico 1970–1971), pp. 332–36 (and also summarizing passages in Luiso, "Studi," p. 284): ". . . Iam vero in ipsa Romana curia, in qua plurimum aetatis tuae versatus es, etsi opinor te in tam variis, tam infinitis hominum cupiditatibus, in tam corruptis et depravatis moribus pro tuo splendore et dignitate, quae non mediocrem tibi invidiam concitabit, hoc vitium saepissime esse perpessum, sic tamen te instituisti ac munisti, ut tibi calumnia refellenda quidem esset, nullo vero modo pertimescenda. . . . Quae quamquam ita sint, erit tibi tamen, meo quidem arbitrio, non inutile Luciani De calumnia praecepta legere et eorum hominum, qui sive caeteris desperatis vitae rationibus sive malignitate naturae ad eam confugiunt, fraudes fallaciasque dignoscere." (See the entry I wrote on Castiglionchio, *Dizionario Biografico degli Italiani,* vol. 22 [1979], pp. 44–51.)

77 The translation, by Dietrich von Plieningen, does not indicate the place of edition: "Hernachvolgen zway Puechlein, das ain Lucianus und das ander Poggius beschriben haben, haltend in ines das man den Verklaffern und haymlichen Ornplonsern klynen Glauben geben soll" (cf. *Opera omnia,* vol. 1, Premessa, p. viii).

78 Cf. Harth, "N. Niccoli," p. 46. This is the Florence, Biblioteca Medicea Laurenziana, MS. Plut. 47, 19. ("Liber Poggii Secretarii apostolici"). Poggio probably revised the text, and the date of the editing falls between 1440 and 1447 (that is, between the composition of *De nobilitate* and *De infelicitate principum*—which follow in the manuscript the *De avaritia*—and the composition of the *Contra hypocritas,* added at another time and written in another hand); cf. also B. L. Ullmann, *The Origin and Development of Humanistic Script* (Rome, 1960), pp. 49 f. (On this subject, cf. also chap. 3, n. 57 below.)

79 L. Valla, *De vero falsoque bono* (cited hereafter as *Dvb*).

80 Cf. G. Mancini, *Vita di Lorenzo Valla* (Florence, 1891), p. 79; and, for a more up-to-date study of the issue, M. Fois, *Il pensiero cristiano di Lorenzo Valla* (Rome, 1969), pp. 14–17, 113–15. (But for the issue in its entirety, cf. chap. 5 below.)

81 There are two letters, dated to August and December 1428, which Filelfo addressed to Bartolomeo Fracanzano (cf. Fois, *Il pensiero,* pp. 125–27; the first is reproduced in E. Garin, *Filsofi italiani del Quattrocento* [Florence, 1942], pp. 158–61). Filelfo aims to outline an interpretation of Epicurean *voluptas* "secundam honestatem," distinguishing between the pleasure of the body and the pleasure of the soul: "Ego eam arbitror laudabilem voluptatem et maxime expetendam quae ex intelligentia veritatis et ex actione totius honestae vitae conflatur" (ed. Garin, p. 160). The connecting point between the sphere of ethics and the cognitive and religious one is pointed out in the adherence to truth: "Veritatem vero in iis rebus sitam existimo, quae sunt

incommutabiles et eternae. Quid autem aliud sit huiusmodi praeter unum et im-
mortalem Deum non intelligo." Petrarch, too, even though he conformed to the
traditional condemnation of the *voluptas*, no differently from Filelfo, pointed out
the purity of Epicurus's life, but especially he showed himself to be sensitive, according to what he drew from Seneca, to the compatibility of some of Epicurus's
maxims with Stoic and even Christian morality (cf. *Familiares* 1.8.3: "cum Epycuri
sententia sit, ab eodem Seneca relata, quicquid ab ullo bene dictum est non alienum
esse sed nostrum"; see also *Familiares* 10.3.48–49; and, in particular, *Rerum memorandarum* 3.77). Along the same lines, and perhaps because he had learned of Diogenes
Laertius, Filelfo attempted a spiritualized interpretation of the entire doctrine of
voluptas (cf. on this subject, G. Radetti, "L'epicureismo nel pensiero umanistico del
Quattrocento," *Grande antologia filosofica*, vol. 6 [Milan, 1964], pp. 840, 849 f.).

82 Raimondi is the only one besides Valla who, rather than seeking to rescue Epicureanism from its secular condemnation by searching for agreements with more traditional philosophical ways of thought, exalted it in opposition to these very teachings—"Academici, Stoici, Peripateticique"—in his letter to Ambrogio Tignosi (ed.
G. Santini, "Cosma Raimondi umanista ed epicureo," *Studi storici* 8 (1899): 159–67;
reproduced by Garin, *Filosofi*, pp. 134–49.) But on this matter, see chap. 5 below.

83 Cf. "Prohemium," pp. 1 f.: "Et de religione quidem dicere in animo non est, de qua
satis abundeque cum alii, tum praecipue Lactantius et Augustinus tractaverunt, quorum alter, ut qui prior fuit, falsas religiones confutasse, alter veram confirmasse prae-
clarius videtur. . . . Ego e contra planum faciam non nostris sed ipsorum philosophorum rationibus nihil cum virtute gentilitatem, nihil recte fecisse."

84 Cf. Fois, *Il pensiero,* pp. 128 f.: "Il 'De vero bono' di L. Valla rifiuta una validità a
queste tendenze, negando qualsiasi valore teoretico e pedagogico alla 'honestas' dei
filosofi, alla 'philosophia,' cioè alla morale stoicizzante intesa sotto questo termine.
Rifiuta inoltre qualsiasi soluzione del 'summum bonum' prescindente dalla rivela-
zione, non impostata cioè sulle virtù teologali, eliminando cosi quella dissociazione
dell'uomo in atto nell'averroismo latino e anche, benché meno visibile, nelle tendenze filosofiche dell'umanesimo, tra 'homo philosophus' e 'homo fidelis' "; and cf.
also pp. 109 f.

85 *Dvb,* p. 15: "Quanto enim evidentius, gravius, magnificentius ab oratoribus illa disseruntur, quam a philosophis obscuris, squalidis et exanguibus disputantur!" This is
the text of the third version; the original one sounds: ". . . quam a dialecticis obscuris
quibusdam squalidis et exanguibus dispuntantur" (p. 157). Moreover, the adoption of
the dialogue genre is in itself at this date meaningful; cf. F. Tateo, "La tradizione classica e le forme del dialogo umanistico," *Tradizione e realtà nell'Umanesimo italiano* (Bari,
1967), pp. 223 ff., and D. Marsh, *The Quattrocento Dialogue* (Cambridge, Mass., 1980).

86 Cf. *Dvb,* p. 1: "Instituenti mihi de causa veri falsique boni dicere, de qua tribus hisce
explicatur, placuit hanc potissimum sequi partitionem, ut duo tantum bona esse cre-
damus, alterum in hac vita, alterum in futura." The original version reads, ibid., p. 151:
"Si quis forte ex amicis . . . hunc admiratus titulum . . . a me postulet quaenam mihi
cupido incesserit scribendi 'De voluptate' . . . sic accipiat, me . . . hosce . . . libros
maluisse 'De voluptate' inscribere quam 'De vero bono,' quod poteram, siquidem de

vero bono, quam eandem voluptatem esse placet, in hoc opere disputamus. . . . Enim vero hoc de quo dico bonum . . . duplex est: alterum . . . ," etc. In opposition to De Panizza Lorch, C. F. Goffis, "Dal 'De voluptate' al 'De vero falsoque bono' di Lorenzo Valla," *Studi e problemi di critica testuale* 7 (1973): 24–57, has argued that the version represented in the edition printed in Basel, "apud A. Cratandrum, 1519," and which bears the title of *De voluptate ac de vero bono libri tres* (which is reproduced in the *Opera omnia* [Basel, 1540]), constitutes not an editorial contamination of the printings in Paris in 1512 and in Cologne in 1509 but rather the author's original revision of the first version of the dialogue. It is not my intention to discuss strictly textual arguments; nevertheless, it seems strange to me that it has not been noted that the title, *De voluptate ac de vero bono* is the one which was established by Josse Bade, the editor of the Parisian press (but note the different title in the colophon: "Finis libri tertii et ultimi dialogorum Laurentii Vallae de Voluptate: In aedibus Ascensianis ad V Idus Martiua MDXII Supputatione Romana"; *Dvb*, p. xv). On the other hand, the title cannot be traced back to Valla, since, as we have seen, he presented the two titles as alternatives. Even though the text may differ, we can be sure that the editors at Basel knew of Bade's version.

87 Cf. *Dvb*, bk. 1, chap. 16, par. 1, p. 22: "ipse non intelligo, cum unum atque idem nomen sit, quo pacto possimus facere rem diversam; atque eo quidem magis quod omnis voluptas non tam corpore sentitur quam animo qui corpus moderatur" (the entire passage is the following: "Constat enim inter nos aliquod genus voluptatis esse laudandum. Quod et antea [*sc.* with respect to Aristotle] Plato dixerat, volens duas esse in animo voluptates, alteram expetendam alteram fugiendam. A quo non dissentio, quamquam omnis voluptas, ut supra ostendi, bona est; et in libris 'De republica' hos ipsos tres fines quos dixi, saepe voluptates appellat. Verum Aristoteles et ipse voluptates facit, unam in sensibus et quandam aliam in mente. At ipse non intlligo [. . .], quod ut opinor sensit Epicurus.") But see also ibid., 1.16.1, p. 22: "Quod igitur voluptas sit bonum, cum multis eminentissimis auctoribus video placuisse, tum ipsa testatur consensio communis, quae vulgato sermone appellat 'bona animi,' 'bona corporis,' 'bona fortunae.' Quorum duo postrema nihil sobrii homines stoici in se boni habere volunt, quasi vero mala sint" (cf. *De finibus* 4.9.22).

88 C. Salutati, *De laboribus Herculis,* ed. B. L. Ullman (Zurich, 1951), vol. 2, p. 488: "Nam utilitatem sic vulgus amplexus est, quod omnis philosophorum scola doceret paupertatem, et divitias, in quibus usitatiore vocabulo versetur utilitas, contemnendas esse; quod et cuncte philosophorum hereses professe quidem, imo secute sunt. Nam et Epycurii et his inverecunda Cynicorum familia turpior non predicabant voluptatem solum, sed amplectebantur et eligebant."

89 Cf. chap. 5 below, for a more analytical explanation of this work.

90 *Dvb* 1.5.7–8, p. 10: "Sed tamen eius [*sc.* virtutis] cura atque amor perquam raris beneficio ac peculiari dono naturae concessus est; plurimis autem eiusdem naturae malignitate non aliter denegatus, quam quod monstruosos, debiles, vitiatos corpore videmus. Excaecavit mentes hominum quae illuminare debebat, ne lucem sapientiae contemplentur."

91 *Dvb* 2.29.5, pp. 82 f.: "Equidem sic statuo existimoque fuisse quosdam homines, ut

hodie quoque, amatores negligentiae et ignaviae, qui tedio rerum comparandarum, quae sunt necessariae, in vivendo praeelegerunt vitam hanc incultam et horridam." It is likely that this passage is echoing the expressions that Poggio used in the *De avaritia*, p. 13: "Non enim ex istis inertibus et larvatis hominibus, qui summa cum quiete feruntur, nostris laboribus sunt nobis civitates constituendae, sed ex his qui sint accommodati ad conservationem generis humani, quorum si unusquisque neglexerit operari quicquid excedat usum suum, necesse erit, ut omittam reliqua, nos omnes agrum colere." The corresponding passage in Raimondi, which in all probability Valla used as a model, attacks, in keeping with the general context of the tract, not the way of the monks' "ignavia" but rather their insensitiveness: "agrestes quosdam atque inhumanos philosophos, quorum sopiti occlusique essent omnes sensus" (*La cultura filosofica,* ed. Garin, p. 89 [but cf. *Rinascimento,* ed. M. C. Davies, 27 (1987): 134]).

92 Cf. *Dvb* 2.5–7, pp. 48–52; and *De civitate* 1.19.23–24. On Regulus, cf. *Dvb*, p. 51: "Ita cum diu superesse non posset, brevis vitae detrimentum multis commodis compensavit vel filiae dote vel gloria."

93 Cf. *Dvb* 2.28.17, p. 79, on the labor and the pleasures of contemplation, understood in terms of studying and learning: "Neque tu, Aristoteles, tam hoc sensisti quam studium tuum iactare voluisti. Ausim deos deasque omnes iurare, nisi tibi gloriae praemium proposuisses, nunquam te fuisse facturum ut in tuis tot librorum sane admirabilium contemplationibus insenuisses tam diu. Gloriae cupidus videri nolebas, studiorum amator videri volebas, cum tamen studia non propter se, sed propter gloriam praecipue amares."

94 Cf. *Dvb* 2.28.20, p. 80. Valla cites the Greek from Gregory Nazianzenus, *Oratio IV contra Julianum,* in Migne, P.L. XXXV, col. 597. The legend had medieval variants, such as the version that records that Aristotle drowned himself in the Nile, "dum causas refluxus capere non valeret" (Dionigi of Borgo San Sepolcro's commentary on Valerius Maximus, VIII, 7, ext. 3, in Arbesmann, *Der Augustinereremitenorden,* p. 33). As Radetti notes (Valla, *Scritti filosofici,* pp. 280 f.), Valla was delighted "to report the fact in his other works, . . . though confessing in the fourth book of the *Antidota* that he followed such story against the historical evidence of Aristotle's death for polemical and edifying ends: ". . . tamen malui in opere christiano christianum hominem sequi.'"

95 Cf. *Dvb* 1.47.2–3, p. 42: "Enumerarem concubitus, incestus, adulteria, id quod a vobis maximi culpatur, cum aliorum deorum tum praecipue Iovis, si enumerari possent. Ubi sunt qui obiurgant choreas, convivia, ludos? Sed has Cato [the speaker, Cato Sacco] ex media philosophia respondens fabulas vocat. Esto, sint sane fabulae! . . . Cur porro summi hominum, poetae, haec diis attribuunt? Necesse est alterum concedas: aut verum dixisse poetas de diis, aut ipsos tales fuisse quales illos esse voluerunt. . . . Aut quis se poetis Homero, Pindaro, Ovidio non dico anteferre audeat, sed conferre et illorum sententiam vitamque reprehendere? I nunc et dic naturam contra multitudinem imperitam irasci, cum videas poetas, ceterorum duces, in voluptatibus versari, aut potius diis contumeliam facere sine ira illorum! An est aliud natura quam dii?"

96 Toward the end of his speech, the defender of Epicurus describes the serenity of the

philosopher, "qui et anteactae vitae gratias agit, et adventantia fata serenis ac placidis oculis intuetur, nec aliter mortem habet invisam quam noctis tenebras post solis occasum" (*Dvb* 2.30.14, p. 84). It is to this passage that the defender of faith refers, at the point of pronouncing his judgment on the debate: ". . . Ne hoc quod sensit Epicurus videar tua magis confessione quam ratione convincere, accipe meliorem quam tu de bestiis ad nos usus es similitudinem. Similis est anima hominum, inquis, animae brutorum. Quod similius quam lumen stellarum lumini lucernae? Et tamen hoc mortale est, illud aeternum. . . . Tu comparasti actionem cum actione, ego substantiam cum substantia . . . Tu, ut dixi, simulator quidam atque iron fuisti et magis Socrates quam Epicurus; Cato autem cuius oratio propius ad veritatem accedere videtur, haud dubie serio locutus est, nec iocandi causa disputationem introduxit. Quid ergo? Dicemus eum errasse? Minime . . . , sed antiquitatis admiratorem se ostendere voluisse. Cui antiquitati concedo litteras, studia doctrinarum, et, quod semper plurimum valuit, dicendi scientiam; ad sapientiam autem et verae virtutis agnitionem nego pervenisse" (ibid., 3.7.4–5, p. 107). It is as if to say that, while from a strictly religious point of view the vindication of pleasure retains the value of a maieutic paradox, the defense of faith—according to the introductory argument— passes through the refutation of "Stoic" philosophic principles, understood as apparent truth, but which, in fact, are specious.

97 The criticism of Boethius is of particular importance and interest. At the same time as he criticizes him in the general arguments of the dialogue, Valla denies him a true Christian inspiration: "patronam philosophiam advocavit et ei propemodum maiorem honorem quam nostrae religioni tribuit" (*Dvb* 3.12.2, p. 112). Valla seems to be aligning himself with the doubts expressed by medieval commentators about the orthodoxy of the *Consolatio* (cf. Courcelle, *La Consolation,* pp. 275 ff.). But apart from the fact that these uncertainties were tempered by the trends of Platonism in the twelfth century and those of Aristotelianism in the fourteenth (Courcelle, ibid., pp. 317 ff.), the concerns were not about ethics but rather about cosmology and Plato's teaching on the soul (ibid., p. 337); and, most of all, they emerged in the context of a search for a Christian interpretation of Boethius—in other words, they were going in a direction entirely opposite to the one Valla was taking. It is, moreover, well known that Boethius occupies a central target in Valla's attack, though, as Fois has correctly pointed out (p. 106), not an exclusive one. Actually this is not owing so much to the devotional motives of the Christian speaker in the *De vero bono,* as it is to the characteristics that modern scholars have recognized in Boethius: that he was the author of the axiom "fidem si poteris rationemque coniunge" (cf. Gilson, *La philosophie,* pp. 150 ff.); just as he who tried "to detach from the pagan religion and compare with the Christian religion" Neoplatonic theology, thus opening "the way to the medieval scholastic" (P. Courcelle, *Les lettres grecques en Occident: De Macrobe à Cassiodore* [Paris, 1948], p. 304; Courcelle, *La Consolation,* pp. 340 f.).

98 Here, as he in his other writings, Bruni, following Aristotle's lead, is concerned with circumscribing the sphere of ethics in a way that excludes theological inferences; cf. his letter to Valla, Florence, 11 September 1433, in Sabaddini, *Cronologia,* pp. 65 f.: "Ego tamen dico de summo bono in quantam hominis, nam post mortem non est homo

amplius." Carlo Marsuppini confirms Platonic distinction between the two Venuses, "Uraniam et Pandemon," on the basis of which, "et duae voluptates tenendae sunt maxime": only on this condition will he approve of the dialogue, "cum . . . verum ac summum bonum in ea posueris voluptate, quae ex honestis actionibus proficiscitur" (from a letter to Valla, 12 September 1433, ibid., pp. 66 f.). Finally, Traversari avoids stating his opinion as Valla had asked him to ("De sententiis non ausim ipse sententiam ferre, quia re vera occupatissimus legi"), although he does make note of the dialogue's attack on the "auctores": "Non itaque improbo si quid contra philosophorum sentiamus inventa, si modo nostra probabilibus verisque rationibus muniamus" (from a letter to Valla, 4 September 1433, ibid., p. 65). Of lesser interest is a letter from P. C. Decembrio, n.d. [but which seems to have been written in Milan, in 1433, ibid., p. 63], which contains warm though general praises for the dialogue. Finally, it seems that the Sienese humanist Agostino Dati (1420–1479) makes reference to the work in his *Sermo de voluptate,* edited in incomplete form in his *Opera omnia* (Siena, 1503), ff. 256r–259v. Dati's inspiration is the traditional one of religious ethical moralism, and Church Fathers such as Augustine and Lactantius are quoted alongside authors like Aristotle and Cicero. It is a didactic dialogue, between "Aporetus," the interrogator, and "Crito," who responds. In the following passage the former makes reference to Valla's argument and is refuted by the latter: "*Aporetus:* Unam semper existimavi esse voluptatem, Crito, quae hominem ipsum iocunditate quadam ac delectatione afficiat . . . *Crito:* Nimium, Aporete, falsus es, siquidem unum solum constituis genus voluptatis. . . . Video sane [unde] is ortus sit error; neque enim arbitraris par esse ut res tam longe inter se diversas atque contrarias eodem omnis vocabulo complectamur, ut si bonum et malum virtutem quispiam appellare velit, cum tamen aliud bonum sit, aliud malum."

3. Poggio Bracciolini and San Bernardino

1   "te factum esse christianum, relicta illa 'iesuitate' quam ascribebas principio litterarum tuarum"; "novam haeresis sectam moliebantur"; "magis ab ambitione et pompa hanc divisionem profectam quam ab ulla sanctimonia ac religione." Cf. letter to F. Barbaro, Rome, 18 December 1429, *Epistolae,* vol. 1, pp. 269 f. [ed. Harth, vol. 2, p. 93]. On the controversy, cf. the entry by R. Manselli, "Bernardino da Siena," *Dizionario Biografico degli Italiani,* vol. 9 (1967), pp. 218 ff. In contrast to the opinions of some biographers, the letters of Poggio mentioned here and further on seem to confirm that after his trial Bernardino in fact put temporary restrictions on the controversial cult. See also A. G. Ferrers Howell, *S. Bernardino of Siena* (London, 1913), pp. 147 ff., 183–87.

2   "Ut, dum vetustatem corrigi quam sequi malunt, in foveam quam meruerunt et quasi in haeresim prolaberentur." Cf. L. Valla, *Collatio Novi Testamenti,* unpublished version ed. A. Perosa (Florence, 1970), pp. 11 f. (to Matthew 1.1), and p. xxxv. According to Perosa's accurate reconstruction, the text was written no later than 1444 (pp. xxxviii f.).

3   A. Morisi, "Andrea Biglia e San Bernardino da Siena," *Bernardino predicatore nella società*

del suo tempo, Convegni del Centro di Studi sulla Spiritualità Medievale, vol. 16 (Spoleto, 1976), p. 338.

4 G. Miccoli, "Bernardino predicatore: Problemi e ipotesi per un'interpretazione complessiva," *Bernardino predicatore,* p. 31.

5 "Nemini parere et praeesse caeteris." Cf. letter to N. Niccoli, 16 December 1429, ed. Tonelli, vol. 1, p. 297 [ed. Harth, vol. 1, p. 92].

6 Cf. ed. H. Sincerus (Lyons, 1679) [*Opera omnia,* vol. 2, pp. 45–80]. It is worth noting that the tract was written around November 1447. (Walser, on the other hand, suggests 1448 as the date [p. 244], grounding his argument on an incorrect identification of the "Arminensis episcopus," a figure mentioned in the tract, as Bartolomeo Malatesta, who died on 5 June 1448. The reference is undoubtedly to his predecessor, Cristoforo of San Marcello, who died in 1444; Poggio in fact had stated that his work dealt only with the already deceased.)

7 Cf. letter to Niccoli, 16 December 1429, ed. Tonelli, vol. 1, p. 298 [ed. Harth, pp. 92 f.]: "Sunt factae praeterea certae constitutiones atque edicta, quorum ego non auctor sed opifex fui, quae tunc videbantur necessaria ad reprimendam insolentiam multorum, inter quae illud fuit decretum praecipuum, ne quis locus pro his fratribus aedificaretur de novo, quoad capitulum fieret." Cf. also L. Wadding, *Annales Minores,* vol. 10 (Quaracchi, 1932), p. 166; Walser, pp. 115 f.

8 "huiusci Pogii authoritate ac eloquentia"; "apud exteros a religione.": Cf. letter by Alberto of Sarteano to N. Niccoli, "ex Cortona 1430," *B. Alberti a Sarthiano . . . Vita et opera,* ed. F. Haroldus and P. Duffius (Rome, 1688), p. 202 [*Opera omnia,* vol. 4, p. 7].

9 Letter to Niccoli, 16 December 1429, p. 300 [ed. Harth, pp. 94 f.]: "Sed totiens deceptus sum, totiens frustratus opinione, ut iam nesciam quid credam aut cui credam. . . . Hac in curia multa innotescunt quae sunt apud alios ignota. Omnium enim vitia huc confluunt, ut sit tanquam speculum in quo plurimorum et facta et mores cernuntur." It is worth underlining the mediating and moderating role adopted by Niccoli, as compared with the intemperance of his friend: an attitude that reflects concerns that made him solicit a revision of the text of *De avaritia;* cf. n. 14 below.

10 Letter to Alberto of Sarteano, 21 February 1430, ed. Tonelli, vol. 1, p. 314 [ed. Harth, vol. 2, p. 99]: "Unum scias, me, quamvis sim malus, tamen abhorrere ab eorum secta, qui simulatione boni non tantum caeteros quantum se ipsos fallunt. . . . Nihil confert vestis sordida ad virtutem, sed mores et vitae sanctimonia"; "Nam ego illorum aut doctrina aut exemplis non egeo." Cf. also Alberto of Sarteano's letter to Poggio, "ex Cortona 1430," pp. 203–19 [*Opera omnia,* vol. 4, pp. 8–24]; and Walser, pp. 118–22. The incidental clause "quamvis sim malus," which Poggio takes from one of Seneca's maxims ("omnes enim mali sumus, ut ait Seneca," letter to Niccoli, ed. Tonelli, vol. 1, p. 300 [ed. Harth, vol. 1, p. 94]; cf. *De ira,* 3.26.4), constitutes a kind of leitmotiv in his polemic against "hypocrisy." Alberto's two letters were actually circulated as an apology for monastic life; a copy, for example, can be found attached to an older MS. copy of a commentary to the *Sententiae:* Florence, Bibl. Laurenziana, Conv. Sopp. 499, ff. 26r–29v (damaged). Cf. Biblioteca Medicea Laurenziana, *Poggio Bracciolini nel VI centenrio della nascita: Codici e documenti fiorentini, Catalogo,* ed. R. Fubini and S. Caroti (Florence, 1981), p. 45, n. 75 (cited hereafter as *Catalogo*).

11 "Ita versatus est plurimis in locis ut nullius erroris aut commotionis in populo causam praebuerit." Cf. letter to Niccoli, 16 December 1429, vol. 1, p. 92].

12 J. Cl. Maire-Vigueur, "Bernardino et la vie citadine," *Bernardino predicatore*, p. 281.

13 Ibid.; and Miccoli, *Bernardino predicatore*, p. 25.

14 There is an accurate record of the different phases of composition and reworking of the text in Harth, "N. Niccoli als literarischer Zensor" (see also my observations on what were other than purely literary motives underlying the revision, chap. 2 above). A stimulating if debatable interpretation of the dialogue is offered by J. W. Oppel, "Poggio, S. Bernardino, and the Dialogue on Avarice," *Renaissance Quarterly* 30 (1977): 564–87; on which cf. H. M. Goldbrunner, "Poggios Dialog über die Habsucht. Bemerkungen zu einer neuen Untersuchung," *Quellen und Forschungen aus italienischen Archiven und Bibliotheken* 59 (1979): 436–52. Cf. also F. Tateo, "Il dialogo 'realistico' di Poggio Bracciolini," *Tradizione e realtà nell'Umanesimo italiano* (Bari, 1967), pp. 251–77; D. Marsh, *The Quattrocento Dialogue, Classical Tradition, and Humanist Innovation* (Cambridge, Mass., 1980), pp. 38–54. References will be made to the text in Poggii Florentini, *Opera . . .* , (Basel, 1538) [*Opera omnia*, vol. 1 (Turin, 1964), pp. 1–31]. Finally, it is worth noting that the original title of the work was "In avaritiam," according to the ms. copy of the *Dialogi* that the author had collected and revised c. 1440: Florence, Biblioteca Laurenziana, Plut. 47, 19. This contains the first version of the work that corresponds to the printed text (not, in other words, to the text revised on the basis of Niccoli's suggestions, as Harth has demonstrated), which Poggio evidently considered as his original text.

15 "homo inter omnes quos audierim mea sententia eloquens et satis eruditus"; "Una in re maxime excellit, in persuadendum ac excitandum affectibus flectit populum et quo vult deducit, movens ad lachrymas et cum res patitur ad risum." Cf. *De avaritia*, p. 2. It is of no small importance to the interpretation of the dialogue that the action, which refers to Bernardino's preaching in Rome after his acquittal, is dated three years earlier than the actual date of the dialogue's composition. In other words, despite the "realistic" elements of the setting, the action is fictional and as such is in keeping with the literary model suggested by Cicero, who backdated his dialogues (cf. M. Ruch, *Le préambule dans les oeuvres philosophiques de Cicéron: Essai sur la genèse de l'art du dialogue* [Paris, 1958], pp. 103 ff.). Both L. Bruni in the *Dialogi ad Petrum Histrum* and later Valla in the *De voluptate* would also follow this model.

16 "Tantum apud animas hominum valet, ut nihil plus eo valere maximi oratores testantur." Cf. Z. Zafarana, "Bernardino nella storia della predicazione popolare," *Bernardino predicatore*, p. 45; Oppel, "Poggio," pp. 568 f. For an ample treatment of this topic, see Nirit Ben-Aryeh Debby, *Renaissance Florence in the Rhetoric of Two Popular Preachers: Giovanni Dominici (1356–1419) and Bernardino da Siena (1380–1444)* (Turnhout, 2001).

17 "Verum in una re (pace sua dixerim) errare mihi videntur et ipse et caeteri huiusmodi praedicatores. Nam cum multa loquantur, non accommodant orationes suas ad nostram utilitatem, sed ad suam loquacitatem"; "cum habeant tres quasdam praemeditatas"; "de rebus reconditis et obscuris"; "quam videas abire multo quam accesserat stultiorem"; "perpauci vel nulli . . . evaadunt eorum sermonibus meliores"; "haesitant atque obmutescunt, aut se respondent nescire." Cf. *De avaritia*, pp. 2 f. The criti-

cisms noted here were hardly isolated, even in the context of the religious orders; for example, according to an anonymous Servite monk author of a Latin report of Bernardino's preaching, "multa dixit inutilia. . . . Nil possum scribere, quia omnia quae dixit nullius fierent roboris" (cf. Zafarana, "Bernardino," p. 69).

18 Cf. C. Delcorno, "L'exemplum' nella predicazione di Bernardino da Siena," *Bernardino predicatore,* pp. 73–103; he identifies in Bernardino a "decisive moment in the secularization of the *exemplum,* though in the context of a reform in the sense of popularizing sacred rhetoric" (p. 107); and also, among others, F. C. Tubach, "Exempla in the Decline," *Traditio* 18 (1963): 417: "the majority of the late medieval *exempla* merged with the new forms of expression which developed out of this new age and which were as such a vital reflection of it: the *Schwank,* the *facetia,* and the sixteenth-century *Spruch.*" A synthesis and bibliography of the subject is found in A. Lumpe, "Exemplum," *Reallexicon für Antike und Christentum* 6 (1966), coll. 1229–1257; and also C. Delcorno, *La predicazione nell'eta comunale* (Florence: Sansoni Scuola aperta, 1974), p. 54. (But see especially C. Brémont, J. Le Goff, J. C. Schmitt, *L'exemplum* [Brepols, 1982], Typologie des sources du Moyen Âge occidental, fasc. 40.)

19 Cf. in particular L. Sozzi, "Le 'Facezie' di Poggio nel *Quattrocento* francese," *Miscellanea di studi sul Quattrocento francese,* ed. F. Simone (Turin, 1966), pp. 412 ff. (it refers to the preface in *Opera,* p. 420: "Verum facessant ab istarum confabulationum lectione . . . qui nimis rigidi censores aut acres existimatores rerum existunt. A facetis enim et humanis . . . legi cupio"; and to the *Invectiva secunda* in L. *Vallam,* ibid., p. 219). Incidentally, the title of the *Facetiae* was the one conventionally adopted, whereas the author had indicated as a more fitting term the title "Confabulationes" ("sic enim eas appellari volo"), which reflected its colloquial and varied nature. Sozzi makes some significant observations "on the differentiating from Poggio's humor," in French adaptations by J. Macho and G. Tardif. According to the latter, in Poggio's "facetia" "n'y pas de sens moral, n'y pas grant sens figuratif, n'y a pas grant sens reductif a moralité" (ibid., pp. 485 f.).

20 *Institutio oratoria* 6.2.8; and 7.2.20: "affectus igitur *pathos* concitatos, *ethos* mites atque compositos esse dixerunt; in altero vehementer commotos, in altero lenes; denique hos imperare, illos persuadere; hos ad perturbationem, illos ad benevolentiam praevalere." Cf. H. Lausberg, *Handbuch der literarischen Rhetorik,* vol. 1 (Munich, 1960), pp. 141 f., § 257, 2a. This graduate scale of oratory is connected with that "sermo facetus ac nulla in re rudis," which Cicero judged "magis proprium humanitatis" (*De oratore* 1.8.32). Cf. on this point Poggio's letter to Antonio Loschi, n.d. [c. 1426], *Opera omnia,* vol. 4, p. 600: "M. Tullius in iudiciis utebatur iocis et salibus, adeo ut quandoque ridiculus diceretur," citing immediately afterwards Cicero's saying, *Philippics* 2.14.39: "Homines quamvis in rebus turbidis sint, si modo homines sunt, interdum animis relaxantur." At this point Poggio adds the following words, which anticipate the introduction of the *Facetiae:* "Haec disciplicent eis de quibus loquimur rusticanis et agrestibus animalibus, quibuscum non iocis et facetiis, sed fustibus et virgis ludendum esset." On the connections between the incident in question in the letter to Loschi and the setting of *De avaritia,* cf. above, chap. 2. Last of all, it is significant that Poggio's criticism of the preacher's style of oratory in *De avaritia* centers on

their incorrect use of the three parts of the "ars dicendi," "ut doceantur auditores, ut delectentur, ut moveantur"; and especially: "ita delectant, ut nil sit ipsorum voce et oratione molestius" (p. 3).

21 Cf. F. Tateo, "Il lessico dei 'comici' nella facezia latina del Quattrocento," *I classici nel Medioevo e nell'Umanesimo: Miscellanea filologica* (Genoa: Universita di Genova, Facoltà di Lettere, Istituto di Filologia classica e medioevale, 1975), pp. 93–109.

22 *De avaritia,* p. 9.

23 "semel dixit in usurarios, magis movens populum ad risum quam ad horrorem tanti criminis." Cf. *De avaritia,* p. 4.

24 "non conscientia peccati, sed timore amittendi parta se foenus relicturum professus." Cf. *Opera,* p. 445.

25 "qui animam profligavit et perdidit"; "Facillime res in suam naturam redit." Cf. *Opera,* p. 486. See also *Facetia* 157 (p. 463), where a usurer insists that the preacher inveigh against usury, so that he might discourage his competition; cf. Tateo, "Il lessico," p. 103.

26 "ò renduto e factomi conscienzia, e però non presto più"; "èmi preso pietà di te, e però va al mio figliuolo che presta." Cf. *Le prediche volgari, VII, Predicazione del 1425 in Siena,* ed. C. Cannarozzi, vol. 2 (Florence, 1958), pred. xxx, p. 121.

27 "verba ampullosa et magnificas sententias." Cf. "Oratio ad Patres reverendissimos," *Umanesimo e secolarizzazione,* p. 315, line 13.

28 "passim discurrunt ac vagantur per varios morborum genera prout fert libido loquendi, in nullius cura insistentes." Cf. *De avaritia,* p. 3.

29 "Quicquid ab ullo bene dictum est, non alienum esse sed nostrum." Cf. *Familiares* 1.8.3; and Seneca, *Ad Lucilium* 12.11; and also 16.7: "Quare autem alienum dixi? Quicquid bene dictum est ab ullo, meum est." On the subject see N. Struever, *The Language of History in the Renaissance: Rhetoric and Historical Consciousness in Florentine Humanism* (Princeton, 1970), p. 147. This way Petrarch revived the ancient Senecan controversy against the empty *quaestiunculae* of school teaching, which, as P. Grimal has pointed out (*Sénèque ou la conscience de l'Empire* [Paris, 1978], p. 365), were unessential to the principle aim, the attainment of an inner equilibrium. "Cet équilibre ne sera atteint qu'au terme d'un long apprentissage, dont le premier stage est . . . la découverte des vraies valeurs: le prix du temps, le sens de la mort, de l'amitié, de la richesse et de la pauvreté . . . Au cours de cette détermination des valeurs fondamentales, Sénèque a récours à tout ce qui peut illuminer l'âme de son disciple, et c'est pour cela qu'il utilise si largement . . . les formules si frappantes et si profondes de l'épicurisme." U. Dotti, "Fonti della 'Familiari' petrarchesche," *Atti dell'Accademia delle scienze di Torino, Classe di Scienze morali, storiche e filologiche,* vol. 108, fasc. II, 1974, pp. 559 f., gives further details on the amplitude of Petrarch's "appropriation" of Senecan sentences and notes the similarities in style of citing the sympathetic author's maxims (Petrarch appropriates Seneca's thoughts in the very guise in which Seneca himself "liked to fit in his own discourse the exemplary sentences of Epicurus"). Likewise, in the tract *De sui ipsius et multorum ignorantia,* Petrarch defines as "true moral philosophers and profitable teachers of virtues" all those who do not limit themselves to teach the essence of virtues and vices ("quid est virtus aut vitium, praeclarumque illud, hoc fuscum

nomen auribus instrepunt") but aim at inculcating upon the human soul the love or aversion for it ("pectoribus inserunt"). Cf. Dotti, ibid.

30 Cf. B. L. Ullman, "Petrarch's Favorite Books," *Studies in the Italian Renaissance* (Rome, 1955), pp. 117–37. Ullman was able to read correctly the sentence placed at the top of the list of "libri peculiares": "ad reliquos (*sc.* libros). non transfuga sed explorator transire soleo," which recalls the famous maxim of Seneca, *Ad Lucilium* 2.5: "soleo enim et in aliena castra transire, non tamquam transfuga sed tamquam explorator." Here, however, it is used in a way opposite to its adoption in the medieval tradition, where the "aliena castra" represented the pagan authors. On the notion of "retorquere," or twisting of ancient moral maxims, cf. B. Smalley, "Moralists and Philosophers in the Thirteenth and Fourteenth Century," *Die Metaphysik im Mittelalter . . .* , Miscellanea Mediaevalia, vol. 2 (Berlin, 1963), pp. 59–67.

31 *Familiares* 4.15. For Petrarch's polemic, generally directed at the *compendia* of doctrinal authorities, both sacred and profane ("multiloquos magis quam multiscios appellant," *Seniles* 5.2, in *Opera,* p. 880), cf. above, chap. 2. On the literature in question, cf. H. M. Rochais and Ph. Delhaye, "Florilèges Spirituels," *Dictionnaire de Spiritualité,* no. xxxiii–xxxiv (Paris, 1964), cols. 435–75; and R. H. Rouse and M. A. Rouse, *Preachers, Florilegia, and Sermons: Studies on the "Manipulus florum" of Thomas of Ireland,* Studies and Texts, vol. 47 (Toronto, 1969).

32 "'Quippe quem fructu deceat gaudere, non floribuis." *Familiares* 4.15.17; *Ad Lucilium* 33.7; also *Familiares* 1.3.4: "quique coetaneis meis est mos, per auctorum vireta captare flosculos"; and *Secretum,* in Petrarch, *Prose,* p. 192: "Nunquam, ex quo pueritiam excessi, scientiarum flosculis delectatus sum." There is a note of irony in the same context, in Augustine's reply to Petrarch: "nec suppellex hec exemplorum displicet, modo non segnitiem afferat . . ." (p. 180).

33 "e tu cogli questo fiore e poi quell'altro e poi quell'altro, e così te ne fai una ghirlandetta, e portitenela in capo quando tu impari quello che ti bisogna imparare." Cf. *Le prediche volgari di San Bernardino da Siena dette nella Piazza del Campo l'anno MCCCCXXVII,* ed. Banchi, vol. 3 (Siena, 1888), p. 455 (in Miccoli, *Bernardino predicatore,* p. 14).

34 Cf. C. Godi, "La 'Collatio laureationis' del Petrarca," *Italia medioevale e umanistica* 13 (1970): 21: "quod inter nubilosum et serenum celum interest."

35 "facete satis et proprie dictum"; "sive enim id Virgilius ipse sensit, sive ab omni tali consideratione remotissimus, maritimam his versibus et nil aliud describere voluit tempestatem." Cf. *Secretum,* pp. 24 f.

36 "De quibusdam fictionibus Virgilii." F. Rico, *Vida u obra de Petrarca: I, Lectura del Secretum* (Padua, 1974), p. 238 f., denies, in opposition to other interpretations (Carrara, Tateo), the irony of the passage, which instead corroborates "la licitud de buscar sentidos moralmente valiosos a un texto quizás escrito por el autor con otras miras," according to the Augustinian model of biblical exegesis in *De doctrina christiana.* It is not clear, however, how such a rigid interpretation is compatible with Petrarch's subtle ambivalence, aimed in short at eluding canons of exegesis and doctrine. So he states in the *Senilis* cited above: "Sunt qui moralem sensum apud Virgilium quaerunt: sic est enim, quisque suum tendit in finem, inque id maxime in-

tendit; itaque de una eadem re pro varietate utentium varii captantur effectus, utque ait Anneus, in eodem prato bos herbam quaerit, canis leporem, ciconia lacertam" (*Opera*, p. 869; cf. E. Müller-Bochat, "Allegorese und Allegorie. Zu Petrarcas Vergildeutung," *Petrarca, 1304–1374: Beiträge zu Werk und Wirkung*, ed. F. Schalk (Frankfurt am Main, 1974), pp. 205 f; cf. Seneca *Ad Lucilium* 108.29). Sacred exegesis cannot escape such relativism, according to the example given: "qualia multa de Moyse in Confessionum libris disputat Augustinus" (p. 869; cf. Rico, *Vida*, p. 239). This gives some indication of the breadth of the issue that Petrarch raises, which links to the more radical criticism of Poggio and Valla and can be traced as far as Montaigne, who in the manifesto of his skepticism, the "Apologie de Raimond Sebond," used very similar terms: ". . . il y a tant de moyens d'interpretation qu'il est mal aisé que, de biais ou de droit fil, un esprit ingenieux ne recontre en tout sujet quelque air qui luy serve à son poinct" (*Essais*, ed. A. Thibaudet [Paris, 1950], bk. 2, chap. 12, p. 661; cf. Müller-Bochat, p. 201 f.). It is no coincidence that a Petrarch verse is incorporated into the same context: "Chi troppo s'assottiglia si scavezza" (p. 627; cf. *Rime* 105.28).

37 *De avaritia*, p. 8: "Quis potuit pingi elegantius forma quadam cuiuspiam animantis quam id vitium est versibus a Virgilio expressum?"; and further on, p. 9, he continues: "Proluvies, expressit apte immensam eius cupiditatem, ex quo ille vulgatus est versus: 'Avarus animus nullo satiatur lucro,' " in reference to the anonymous passage in a comedy cited by Seneca *Ad Lucilium* 94.43, but probably as a counterpart to Dante *Inferno* 1.99, cited by Bernardino in his Florentine sermon "De' ma' contratti" ("On bad contracts"): ". . . come disse il vostro poeta volgare: 'e dopo il pasto ha piu fame che pria' "; cf. *Le prediche volgari: Quaresimale del 1425*, ed. C. Cannarozzi, vol. 2 (Florence, 1940), sermon XLIV, p. 430 (but cf. also n. 41 below).

38 "perridicula atque inepta . . . et indigna docto viro"; "Itaque contempsi semper hanc insulsam auctoritatis et sapientiae suspicionem, quam nonnulli superstitiosa ambage poetarum fabulis inclusam suspicantur." The passage appears only in the revised version (cf. Harth, "N. Niccoli," p. 30); it is in *Prosatori latini*, ed. E. Garin, pp. 1129 f.; and see Garin, *La cultura filosofica*, pp. 36 f. It is worth noting that here, as in Petrarch, there is a reference to the almost unfailing authority of Seneca: "cum et ipse Seneca etiam dicat, hoc esse propositum poetis, ut oblectent aures et fabulas connectant"; cf. *De beneficiis* 1.4.5.

39 Garin, *La cultura filosofica*, pp. 35 ff., notes Salutati's dependence on Bernard Silvester's exegesis of Virgil, from which he derives "l'indicazione del carattere introduttivo della poesia rispetto alla filosofia." But cf. especially *De laboribus Herculis*, ed. B. L. Ullman, vol. 1 (Zurich, 1951), p. 235: "Unde et avari finguntur Furias pati, qui abstinent partis" (with reference to Servius, *Ad Aeneidem* 3.209). The allusion to Salutati is further confirmed by the following words: "Hunc ego omnia Herculis monstra . . . exsuperare confitear" (*De avaritia*, p. 10).

40 *De avaritia*, p. 8: "Dixit volucres vultu virgineo, non hominem significans esse avarum sed monstrum. . . . Vultus virginei testantur viriscentem semper cupiditatem. . . . Volucres finxit propter appetitum, mobilitatem velocitatemque. Proluvies expressit apte immensam eorum cupiditatem" etc. (precisely like the ritual subdivisions of the "thema" of a sermon, "puisque il ne s'agit plus de diviser un texte, mais de

diviser et subdiviser des idées"; cf. É. Gilson, "Michel Menot et la technique du sermon médiéval," *Les idées et les lettres* [Paris, 1932], p. 130). For the equation Bernardino
makes between the Gospel and moral precepts, and the relative allegorical interpretation of the text (the "midolla" as opposed to the "letteracce di fuori"), cf. Zafarana,
"Bernardino," p. 55.

41 Cf. *Quaresimale del 1425,* vol. 2, sermon XLIV, pp. 425 ff.; and Marsh, pp. 46 f. In
De avaritia, the cue for the allegory of the Harpies is the theme of the "avarus
senex" (p. 8), on which Bernardino also dwells, p. 430: "L'avaro quanto più invecchia
nell'avarizia, tanto più trafigge e morde."

42 Cf. *De avaritia,* p. 9, about the "facetia" of the noble miser from Florence, who has the
table cleared of the chicken that has just been set on it; or the other one, who, against
the advice of his doctor, feeds on beef and not on the "pullis gallinaceis" that cost
more, etc. (the reference to the *Aulularia* is made in the austere context of Andrea's
discourse, p. 30). Cf. also *Le prediche volgari: Quaresimale del 1424,* ed. C. Cannarozzi,
vol. 1 (Pistoia, 1934), p. 82.

43 "Oratio ad Patres reverendissimos," *Umanesimo e secolarizzazione,* p. 323, line 172:
"Sed nimirum personati sunt quidem homines isti, qui haec tam grandia in pulpito
loquuntur." We may recall the more traditional criticism directed at the preachers'
exaggerated search for rhythmic and mimic effects ("quae praedicatio theatralis est
et mimica, et ideo omnifarie contemnenda," according to Alain of Lille; cf. Gilson,
"M. Menot," p. 99); and the same kind of censure had been repeated more recently
by Salutati (*De seculo et religione,* ed. B. L. Ullman [Florence, 1957], pp. 45 f.; cf. Harth,
"N. Niccoli," p. 42). But the source of Poggio's image must better be sought, once
again, in Petrarch's moral and rhetorical conceptions. In fact he contrasts the "aliena
dicta et monita" and peculiarity of personal style: "Omnis vestis histrionem decet,
sed non omnis scribentem stilus" (*Familiares* 22.2.17; cf. H. Gmelin, "Das Prinzip der
Imitatio in den romanischen Literaturen der Renaissance," *Romanische Forschungen* 46
[1932]: 123).

44 Cf. Quintilian, *Institutio oratoria* 10.2.27: "Imitatio per se ipsam non sufficit, vel quia
pigri est ingenii contentum esse iis quae sint ab aliis inventa." Cf. Gmelin, *Das Prinzip,* pp. 120 f.; Struever, pp. 145 f.; and P. De. Nolhac, *Pétrarque et l'Humanisme,* 2d.
ed., vol. 2 (Paris, 1907), p. 89.

45 L. Valla, *De vero bono,* p. 45 (bk. 2, introd., 2): "Ea namque est argumentorum inculcatio, ea exemplorum redundantia, ea rerum earundem repetitio, is flexus orationis
quicquid occurrit more vitium apprehendentis, ut an inutilius sit an turpius nesciam." Cf. in general, on the sermon and its relative symbolism, T. M. Charland, *Artes
praedicandi: Contribution de la rhétorique au Moyen Age* (Paris and Ottawa, 1936).

46 "ab aliqua sententia incipiunt, deinde aliorum dictis intexunt orationes suas"; "re-
formari haec oportere, alioquin evenire rerum omnium perturbationem." Cf. "Oratio ad Patres reverendissimos," *Umanesimo e secolarizzazione,* pp. 323 f., lines 179 ff.
Even Salutati, combining in his usual way traditional themes with more pressing
criticisms, takes a polemical tone when describing the behavior of preachers: "aliquod divinarum scripturarum oraculum reassumens [*sc.* religiosus] pulcerrimum,
totum in sua . . . membra decerpit . . . et membra subdividit, subdivisa distinguit, et

rebus inops ac sententiis inanis maxima verborum inculcatione lascivit" (*De seculo,*
pp. 45 f.). The criticism should also be understood as an expression of his criticism of
the role claimed by the regular orders, "postquam omiserunt episcopi monere popu-
los," in a pessimistic vision of the actual state of the Church, and not much different
from the one presented by Poggio (Salutati was writing in 1381). In contrast to Poggio, however, the discourse is inserted and blended into the context of a discussion
"de contemptu mundi" ("Quod mundus sit spectaculum delictorum") and in this
sense is very different from the genuine distrust of sacred oratory that emerges from
Poggio's Oration at Constance.

47 Letter to Niccoli, 13 June 1420, ed. Tonelli, vol. 1, p. 33 [ed. Harth, vol. 1, p. 11]: "Nisi
nos praeteritorum et dicta et facta magis iuvarent quam praesentium perdita exempla, fides procul dubio perditum iret." The statement is illuminated by a particular passage in the Oration at Constance, which claims that the "difficult" precepts
of Christ ("res quaedam durissimae legis . . . et similia austera . . . a sensu nostro
quodammodo abhorrentia") could not have been corroborated without the highest example of the Apostles; since "contra molliora erant et multo faciliora, certe
ad naturam humanam magis accommodata legis gentilium praecepta, firmata usu
quotidiano et legibus sancita" ("Oratio ad Patres reverendissimos," in *Umanesimo e
secolarizzazione*, pp. 319 f., lines 102 ff.). Cf. also *De avaritia*, p. 22, concerning Augustine's reproach of Carthaginian clergy: "Quod si tunc accidebat cum recens aestuaret
fidei fervor, . . . quid in hac foece temporis, quid in hac morum perversitate, in hac
hominum corruptela et quasi senescente fide fieri putamus?"

48 *De avaritia*, p. 4: "Hanc Bernardinus . . . nunquam tetigit, semel dixit in usurarios,
magis movens populum ad risum quam ad horrorem tanti criminis. Avaritiam vero,
quae foenus persuadet, intactam reliquit."

49 Ibid., p. 5: "Quare tentemus et ipsi, si quid possumus prodesse hoc sermone nostro,
etsi non caeteris, vel saltem nobis." According to Seneca's precepts, Poggio would be
referring to the "vis et natura" of vice, which, were they known, would be easy to
avoid (cf. Harth, "N. Niccoli," p. 43; and also Grimal, pp. 276 ff.). See also further
on, p. 6: "non quaeremus philosophica et acuta quaedam, sed quae sunt huius et loci
et temporis."

50 *De avaritia*, p. 10: "ego tamen sequens morem Academicorum" (the words with which
Loschi introduces his speech). But cf. Cicero's definition, *De natura deorum* 1.11: "Haec
in philosophia ratio contra omnia disserendi nullamque rem aperte iudicandi profecta ab Socrate" etc. (cf. Ruch, *Le préambule*, pp. 58 ff.). Marsh, pp. 1–23, 28 ff., emphasizes that the Augustinian propositions in the *Contra Academicos* are overcome in
the framework of the humanists' dialogue. I agree, however, only in part with the
argument according to which "this simple, three-part debate on the moral topic of
avarice follows in part the model of Cicero's discussion *in utramque partem*, while
the final role of Andreas reflects the influence of Augustine's Cassiciacum dialogues"
(p. 39). Poggio, transcribing the *Contra Academicos* with his own hand, had signalized
in the margins Augustine's statement, 3.8.17: "quanto minus malum sit indoctum
esse quam indocibile" (Florence, Biblioteca Laurenziana, S. Marco 665, c. 29 v; cf.
Catalogo, pp. 17 f., n. 3); and, in fact, the instruction of philosophy remains a con-

stant theme in, among other writings, the *De avaritia* itself. (On this point, see also Ch. B. Schmitt, *Cicero Scepticus: A Study in the Influence of the Academica in the Renaissance* [The Hague, 1972], pp. 48 ff., who notes the absence of "an outbreak of scepticism" in the early Renaissance). Moreover, as Marsh himself demonstrates, the various discourses in the dialogue are closely related, and it is only in terms of this connection—in which there is no evidence of a specific classical model—that they can be understood. If they are isolated from one another, it is impossible to avoid the contradiction which more recently Goldbrunner has encountered, according to whom "the new element is represented . . . by the extraordinary power in which Loschi, with an analysis largely free from moral categories, describes avarice as the propelling influence of every human action"; while Poggio's own position is not "at all ambivalent" but instead corresponds "completely to Andreas of Constantinople's" (p. 452, "summary"): as if to suggest that the characters existed independently of their roles in the context of the dialogue. Lastly, it should be pointed out that there is a clear distinction, even on a rhetorical level, between Poggio's dialogue and the popular contemporary genre of the *declamationes* pro and con, such as Buonaccorso of Montemagno's popular debate "De nobilitate."

51 *De avaritia,* p. 4: "Nam luxuria, licet multorum malorum causam sapientes dixerint, est tamen aliqua ex parte ut posset fieri, veluti quae admiscetur procreatione liberorum, blandum malum, sed sibi soli nocens, non alteri neque alienum a conservatione generis humani." In the Oration to the Fathers at the Council at Constance, Poggio, no differently from Bartolomeo, had judged avarice, "illa malorum omnium parente atque effectrice," to be a more serious sin than lust, "blandum humani generis malum . . . que nos redderet simillimos beluis, qua ab omni ratione sensuque avocaret" (cf. *Umanesimo e secolarizzazione,* p. 317, lines 43 ff.). The severity of his discourse, however, is softened in the passage cited from *De avaritia* and as such recalls the indulgence that Poggio claimed for himself on this matter: "unusquisque iudicet ut vult, ipse quoque iudicandus. . . . Ista ut scis, nunquam abhorrui: homo enim sum" (cf. letter to Niccoli, 30 November 1421, ed. Tonelli, vol. 1, p. 50 [ed. Harth, vol. 1, p. 25]). Loschi, on the other hand, counters rhetorically in his speech that lust is more serious than avarice, and although he brings up the argument of how lust unsettles the soul and the body, his judgment is imprinted with general human criteria; he does not claim that lust transforms man into a beast but rather that it unnerves his highest faculties, "adeo ut luxuriosos videas insulsos, effoeminatos, imbelles" (p. 10). Through such a rhetorical see-saw of definitions, it manifests Poggio's intention to relativize the traditional classifications of the virtues and vices.

52 "ducimurque omnes lucri cupiditate"; "ad futuros casus atque impetus fortunae." Cf. *De avaritia,* p. 13. This is the same argument, drawn from Cicero and Petrarch (*Secretum,* p. 88: "Senectutis pauperiem ante prospiciens si fatigate etati adiumenta conquiro, quid hic tam reprehensibile est?"; cf. Marsh, pp. 47, 126, nn. 16–17). But quite typical of Poggio is what he writes on the subject of the *avarus senex:* "Quod si quis etiam senilem avaritiam turpem duceret, non hominis consilium qui se communit ad insperatos improvisosque casus, sed naturae fragilitatem decet culpari, quae tot nos discriminibus subiecit, tot addixit necessitatibus, tot difficultatibus circum-

dedit, quarum rerum nisi inaniter et verbis magis quam re velimus philosophari, a divitiis necesse est suffragia postulentur" (p. 17).

53 Ibid., p. 15. The practical wisdom of the "legislators" is this way opposed to "philoso-phy." The reference here is to the Stoic doctrine, according to which the *semina divina,* which nature had infused in man, had been corrupted by human malice (cf. Seneca *Ad Lucilium* 73.16); or, more specifically, to Aristotle's authoritative statements in connection with the doctrine of money as a measurement suited for evaluation of things on equal terms, as a safeguard of equity in human society (cf. *Ethics to Nico-machus* 8.1133b, 14). Loschi overturns this statement: "Quicquid tractamus, operamur, agimus eo spectat, ut quam multum commodi ex eo capiamus; quod, quo amplius fuerit, eo maiori afficimus laetitia, atque commoda nostra fere pecunia pensantur:" (p. 11). It is possible to recognize here an echo of the stimulating ideas of Pietro di Giovanni Olivi on economics, which Bernardino adopted in his preaching. Accord-ing to Olivi's subjectivist view, "valor et pretium rerum venalium potius pensan-tur in respectu ad nostrum usum et utilitatem quam secundum absolutum valorem suarum essentiarum." Cf. A. Spicciani, "La mercatura e la formazione del prezzo nella riflessione teologica medioevale," *Atti dell'Accad. Naz. dei Lincei, Memorie della Classe di Sc. mor. stor. e filol.,* ser. 8, XX, no. 3, vol. 374 (Rome, 1977), pp. 143, 196; cf. also further on, n. 46. In the same way, Loschi's speech opposes Aristotle's conception of unnatural "chrematistic" (or exchange of goods), which was based on unneces-sary and unjust exchanges, insofar as "practiced by the one at the others' expense" (*Politica,* bk. 1, chap. 8, col. 1258b; cf. Spicciani, pp. 144 f.). Directly opposing this doctrine, Loschi states: "Sin autem ideo habes infensam avaritiam, quod ea importet secum multorum damna quibus parantur divitae, mercaturam quoque et quicquid est aliud in quo lucrum quaeritur oderis necesse est: nullum enim fit lucrum sine alicuius detrimento, cum quicquid emolumenti uni additur detrahatur alteri" (pp. 16 ff.). Avarice is understood as being both "private and public." Echoing Augustine (*De civitate Dei* 4.4), Loschi thus adds: "Sed quid ego de singulis hominibus disputo? Civitates, respublicae, provinciae, regna quid aliud sunt, si recte animadvertas, prae-ter publicam avaritiae officinam?" (p. 13). Bernardino also cited "Augustino in libro De civitate Dei . . . . : Che so' i regni senza la giustizia? So' una grandissima ladron-celleria" (Banchi, ed., *Le prediche volgari,* vol. 2, sermon 17, p. 28). The difference is that the connection between the individual and the state, which in theological and scholastic tradition consisted in the foundation of justice, is here based on its exclu-sion.

54 "Cupiditas vehemens quae excedit modum." Cf. *De avaritia,* pp. 18 ff. (but cf. also n. 79 below.)

55 Cf. ibid., pp. 27 ff.

56 Ibid., p. 20; and in general, Goldbrunner, pp. 449 f.

57 "omissa definiendi solertia"; "ut res mortalium ad eius voluntatem circumagi videan-tur nullo ordine ductae." Cf. *De varietate fortunae,* ed. D. Georgius (Paris, 1723), pp. 31 f. [*Opera omnia,* vol. 2, pp. 533 f.]. On this close examination of the concept of fortune (ibid., pp. 25–36), cf. Tateo, pp. 276 f. [and here below, chap. 4, nn. 227 ff.]. On the connection between these views and ethical ideas, see the comments here

attributed to Loschi: "Omittamus . . . principum vitia, quae magis reprehendi quam corrigi possunt" (p. 67). Struever, p. 195, has suggested a connection between Poggio's views and the ancient doctrine of the Sophists, "that it is impossible to teach virtue." Nevertheless, the same criticism made in connection with skepticism also applies to this point. Poggio's skepticism does not derive from rhetorical or logical doctrines, but rather is, if I can say so, of a practical nature, based, from an empirical point of view, on a crisis of trust in the ends.

58 Cf. the clear exposition by Spicciani, pp. 154 ff., which, among other things, notes (as is expedient in the context of analyzing *De avaritia*) that the canon of the *Decretum Gratiani* is included in the "distinction" that prohibits clerics from taking part in commerce ("Episcopi et ecclesiastici saecularia negotia non curent"). Cf. also Oppel, pp. 575 ff.; Goldbrunner, pp. 439 ff. On the rhetorical variations related to this theme, cf. nn. 62, 63, and 64 below.

59 "quod in mercatione concurrunt multa pro reipublicae servitio et utilitate"; "quia duo vel tres in una civitate magna corrumpunt totam multitudinem mercatorum." Cf. Oppel, p. 575, in reference to Bernardino's *Quadragesimale de Evangelio Aeterno,* sermon 33, "De mercatoribus et artificibus." The comments were repeated by Bernardino in the context of his popular preaching. Cf. for example, Banchi, ed., *Prediche,* vol. 3, sermon 38, pp. 249 f.: "Oh! chi se lo vorrebbe fare a questi tali? Eglino si vorebono sbandire, o fare uno statuto e confinargli"; cf. also D. Scaramuzzi, *La dottrina del B. G. Duns Scoto nella predicazione di S. Bernardino* (Florence, 1930), pp. 32 f.

60 Oppel, pp. 585 f.

61 Goldbrunner, pp. 445 f., has Harth's essay in mind when he objects "dass der unmittelbare Bezug von *De Avaritia* Zur Volkspredigt der Bettelmönche und zur Aktivität des hl. Bernardino nur in der Urfassung, nicht aber in der unter dem Einfluss von Niccoli entstanden entgultigen Fassung des Dialoges trasparent ist." It should therefore be clarified: (a) That the reference to, or rather the citation of, Bernardino ("semel dixit in usurarios") was clearly made not by accident but rather in order to create the opportunity of presenting a competing discussion ("quare tentemus et ipsi," etc.); and that Poggio provides a fuller articulation of these aims in a letter he wrote to Niccoli, on 8 June 1429, in Harth, "N. Niccoli," p. 35: "Nam quod mentio fratris Bernardini displicet eaque in dialogum introductio, id ego non feci ad eum laudandum, sed ad exagitandum paulisper hos molestos latratores ac rabulas foraneos. Simul per eorum ineptias visum est *apte subici posse quibus in rebus delinquant,* cum non reprehendant ea vitia quae magis vulgo nocent. Scis morem dialogorum eum esse, *ut vel veris rebus vel similibus veri niti debeat,* et saepius alia res ex alia cadat" (italics mine). (b) That Niccoli's "censure" was not, as it has been considered by Harth, merely literary in nature but rather stems from his concern about the explicitness of Poggio's attack, to the extent that he urged Poggio to present the same material in an indirect and allusive way ("Sed alia via aggrediamur"). The result was the so-called "definitive" version, in reality, as has been noted (above, n. 14), a makeshift version. (c) That the explicit reference to Bernardino is a sign of Poggio's interest in issues of preaching, even if it would be rather futile to expect to find exact parallels with texts of preachings or sermons, whose circulation at that time we know little about

(Goldbrunner's concerns, p. 438, to establish precise points of criticism and chronology cannot be of decisive importance; in any case, it should not be forgotten that the context of the 1426 dialogue is fictional). Poggio's reference to the doctrines that Bernardino was then spreading in his preaching should be thought in terms of suggestion; but not — I believe — in terms of arbitrary inferences. In conclusion, it would be making an arbitrary conclusion to distrust the author's statement, that he had been moved by Bernardino's preaching to discuss the relationship between moral ideas and economic activity (an issue not to be found elsewhere in Poggio's works), maintaining close similarities to Bernardino's themes and terminology, which scholars have not failed to point out (cf. Harth, "N. Niccoli," p. 41: "enge thematische Berührungspunkte"; Goldbrunner, p. 441: "Eben diese Motive spielen im Dialogue eine wichtige Rolle . . . unmittelbar von Anfang an," contradicting to some extent the observation cited above).

62   "tamquam seminarium malorum." Cf. *De avaritia*, p. 8; cf. also Goldbrunner, p. 441.

63   Ibid., p. 13: "Nam qui inhabitabunt illas [*scil.* civitates] expulsis avaris? Nos quippe eiiciemur" etc.; and further on, p. 14: ". . . ut si avaros existimes redarguendos, universus tibi reprehendendus sit terrarum orbis, totumque humanum genus immuntandum in alios mores, in aliam vivendi institutionem" (precisely the particular "statute" which Bernardino invoked; cf. n. 55).

64   Ibid., p. 27: ". . . sicut Plato e republica, quam iustam suis libris describit, expulit quos [quod, *ed.*] eorum verbis et doctrina infici putaret vitam adulescentum ac civitatum mores." It would perhaps have been preferable if, in order to preserve the Roman republic, Cicero had also threatened banishment: "sed vir prudentissimus, obsecutus forsan temporibus, solummodo mulcta plectendam avaritiam censuit, non addens graviorem poenam" (cf. Cicero, *De legibus* 3.3.6).

65   "ratione et mensura indivisibili in plus et minus"; "sub aliqua latitudine competenti respectu temporum, locorum, personarum." Cf. Spicciani, p. 195; and also Scaramuzzi, *La dottrina,* p. 195. Oppel, p. 572, claims to see in Bernardino's Latin treatises "a more permissive, less censorious view of social questions than he [Bernardino] did in his more popular moralistic sermons" (an opinion which Goldbrunner refutes easily, p. 438).

66   Cf. *De avaritia,* p. 10. In this sense, there is some truth to Oppel's claim to find an echo of Bernardino's doctrines in Loschi's remarks. It is worth noting that the statement according to which, in contrast to avarice, laws and judgments were established "in luxuriam" may allude to the canon *Fornicari,* D. 88, c. 10: "Fornicari hominibus semper non licet, negotiari vero aliquando licet, aliquando non licet," according to a statement of Augustine, on whose authority Bernardino tempered the harshness of the subsequent canon, *Eiciens.;* cf. R. De Roover, *San Bernardino and Sant'Antonino of Florence: The Two Great Economic Thinkers of the Late Middle Ages* (Boston, 1967), p. 10. On the other hand, theological speculation had distinguished between God's law and civil law. This last was "made for anyone and not only for the virtuous, and therefore could not prohibit everything contrary to virtue, but might limit itself to prohibiting what would subvert the general welfare." This was the basis for the latitudinarianism of Franciscan doctrines, which sought to define the terms for the

freedom to bargain, sanctioned in *Digesta* 35.2.70 (cf. De Roover, p. 20; Spicciani, pp. 190 f., 205 f.). Nevertheless, it should not be overlooked that these theories, even though present and utilized in *De avaritia*, are reduced to paradoxical assumptions in the context of dialogical debate, as if Poggio would compete with juridical and theological doctrinairism. In fact his aim is not so much to evaluate the merit per se of such doctrines as it is to empty them of their ethical and theological content. In other words, his main intention is to deny their relevance in the context of a moral discourse. The lack of any reference to the rules against monopolies, another principle point of Bernardino's "economic" preaching, would seem to emphasize this point.

67 "plus velle quam quod satis est." Cf. *De avaritia*, p. 17 f.; and also, in connection with this, Goldbrunner, p. 443; see chap. 2, n. 64 above.

68 Bruni, *Humanistisch-philosophische Schriften*, pp. 120 f.: "Sunt vero utiles divitiae, cum et ornamento sint possidentibus et ad virtutem exercendam suppeditent facultatem"; cf. H. Baron, "Franciscan Poverty and Civic Wealth as Factors in the Rise of Humanistic Thought," *Speculum* 13 (1938): 1–37 [now, in a developed form, Baron, *In Search of Florentine Civic Humanism* (Princeton, 1988), vol. 1, pp. 158–257]; J. F. McGovern, "The Rise of New Economic Attitudes: Economic Humanism, Economic Nationalism During the Later Middle Ages and the Renaissance," *Traditio* 26 (1970): 236 ff.; Goldbrunner, p. 447. Bruni's comments are, in fact, repeated in *De avaritia*, p. 12: "Est enim peroportuna ad usum communem et civilem vitam pecunia, quam necessario Aristoteles inventam tradit ad commercia hominum resque mutuo contrahendas," clearly abstracting from Aristotle's specific doctrine about equal exchange and unnatural "chrematistic." Moreover, it is worth noting the repeated allusions made to Bruni and to his translations beginning with the preface of the dialogue, not to mention Poggio's concern not to offend him as "avaricious," a quality that is somewhat allusively attributed to Aristotle himself (p. 11).

69 "ut saepius alia res ex alia cadat." Cf. Harth, "N. Niccoli," p. 36.

70 Cf. J. Soudek, "L. Bruni and His Public: A Statistical and Interpretive Study of His Annotated Latin Version of the (Pseudo)-Aristotelian Economics," *Studies in Medieval and Renaissance History* 5 (1968): 51–136; H. M. Goldbrunner, "Leonardo Bruni Kommentar zu seiner Uebersetzung der pseudo-aristotelischen Oekonomik: ein humanistischer Kommentar," in *Der Kommentar in der Renaissance, Mitteilungen der Kommission für Humanismusforschung*, ed. A. Buck, vol. 1 (Boppard, 1975), pp. 99–118; Goldbrunner, "Poggios," p. 444.

71 "oblitus publici commodi"; "publicus omnium hostis." Cf. *De avaritia*, pp. 7 f.; and also Spicciani, pp. 197 ff.; Goldbrunner, p. 441. Cf. in particular Banchi, ed., *Le prediche volgari*, vol. 3, sermon 28, p. 216: "per lo ben comune si diè esercitare la mercantia."

72 "Dicuntur eiusmodi nonnulla a philosophis de praeponenda utilitate communi, magis speciose quam vere. Sed vita mortalium non est exigenda nobis ad stateram philosophiae." Cf. *De avaritia*, p. 16.

73 "Non aurificis statera, sed populari quadam trutina." Cf. Cicero *De oratore* 2.38.159; and also Marsh, p. 50.

74 "E quanti essempli ài, avaro! Credi a chi à bilanciato il mondo!"; "Io so' andato colla

mia bilancia bilanciando Italia." Cf. Banchi, ed., *Le prediche volgari,* vol. 3, sermon 38, p. 225; and also vol. 1, sermon 11, pp. 274 f.; sermon 14, p. 333.

75 Harth, "N. Niccoli," p. 44 (cf. also chap. 2, n. 61 above). The substituted passage, still unpublished, can be characterized by the following sentences: "Sed nimis remota illa est sententia a sensibus nostris et communi prudentia, nullum esse peccatum aliud alio maius, et eque peccare qui unam quondam ediculam et qui patriam incenderit. Nostri dispares esse volunt virtutes et vitia multumque inter se distare et pondere et magnitudine" (Florence, Bibl. Naz. Centr., Conv. Soppr. J I 16, f. 189 v; cf. in connection with this Cicero *De finibus* 4.24.68). This, then, is that "other road" with which Poggio "assails" the same argument (cf. here above, n. 61).

76 *De avaritia,* p. 16. Cp. also the MS. note of a contemporary owner of a *De avaritia* copy, who was seemingly attracted by Poggio's paradoxes: "De veteri consuetudine preferendi utilitatem privatam publice." Cf. Florence, Bibl. Naz. Centr. Conv. Soppr., J I 31, f. 164r; cf. *Catalogo,* p. 27, n. 30.

77 "Nisi malumus magnifica loqui quam consueta." Cf. *De avaritia,* p. 16.

78 Cf. R. W.-A. J. Carlyle, *Il pensiero politico medievale,* trans. in Italian by L. Firpo, vol. 1 (Bari, 1956), pp. 36 ff., in connection with, among others, Seneca, *Ad Lucilium* 90.39: "inrupit in res optime positas avaritia"; and also Spicciani, pp. 132, 221 ff., with bibliography. The doctrine, moreover, was common knowledge; cf. *Giovanni Rucellai e il suo Zibaldone,* vol. 1: *"Il Zibaldone quaresimale,"* selections by A. Perosa (London, 1960), p. 12: "Et se io fussi domandato perché a richo è richiesta la cortesia, sappiate ch'ella è richiesta a ogni huomo, ma spetialmente a colui che è richo, perciò che la terra et le possessioni et l'avere, le quali cose sono tutte terra, si sono comuni tra le genti secondo le ragioni naturali, ma perché dalle dette cose nascevano molte discordie e erano neghettite et abandonate, si fu trovato e ordinato per le genti la signoria delle cose, acciò che quelle discordie e negligentie cessassero."

79 *De avaritia,* p. 18: "Nihil habet haec reprehensionis cupiditas modica et temperata, quam non aberrabis si dixeris naturalem"; avarice was another matter, "immensa, insatiabilis cupiditas habendi ultra quam decet, plus quam oporteat." St. Thomas Aquinas, *De regimine principum* 1.2, had legitimated profit in consideration of its ends: "unde nihil prohibet lucrum ordinari ad aliquem finem necessrium vel etiam honestum." Cf. on this point Spicciani, pp. 157 f.: "Tommaso pensa forse di superare . . . la logica aristotelica operando una distinzione fra 'cupidità e 'guadagno.' Il 'lucrum,' in se considerato, gli appare né buono né cattivo. . . . È la cupidità che lo rende condannabile, moltiplicandolo oltre misura a prescindere dalle effettive necessita degli uomini." Andreas's appeal for a just measure, even in its use of a somewhat similar terminology, is only apparently inspired by Aristotelian and Thomistic doctrines, insofar as it breaks away from an objective consideration of ends and instead retreats to a Stoic vision of the subjective control of the passions. It does not even seem possible to discern, as does Tateo, pp. 259 f., the "concetto ciceroniano del necessario accordo di 'utile' e 'onesto' "; in truth, it represents a simple assertion of the incompatibility of *virtus* and *avaritia,* and the studied evasiveness and eclectic terminology once again serves to indicate that the solution cannot be doctrinal in nature.

80 "Legunt sed non servant verba Isidori, qui iubet eos fugere amorem pecuniae." Cf.

De avaritia, p. 22; cf. the letter to Niccoli, 10 June 1429, in Harth, "N. Niccoli," p. 35: "Mentionem autem Isidori factam scias non inopia auctoritatum, sed quia in culpanda avaritia sacerdotum ii potissime apti videbantur quos illi dignificant quosque in suis legibus et decretis quotidie legunt." The reference was, in fact, suppressed in the revised version (cf. Harth, p. 46), demonstrating once again the precautionary motives underlying Niccoli's intervention.

81 Cf. Tateo, pp. 270 f.; Marsh, pp. 47 f.; There is, moreover, an explicit reference to Petrarch: "Recte Franciscus Petrarcha, vir suae aetatis optimus ac praestantissimus, avaram [um, *ed.*] Bablyoniam nuncupavit, vidit quam insita esset huic generi hominum avaritia, quam infinita cupiditas, quanta libido quaestus."

82 Cf. Goldbrunner, p. 477. According to Oppel, pp. 586 f., the contradiction is "only apparent," since it "is consistent that Poggio, a layman and a citizen, should apologize for and endorse this-worldy values in the civic sphere and condemn them in the church. . . . Most important for an understanding of this work is the special position of the humanist secretaries" etc. We recognize the obvious and almost tautological tendency to evaluate on the basis of preconceived generalizations; in this case "civic humanism" on the one hand and the newly coined term "humanist secretaries" on the other. In other words, inasmuch as we substitute the concern for the individual with such generalizations, the issue is emptied of meaning, real though its terms may be.

83 Letter to Cardinal Giuliano Cesarini, 10 July 1432, in *Opera omnia,* vol. 4, p. 49 [ed. Harth, vol. 2, p. 145]: "Ego iamdudum decrevi certum vitae cursum. . . . Nolo esse sacerdos, nolo beneficia . . . decrevi procul a vestro ordine consumere quicquid superest temporis peregrinationis meae." Goldbrunner relies on a passage from a letter by Poggio to Niccoli (9 February 1426, ed. Tonelli, vol. 1, p. 174 [ed. Harth, vol. 1, p. 169]: "Ego et clericus sum et beneficium possideo, nec ullum est mihi patrimonium"), which in reality demonstrates the opposite. Actually Poggio is protesting precisely in his capacity as a citizen, not to enjoy other goods subject to taxes, apart from the immune returns of his benefice, as Niccoli should make clear "cum officialibus ad id deputatis."

84 Cf. "Oratio ad Patres reverendissimos," in *Umanesimo e secolarizzazione,* p. 329, lines 305 ff.: "incipite a vobismet ipsis. Vos vero mihi traditis doctrinam minime profuturam"; and p. 316, line 41: "Experti sumus ista nimium diu in multis," etc. Elsewhere, the "nos" includes the community of the faithful, laymen and clerics alike, in contrast to the empty pride of the latter; ibid., p. 337 f., lines 454 ff.: "Nescitis enim qua hora venturus [*scil.* terminus] sit, ne cum venerit vos inveniat dormientes. Mors quidem nos circumstat . . . danda est opera ne incautos nos opprimat. Ad maiora quaedem geniti sumus" etc. The same shift from "vos" to "nos" happens between the first and the second version of the *De avaritia* in Andreas's concluding peroration; cf. p. 31: "Cum migrabitis a vita, destituent vos abibitisque nudi, inopes, deserti"; whereas in the revised version "Andreas die Anwesenden hier durchgehend in Wir-Form anspricht, seine eigene Person einbegreifend" (Harth, "N. Niccoli," pp. 45 f.).

85 "Sed mirum est, cum tot monita excellentium virorum, tot sana consilia, tot plenas auctoritatis gravitatisque sententias habeamus ante oculos positas, quibus permoveri

mentes mortalium deberent, tamen existere aliquos, qui ratione posthabita cupiditati dedicent se tamquam deo." Cf. *De avaritia*, p. 31.

86 The assimilation of Christian and ancient precepts, according "non unius aut alterius voces, sed naturae et ipsius veritatis," was another of the controversial points, later suppressed after Niccoli's "censure." The sentence with which it was substituted was: "Tum Bartholomeus: Plurima in hanc sententiam—inquit—scripta praeclare monumentis litterarum viri sapientissimi tradiderunt. Ad quae si homines adhiberent aures animumque intenderent, procul dubio substisterent paulisper nec ita proni coecique in cupiditatum pelagus deferrentur" (Harth, "N. Niccoli," p. 46). Clearly, the more vague terminology that Poggio adopts here does not prevent him from intensifying his emphasis on the conditional and optative forms of the verb.

87 "Oratio ad Patres reverendissimos," in *Umanesimo e secolarizzazione*, p. 335, lines 425 f.: "Tamen nihil ista tam multa proficiunt; ducimur a vitiis neque ullum auxilium imploramus."

88 Ibid., p. 331, line 337, concerning the opposition between the apostolic examples of the apostles and the corruption of the time, in one of the most authoritative MSS. appears the following alternative: ". . . gaudebant illi paupertate, vos divitiis; illi potentiam mundanam aspernabantur, *humanitatem seu humilitatem* sequentes, vos dominia et elatio delectant." One branch of the manuscript tradition reads "humanitatem," whereas another gives the reading "humilitatem," so that we can suppose we are dealing with an author's variant. But see also, as significant to this issue, Poggio's "Oratio ad summum pontificem Nicolaum V," *Opera*, p. 289: "Ad humanitatem quoque adhortandi [*sc.* pontifices]. . . . Est enim virtutum omnium condimentum. Admonendi sunt, ut meminerint se homines esse . . . licet sanctissimi et beatissimi appellentur. Quae cogitatio, si saepius mentem subeat, non sinet principes ultra humanam conditionem efferri." The passage once more corresponds significantly to "Oratio," p. 325, lines 206 f., concerning the "flagitia" of the popes: "mihi quidem ipsi haec aliena videntur ab ipsius lege naturae, indigna homine etiam facinoroso, nedum eo qui se velit sanctissimum ac beatissimum appellari." From an opposite perspective, human instincts are considered, which are barely concealed by social convention—precisely the "semina avaritiae" in the dialogue: "Nam plures pudore peccandi quam bona voluntate prohibiti abstinent. Semina in te sunt eadem: detur facultas, detur potestas perficiendi, eris, mihi crede, improbior" ("Oratio," p. 328, lines 278 ff.). This puts into particular relief his accusation of hypocrisy, "quae totum mundum falsa bonitatis specie subornavit" (ibid., p. 317, line 57), which is so prominent that, as noted earlier (above, n. 9), Poggio asks himself: ". . . ut iam nesciam quid credam aut cui credam." The impact of these themes on contemporary opinion (both in Italy and elsewhere) is a topic worthy of investigation: in the Munich codex, Staatsbibl., lat. 418, the oration is followed by Bruni's invective *Contra hypocritas* (ff. 181 ff.), while von Eyb's edition contaminates the two (on the subject see *Umanesimo e secolarizzazione*, pp. 303–14). An Italian copy of Poggio's *Contra hypocritas* (of the second half of the fifteenth century), in the course of radicalizing the polemic, associates the theme of hypocrisy with one of superstition, in keeping with the title given to the work: "De hypocritis et superstiosis" (Florence, Bibl. Laurenziana, MS. Acquisti e Doni 333, f. 26 r.; cf. *Catalogo*, p. 31 n. 40). The title actually corresponds to that of

a brief chapter in Platina's *De principe*, with the exact title of "Contra superstitionem et hypocrisim," which at various levels shows itself to be indebted to Poggio's *Dialogi;* cf. B. Platina, *De principe*, ed. G. Ferraù (Palermo, 1979), pp. 61 ff.

89   "Incipiamus ergo a partibus, illas componamus, tum facile corpus componetur ("Oratio ad Patres reverrendissimos," p. 329, lines 303 ff.); cf., in connection with this, Fubini, "Papato e storiografia nel Quattrocento . . . ," *Studi Medievali*, 3a ser., 18 (1977): 329.

90   "Quale si converrà sostenere per amicizia dello imperadore, e quale per amicizia di re e di baroni, e quale per amicizia dei cardinali o d'altri signori e prelati di S. Chiesa . . . Non si fe' mai riformazione di Chiesa generale, ma sì particulare . . . Aumenta e dà favore a' buoni, e basta." Cf. *Quaresimale del 1424*, ed. Cannarozzi, vol. 1, pp. 220 f.; cited by Miccoli, *Bernardino predicatore*, p. 35.

91   "Non est reformatio haec, sed deformem fieri; adversari per contumeliam Pontificis mandato non est ponere pacem, sed gladium in populo. . . . Sub velamento concilii aliud quiddam moliuntur"; "Scio difficillimum esse compescere iram, odia, cupiditates. . . . Caput is est: si quid deliquerit, tuum est quid sentias loqui et efficere ut sis extra noxam; hoc tamen praestare debet vir sapiens, ut vacet culpa . . . Reliquum est ut oboediens dicto sis: egisti ut fore utile iudicabas." Cf. letter to G. Cesarini, 31 December 1432, ed. Tonelli, vol. 2, pp. 22–31 [ed. Harth, vol. 2, pp. 148–50; I accept the date established by Harth]. On the surrounding circumstances, see J. W. Stieber, *Pope Eugenius IV, the Council of Basel, and the Secular and Ecclesiastical Authorities in the Empire* (Leiden, 1978) (Studies in the History of Christian Thought, 13), pp. 12–19.

4. The Theater of the World in the Moral and Historical Thought of Poggio Bracciolini

1   For recent contributions and definitive summaries, cf. B. L. Ullman, *The Origins and Development of Humanistic Script* (Rome, 1960), pp. 21–57; T. Foffano, "Niccoli, Cosimo e le ricerche di Poggio nelle biblioteche francesi," *Italia medioevale e umanistica* 12 (1969): 113–28; S. Rizzo, *Il lessico filologico degli umanisti* (Rome, 1973), pp. 327–38 and passim; A. De La Mare, *The Handwriting of Italian Humanists,* vol. 1, pt. 1 (Oxford, 1973), pp. 62–84; other information may be found in Biblioteca Medicea Laurenziana, *Poggio Bracciolini nel VI centenario della nascita: Mostra di codici e documenti fiorentini,* ed. R. Fubini and S. Caroti (Florence, 1980) [hereafter cited as *Catalogo*]; on this cf. also R. Fubini, "Poggio Bracciolini attraverso l'esposizione dei suoi codici," *Accademie e Biblioteche d'Italia* 49 (1981): 79–89. The preeminent interest in his manuscript discoveries is still attested to in R. Roedel, "Poggio Bracciolini nel quinto centenario della morte," *Rinascimento* 11 (1960): 51–67; and in *Two Book Hunters: Letters of Poggius Bracciolini to Nicolaus de Nicolis,* trans. and notes by Ph. W. Goodhart Gordan (New York, 1979). See also E. Bigi and A. Petrucci, "Bracciolini, Poggio," *Dizionario Biografico degli Italiani,* vol. 13 (1971), pp. 640–46.

2   C. G. Gutkind, "Poggio Bracciolinis geistliche Entwicklung," *Deutsches Vierteljahrschrift für Literaturwissenschaft und Geistesgeschichte,* 10 (1932), pp. 548–596; especially p. 573.

3   See above, chap. 2; and also my essay, "Osservazioni sugli 'Historiarum Florentini

populi libri XII' di Leonardo Bruni," *Studi di storia medievale e moderna per Ernesto Sestan,* vol. 1 (Florence, 1980), pp. 403–48.

4 Cf. R. Fubini, "Biondo, Flavio," *Dizionario Biografico degli Italiani,* vol. 10 (1968), p. 547 f.; Fubini, "Papato e storiografia nel Quattrocento," *Studi medievali,* 3a ser., 18 (1977), pp. 326, 329 f.

5 Cf. P. O. Kristeller, *Studies in Renaissance Thought and Letters* (Rome, 1969), p. 553 ff.; and also, Kristeller, *La tradizione classica nel pensiero del Rinascimento* (Florence, 1965); *Concetti rinascimentali dell'uomo e altri saggi* (Florence, 1978), pp. 81ff; J. R. Seigel, "'Civic Humanism' or Ciceronian Rhetoric? The Culture of Petrarch and Bruni," *Past and Present* 34 (1966): 3–48; Seigel, *Rhetoric and Philosophy in Renaissance Humanism* (Princeton, 1968).

6 E. S. Piccolomini, *De viris illustribus* (Stuttgart, 1842), p. 24: "Hoc etiam tempore magnus est habitus Poggius, qui licet lingua ignarus fuerit, nulli tamen in dicendo fuit inferior. . . . Scripsit 'de avaritia' elegantem tractatum, quamvis ipse more hominum qui aliena potius quam sua praenoscunt vitia nequaquam liberalis esset. Scripsit 'de infelicitate principum,' 'de nobilitate et confabulatione,' quae suis moribus potius quam famae consentiunt" etc.

7 P. Cortesi, *De hominibus doctis dialogus,* ed. G. Ferraù (Palermo, 1979), p. 135 f.; Desiderio Erasmo, *Il Ciceroniano,* ed. A. Gambaro (Brescia, n.d.), p. 216: "Naturae satis erat, artis et eruditionis non ita multum."

8 Pauli Iovii, *Elogia virorum illustrium,* ed. R. Meregazzi, *Opera,* cura et studio Societatis Historiae Novocomensis denuo edita, VIII (Rome, 1972), p. 46: ". . . erat consilio gravis et, quum luberet, facetiarum sale perurbanus, ita ut mira et saepe subita varietate ad ciendum risum modo praetextatis verbis uteretur, modo gravibus et malignis scommatibus alienae famae nomen perstringeret. . . . Erat quoque Pogius adeo intemperans obiurgator" etc.

9 Poggius Bracciolini, *Opera omnia,* ed. R. Fubini, 4 vols. (Turin, 1964–69): volume 1, with an introduction by R. Fubini, *Scripta in editione Basilensi MDXXXVIII collata* (1964) [cited here as *Opera*]; volume 2, *Opera miscellanea edita et inedita* (1966) [cited here as *Opera omnia,* vol. 2]; volume 3, *Epistolae curante Thomas de Tonellis;* volume 4, *Epistulae miscellaneae: Accedunt epistulae aliquot ineditae et tabula epistularum a Poggio et ad ipsum conscriptarum* (1969) [cited here as *Opera omnia,* vol. 4]. The letters edited by Tonelli will be cited with the abbreviation ed. Tonelli, vol. 1, 2, or 3, according to whether they are in the first, second or third volume of his edition, included the reprinted volume 3 [the reference to Poggio's letters must now be extended to include the new edition, which, nevertheless, by limiting it to the collections approved by the author, does not completely replace the earlier one: Poggio Bracciolini, *Lettere,* ed. H. Harth, vol. 1, *Lettere a Niccolo Niccoli* (Florence, 1984); vol. 2, *Epistolarum familiarium libri* (1984); vol. 3, *Epistolarum familiarium libri, secundum volumen* (1987); references to this edition will be made with the abbreviation ed. Harth]. In references to individual works found in volume 2 and volume 3, the page number of the original edition will be cited, followed in square brackets by the page number in the pertinent volume (for example, *De varietate fortunae,* ed. D. Giorgi (Paris, 1723), p. 30 [*Opera omnia,* vol. 2, p. 532]). [The collection of the *Opera Omnia* has now been

completed with some supplementary works: M. C. Davies, "Poggio Braccolini as Rhetorician and Historian: Unpublished Pieces," *Rinascimento* 22 (1982): 153–82.]

10 L. Martines, *The Social World of the Florentine Humanists* (Princeton, 1963), pp. 15 f., 123 ff., 258.

11 The contributions by Harth, Oppel, and Goldbrunner are quoted and discussed in chap. 3 above.

12 Cf. Tateo, pp. 251–77; D. Marsh, *The Quattrocento Dialogue*, pp. 38–58.

13 Cf. H. Harth, "Eine kritische Ausgabe der Privatbriefe Poggio Bracciolinis," *Wölfenbütteler Renaissance-Mitteilungen*, vols. 2 and 3 (1978), pp. 73–75 (it anticipates the critical edition, as well as a more thorough study of Poggio's correspondence). [Cf. Harth, "Poggio Bracciolini und die Brieftheorie des 15. Jahrhunderts: Zur Gattungsform des humanistischen Briefs," *Der Brief im Zeitlater de Renaissance*, ed. F. J. Worstbrock (Wienheim, 1983), pp. 81–99.]

14 Cf. F. Tateo, "La raccolta delle 'Facezie' e lo stile 'comico' di Poggio," *Poggio Bracciolini, 1380–1980: Nel VI centenario della nascita* (Florence, 1982), pp. 207–33; L. Sozzi, "Le 'Facezie' e la loro fortuna europea," ibid., pp. 235–59.

15 Cf. N. Rubenstein, "Poggio Bracciolini cancelliere e storico di Firenze," *Atti e Memorie dell'Accademia Petrarca di Arezzo*, n.s., 37 (1958–1964): 1–25; D. Wilcox, *The Development of Florentine Humanist Historiography in the Fifteenth Century* (Cambridge, Mass., 1969), pp. 130–76; and also E. Garin, Introduction to *Historia fiorentina*, by Poggio Bracciolini, trans. by his son, Jacopo (Arezzo, 1980 [reprint of the Venice edition of 1476]), pp. not numbered. (See also my essay, "Cultura umanistica e tradizione cittadina nella storiografia fiorentina del '400," *La storiografia umanistica*, vol. 1, Convegno internazionale di studi [Messina, 1992], pp. 399–443; in particular, pp. 415–23.)

16 Struever, "Rhetoric, Ethics, and History: Poggio Bracciolini," in her *The Language of History . . .* , pp. 144–99; cf. especially p. 197.

17 G. Holmes, *The Florentine Enlightenment, 1400–1450* (New York, 1969).

18 L. Bruni, *Commentarius rerum suo tempore gestarum, R.I.S.,* 2d ed., XIX, 2, ed. C. Di Pierro (Bologna, 1926). The work ends with the battle of Anghiari (1440).

19 Cf. Fubini, *Papato*, p. 324; the first core of the work was written earlier, in 1437.

20 His competitive attitude could be understood from the following words of the preface, ed. D. Giorgi (Paris, 1723), p. 2 [*Opera Omnia*, vol. 2, p. 504]: "Si vero commendatione historia digna est, haec nostra est profecto, in qua fortunae instabilis favor describitur" etc. The original core of the work (what now makes up more or less books 2 and 3) was composed before 1443; cf. the letter to Pietro del Monte, 14 September 1443, ed. Tonelli, vol. 2, p. 281 [ed. Harth, p. 427]: "Composui duos libros de varietate fortunae, sed nondum edidi" etc; but cf. also the letter to Cardinal G. Cesarini, 7 May 1431, ed. Tonelli, vol. 2, p. 346 f. [ed. Harth, vol. 2, p. 116]: "Scias me . . . tanquam in commentaria coniecisse usque ad haec tempora fortunae varietatem . . . licet Oddo noster se ultro nobis offerat, a quo velit exordium sumi" (with reference to the uproar provoked by the arrest of the interim cardinal, Ottone Poccia, upon the accession of Eugenius IV). Cf. also Biondo Flavio, *Historiae* (Basel, 1559), p. 458f.: "Habuit vero huiusce fastigii fortuna, quod semper in rebus contigit humanis, admixtam infelicitatis partem, et, quod ea tempestate non insulse est iactatum, quae res

defuncti olim pontificis omnium iudicio sapientissimi maximas cumulavit laudes, eadem suffecti opulentissimam labefecit fortunam" (in reference to the dispute over the treasure of Martin V, which had remained in the custody of the Colonna). The *De varietate* dwells on this issue, p. 89f. [*Opera omnia,* vol. 2, p. 591 f.]. [But on the composition of *De varietate fortunae,* see now the new edition: Poggio Bracciolini, *De varietate fortunae,* edizione critica e commento a cura di O. Merisalo (Helsinki, 1993) (Annales Academiae Scientiarum Fennicae, Ser. B, Tom. 265].

21 E. Walser, *Poggius Florentinus: Leben und Werke* (Leipzig, 1914), pp. 309, 323.

22 Ibid., pp. 37, 65, 83.

23 Ibid., p. 126.

24 Ibid., pp. 240, 258, 308.

25 Letter from Coluccio Salutati to Poggio, 17 December 1405, *Epistolario,* vol. 4, bk. 1, pp. 126–45. It refers to the panegyric of Petrarch, which Salutati addressed several years before to G. Bartolomei d'Arezzo, 13 July 1379, ibid., vol. 1, pp. 334–42, in connection with the project to publish Petrarch's works (cf. G. Billanovich, *Petrarca letterato* [Rome, 1947], pp. 300 f.), and which, as Novati explains (vol. 4, p. 130), "era . . . stata da molti aggiunta quasi condegna illustrazione ai codd. racchiudenti le opere del Petrarca"). On this issue, cf. M. Aurigemma, "Il giudizio sul Petrarca e le idee letterarie di Coluccio Salutati," *Accademia dell'Arcadia, Atti e Memorie,* ser. 3, VI, 4 (1975–1976), pp. 67–139.

26 Cf. Baron, *The Crisis,* pp. 225 ff.; and L. Bruni, *Dialogi ad Petrum Histrum,* in *Prosatori latini,* ed. E. Garin, p. 94.

27 F. Simone, *Il Rinascimento francese: Studi e ricerche* (Turin, 1961), p. 253; cf. also A. Coville, *Gontier et Pierre Col et l'Humanisme en France au temps de Charles VI* (Paris, 1924), pp. 104, 147; Jean De Montreuil, *Opera,* I, 1, *Epistolario,* ed. E. Ornato (Turin, 1963), p. 315.

28 "Cum plures . . . mali quam boni sint mortales, et oratores convenit esse bonos, per predicta ergo . . . eloquentiam non expedit esse aut rhetores." Cf. Jean de Montreuil, *Opera,* p. 192; and also E. Ornato, *Jean Muret et ses amis, Nicolas de Clémenges et Jean de Montreuil: Contribution a l'étude des rapports entre les humanistes de Paris et ceux d'Avignon* (Geneva and Paris, 1969), p. 233. The reference is to Petrarch, *Familiares* 24.3: On the issue cp. my observations in *Rivista Storica Italiana,* 88 (1976): 867 ff.

29 "non religione solum fide et baptismate christianum, sed et eruditione theologum et gentilibus illis philosophis preferendum." Cf. letter from Salutati to Poggio, 17 December 1405, p. 135. He refers in particular to the *Secretum.*

30 "Nimis tu et tuus ille peritus, ut scribis, amicus defertis et conceditis vetustati. Et ut ad primum veniam, quos priscos illos viros eruditissimos dicis, Christicolas an Gentiles?" Cf. ibid., p. 131.

31 Cf. Salutati's letter, in reply to Poggio's response of 26 March 1406, *Epistolario,* vol. 4, 1, pp. 158–170. Of particular interest in this context is the accusation of a lack of religious conviction ("nondum enim video quod doctrine christiane perfectionem agnoscas," p. 159 f.), and above all that he was concealing his own opinions from public view: "principio quidem non videris illius tui maleloquii penitere, qui defendere coneris quod ea domestice et per fidum delatorem . . . caute scripseris Nicolao, quasi

reprehenderim quod in scribendo minus adhibueris cautionis . . . , quasi ponderandum sit non consilium sed eventus" (p. 160). Salutati is referring in this instance to Seneca's precept, *Ad Lucilium* 3.2–3: "tu quidem ita vive, ut nichil committas nisi quod committere etiam inimico tuo possis," from which he amends Poggio's unilateral interpretation of this sentence, concerning the private sphere of friendship ("diu cogita, an tibi quis in amiciciam recipiendus est . . . : tam audacter cum eo loquere quam tecum"). In another place Seneca had exhorted Lucilius to conform to the conduct of the common norm, in order not to stir up the hostility against philosophy: "Satis ipsum nomen philosophiae, etiam si modeste tractetur, invidiosum est. . . . Intus omnia dissimilia sint, frons populo nostro conveniat" (Seneca *Ad Lucilium* 5.2). The passage had been adopted by Petrarch, in his defense against accusations of concealed profane preferences: "Mirari solitum te ais, quod mundum . . . sic artificiose decipiam. . . . Dicis me non modo vulgus insulsum sed celum ipsum fictionibus tentare; itaque Augustinum . . . simulata quadam benivolentia complexum, re vera a poetis et philosophis non avelli" (*Familiares* 2.9.2 and 8). Petrarch, however, boasts of his own deceit: "In hoc igitur ancipiti et lubrico itinere, si quem forte tam cautum vel natura vel studium fecisset, ut, fraudibus elusis, mundum ipse deciperet, frontem scilicet ostendens populo similem, tota intus mente dissimilis, quem tu hunc virum diceres?" (ibid., 5). Clearly, we are in a sphere of ideas no different from the one for which Salutati had reproached Poggio: except that what mattered to Petrarch as an individual norm of conduct appears now in Poggio as a norm of "caution" within a clique, as if in a kind of intellectual nicodemism inspired by Seneca's ancient sayings. The influence of Seneca (and Petrarch) on this point along the vicissitudes of humanism is a topic that still demands adequate analysis.

32 Cf. Grimal, *Sénèque ou la conscience de l'Empire* (Paris, 1978), p. 365; see, on this issue, Petrarch, *Familiares* 1.8.3: "Quanquam quid ego alienum aliquid dixerim, licet ab aliis elaboratum est, cum Epicuri sententia sit ab eodem Seneca relata, quicquid ab uno bene dictum sit non alienum esse sed nostrum?" (which repeats the basic maxim of Senecan "appropriation," where reference was made to Epicurus; cf. *Ad Lucilium* 1.5.16, 7. See also chap. 3 above. For Petrarch's reevaluation of Epicurus on the trusted model of Seneca, cf. also G. Radetti, "L'epicureismo nel pensiero umanistico del Quattrocento," *Grande antologia filosofica*, vol. 6 (Milan, 1964), p. 843. In this connection it is useful to make a comparison between the medieval and Trecento tradition, which did not mediate between the philosophical and patristic condemnation of the philosopher of "voluptas," and Seneca's authoritative opinion; cf. G. C. Garfagnini, "Da Seneca a Giovanni di Salisbury: 'Auctoritates' morali e 'vitae philosophorum' in un ms. trecentesco," *Rinascimento*, 2a ser., 20 (1980): 205, 215 f., 221, 230 ff.

33 I diverge from the more recent and authoritative interpretation by F. Rico, *Vida u obra de Petrarca: I, Lectura del "Secretum"* (Padua, 1974), according to whom "Petrarca asumia los factores negativos y los espiaba a beneficio de inventario penitencial" (p. 527). Rico's meticulous exegesis alone demonstrates the contradictions this statement comes up against and how much the author must himself add in order to strengthen it, to the point that he admits immediately afterward that "el humanista non reprimiera un leve suspirio, tambien atestiguado por el apografo: 'facturus to-

tidem libros de secreta pace animi, si pax erit,' 'si pax sit usquam' " (p. 528). On the limits of Petrarch's adhesion to Augustine, the basic text remains: P. Courcelle, *Les Confessions de Saint Augustin dans la tradition litteraire* (Paris, 1963), pp. 329 ff.

34 "qui iampridem ab ipsis gentium philosophis discere debuissem, nichil preter animum esse mirabile." Cf. *Familiares* 4.1.28 (and Seneca, *Ad Lucilium* 8.5). The passage rings out as a sharp denial of the legend of Seneca's Christianity, confirmed and diffused, it would seem, beginning with Giovanni Colonna's *De viris illustribus* (c. 1332); cf. A. Momigliano, "Note sulla leggenda del cristianesimo di Seneca," *Contributo alla storia degli studi classici* (Rome, 1955), pp. 23 ff. Incidentally, the fundamental relationship between Petrarch and Seneca demands new analysis, following the pages of De Nolhac, *Pétrarque*, vol. 2, pp. 115–26; A. Bobbio, "Seneca e la formazione spirituale del Petrarca," *La Bibliofila* 43 (1941): 224–91; and Dotti, *Fonti*, pp. 539–84; it is clearly insufficient to consider Seneca in relation to Petrarch only as "an ally in his hostility to scholasticism" (G. M. Rossi, "Seneca's Philosophical Influence," *Seneca*, ed. C. D. N. Costa [London, 1974], p. 142) without at least considering his purpose in competition with Seneca's (and apocryphas') reputation as teacher of ascetics, on which cf. C. G. Meersseman," Seneca maestro di spiritualità nei suoi opuscoli apocrifi dal XII al XV secolo," *Italia medioevale e umanistica* 16 (1973): 43–135.

35 "Contra ostentatores scientie non sue ac flosculorum decerptores." Cf. *Familiares* 4.15. On the attack made here against Valerius Maximus, and thus against the model of collections of exempla of an exterior and compilatory nature, not to mention its contemporary success especially in ecclesiastical contexts (think of the institutional comment of Dionigi di Borgo San Sepolero), see above, chap. 2 and 3.

36 "neque is ego sum qui . . . de prestantia excellentium virorum profitear me sententiam laturum"; "Sed inest quiddam mentibus hominum ipsa inditum natura, ut facilius quid in quaque re vitii sit animadvertunt quam corrigant errata, cum quid rectum sit pernoscere paucorum videamus intelligentie attributum. Ob quam causam Achademici fortasse ad refellendum promptiores fuere quam ad asserendum." Cf. Walser, p. 435 f. [*Opera omnia*, vol. 4, p. 439 f.]; the letter is dated Florence, 27 October 1413.

37 Cf. G. Martellotti, "Introduction" to F. Petrarca, *De viris illustribus* (Florence, 1964), p. li f. Rinuccini's text is now edited in Lanza, *Polemiche e berte letterarie*, pp. 261–67 (especially p. 264). Cf. also G. Tanturli, "Cino Rinuccini e la scuola di S. Maria in Campo," *Studi medievali*, 3a ser., 17 (1976): 625–74.

38 "initium est salutis notitia peccati"; "et hoc nonnullam spem mei corrigendi aliquando affert." Cf. letter to F. Pizolpasso, 5 August 1424, ed. Tonelli, vol. 1, p. 136 [ed. Harth, vol. 2, p. 44]. Cp. Seneca *Ad Lucilium* 28.9.

39 Cf. De La Mare, *The Handwriting*, p. 77, n. 12; *Catalogo*, p. 17 f., n. 3.

40 "Dux et magistra vitae bene degendae." Cf. *De avaritia*, *Opera*, p. 20; and above, chap. 3.

41 Cf. letter to Guarino, 15 March 1416, ed. Tonelli, vol. 1, p. 23 [not in ed. Harth]. Curiously, Walser, misunderstanding Poggio's remarks, infers that he "versichert ausdrücklich, kein schüler des Chrysoloras zu sein," p. 10, n. 1; and p. 228. Gutkind following him repeats that in Chrysoloras's circle "hatte der arme Poggio keinen

Zutritt" ("Poggio Bracciolinis," p. 556). As it has been shown, Poggio states the opposite; while in the other evidence cited by Walser (a letter to Guarino, c. 1454–55, ed. Tonelli, vol. 3, p. 179 f. [ed. Harth, vol. 3, p. 348]), he limits himself to mentioning that he had not composed the funeral eulogy for Chrysoloras that Cencio Rustici had anticipated, "qui eius laudandi munus sibi desumpsit." This does not mean that Poggio was extraneous to the group of the Greek teacher's followers, but it shows instead the cohesiveness of the group itself, if it could be represented by the funeral oration of only one of its members. This is confirmed by the repetition of the episode, according to Poggio, at the death of Antonio Loschi, "cuius laudationem me scripturum professus essem," only to be anticipated once again by Cencio, "quasi aegre laturus si quid a me scriberetur" (ibid.). Elsewhere, Poggio attests to his own albeit brief apprenticeship in Greek: his reading of Aristotle had had this effect: "cur amor graecarum litterarum *redierit*" (letter to Niccoli, 17 July 1420, ed. Tonelli, vol. 1, p. 39 [ed. Harth, vol. 1, p. 16]; italics mine). On the subject, I was not able to consult L. Ropes Loomis, "The Greek Studies of Poggio Bracciolini," *Medieval Studies in Memory of Gertrude Schoeperle Loomis* (Paris, 1927).

42 Cf. Walser, p. 228 f.

43 In his letter to Guarino, 15 March 1416, Poggio joins in deploring Leonardo Teronda's impertinent request for a tract supposedly written by Guarino himself, "in quo dicebaris te collegisse eorum errores, qui graeca contulerunt in latinum" (p. 24). As it also appears from Guarino's letter to Barolomeo of Montepulciano, to which Poggio makes reference (cf. Guarino, *Epistolario,* vol. 1, pp. 101 f.), Guarino's writing was a defense of L. Bruni's style of translation.

44 "prae caeteris"; "ad hominum imperitorum normam." Cf. letter to Antonio Loschi, 20 June 1424, ed. Tonelli, vol. 1, p. 114 [ed. Harth, vol. 2, p. 6], and to the same, c. 1426, in *Opera omnia,* vol. 4, p. 598.

45 Sometimes also in a literal sense: for example, Bruni asked Poggio to write his most confidential comments in Greek characters; cf. Walser, p. 228; and letter from Bruni to Poggio, April 1417, ed. Mehus, p. 110 (to be used alongside Luiso, *Studi,* p. 87), in connection with news from the Council: "si quid occultius fuerit, ἑλληνικῶς adnotabis." This, incidentally, is the context in which Bruni, in regard to the letter about Jerome of Prague's death, recommends to Poggio that he use caution: "Ego cautius de hisce rebus scribendum puto."

46 Hesiodus, *Opera et Dies,* 289–91. On the tradition of the sentence, cf. J. Bompaire, *Lucien écrivain: Imitation et création* (Paris, 1958), pp. 391 f. A. Otto, *Die Sprichwörter und sprichwörtlichen Redensarten der Römer* (Leipzig, 1890), p. 181, notes its recurrence only in Horace *Satires* 1.9.59 (but without mentioning Hesiod), and in Priscian, *Praeexercitamina,* 432–33 K: "Hesiodus quidem dixit: . . . virtutis sudorem di longe posuere" (which translates literally from *Opera,* 289: Τῆς δ᾽ ἀρετῆς ἱδρῶτα θεοὶ προπάροιθεν ἔθηκον). H. Walter, *Proverbia sententiaeque latinitatis Medii Aevi,* vol. 2, 5 (Göttingen, 1967), nos. 33694 and 33715, records the saying as anonymous, but from late repertoires, not before the sixteenth century ("virtus sudore paratur"; "virtutem posuere dii sudore parandam").

47 *Familiares* 4.1.13: "Equidem vita, quam beatam dicimus, celso loco sita est; arcta, ut

aiunt, ad illam ducit via." It refers to Matthew 7. 14: "quam angusta porta et arcta via est quae ducit ad vitam." But cf. also Seneca, *De vita beata* 7.3: "Altum quiddam est virtus, excelsum et regale" etc.

48 On the oration, which will be cited further on as "Oratio ad Patres reverendissimos," cf. R. Fubini, *Un'orazione;* and the edition of the text in *Umanesimo e Secolarizzazione,* pp. 303–38; my citations will follow both the numbering of the pages and the lines in my edition and its apparatuses.

49 "Ante ipsam poeta nobilis inquit Hesiodus deos sudorum posuisse, quam difficilis eius consequendae facultas esset ostendens." Cf. "Oratio ad Patres reverendissimos," *Umanesimo e secolarizzazione,* p. 316, lines 25–26.

50 Plato, *Protagoras,* 340 D: τῆς γάρ ἀρετῆς ἔμπροσθεν τοὺς θεοὺς ἱδρῶντα θεῖναι. As can be seen, the paraphrase of Plato, in accordance with the variant in which the gods do not place in front, as they do in Hesiod, "the sweat of virtue" but "the sweat in front of virtue" (whereas elsewhere in Plato, as in *Republic* 364 D, for example, the passage is cited literally), is followed strictly by Poggio, not without some harshness of his Latin version: "Ante ipsam . . . deos sudorem posuisse." Poggio's dependence on Plato's text should be no surprise: the Florentine circle in fact had longed early on for a complete version of Plato, and as if introducing his plan, Bruni had preceded his translation of the *Phaedo* with an *Epistola communis ad libros omnes Platonis* (ed. Mehus, vol. 1, p. 8, dated by Luiso, *Studi,* p. 3, to 5 September 1400, but really between 1404 or 1405). Moreover, he proceeded with a translation of the *Gorgias* (1409), of particular interest for its discussion on the Sophists ("disputatio cum Gorgia invehens contra oratores sive artem dicendi," according to the title of one MS.); cf. E. Garin, "Ricerche sulle traduzioni di Platone nella prima metà del secolo XV," *Medioevo e Rinascimento: Studi in onore di Bruno Nardi* (Florence, 1955), vol. 1, pp. 361 ff. [But cf. more recently J. Hankins, *Plato in the Italian Renaissance.* vol. I, second impression with addenda and corrigenda (Leiden, 1991), pp. 29–101; vol. 2, pp. 367–400]. There clearly must have been the same kind of interest in the not yet translated *Protagoras,* where the citation to Hesiod is introduced precisely in the economy of a discussion of the Sophists, according to whom the "very difficult" possession of virtue also makes its teaching problematic (in opposition to Hesiod's simplistic statement, "that when one reachs its heights, it becomes easy to possess it"). Ch. Trinkaus, "Protagoras in the Renaissance: An Exploration," *Philosophy and Humanism: Renaissance Essays in Honor of P. O. Kristeller,* ed. E. P. Mahoney (Leiden, 1976), pp. 190–213, has no connection with the issue discussed here.

51 Cf. Bompaire, *Lucien,* p. 392.

52 Cf. E. Mattioli, *Luciano e l'Umanesimo* (Naples, 1980), pp. 127–35; and also *De avaritia, Opera,* p. 11; *De infelicitate principum,* p. 417 f. Note also the ironic ban in *De avaritia,* p. 27: "Avari in urbibus ne sunto, qui fuerint publico edicto eiiciantur," which, albeit in a different context, seems to imitate the "Decretum" against the misers in Lucian's *Menippus* 20, to which moreover the *De infelicitate* makes open reference, p. 395: "Accusatae apud Lucianum divitiae, quod nunquam se ad honestos viros conferant."

53 "Nam si quis eorum quenpiam vidisset in fabula representanda ornatu regio inceden-

tem, verba proferentem gravia, magnifica, superba, rege digna, satellitibus imperan-
tem, tenentem sceptrum, regem profecto inscius credidisset. Detrahe illi ornatum,
admove cultum vestimentorum, summove personam, nempre servus relinquetur et
fortasse nequissimus." Cf. "Oratio ad Patres reverendissimos," *Umanesimo e secolarizzazione,* p. 323, lines 173–77.

54 "Multiloquos magis quam multiscios appellant." Cf. *Seniles* 5.2 *Opera,* vol. 2, p. 880
(ed. Fracassetti, vol. 1, p. 280).

55 "ab aliqua sententia incipiunt, deinde aliorum dictis intexunt orationes suas." Cf.
"Oratio ad Patres reverendissimos," pp. 323 f., lines 179 f.

56 Cf. Seneca, *Ad Lucilium* 76.31.

57 Iohannis Chrysostomi, *De Lazaro* 2.3, in Migne, P.G. XLVIII, col. 986. On this issue,
cf. R. Helm, *Lucian und Menipp* (Leipzig, 1906), pp. 46ff.; and J. Jacquot, "Le théâtre
du monde de Shakespeare à Caldéron," *Revue de littérature comparée* 31 (1957): 348 ff.

58 *Menippus,* 16; cf. Helm, *Lucian,* pp. 44 ff; Bompaire, *Lucien,* pp. 436 ff. ("sur la dé-
senvolture avec laquelle les figurants deviennent de roi esclave et inversement"), and
on the particular emphasis Lucian gives to the image of the theater: "elle l'a accom-
pagné pendant toute sa carrière . . . , en lui elle s'est épanouie." The king-slave antithesis also reappears in Seneca *Ad Lucilium* 80.7, but as a complementary motive in
order to illustrate metaphorically the contrast between rich and poor.

59 Cf. Chrysostom's *De Lazaro* (in the Latin translation of Migne): "Quod si detraxeris
illi personam, si conscientiam explices et ingrediaris animum, multam illic offendes
virtutis inopiam comperiesque omnium hominum abiectissimum"; and above, n. 53.

60 "difficile est bonum esse veteri Graecorum sententia." Cf. letter to Richard Petworth,
18 October 1425, ed. Tonelli, vol. 1, p. 141 f. [ed. Harth, vol. 2, p. 36]. It is worth
noting that in this context Hesiod's saying is presented as something that must have
sounded to his correspondent as unheard of: ". . . ut sapientissime scripsit Hesiodus, quem tu raro suscipies, ut opinor." For the letters mentioned in the text, cf. the
correspondence in Harth's edition, in order: vol. 2, pp. 34–37; 96–99; 412–14.

61 Letter to Niccoli, 18 May 1416, ed. Tonelli, vol. 1, p.1 f.[ed. Harth, vol. 1, p. 128]:
". . . quam [*scil.* disciplinam] etsi nullius usus esse conspiciam ad sapientiae facultatem,
confert tamen aliquid ad studia nostra humanitatis, vel ex hoc maxime, quia morem
Hieronymi in transferendo cognovi" (cf. on this point, above n. 42). Such a comment
is similar to Bruni's, in letter to Giovanni Cirignani, 12 September 1442 (ed. Mehus,
vol. 2, pp. 160–64; cf. Luiso, *Studi,* p. 156), which Mehus thus synthesizes: "Hebraicas
litteras inutiles, Graecas Latinasque utilissimas esse ostendens," insofar as moral and
religious doctrine can be derived sufficiently from translation. Finally Bruni concludes: "deinde quid simile habet Graecorum eruditio cum Judaeorum ruditate?"
Elsewhere Bruni, in his *De studiis et litteris* (1422), distinguishes moral from religious
discipline, "quorum alterum ad religionem, alterum ad bene vivendum spectat": Cf.
Humanitisch-philosophische Schriften, p. 12. Cp. on the issue my essay, "L'Ebraismo nei
riflessi della cultura umanistica," *Medioevo e Rinascimento: Annuario del Dipartimento di
Studi sul Medioevo e il Rinascimento dell'Università di Firenze,"* vol. 2 (1988), pp. 283–324
(especially 285–90).

62 "schola epicureae factionis"; "nostras execror animi perversitates . . . dum futuras

expavescimus calamitates, continuis in calamitatibus anxietatibusque iactamur;" "Ita hac sola ditantur sententia: vixit, dum bene vixit." Cf. letter to Niccoli, 18 May 1416 [ed. Harth, vol. 1, p. 134]: The reference is to the maxim of Terence, *Hecyra*, 461; but cf. also Seneca *Ad Lucilium* 22.13–17.

63 Cf. letters to Niccoli, 30 November 1420, ed. Tonelli, vol. 1, p. 50 f. [ed. Harth, vol. 1, p. 25]: "sicut homo peraegre profectus, si quid viatici oblatum est, coepi, non devians a recto itinere" (in regard to the pleasure of the senses); 21 October 1427, ibid., p. 214 [ed. Harth, p. 83]: he aspires to "quiescere" in his "achademia valdarnina, . . . si tamen quies aliqua haberi potest in hoc procelloso mari"; 13 August 1429, ibid., p. 291 [ed. Harth, p. 85]: "Affirmo tibi confirmoque sententiam . . ., me non expansurum vela in altum sed contracturum: mare magnum est et procellosum"; 28 December 1430, ibid., p. 336 [ed. Harth, p. 199]: ". . . ut non plus torqueamur publicis malis quam nostra ferat portiuncula." In the same period Poggio insists that Niccoli give back his copy of Lucretius, which he had not been able to finish completely: "Cura ut habeam Lucretium, si fieri potest: non enim adhuc potui universum librum legere, cum semper fuerit peregrinus; vellem ut civis efficeretur" (letter of 13 December 1429, p. 295 [ed. Harth, vol. 1, p. 89]; the request had not yet been fulfilled by 27 May 1430 [ibid., p. 103]: "Cupio legere Lucretiam, at ego privor illius praesentia; nunquid etiam alium decennium tenere velis?" Niccoli's reluctance in all likelihood was owing to those doctrinal motives he had noted in the margins of his own apograph: "Mundum non esse ab diis constitutum" (cf. *Firenze e la Toscana nell'Europa del Cinquecento, La rinascita della Scienza,* Catalogo, ed. P. Galluzzi [Florence, 1980], p. 136. For what follows, cf. also A. Buck, "Democritus ridens und Heraclitus flens," in *Wort und Text: Festschrift für Fritz Shalk* (Frankfurt am Main, 1963).

64 "me ipsum rideo"; cf. ed. Tonelli, vol. 1, p. 82 [ed. Harth, vol. 1, p. 57]; "risi ineptitudinem tuam;" cf. ed. Tonelli, vol. 1, p. 187 [ed. Harth, vol. 1, p. 171]; "risimus omnes ineptitudinem verborum et petulantiam"; cf. ed. Tonelli, vol. 1, p. 206 [ed. Harth, vol. 2, p. 85].

65 "satius est ridere, ut Democritus ille, communem insaniam quam fletu eam persequi"; cf. ed. Tonelli, vol. 1, p. 337 [ed. Harth, vol. 1, p. 200].

66 Cf. in particular letter to cardinal Giuliano Cesarini, Rome, 2 November 1431, ed. Tonelli, vol. 1, pp. 365–67 [ed. Harth, vol. 2, pp. 130–32].

67 Walser, p. 65; letter to Bruni, 30 May 1416, ed. Tonelli, vol. 1, pp. 11–20 [ed. Harth, vol. 2, pp. 157–63]; see R. Neu Watkins, "The Death of Jerome of Prague: Divergent Views," *Speculum* 42 (1967): 104–29, and also the observations by E. Flores, *Le scoperte di Poggio Bracciolini e il testo di Lucrezio* (Naples, 1980), pp. 11 ff.

68 "vitam suam et studia exposuerat officii plena et virtutis." Cf. letter to L. Bruni, Constance, 30 May 1416, ed. Tonelli, p. 16 [ed. Harth, vol. 2, p. 161].

69 "ita enim erant verisimiles, ut excepta fidei causa parva illis testimoniis fides adhibenda esset"; ibid.

70 "vereor ne haec omnia in pestem suam fuerint a natura concessa"; ibid. p. 18 [ed. Harth, vol. 2, p. 163].

71 Cf. Cicero *Laelius* 79. Cf., for example, letter to A. Loschi, 23 June 1424, ed. Tonelli, vol. 1, p. 117 [ed. Harth, vol. 2, p. 8]: ". . . omnia praeclara rara . . . non solum nostra sed superiorum quoque temporum memoria."

72 "iam multis saeculis obliteratae et paene sepultae, atque ab omnibus philosophis re-
probatae." Cf. letter to Guarino, 17 October 1433, ed. Tonelli, vol. 2, p. 47 [ed. Harth,
vol. 2, p. 178].

73 "hoc et utillimum tibi, et amicis tuis et praesertim mihi erit gratissimum." Cf. letter
to Panormita, July 1426, ed. Tonelli, vol. 1, p. 185 [ed. Harth, vol. 2, p. 58].

74 Cf. "Prohemium ad Pogium," to "Liber quartus" of the *Intercoenales*. Cf. L. B. Alberti,
Intercenali inedite, ed. E. Garin (Florence, 1965), p. 24 f.; and also E. Garin, *Rinascite e
rivoluzioni* (Bari, 1975), pp. 131 ff.

75 "Non quaero . . . bonum et sapientem illum stoicorum, qui nondum est inventus,
hos sentio bonos, quos usus et vita hominum comprobat, in quibus satis est inesse
aliquam, etsi non perfectam virtutem, at saltem speciem et adumbratam effigiem
earum virtutum, quas civilis vitae ratio perquirit" (cf. Cicero *De officiis* 1.15.46: "Quoniam autem vivitur non cum perfectis hominibus, sed cum his in quibus praeclare
agitur si sunt simulacra virtutis, etiam hoc intelligendum puto, neminem omnino
esse negligendum in quo aliqua significatio virtutis appareat, colendum autem esse
ita quemque maxime, ut quisque maxime virtutibus his lenioribus erit ornatus, modestia, temperantia, hac ipsa de qua multa iam dicta sunt, iustitia"). Cf. "De infelicitate principum," *Opera,* p. 411 (but see the critical edition: Poggio Bracciolini, *De
infelicitate principum,* a cura di D. Canfora [Rome, 1998] [Edizione Nazionale dei Testi
Umanistici, 2]).

76 On this issue, cf. Grimal, pp. 351 f.

77 Cf. letter to Niccoli, London, 12–17 December 1421, ed. Tonelli, vol. 1, p. 55 [ed.
Harth, vol. 1, p. 3]: "in hoc eodem laberyntho."

78 "Oportuit enim parere tempori, quod, cum non sit semper idem, ex eius varietate
decet mutare et consilia." Cf. letter to Niccoli, 12–17 December, ed. Tonelli, vol. 1,
p. 56 [ed. Harth, vol. 1, p. 32]. The expression is shaped in particular on Cicero *Ad familiares* 4.9.2: "Primum tempori cedere, id est necessitati parere, semper sapientis est
habitum"; but cp. also *De finibus* 3.22.73: "Quaeque sunt vetera praecepta sapientium,
qui iubent tempori parere et sequi deum" etc. The latin proverb was also transmitted
to Middle Ages through Ovid, Seneca, and *Disticha Catonis;* cf. for instance Walter,
Proverbia sententiaeque, no. 31264: "temporibus mores sapiens sine crimine mutat."

79 "Hanc mediocritatem cupimus sectari, in qua Deum sequentes, non omnino mundo
serviamus." Cf. letter to Niccoli, London, 25 June 1422, ed. Tonelli, vol. 1, p. 83 [ed.
Harth, vol. 1, p. 58].

80 "in omnibus statuendus est modus cupiditati"; cfr. letter to F. Pizolpasso, 5 August
1424, ed. Tonelli, vol. 1, p. 133 [ed. Harth, vol. 2, p. 43]; "statui modum desiderio
meo . . . appetens quod est satis"; and letter to R. Petworth, 18 October 1425, ed. Tonelli, vol. 1, p. 140 [ed. Harth, vol. 2, p. 35]. Cf. also *De avaritia,* p. 13; and chap. 3 above.

81 "Si tamen aliquod ad incertos temporum casus et fortunae impetus servares . . . non
est vituperandum. Tamen modus adhibeatur rerum omnium moderator." Cf. letter to
John, canon of Rheims, c. 1455, ed. Tonelli, vol. 3, p. 155 [ed. Harth, vol. 3, p. 319]. In its
brevity the statement summarizes the very theme of the *De avaritia.* Incidentally, the
"moderation" that Poggio recommends must not be confused with the Aristotelian
concept of *medietas,* which, in the margins of his *Nicomachean Ethics,* Poggio makes
note of as a difficult achievement: "Arduum est medium consequi," "Nil firmum in

agendis." Cf. *Catalogo,* p. 22, n. 16; and tav. II/a (*Nicomachean Ethics* 2.9.1109a). On one occasion only, in drawing a comparison between Stoics, Epicureans, and Peripatetics, Poggio had declared his own preference for the last ("mediocritatem Peripatetici servant, admittunt divitias, dignitates non aspernantur: hos censeo amplectendos"; cf. letter to Pietro Donato, 24 July 1424, ed. Tonelli, vol. 1, p. 124 [ed. Harth, vol. 2, p. 17], probably under the influence of L. Bruni's *Isagogicon moralis disciplinae.* But cf. H. Baron, "The Date of L. Bruni's '*Isagogicon moralis disciplinae,*'" *Yearbook of Italian Studies* (Florence, 1971), pp. 67–74, which proposes that the tract should be postdated.

82 "Nam cum pluribus virtutibus vitia quaedam proxima et ferme similia videantur . . . , si quis non recte discreverit . . . necesse est dilabi in errores permultos." Cf. letter to Giovan Francesco Gonzaga, 13 November 1437, ed. Tonelli, vol. 2, pp. 131 f. [ed. Harth, vol. 2, pp. 261 f.]: The somewhat unusual and reductive comparison between "discretio," as Poggio reads in John Cassian's *Conferences,* and "prudence" ("ea, ut opinor, prudentiam caeteri appellant") rings true as a devaluation of this last virtue, in the classical sense, to cite the contemporary authority of Matteo Palmieri, of "ogni nostro pensiero et ogni nostra azione con ragione dirizzare in laudabile et honesto fine" (*Della vita civile,* ed. F. Battaglia [Bologna, 1944], p. 43). The aim of the letter is actually to dissuade the marquis from enforcing punishment, albeit deserved, on his son, in recognition of the weakness of human nature and the unknowns of political life. It is useful to compare Poggio's letter to the corresponding passage by John Cassian, to whom he so unusually refers. Cf. *Conlationes* 2.2: "Quid discretio sola conferat monacho." This virtue is praised far and beyond the other merits of monks (fasts, vigils, the contempt of this world, the charity toward our neighbors), insofar as it is the only one capable of avoiding excesses and deficiencies: "ita videmus repente deceptos, ut arreptum opus non potuerint terminare. . . . In illis namque cum exuberaret praedictarum opera virtutum, discretio sola deficiens ea durare non sivit" etc. (ed. M. Petschenig [Vindobonae, 1886], p. 41). Note the subtlety with which Poggio moves away from a spiritual meaning of the concept to an intellectual and moral one, in order to dilute the classical concept of "prudentia."

83 "longum est iter per praecepta, per exempla vero breve, efficax et apertum"; cf. "Orario ad Patres reverendissimos," p. 319, lines 90 f.; "prius facere coepit quam docere"; cf. letter to F. Pizolpasso, 5 August 1424, ed. Tonelli, vol. 1, p. 133 [ed. Harth, vol. 2, p. 42].

84 Videbantur res quaedam durissimae legis illa verba divinae: relinque patrem et matrem; vende omnia bona tua et da pauperibus; tolle crucem tuam et sequere me; diligite inimicos vestros, benefacite his qui oderunt vos; ad iniuriam vos praebete, et similia, austera haec quidem, et a sensu nostro quodammodo abhorrentia"; "at contra multo molliora erant et multo faciliora, certe ad naturam humanam magis accommodata legis gentilium praecepta, firmata usu cotidiano et legibus sancita." Cf. "Oratio ad Patres reverendissimos," p. 319, lines 98–105.

85 "Nisi nos praeteritorum et dicta et facta magis iuvarent quam praesentium perdita exempla, fides procul dubio perditum iret." Cf. letter to Niccoli, London, 13 June 1420, ed. Tonelli, vol. 1, p. 33 [ed. Harth, vol. 1, p. 11].

86 "nam horum studiorum principia inania sunt, partim ambigua, partim falsa, omnia

ad vanitatem. Sacri vero eloquii principium est veritas, qua amissa nihil rectum tenere, nihil operari possumus." Cf. letter to Niccoli, 12 February 1421, ed. Tonelli, vol. 1, pp. 60–64 [ed. Harth, vol. 1, pp. 34–37]. Cf. on this Walser, pp. 79 ff.

87 "voluntas adest, sed perficere non est in me." Cf. letter to Niccoli, 12 February 1421, ed. Tonelli, vol. 1, p. 62 [ed. Harth, vol. 1, p. 35]; and Romans 7.18: "Nam velle adiacet mihi: perficere autem bonum non invenio."

88 "Neque enim sum ex iis perfectis, qui iubentur relinquere patrem et matrem, vendere omnia et dare pauperibus: paucorum illud fuit et apud saeculum prius." Cf. letter to Niccoli, 12 February 1421, ibid.

89 "id quondam fuit et apud saeculum prius"; cf. letter to Niccoli, London, 25 June 1422, ed. Tonelli, vol. 1, p. 80 [ed. Harth, vol. 1, p. 58]. "Si virtutes cum bonis et sanctis viris pereunt, iamdudum cum Petro et Paulo reliquisque Apostolis perierunt"; cf. the letter (or, better, invective) to Francesco of Velate, Rome, 18 December 1428, ed. Tonelli, vol. 1, pp. 254 f. [not in Harth edition].

90 "Felix si essem ex prima nota, qui inciperem abstinere a vitiis iis, quae nos privant regno Dei, vivens parce et sobrie." Cf. letter to Niccoli, London, 12 February 1421, ed. Tonelli, vol. 1, p. 62 [ed. Harth, vol. 1, p. 35].

91 Seneca *Ad Lucilium* 52.5: "non ituros si nemo pracesserit, sed bene secuturos"; "nos ex illa prima nota non sumus; bene nobiscum agitur, si in secundam recipimur." Another indirect reference to Epicureanism is given by the adaptation of Ciceronian expressions pertinent to the deprecation of "voluptas." Cf. *De officiis* 1.30.106: "Atque etiam si considerare volemus quae sit in natura excellentia et dignitas, intellegemus quam sit turpe diffluere luxuria et delicate ac molliter vivere, quamque honestum, parce, continenter, severe, sobrie." Typically in Poggio, the opposition of "dignitas" with turpitude, of "honestum" with "voluptas," dissolves into a pure statement of moderation, where Stoic and Epicurean perspectives converge, precisely on the issue of living "parce ac sobrie."

92 "illam quaero libertatem . . . in qua paucioribus sim subiectus, quam Tullius ait vivere ut velis." Cf. letter to Niccoli, 25 June 1422, ed. Tonelli, vol. 1, 22, p. 83 [ed. Harth, vol. 1, p. 58]; cf. Cicero *Paradoxa* 5.1.

93 "quem ego iudico felicissimum: reputat enim omnia ut stercus, ut Christum lucri-faciat." Cf. ibid. and Philippians 3.8.

94 Cf. Vespasiano da Bisticci, *Le vite,* ed. A. Greco, vol. 1 (Florence, 1970), p. 458. Bruni's *Contra hypocritas* was written in 1417; cf. also Poggio, *Contra hypocritas,* ed. H. Sincerus (Lugduni, 1679), p. 35 [*Opera omnia,* vol. 2, p. 79]. Cf. also on this issue L. Gualdo Rosa, "Leonardo Bruni, l' "Oratio in hypocritas" e i suoi difficili rapporti con Ambrogio Traversari," *Vita Monastica* 41 (1987): 89–111.

95 "quae totum mundum falsa bonitatis specie subornavit." Cf. "Oratio ad Patres reverendissimos," p. 317, line 58.

96 "illi potentiam mundanam aspernabantur, humanitatem (*alias* humilitatem) sequentes, vos dominia et elatio delectant." Cf. ibid., p. 331, lines 336–37. Alongside its manuscript tradition, a twofold series of the Oration's testimonies alternatively confirms the two readings of the Belluno ms.

97 "quidam humilitatem in superbiam, . . . caritatem in odium converterunt." Cf. let-

ter to Scipione Mainenti, Bologna, 20 July 1427, ed. Tonelli, vol. 2, p. 89 [ed. Harth, vol. 2, p. 216].

98 "Ad humanitatem quoque adhortandi [*scil.* pontifices]. . . . Est enim virtutum omnium condimentum. Admonendi sunt ut meminerint se homines esse . . . licet 'sanctissimi et beatissimi' appellentur." Cf. "Oratio ad summum pontificem Nicolam V," *Opera,* p. 289.

99 "Unam mehercule nostram confabulationem papatui anteferrem." Cf. letter to Niccoli, Rome, 6 November 1423, ed. Tonelli, vol. 1, p. 99 [ed. Harth, vol. 1, p. 73].

100 "cupio enim liber esse, non publicus servus." Cf. letter to Niccoli, London, 22 February 1422, ed. Tonelli, vol. 1, p. 72 [ed. Harth, vol. 1, p. 46].

101 Cf. for example, in regard to the dispute with the marquis of Mantova, who took offense at Poggio's remarks (see above n. 82), the letter to Carlo Brognolo, 5 May 1438, ed. Tonelli, vol. 2, p. 267 [ed. Harth, vol. 2, p. 292]: "Tutissimum est vobis, qui ex alterius nutu pendetis, loqui ad principis voluntatem. . . . Mihi vero est alia vitae institutio." See moreover, in this same sense, the dispute with Guarino over Scipio and Caesar (cf. J. W. Oppel, "Peace vs. Liberty in the Quattrocento: Poggio, Guarino, and the Scipio-Caesar controversy," *Journal of Medieval and Renaissance Studies* 4 (1974): pp. 221–65; but especially G. Crevatin, "La politica e la retorica: Poggio e la controversia su Cesare e Scipione," *Poggio Bracciolini. . . . ,* (Florence, 1982), pp. 281–342.

102 "Hunc morem priscis doctissimis viris ac sanctissimis fuisse, ut in rebus fidei invicem sententiis discreparent, non ad pessundandam fidem, sed ad veritatem fidei recipiendam" (ed. Tonelli, vol. 1, p. 16 [ed. Harth, vol. 2, p. 161]).

103 "disceptando enim in utramque partem veritas elici consuevit"; cf. letter to Gherardo Landriani, Florence, November 1442, ed. Tonelli, vol. 2, p. 267 [ed. Harth, vol. 2, p. 412].

104 Cf. on this issue Marsh, *The Quattrocento Dialogue,* pp. 38, 50 f.

105 Cf. letter to Niccoli, 30 November 1412, ed. Tonelli, vol. 1, p. 50 [ed. Harth, vol. 1, p. 25], about his refusal to embrace the status of priest: "Gravissimum est consilium, in quo de omni futura vita deliberandum sit; ubi, si quis fallitur, quod saepius accidit, non sine ignominia relinquitur quod inceptum est"; and to the same, 25 June 1422, ibid., p. 82 [ed. Harth, vol. 1, p. 57], on the responsibilities of the priesthood. But above all, see his resolute assertion of the layman's life, in the letter to Cardinal G. Cesarini, who had warned him to come to a decision: "Quod de instituendo vitae genere scribis, ego iamdudum decrevi certum vitae cursum, quo et proficiscor, non devians ab itinere constituto" (letter dated 10 July 1432, in *De varietate fortunae,* p. 211 [*Opera omnia,* vol. 4, p. 49; ed. Harth, vol. 2, p. 141]. On this issue, cf. R. Fubini, *Introduzione alla lettura del 'Contra hypocritas' di Poggio Bracciolini* (Turin, s.d.[1970]), pp. 29–33.

106 "ego homo sum ad lenitatem ac familiaritatem propensior." Cf. letter to Niccoli, Rome, 2 October 1428, ed. Tonelli, vol. 1, p. 222 [ed. Harth, vol. 1, p. 183].

107 "Cum magna in me commutatio facta sit, volui eam tibi notam esse. . . . Scis me hactenus incertum quasi vitae cursum degisse, cum neque saeculum fugerem neque clerum sequerer. Cum tamen natura mea sacerdotium semper abhorruisset, inque ea essem aetate ut aliquando mihi certa vivendi formula capessenda esset, decrevi

uxorem ducere." Cf. letter to Nicholas Bildeston, 6 February 1436, ed. Tonelli, vol. 2, p. 72 [ed. Harth, vol. 2, p. 202]; and also letter to Guarino, 18 May, ibid., p. 77 [ed. Harth, vol. 2, p. 205]: "Et quemadmodum poetae extremum actum politiorem per-fectioremque efficiunt, itidem ego, quod temporis superest, perfectiori vitae dedi-cavi." Using a different tone from the confidential one he uses with his friends, Pog-gio expresses himself to Cardinal Cesarini, 26 May, ibid., p. 79 [ed. Harth, vol. 2, p. 208]: "satius certe duxi, non quidem contemnere superiorem vitae institutionem, sed posteriorem sectari, quae aptior meis moribus videbatur."

108   "me esse unum in cuius litteris nihil esset ambiguum." Cf. letter to F. Barbaro, Rome, 18 December 1429, ed. Tonelli, vol. 1, p. 261 [ed. Harth, vol. 2, p. 93].

109   Cf. letters to Niccoli, Rome, 3 April 1429, ed. Tonelli, vol. 1, p. 271 [ed. Harth, vol. 1, p. 207]; to Pietro Tommasi, Rome, summer 1446, ed. Tonelli, vol. 2, p. 331 [ed. Harth, vol. 3, p. 36]; to Domenico Capranica, Florence, summer 1458, ed. Harth, vol. 3, p. 507.

110   "prodeunt statim et veluti cohorte facta magno impetu erumpunt"; "humilis, benig-nus atque omnibus gratus, facilis et humanissimus"; "vere possunt dici ceremonias, quae cum sint dictae 'a carendo,' non solum omni virtute careant, sed etiam umbra virtutum." Cf. the "invective" letter to Francesco of Velate, "Scriptori apostolico," 18 December 1428, ed. Tonelli, vol. 1, pp. 224–63.

111   "qui vero, Pater Sancte, tuas laudes, quae quidem exquisitae sunt, sua oratione com-plectuntur, quamvis vere id et tuo merito videantur posse facere, tamen meo iudicio aut verborum ostentatores aut assentatores improvidi censendi sunt." Cf. "Oratio ad summum pontificem Nicolaum V," Opera, p. 288. Poggio is probably referring to the solemn encomium that Giannozzo Manetti pronounced on behalf of the Florentine embassy of obedience, in a widely circulated oration, which collections sometimes associate with Poggio's; cf. H. W. Wittschier, Giannozzo Manetti: Das corpus der Ora-tiones (Cologne, 1968), pp. 79–84; Fubini, Papato, p. 334; Catalogo, p. 30, nn. 37–38.

112   "quid episcopum deceat, quod eius sit officium, quae actio, quod munus." Cf. let-ter to Scipione Mainenti, Bologna, 26 July 1437, ed. Tonelli, vol. 2, p. 89 [ed. Harth, vol. 2, p. 216].

113   "postquam video quot et quanta iudicio sapientum requirat uxorium munus, quae magis optare licet quam ea nos consequi posse." Cf. letter to Guarino, 15 March 1416, ed. Tonelli, vol. 1, p. 22 [not in Harth edition]. The sources of Barbaro's tract are identified by A. Gnesotto, "Francisci Barbari De re uxoria liber," Atti e Memorie della R. Accademia di Scienze e Lettere di Padova, 32 (1915).

114   "eiusmodi esse rationes de quibus nulla doctrina tradi possit: nam magis experiendo quam legendo cognoscuntur. . . . Consilia enim cum sint temporum et in diem nasci debeant, non ad certam formulam possunt redigi, praesertim in re dubia, in qua nor-mam et rationem praestare difficile esse consuevit." Cf. letter to Bartolomeo Guasco, autumn 1439, ed. Tonelli, vol. 2, p. 210 f. [ed. Harth, vol. 2, p. 35]; and also letter to Pietro del Monte, 18 July 1437, ibid., p. 121 [ed. Harth, vol. 2, p. 250]: "uxor vero cu-rarum ac voluptatum conscia tecum laetatur ac condolet"; and lastly, letter to Guasco, ibid., p. 210: "Sicut enim una vestis non omnibus apta sit, ita nec unica cum uxore vivendi ratio."

115   Cf. Opera omnia, vol. 2, p. 675.

116 "Deus ille est qui tribuit unicuique ut vult." Cf. letter to Scipione Mainenti, 20 December 1438, ed. Tonelli, vol. 2, p. 198 f. [ed. Harth, vol. 2, p. 339]. Poggio's fatalism is even more marked in his confidential letter to Cencio Rustici, 16 December, ibid., p. 195 [ed. Harth, vol. 2, p. 336]: "Deus sive sidera aut coeli."

117 "Dicit homo fanaticus se omnem moralis philosophiae materiam suis libris complexurum, ingens certe promissum et Ciceroni et Aristoteli grave, nedum impudentissimo rabulae Philelpho!" Cf. Poggio's letter to Tommasi, 19 August 1446, Walser, p. 465 [*Opera omnia*, vol. 4, p. 469]; and also letter by Filelfo to Tommasi, 26 May 1446, ibid., p. 459 [p. 463]. Cf., moreover, the letter from Tommasi to Filelfo, ibid., p. 456, which complains about the polemical part and negative premise of the philosophical debate, "de finibus . . . bonorum et malorum, deque felicitate et summo bono. . . . De infamia preterea et calamitate et oppositis reliquis opportunum fuit te dicere ad complementum doctrinae, quantum contrariorum eadem est disciplina, ut idem [*scil.* Aristoteles] ait." The part about "infamy," "exile," and "poverty" was the only one actually written; cf. *Testi inediti e rari di Cristoforo Landino e Francesco Filelfo*, ed. E. Garin (Florence, 1949), pp. 39–41; and *Prosatori latini*, pp. 491 ff.

118 On Poggio's mockery of Filelfo's political compromising ("partium causae homo rusticus et peregrinus te dedicaras"), cf. *Opera omnia*, vol. 4, p. 611.

119 *De avaritia, Opera*, p. 16.

120 "ego non quid fieri possit pervestgatus sum . . . nam plura fieri possunt quae numquam sunt facta, sed quid hactenus fieri consuevit." Cf. letter to Gherardo Landriani, November 1442, ed. Tonelli, vol. 2, p. 268 [ed. Harth, vol. 2, p. 413].

121 This is the subject of his letter to A. Loschi, 20 June 1424, ed. Tonelli, vol. 1, pp. 112–19 [ed. Harth, vol. 2, pp. 5–10], his first lengthy reflection on the theme of fortune, and the small margin of freedom conceded to moral reflection, against a background of a troubled state of affairs and recent political misfortunes: "nihil est certum, nihil exploratum nobis, quo constitutum habeamus vel agendi vel quiescendi tempus, suspensi animis atque iis rebus intenti, quae parum habeant commercii cum virtute" (p. 113). Cf. also the letter to Niccoli, 28 May 1423, ibid., pp. 89–91 [ed. Harth, vol. 1, p. 64 f.], on the rekindling of Florence's wars with the Visconti. Cf. also n. 263 below.

122 Cf. letter to Niccoli, Rome, 6 May 1429, ed. Tonelli, vol. 1, p. 273 [ed. Harth, vol. 1, p. 208]: "Hoc primum est opusculum quod tanquam in campum atque in palaestram sit perventurum" etc.

123 On this, refer to chap. 3.

124 Cf. letters to Niccoli, 3 September, 28 November 1430, ed. Tonelli, vol. 1, pp. 319–22, 333–37 [ed. Harth, vol. 1, pp. 106–08, 197–200].

125 Cf. letters to G. Cesarini, cardinal of S. Angelo, 3 May 1431; 2 November, 31 December 1432, ed. Tonelli, vol. 1, pp. 345–49; 365–67; vol. 2, pp. 22–31 [ed. Harth, vol. 2, pp. 115–17; 130–32; 146–52]. He forsees the bad end, later fulfilled, of the expedition against the Hussites and then exhorts the cardinal, president of the Council of Basel, to obey the pope. On these circumstances, cf. Walser, pp. 151–55; J. W. Stieber, *Pope Eugenius IV, the Council of Basel, and the Secular and Ecclesiastical Authorities in the Empire* (Leiden, 1978), pp. 12–19; G. Christianson, *Cesarini, the Conciliar Cardinal: The Basel Years, 1431–1438* (St. Ottilien, 1979).

126 "Verum ea nos agunt tempora, ii rerum motus parantur, ut unumquemque, ut video, taedat conditio fortunae suae." Cf. letter to Niccoli, 28 November 1430, p. 333 [ed. Harth, vol. 2, p. 197]. On the one hand, the letter, taking up again the issues in the preceding one of 3 September, expresses a distrust in the popular government: "recte Aristoteles democratiam dixit omnibus peiorem" (ibid., p. 321 [ed. Harth, p. 108]); "arduum quippe est contra ire fatis ac maius quippiam quam cadat in arbitrium plebis. . . . Vicit tamen maior pars meliorem," (ibid., p. 334 [ed. Harth, pp. 197 f.]). On the other hand, it seems to echo the accusations of demagogy and private interest ("dum nonnulli privatam rem publicae utilitati anteponentes, quidvis aliud quam hostem nostrum succumbere malebant"; ibid., p. 335 [ed. Harth, p. 198]), which at the time had been directed at Neri Capponi above all, but from which not even the Medici themselves were exempted (cf. G. Brucker, *The Civic World of Early Renaissance Florence* [Princeton, 1977], pp. 496–500; D. Kent, *The Rise of the Medici: Faction in Florence, 1426-1434* [Oxford, 1978], pp. 256–88; and n. 261 below). In his *Florentine Histories* Poggio would later, and not without a good historical grounding, represent the struggle over war and peace in the speeches of Rinaldo degli Albizzi and Niccolò da Uzzano respectively. Cf. Oppel, *Peace vs. Liberty*, pp. 227 ff., who suggests that Poggio's condemnation of Caesar (in a rhetorical comparison with Scipio) was an implicit attack on the position of the Albizzi, creating almost a propagandistic theme in favor of the Medici, lovers of peace as the ancient Scipio had been. The *Historiae*, however, are completely silent on the role played by the Medici; whereas Poggio's letters to Cosimo, "consolatory" in his exile, and "congratulatory" upon his return (ed. Tonelli, vol. 2, pp. 37–46; 67–71 [ed. Harth, vol. 2, pp. 181–88, 192–97]) are limited to moral exhortation—for Stoic resignation and for civic pacification respectively. "L'esempio di Scipione, che Cosimo è invitato a seguire, serve a Poggio appunto per esortare il vincitore a mantenersi nei limiti stabiliti dal rispetto della volontà comune e a non prevaricarla" (Crevatin, *La politica e la retorica*, p. 290).

127 "Nunc autem quem dabis ad quem confugiat, ut non tanquam ad scopulum allidatur? Communis quasi insania omnes pervasit." Cf. letter to Cesarini, 2 November 1432, p. 336 [ed. Harth, vol. 2, pp. 130 f.].

128 "ut dolendum sit maxime ac deplorandum nobis Spiritum Sanctum (si tamen is nusquam apud nos est) adeo immutasse naturam suam, charitatemque ac dilectionem, ex quibus totus est, in odium ac malivolentiam convertisse." Cf. letter to Cesarini, 28 January 1433, ed. Tonelli, vol. 2, p. 55 [ed. Harth, vol. 2, p. 191]; the letter was written to accompany and explain his dissuasions from the Council, stated in letter of 31 December (see n. 125 above), and which he had held back at an earlier time.

129 "Omnia tamen mallem quam iniri bellum novum cum duce, cuius exitus difficilis est coniectura; et mihi crede, ruina illius trahet secum nostram . . . Trade hoc memoriae: videbis Italiam ante quatuor annos refertam barbaris, et multos dari in praedam nisi abstineatur a bello." Cf. letter to Niccoli, 6 January 1431, ed. Tonelli, vol. 1, p. 340 [ed. Harth, vol. 1, p. 98]. In the previous years, Poggio had worked in the curia as a mediator between Milanese agents and Florentine ambassadors, also because of his suspicion of the Venetian alliance; cf. Walser, p. 134 f. Notable in a more general sense are his concerns about the collapse of the political and diplomatic balance. Florence

and the Church found themselves in the same boat, "non potest ruina unius, quae iam imminet, semota esse ab alterius calamitate. . . . Italiae calamitas me movet . . . per oppressionem nostram et alterius ambitionem [that is obviously, the emperor Sigismund], cui si libuerit quantum licet, recte quidem erit." Cf., moreover, his letter to Cesarini, 28 January 1433, ibid., p. 54 [ed. Harth, vol. 2, p. 141]. According to Poggio, the "scissuram Ecclesiae" was foreshadowed in Germany; cf. the letter to the same, 31 December 1432, p. 26 [ed. Harth, vol. 2, p. 149].

130 Cf. letters to Niccoli, 15 May 1423, ed. Tonelli, vol. 1, p. 88 [ed. Harth, vol. 1, p. 63]; 28 May, ibid. p. 91 [ed. Harth, vol. 1, p. 65].

131 "me . . . tanquam in commentaria coniecisse usque ad haec tempora fortunae varietatem, ne quae conceperam laberentur e memoria." Cf. letter to Cesarini, 7 May 1431, p. 346 [ed. Harth, vol. 2, p. 116]. Cf. now I. Kajanto, "Poggio Bracciolini and Classicism," *Annales Academiae Fennicae,* ser. B, 238 (Helsinki, 1987), p. 37: "*De varietate fortunae* 1–2 were . . . not yet written in May 1431. The chronology of the events recorded in book two suggests that they were written down between 1432–1435."

132 *De varietate fortunae,* p. 77 [*Opera omnia,* vol. 2, p. 579]. But on the new edition, see n. 20 above.

133 "De hac silui inopia historiarum . . . ne aliquid incertum affirmarem." Cf. letter to Niccoli, 19 August 1433, ed. Tonelli, vol. 2, pp. 31 f. [ed. Harth, vol. 1, p. 126].

134 Letter to the same, 4 June 1433, p. 15 [ed. Harth, vol. 1, p. 119].

135 Letter to Leonello d'Este, 17 August 1436, ed. Tonelli, vol. 2, p. 82 [ed. Harth, vol. 2, p. 210 f.]; *De varietate fortunae,* pp. 36 ff. [*Opera omnia,* vol. 2, pp. 538 ff.]; cf. also J. Jacquot, "Le pensée de Marlowe dans 'Tamburlain the Great,'" *Études Anglaises* (1953), pp. 332–45.

136 "Nescio enim quomodo semper existimentur ampliora quae audit auris quam quae oculis cernuntur: credo quia fama persaepe mentitur, oculus iudicat ex vero. Tum prisca augustiora quaedam putantur semperque praeterita commendamus praesentium taedio"; "an tu . . . ita insulsus es, ut omnia quae antiquitas tulit, perinde atque ab illis narrantur, putes gesta magnifice, et non multum decoris atque ornamenti scribentium facultate additum?" Cf. *De varietate fortuna,* ibid. Note the loaded implicit reference to the famous passage in Titus Livius, *Praefatio* 6–7: "Quae ante conditam condendamve Urbem poeticis magis decora fabulis quam incorruptis rerum gestarum monumentis traduntur, ea nec adfirmare nec refellere in animo est. Datur haec venia antiquitati, ut miscendo humana divinis primordia urbium augustiora faciat" etc. The passage would actually become a point of reference in the attitude humanist historiography affects toward tradition and its moral value; cf. my *Osservazioni sugli 'Historiarum Florentini populi' di L. Bruni,* pp. 442 ff. Poggio's comparison between things that are seen and things that are heard, between the eye and the ear, probably has its origin in Seneca's moral teachings (cf. *Ad Lucilium* 6.5), which illustrates well the connections in the twofold meaning of credibility, in both the moral and historiographical sense. On this point see also Lucian *De historia conscribenda* 29 (translation and commentary by L. Canfora, *Teorie e tecniche della storiografia classica* [Bari, 1974], p. 63), which is freely taken up by Guarino, *Epistolario,* vol. 2, p. 46. Guarino contaminates it with suggestions from Horace's *Ars Poetica* (180–81): "Cer-

tior aure arbiter est oculus." On the epistemological value of the ancient *querelle*, cf. M. Laffranque, "L'oeil et l'oreille: Polybe et les problèmes de l'information en histoire à l'epoque hellénistique," *Revue philosophique de France et de l'Étranger* 158 (1968): 263–72.

137 "duplici fruor voluptate, altera cernens quae oblectant oculos, cum sint procul ab usu nostro remota; altera complectens cogitatione superiora illa quae legendo admiramur"; "ea inest in vultu comitas ac maiestas, ut qui illum ignorarent . . . caeterorum regem opinarentur." Cf. letter to Niccoli, 4 June 1433, pp. 13, 18 [ed. Harth, vol. 1, pp. 120, 122].

138 "adulatorum scriptorum omnium adulantissimus": Cf. *De infelicitate principum, Opera*, p. 397. On Neapolitan historiography, cf. G. Resta, Introduction to A. Panormita, *Liber gestarum Ferdinandi regis* (Palermo, 1968), pp. 5–58.

139 Letter to Bartolomeo Facio, 23 November 1447, ed. Tonelli, vol. 2, p. 347 [ed. Harth, vol. 3, p. 54]; to the Count of Celano, summer 1451, ed. Tonelli, vol. 2, p. 347 [ed. Harth, vol. 3, p. 135]: "Ea vero Xenophontis historia non usquequaque vera est: non enim historiam Cyri conscribere voluit, sed optimum principem, qualis nunquam fuit, effingere." The fact that on account of political and personal events the dedication to the Aragonese king was at an earlier point crossed out and then reconfirmed (cf. *Opera omnia*, vol. 4, pp. 671–73) does not have a significant bearing on the ambiguity of the homage itself, with the idea being understood that the image of princely virtues is utopian and thereby also of doubtful pedagogical value, except insofar as it points out the discrepancy between what should be and what actually is.

140 Cf. "Proemium" (1449), *Opera omnia*, vol. 4, p. 683: ". . . Ab hoc veluti historiarum fonte qui postmodum secuti sunt in priscis historiis fabulisque recensendis hausere, unde ad caeteros transfundere valerent." On the success of Poggio's version, cf. *Catalogo*, pp. 10, 35 f., nn. 49–51; R. Fubini, *P. Bracciolini attraverso l'esposizione dei suoi codici*, pp. 83 f.

141 See on this point Poggio's observations, in the course of his account of Niccolo de' Conti's voyages in India, "on the misinformation, the fables that pass for knowledge"; cf. L. Davis Hammond, Introduction to *Travelers in Disguise: Narratives of Eastern Travels by Poggio Bracciolini and Ludovico de Varthema* (Cambridge, Mass., 1963), p. xiii. The version of the *Verae historiae* of Lucian, which may be considered as belonging to a similar range of thoughts, and attributed to Poggio by a certain manuscript tradition (and hence in Walser, p. 231; *Opera omnia*, vol. 4, pp. 665–69), is actually Lilio Tifernate's; cf. K. Sidwell, "Lucian in the Italian *Quattrocento*" (Ph.D. diss., Harvard University, 1975), pp. 30–32; D. Marsh, "Poggio and Alberti: Three notes," *Rinascimento* 23 (1983): 189. On Conti's voyages, see especially the rich commentary by Merisalo, in her edition of *De varietate*, n. 20 above.

142 Cf. letter to Pietro Donato, Rieti, 23 July 1424, ed. Tonelli, vol. 1, p. 125 [ed. Harth, vol. 2, p. 18]: "Hic vero his inanibus fabellis ac molestiis vacamus"; he adds: ". . . Nam licet hic quoque loci Epicurum fieri."

143 "Superiora vero, quia recentissima sunt, retuli mecum ipse admiratus rerum mortalium mutationem varietatemque fortunae . . . Quis ad huiuscemodi ludum imbecillitatis humanae non expavescere debet?" Cf. letter to A. Loschi, 26 June 1424,

ibid., p. 116 [ed. Harth, vol. 2, p. 8]; and also to Niccoli, London, 13 June 1420, ed. Tonelli, vol. 1, p. 34 [ed. Harth, vol. 1, p. 8]: "Hic est ludus rerum humanarum, ut est versus Nevii: 'Pati necesse est multa mortalem mala.'"

144   "praeclara sui favoris spectacula praebet"; "detracta enim basi, in qua illos in sublimi conspiciendos tanquam in scaena mimos alienis ornatos vestibus locarat, reddidit ridiculos ac spernendos"; cf. *De varietate fortunae*, p. 73 [*Opera omnia*, vol. 4, p. 375]. Cf. also *Proemium*, p. 2 [p. 504]: "quem in summo veluti theatri campo . . . tanquam personatum quendam regem constituisset."

145   "Nam pontifices ipsos, praeter admodum paucos . . . quid aliud quam fortunae mirandam potentiam dices? quos, tanquam reges Aegyptios, e infimo quandoque hominum genere, nulla in re praestantiores reliquis, . . . ad tantum fastigium sublatos nostra saecula conspexerunt, ut saepius addubitare cogar Dei ne providentia ac nutu tanta imperii moles, an fato casuque temere ducatur." Cf. ibid., p. 80 [*Opera omnia*, p. 582].

146   "nihil esse in rebus humanis certi exploratum consiliaque nostra parum proficere ubi obsistat fortuna." Cf. ibid., pp. 64 f. [*Opera omnia*, pp. 566 f.].

147   "Constat enim vitam principum tragoediam esse calamitatum plenam, ex qua multi actus confici possent ad repraesentandam tanquam in theatro eorum infelicitatem." Cf. *De infelicitate principum, Opera*, p. 416. See in this connection the example of Richard II of England, *De varietate fortunae*, pp. 44 f. [pp. 546 f.]: "Huius regis fortunam nulla certe antiquorum tragoedia superat vel varietate rerum vel regni magnitudine."

148   Seneca, *Ad Lucilium* 80.8: "omnium istorum [*scil.* divitum] personata felicitas est." Cf. also the maxim in *De tranquillitate animi* 13.2: "Nam qui multa agit saepe fortunae potestatem facit" (which reappears again in *De varietate*, p. 30). As Grimal, *Sénèque*, p. 413 f., observes, the maxim takes up Democritus' precept, of "not getting involved in many affairs" (*mè pollà prèssein*).

149   A. Doren, "Fortuna im Mittelalter und in der Renaissance," *Vorträge der Bibliothek Warburg*, part 1 (Leipzig, 1922–23), pp. 111 f.

150   "qui virum bonum nimis arctis cicumscribunt spaciis." Cf. *De infelicitate principum*, p. 415. Note the only partial reception of Seneca's thought. In fact in *De tranquillitate animi*, according to P. Grimal's words, p. 414 f., Democritus's renunciatory maxim is overcome by the gradual discovery of "personal autonomy, the *autarcheia*, which is the basic attitude of the Sage."

151   "Ita rara videtur societas . . . cum virtute, ut seclusi ab hac felicitate esse putentur." Cf. the letter to Richard Petworth, 24 May 1440, ed. Tonelli, vol. 2, pp. 234 f. [ed. Harth, vol. 2, p. 379], commenting on the *De infelicitate*.

152   *De providentia* 2.9: "ecce spectaculum dignum ad quod respiciat intentus operi suo Deus, ecce par Dei dignus"; cf. Grimal, pp. 77 and 407.

153   *Enarrationes in Psalmos* 39.6: "Miracula hominum intuebatur, intendat mirabilia Dei"; cf. M. H. Marshall, "Boethius' Definition of 'Persona' and Mediaeval Understanding of the Roman Theater," *Speculum* 25 (1950): 471, 479.

154   *De symbolo* 2, in Migne, P.L., XL, col. 639; cf. Marshall, p. 479.

155   *Enarrationes in Psalmos* 137.6, in Migne, P.L., XXXVII, col. 1686: "Agamus et nos mimum nostrum. Mimus est enim generis humani tota vita tentationis"; cf. Helm, *Lucian*, pp. 48 ff.; Jacquot, *Le théâtre du monde*, p. 352.

156　Hrabanus Maurus, *De universo* 22.36, Migne, P.L., CXI, col. 553: "Spectaculum sumus facti in hoc mundo angelis et hominibus propter Deum"; Honorius Augustodunensis, *De Gemma aurea*, 1.83, in Migne, P.L., CLXXII, col. 570: "Sic clericus noster pugnam Christi populo christiano in theatro Ecclesiae gestibus suis repraesentat." Cf. D. Bigongiari, "Were There Theaters in the Twelfth and Thirteenth Centuries?" *The Romanic Review* 27 (1946): 212.

157　"ingens videlicet virtutis et conscientiae theatrum." Cf. letter to Cosimo de' Medici, Rome, 31 December 1433, ed. Tonelli, vol. 2, p. 41 [ed. Harth, vol. 2, p. 183].

158　"qui si tibi laudandi essent, magnas nobis tragoedias excitares." Cf. letter to Francesco of Velate, ed. Tonelli, vol. 1, p. 253.

159　"At vero cum potentes rerum illius favoribus inflati virtutem aspernari plurimum soleant, . . . fortunae theatrum ingressi praeclara sui favoris spectacula vulgo praebent. Illa enim, quos fovit, suo iure utens, primum deiicit, tum eorum stultitiam detegit." Cf. *De varietate fortunae*, p. 2 [*Opera omnia*, vol. 2, p. 504].

160　Struever, p. 188.

161　"ut res mortalium ad eius voluntatem circumagi videantur nullo ordine ductae." Cf.: *De varietate fortunae*, p. 33 [*Opera omnia*, vol. 2, p. 535]; here is an echo of the verses by Seneca, *Phaedra* 977–978: "res humanas ordine nullo / Fortuna regit."

162　Cf. H. R. Patch, *The Tradition of Boethius: A Study of His Importance in Mediaeval Culture* (New York, 1935), pp. 73 ff., 103 ff.; P. Courcelle, *La consolation de Philosophie dans la tradition littéraire* (Paris, 1967), pp. 317 ff.; cf. also *Lamenti storici dei secoli XIV, XV, e XVI*, collected by A. Medin and L. Frati, vol. 1 (Bologna, 1887), pp. 66–69.

163　"existimatur esse maior et ordinatior quaedam vis volvens ac versans res humanas pro libidine, nihil a se firmum, nihil tutum ducens." Cf. *De varietate fortunae*, p. 29 [*Opera omnia*, vol. 2, p. 531]. A sign that Poggio had Boethius implicitly in mind is in the allusion: "unde et tragoedus viris fortibus eam invidere dixit" (p. 33 [p. 535]), and also p. 26 [p. 528]: "Idem tragoedi quoque et reliqui rerum scriptores sentiunt"), which could be a reference to Pacuvius, cited in the *Rhetorica ad Herennium* 2.23.36, and taken up again in Boethius *Consolatio* 2, pr. 2, 33: "Quid tragoediarum clamor aliud deflet, nisi indiscretu ictu Fortunam felicia regna vertentem?"; cf. Courcelle, *La consolation*, p. 105. However it could also be an indirect borrowing of the passage.

164　Cf. Doren, *Fortuna*, p. 93; and also W. Map, *De nugis curialium*, cited by H. R. Patch, *The Goddess Fortuna in Medieval Literature* (Cambridge, Mass., 1927), p. 59: "Si quod Boetius de Fortuna veraciter asseruit de curia dixerimus, recte quidem et hoc, ut sola sit mobilitate stabilis."

165　"Nam cum mecum ipse cogito quod hi quos modo retulimus, quod alii praeterea sentiant, quatenus fortunam potentem faciant . . . , non accidens quidpiam aut praeter intentionem, sed firmum quid ac stabile diuque in multis rebus ante praemeditatum videtur"; Cf. *De varietate fortunae*, p. 27 [*Opera omnia*, vol. 2, p. 529]; and also ibid., p. 85 [p. 587]: "Ita hominum vaesania auctoritatem tribuit fortunae et horrendam fecit."

166　"quos antea in vulgus tanquam stolidos asinos notari videbamus; qui, ut animal est tardum, stupidum, iners, desidiosum . . . ita, quum ad stultitiam additur indulgentiam beneficiumque fortunae, haud indigne humanum corpus asini fingitur cervice." Cf. ibid., p. 33 [*Opera omnia*, vol. 2, p. 535]. On the passage from S. Bernardino, cf. G. Bronzini, "Bernardino e le tradizioni popolari," *Bernardino predicatore*, p. 133:

"Prima nel fondo suo è tutto uomo, et al salire suo più su diventa mezzo asino, et alla sommità della ruota elli è tutto asino, et è colla cornamusa e suona" etc. Poggio could also be alluding here to the traditional "festivals of the fools" and their relative animal masks; cf. E. K. Chambers, *The Medieval Stage*, vol. 1 (Oxford, 1903), pp. 275 ff.; and more generally, G. Cocchiara, *Il mondo alla rovescia* (Turin, 1963); *L'image du monde renversé et ses représentations littéraires et para-littéraires de la fin du XVI siècle au milieu du XVII*, Études réunis et présentées par J. Lafond et A. Redondo (Paris, 1979).

167 See n. 120 above.

168 "addamus aliam [*scil.* definitionem] haud repugnantem theologis nostris, dicamusque nihil aliud fortunam esse quam divinae nutum voluntatis singula aut permittentis aut imperantis fieri." Cf. *De varietate fortunae*, p. 31 [*Opera omnia*, vol. 2, p. 533].

169 "in quo vir ille doctissimus de fato et providentia cum ipso Iove ludere videtur." Cf. the dedicatory letter to Tommaso of Sarzana (1443–44) in *Opera omnia*, vol. 4, p. 663 (Poggio's version is edited in C. Carini, "Una traduzione latina inedita di Poggio Bracciolini," *Giornale italiano di filologia*, n.s., 26 [1974]: 263–77; and Marsh, *Poggio and Alberti*, pp. 189–97). On the subject, cf. Bompaire, *Lucien*, who illustrates the Epicurean and Cynical background of Lucian's satires on the Stoic doctrine of providence.

170 "omissa definiendi solertia." Cf. *De varietate fortunae*, p. 31 [*Opera omnia*, vol. 2, p. 533].

171 "quibus tecti ac praemuniti illius tela refringamus." Cf. *De varietate fortunae*, p. 32 [*Opera omnia*, vol. 2, p. 534].

172 Cf. in particular Jacquot, *Le théâtre du monde*, pp. 350 ff.; and also Helm, *Lucian*, p. 53; F. A. Yates, *Theatre of the World* (Chicago, 1969), pp. 162 ff.

173 "quae talis est suapte natura, ut etiam bonos reddat malos usu eius et consuetudine." Cf. letter to Gherardo Landriani, November 1442, ed. Tonelli, vol. 2, p. 268 [ed. Harth, vol. 2, p. 413]. (On *De infelicitate principum*, see the introductory essay by D. Canfora to the critical edition [n. 75 above], pp. xv–lxvi; and also O. Merisalo, "Poggio e i Principi: Osservazioni su alcuni temi del 'De varietate fortunae' di Poggio Bracciolini," *Medioevo e Rinascimento*" 4 [1992]: 203–21.)

174 P. Grimal, "Les tragédies de Sénèque," *Les tragédies de Sénèque et le théâtre de la Renaissance: Études réunis et presentées par J. Jacquot* (Paris, 1964), p. 10.

175 Note the autograph "notabilia" in Poggio's own copy, Biblioteca Medicea Laurenziana, MS. Plut. 37, 11 (cf. *Catalogo*, p. 21, n. 14). The codex can be identified with the one acquired through Niccoli, "VII aureis"; cf. letters to Niccoli, 29 September, 20 October 1425, ed. Tonelli, vol. 1, pp. 164 f. [ed. Harth, vol. 1, pp. 161 and 163]). See, for example, the indication ("No.") to *Hercules furens* 255–57: "Prosperum ac felix scelus / virtus vocatur, sontibus parent boni / ius est in armis, opprimit leges timor" (f. 4r). On this regard, cf. the didactic commentary on this passage by N. Trevet, *Expositio Herculis furentis*, ed. V. Ussani Jr., vol. 2 (Rome, 1959), p. 46: " 'scelus prosperum ac felix,' id est prospere ac feliciter gestum; 'virtus vocatur' scilicet a vulgo . . . ; 'ius est in armis,' id est quod quis adquirit vi armorum reputat ad ius suum pertinere; 'opprimit leges,' id est legum iusticiam; 'timor,' scilicet armorum." The aim of Trevet is stated in the introduction of his *Expositio*: "in quantum hic narrantur quedam laude digna, quedam vituperio, potest aliquo modo liber hic supponi ethice, et tunc finis eius est correctio morum per exempla hic posita" (ibid., vol. 1, p. 4 f.). Note

also Poggio's notations in *Troades* 333–34, in the margin of a stichometric comparison between Pyrrus and Agamennon: "Lex nulla capto parcit aut penam impedit. / Minimum decet libere cui multum licet" (f. 92v). Here also Trevet had moralized: "Agamennon honestissima sententia dictum Pirri refellit" etc. (N. Trevet, *Commento alle 'Troades' di Seneca*, ed. M. Palma [Rome, 1977], p. 27).

176 Cf. n. 163 above.

177 *Etymologiae* 18.43: "Tragoedi sunt qui antiqua gesta atque facinora sceleratorum regum luctuoso carmine spectante populo concinebant." Cf. W. Cloetta, *Beiträge zur Literaturgeschiche des Mittelalters und der Renaissance, I, Kömädie und Tragödie im Mittelalter* (Halle, 1890), pp. 17 ff.

178 Cf. M. Pastore Stocchi, "Un chapitre d'histoire littéraire aux XIV et XV siècles," *Les tragédies de Sénèque*, pp. 24 ff., in reference to *Evidentia tragediarum Senece* and to *Ecerinis* by A. Mussato. The author mentions the distinction that Boccaccio proposed, and accepted for a long time afterward, between the figure of Seneca the tragedian and Seneca the moral philosopher. There is, however, no trace of such distinction in Poggio, who evidently rejected it. Cf., for example, the citation from the *Thyestes* in ep. II, 17, ed. Tonelli, vol. 1, p. 128 f. [ed. Harth, vol. 2, p. 38 f.].

179 Cf. H. R. Patch, "The Tradition of Goddess Fortuna in Roman Literature and in the Transitional Period," *Smith College Studies in Modern Languages* 3, no. 3 (1922): 210; Patch, *The Goddess*, p. 60.

180 Patch, *The Goddess*, pp. 58 f. Cf., moreover, A. Medin, "Ballata della Fortuna," *Il Propugnatore*, n.s., 2 (1889): 121 f.: "La Santa Chiesa la Fortuna mena / con papi due già è sedici anni" etc.; and also *Il vanto della Fortuna*, ed. T. Casini, *Nozze De Simone-Sestini* (Florence, 1896), p. 14: "Il mondo guasta e strugge per contraro / li re sommette al cristian Pastore / che ha tolto l'onore / del santo imperio e nomasi Vicaro / di Cristo, signor caro: / pace discaccia, solo intende a guerre / il santo padre e a pigliare terre." The versifier, who wrote this at the end of the Trecento or the beginning of the Quattrocento, seems to have been inspired by astrological determinism: "a le virtù de' cieli ognun soggiace."

181 On the spread of the *De casibus* throughout Europe, cf. especially H. Bergen, Introduction to *Lydgate's Fall of Princes*, ed. H. Bergen, 4 vols. (London, 1924–27; repr., 1967), vol. 1, pp. ix–xxvii. Bergen's observation remains valid, that "practically the entire literature of the Fall of Princes has yet to be investigated" (p. xxiii); but cf. P. M. Gathercole, "Illuminations on 'De cas des nobles' (Boccaccio's *De casibus*)," *Studi sul Boccaccio* 2 (1964): 343–56; Gathercole, "Lydgate's Fall of Princes and the French Vision of Boccaccio's 'De casibus,'" *Miscellanea di studi e ricerche sul Quattrocento francese*, ed. F. Simone (Turin, 1967), pp. 167–78; and also Laurent de Premierfait's *De cas des nobles hommes et femmes*, bk. 1, ed. P. M. Gathercole (Chapel Hill, 1968).

182 Bergen, Introduction, p. x. Still useful on the subject are A. Hortis, *Studi sulle opere latine del Boccaccio* (Trieste, 1879), pp. 117–51; H. Hauvette, *Boccace: Étude biographique et littéraire* (Paris, 1914), pp. 348–52; cf. also M. Miglio, "Boccaccio biografo," *Boccaccio in Europe: Proceedings of the Boccaccio Conference* (Louvain, December 1975), ed. G. Tournoy (Louvain, 1977), pp. 149–63; A. Carraro, "Tradizioni culturali e storiche nel 'De casibus,'" *Studi sul Boccaccio* 12 (1980): 197–262.

183 The text of the twofold preface is edited in Bergen, Introduction, pp. xlvii–xlix; and

also G. Boccaccio, *Opere in versi . . . Prose latine, Epistole,* ed. P. G. Ricci (Milan, 1965), pp. 786–97. On the problem of the date and the twofold version (only the second was dedicated to M. Cavalcanti, around 1373), cf. V. Zaccaria, "Le due redazioni del 'De casibus,'" *Studi sul Boccaccio* 10 (1977–78): 1–26.

184 Cf. in order *De casibus* 1.11 (ed. P. G. Ricci–V. Zaccaria, pp. 58 ff.): "Adversus nimiam credulitatem," in other words, against the adulation which makes princes less circumspect than an ordinary citizen or villager; ibid., 4.4 (pp. 395 ff.): "In cives minus reipublicae amatores"; ibid., 9.7 (pp. 779 ff; and also *Lydgate's Fall,* ed. Bergen, vol. 4, pp. 359 f.): "De Ioanne papa XII." Cf. Miglio, *Boccaccio biografo,* p. 154, who points out the polemical element, in connection with a "contesto politico rifiutato in tutte le sue componenti." This scholar, nevertheless, takes his argument too far, as Boccaccio's moralistic condemnation of the bad habits of citizens certainly does not exclude a genuinely civic concern, on whose standard of judgment Boccaccio reproves the evil actions of princes. Think of his praise of "romana libertas," his warm recommendations to love one's *patria,* civic freedom, and moderation in habits, etc. The dedication to Cavalcanti, moreover, implies that Boccaccio's fellow citizens, unlike princes, are the ideal ones to whom the work should be addressed, in the belief that their customs were actually "corrigibiles."

185 *De casibus* 6.pref. [ed. Ricci–Zaccaria, p. 470; and also *Lydgate's Fall,* ed. Bergen, vol. 4, pp. 246–50]: "ad gremium tuum humanarum rerum confertissimum . . . , unde vates egregii adque hystoriographi illustres tam canendi quam scribendi indeficientem materiam iam sumpsere." Note the appeal to experience: "experientia quippe docemur"; it is also noteworthy that the appeal to "vates egregii adque hystoriographi" seemed inappropriate to Laurent de Premierfait, and, after him, to J. Lydgate; so that they both modified Boccaccio's comment, albeit using different turns of phrase and attributing the speech to Fortune: "Je vueil que tu sache que *les philosophes et les historiens* anciens ont en ceste chose labouré et ont failly"; "Al the labour off *philosophers* olde, / Travaile off *poetis* my maner to deprave, / Hath been of yore to seyn lik as thei wolde / Over my fredam the souereynte to have" (italics mine). Cf. *Lydgate's Fall,* ed. Bergen, vol. 3, p. 679; vol. 4, p. 247.

186 Cf. *De casibus* 2.pref.; and also 6.1.10 (ed. Ricci–Zaccaria, pp. 104, and 470–72): "Sed non talibus tantum hic adsumptus est labor. Sunt plurimi adeo rebus praeteritis innixi, ut vix etiam strepentem adsiduis tonitruis aerem sentiant, nedum facili sono labentia verba percipiant."

187 Cf. *De infelicitate principum, Opera,* p. 409. On the biographical aspects of the *De casibus,* cf. V. Branca, *Giovanni Boccaccio, Profilo biografico* (Florence, 1977), pp. 24, 73, 107, 175, and passim. It should be added that implicit references to the *De casibus,* which was widely diffused in Poggio's time (Zaccaria, *Le due redazioni,* p. 26, counts seventy-four mss. of the work), can also be recognized elsewhere in Poggio's writings. In fact, Boccaccio could have given Poggio the idea to associate the discussion of fortune and the unhappiness of princes with the other one of nobility. With respect to C. Marius, Boccaccio had introduced "some reflections on nobility" ("Pauca de nobilitate;" cf. 6.3, ed. Ricci–Zaccaria, p. 488). Actually the definition of nobility presents a certain phraseological affinity with the one later formulated by Poggio: "Arbitror

quippe nil aliud nobilitatem esse quam *quoddam splendidum decus,* in recte prospicientium oculos morum facetia et affabilitate refulgens, *surgens ex alicuius habituata animi voluntate,* et opere pro viribus executioni mandata spernendi vitia imitandeque *virtutis."* Cf. Poggio's *De nobilitate, Opera,* p. 79: "Est enim nobilitas *quasi splendor quidam ex virtute progrediens,* qui suos possessores illustrat ex quacumque conditione emergentes" (italics mine).

188 *De varietate fortunae,* p. 34 [*Opera omnia,* vol. 2, p. 536]: "Dies me deficeret, si omnia recensere vellem *illustrium virorum* exempla, in quibus fortunae licentia versata est: referti enim sunt libri eiusmodi historiis, quas memoriae posterorum mandavit antiquitas" (italics mine).

189 "L'ultimo avvenimento storico menzionato è l'arrivo in Inghilterra il 24 maggio 1357 di Giovanni il Buono, fatto prigioniero nella battaglia di Poitiers del 1356" (cf. Zaccaria, *Le due redazioni,* p. 19). From this is inferred the *terminus a quo* for the composition of the first version, but, as Zaccaria observes, Boccaccio was still working on it around 1370. The revised version, on the other hand, can be dated sometime around 1373–74 (ibid., pp. 20, 25). Whatever the date of its composition, the work was not publicly circulated until the early 1370s, and thus a reasonable distance from the last events it records.

190 "ut saltem aetatem hanc scribendo complectatur." Cf. *De varietate fortunae,* p. 35 [*Opera omnia,* 537].

191 The first version of Laurent de Premierfait's *Les Cas des nobles hommes* (1400) was dedicated to Louis de Bourbon, and the second version (1411) to Jean, Duc de Berry; *The Fall of Princes* by John Lydgate (the poet of the royal court) was dedicated around 1430 to Humphrey, Duke of Gloucester.

192 Cf. letter to R. Petworth, 30 July 1442, in Walser, p. 454 [*Opera omnia,* vol. 4, p. 458]: "Libellum autem vellem ut duci Gloucestrie monstrares et post transcribi faceres eundem" (it is doubtful, however, that the tract really did arrive at its destination; the only work of Poggio's found in the Duke's library was *De avaritia;* cf. A. Sammut, *Unfredo di Gloucester e gli umanisti italiani* [Padua, 1980], pp. 3, and 93). Among the other important English figures who knew the *De infelicitate* early on should be mentioned William Gray, chancellor of Oxford and later bishop of Ely, whom Poggio had met during his sojourn in the Curia, and who afterward became his correspondent (cf. letter to him, Florence, summer 1454, ed. Tonelli, vol. 3, pp. 112 ff. [ed. Harth, vol. 3, pp. 242–44]). His own manuscript of Poggio's dialogue (now at Oxford, Balliol 146) was acquired in Ferrara and is dated 28 January 1446; cf. P. T. Eden, "William Gray, Bishop of Ely, and Three Oxford Manuscripts of Seneca," *Classica et Medievalia* 21 (1960): 40.

193 Cf. letter to Pietro del Monte, Rome, 14 September 1443, ed. Tonelli, vol. 2, p. 28 [ed. Harth, vol. 2, p. 427 f.]: he thanks him "quod me celebrem apud Gallos reddisti quodque opuscula mea voluisti nota esse regi" (but cf. also nn. 194 and 206 below); the letter to Alonso, bishop of Burgos, 10 May 1443 (about whom see n. 207 below). Cf. moreover letter to King John II of Castile, 1453, ed. Tonelli, vol. 3, p. 66 f. [ed. Harth, vol. 3, p. 173 f.]: "Narravit mihi venerabilis vir mihique amicissimus Nicolaus Vinch, quia ad tuam Serenitatem veniens hac iter fecit, te res meas summo cum

desiderio legere eisque plurimum delectari"; and also the letter to Dalmau de Mur, archbishop of Saragossa, 1 May 1446, ed. Tonelli, vol. 2, pp. 320 f. [ed. Harth, vol. 3, p. 27 f.]: "Libellum item de nobilitate, unum aliud de principum infelicitate, qui an in manus tuas pervenerint ignoro, a multis probantur nescio an recte."

194 Cf. letter to Pietro del Monte, 14 September 1443, pp. 281 f. [ed. Harth, vol. 2, p. 427]: he announces the composition of two books "de varietate fortunae . . . et in hos regni Franciae varietatem fortunae, quae illud diutius quassavit, conieci. Tuo consilio utar, cui dicandus videatur, istine quem laudas an alteri." The finished work would later be announced in advance at the court of Naples; cf. letter to Panormita, 28 February 1448, ed. Tonelli, vol. 2, p. 351 (ed. Harth, vol. 3, p. 59); and at the English court; cf. letter to R. Petworth, 12 July 1448, p. 363 [ed. Harth, vol. 3, p. 71].

195 Cf. *De casibus* 9.7: "De Ioanne papa XII" (ed. Ricci-Zaccaria, pp. 778–84; cf. also *Lydgate's Fall,* ed. Bergen, vol. 4, pp. 359 f.). On Boccaccio's comments about the contemporary pope John XXII, cp. *VI Centenario della morte di G. Boccaccio: Mostra di Manoscritti, Documenti e Edizioni* . . . , *I, Manoscritti e Documenti,* ed. E. Casamassima, D. De Robertis, F. Di Benedetto (Certaldo, 1975), p. 127, n. 103. Here the editors publish a gloss by him to Paolino Veneto's chronicle about, precisely, the papacy of John XXII, which may be taken also as a testimony of *De casibus*'s informator spirit: "Iste venetus adulator nicil dicit de tyrampnide gesta per papam istum, de trucidatione christianorum facta suo iussu, de partialitate animosa eiusdem et de quamplurimis aliis dyabolicis gestis eiusdem. Expectabat quidem bergolus iste pilleum rubeum veritatem tacendo et exprimendo mendacia. Vir quidem sanguinum fuit iste Iohannes, nec ecclesia Dei satis dignus."

196 "in mollitiem et socordiam adque supercilium grave nostri seculi pontificum scribere." Cf. *De casibus,* ibid., ed. Ricci-Zaccaria, p. 784.

197 *De casibus* 9.8: "Concursus dolentium" (ed. Ricci-Zaccaria, p. 786). Cf. also *Lydgate's Fall,* ed. Bergen, vol. 4, p. 361; and Miglio, *Boccaccio biografo,* p. 155 f. This is obviously why medieval political satire, from John of Salisbury to Walter Map, is addressed to the court but does not touch the king; cf. E. Türk, *Nugae curialium: Le règne d'Henri II Plantagenêt (1145–1189), et l'éthique politique* (Geneva, 1977).

198 Cf. Grimal, p. 438: "Sénèque non songe pas à supprimer les hiérarchies établies . . . ; mais il refuse d'accorder à ces hiérarchies une importance spirituelle." Individualism and the predominance of a moral criterion for judgment over a political one are taken up again by Petrarch, both in the context of criticism (such as in the invectives against the Avignon papacy, mentioned by Poggio in the *De avaritia,* p. 22); and also in the precepts for a prince, directed to his personal more than to his public dimension, and not without hints of an empirical and utilitarian nature, such as those in *Seniles* 14.1, to Francesco of Carrara, which seems to foreshadow the patriarchal utopia of the small principate, as it would be later developed by L. B. Alberti. The exception, in this sense, to the principles of public ethics and to the organic conception of the state is opportunely discussed by W. Berges, *Die Fürstenspiegel des hohen und späten Mittelalters,* 2d ed. (Stuttgart, 1952), pp. 283–88.

199 *De infelicitate principum,* p. 393: "cum enim 'sanctissimi ac beatissimi' appellentur . . . consentaneum videtur pontifices omnes . . . recte felices appellari posse."

200 Ibid., p. 400: "Quos tu quidem tyrannos appelles nescio: hoc certe scimus, nonnullos eorum regum fuisse meliores iustiusque in subditos imperium exercuisse. Non enim nomine sed re distinguuntur." To the *De casibus* 2.5: "In tyramnidem versi sunt regii mores, et despecta impotentia subditorum" (ed. Ricci-Zaccaria, p. 118), Laurent de Premierfait had added a precise definition of tyranny: "Celluy certes est tyrant, qui contre le droit divin et humain gouvernent la chose publicque du pays subgect a luy," in celebration of the merits of tyrannicide ("de faire coniuration, de prendre armes, de mettres espies, de employer ses forces contre ung tel roy"), in clear reference to the *Policraticus;* cf. Bergen, vol. 1, pp. 173 ff. On the success of John of Salisbury in the fifteenth century, cf. A. Linder, "The Knowledge of John of Salisbury in the Late Middle Ages," *Studi Medievali,* 3a ser., 18 (1977): 315–66.

201 "Naturalia enim etiam repugnantibus nobis vim suam exercent"; "principatus re ipsa et licentia malus est"; cf. *De infelicitate principum,* pp. 397, 400; and also p. 394: "Semper etiam priscis temporibus eiusmodi mores cogitationesque dominantium exiterunt."

202 "et Christianos quoque . . . felicitate caruisse contendam"; "Non attingit nostra sapientia haec Altissimi secretiora consilia." Cf. *De infelicitate principum,* p. 414.

203 "quibus parvula licent qui legibus coercerentur"; "si tranquillioribus rebus uti unquam licebit." Cf. ibid., pp. 395, 419.

204 "disputatiunculae, controversiae et iis ipsis qui ea tractant inutiles"; "praecepta ad bene vivendum accommodata." Cf. letter to Petworth, 30 July 1442 (n. 192 above). The *De infelicitate* had been announced beginning with the letter of 24 May 1440, ed. Tonelli, vol. 2, p. 234 [ed. Harth, vol. 2, p. 379].

205 Cf. L. K. Born, "The Perfect Prince: A Study in Thirteenth and Fourteenth Century Ideals," *Speculum* 3 (1928): 499.

206 Cf. S. Caroti, "La critica contro l'astrologia di Nicola Oresme e la sua influenza nel Medioevo e nel Rinascimento," *Atti dell'Accademia Nazionale dei Lincei, Memorie, Classe di scienze morali, storiche e filologiche,* 8a ser., 23, 6 (Rome, 1979), p. 654. In 1491 Basin reacted with these words to Paul of Middleburg's astrological interpretation of the two Italian authors, who instead, as he correctly points out, were appealing to the customary reality of history. In the meantime, however, he testifies precociously in French culture to a political, and not purely moralistic, reading of Boccaccio's work, opportunely associated with Poggio's. Cf. for later evidences of this trend, L. Sozzi, "Boccaccio in Francia nel Cinquecento," *Il Boccaccio nella cultura francese,* ed. C. Pellegrini (Florence, 1971), pp. 253 f. On Basin (1412–1490), cf. the lengthy discussion by B. Guenée, *Entre l'Église et l'État: Quatre vies de prélats français à la fin du Moyen Âge* (Paris, 1987), pp. 301–435.

207 Cf. K. A. Blüher, *Seneca in Spanien: Untersuchungen zur Geschichte der Seneca-Rezeption in Spanien vom 13. bis 17. Jahrhundert* (Munich, 1969), pp. 99 f., 103 f. Cf. also, on the function of the "letrados" at the court of Castile, J. A. Maravall, "Le origini dello stato moderno," *Lo stato moderno: I, Dal medioevo all'eta moderna,* ed. E. Rotelli and P. Schiera (Bologna, 1971), pp. 69–90. In my following discussion, I refer chiefly to Poggio's letter to Alonso, 10 May 1443, ed. Tonelli, vol. 2, pp. 274–76 [ed. Harth, vol. 2, p. 419 f.].

208 Cf. Blüher, *Seneca,* pp. 101, 103, 167 (and also n. 161 above). On Mannelli's repertory,

cf. T. Kaeppeli, "Luca Mannelli (+ 1362) ed la sua 'Tabulatio et expositio Senecae,' " *Archivum fratrum praedicatorum* 18 (1948): 237–64.

209 Cf. A. Birkenmajer, "Vermischte Untersuchungen zur Geschichte der mittelalter-lichen Philosophie: V, Der Streit des Alonso von Cartagena mit Leonardo Bruni Aretino," *Beiträge zur Geschichte der Philosophie des Mittelalters, Texte und Untersuchungen*, 20, vol. 5 (Münster in Westfalen, 1922). In this context Alonso had also emphati-cally subordinated eloquence to moral doctrine and in the traditional way had made Seneca's salutiferous exhortation a function of Christian truth (ibid., p. 174 f.). Cf. also chap. 3, n. 34 above.

210 "Multa et gravia et sapienter scripta in tuis litteris continentur, quibus si singulis velim respondere, longus mihi libellus esset conficiendus . . . Quod me hortaris ut de gloria principantium aliquid scribam, quo magis illi ad bene imperandum ani-mentur, agam id forsitan si requies animo erit." Cf. letter to Alonso, 10 May 1443, ed. Tonelli, vol. 2, p. 275 [ed. Harth, vol. 2, p. 419].

211 Cf. Blüher, *Seneca*, pp. 103, 106. On the medieval tradition in Spain of the *De clementia* as a set of political precepts, see ibid., pp. 76 ff.

212 "Sed eorum qui rerum potiuntur aures ita mihi surdae videntur, ut mea verba parum sint illis profutura. 'Trahit enim sua quemque voluptas.' Et quamvis persaepe proferant verba et sententias sapientum, tamen longe abest eorum vita e praecep-tis sapientiae." Cf. letter to Alonso, p. 276; the citation in Poggio's text is from the proverbial Virgil *Eclogues* 2.65. Poggio's epistle concludes: "Libellum meum ad uti-litatem legentium scripsi, ut homines abiecta ambiendi cura virtutem appetant. . . . Quod si secus senserint, sentiant ut libet" etc.

213 Letter to Gherardo Landriani, bishop of Como, after 13 November 1442, ed. Tonelli, vol. 2, p. 267 [ed. Harth, vol. 2, p. 413]: "non credis me putare, ut scribo, principes omnes esse infelices, sed tantummodo malos." Francesco Barbaro, when asked his opinion on the *De infelicitate* by the Milanese humanist Lodrisio Crivelli, distin-guished between those rulers who become meritorious "de rebus humanis" when-ever "naturam et virtutem sequantur," and those which instead only pursued their own usefulness. In so doing, however, he agreed with the pedagogical expediency of Poggio's tract: "Sed bene consultum rebus suis videretur, si infelicitates eorum, qui male profuerunt, tam brevi volumine continerentur" (the indirect reference is obviously to F. M. Visconti). Cf. letter to Leodrisio Crivelli, Venice, 24 December 1444, in R. Sabbadini, *Centotrenta lettere inedite di F. Barbaro* (Salerno, 1884), pp. 39, 118. This passage was pointed out to me by my friend G. Ianziti.

214 Cf. Tateo, "La disputa sulla nobiltà," *Tradizione e realtà*, pp. 355–421, in particular p. 365; cf. also C. Donati, "L'evoluzione della coscienza nobiliare," *Patriziati e aristocrazie*, ed. C. Mozzarelli and P. Schiera (Trento, 1978), pp. 13 ff. But see also the more ex-haustive treatment by Donati, *L'idea di nobiltà in Italia, secoli XIV–XVIII* (Bari, 1988), pp. 11 f. The volume is interesting also for some references to the later impact and discussions of Poggio's dialogue. On Dante, see especially the entry by D. Consoli, "Nobiltà e nobile," *Enciclopedia dantesca*, vol. 4 (Rome, 1973), pp. 53–62. As for the con-ception and debates on nobility in fourteenth-century Italy, see especially *Epistola o sia ragionamento di messer Lapo da Castiglionchio giureconsulto del secolo XIV*, ed. L. Mehus (Bologna, 1753).

215 "Nulla est virtus quae vocetur nobilitas." Cf. *De nobilitate, Opera,* p. 72.

216 "Nulla habita virtutis ratione." Cf. ibid., p. 69.

217 "nomen quidem apud omnes convenit, res admodum discrepat." Cf. ibid., p. 66.

218 "istam nobilitatem Stoicorum pauci quaerunt, pauciores adipiscuntur." Cf. ibid., p. 82.

219 "Utrius autem verior sit sententia, hi viderint quibus est acrius ingenium ad disputandum." Cf. ibid. p. 83.

220 P. O. Kristeller, Introduction to "Tre trattati di Lauro Quirini sulla nobiltà," ed. K. Krauttner in collaboration with P. O. Kristeller and H. Roob, *Lauro Quirini umanista,* ed. V. Branca (Florence, 1977), p. 35.

221 "velut factio quaedam ab reliquo populo distincta." Cf. *De nobilitate,* p. 67; and also Poggio's response to Gregorio Correr, 8 April 1440, ed. Tonelli, vol. 2, pp. 223–28 [not in Harth edition]. Among other reasons, Correr had become indignant at Poggio's allusion to the fact that people stained by criminal actions were on occasion granted the honorific title of Venetian citizen; something which, to quote Poggio, was not said to the detriment of the Venetian nobility, "cum etiam multa fieri a sapientibus possint, a quibus illos videmus abstinere." It was true, as Correr had stated, that kings, princes, and gentlemen had been invested with citizenship, and that also as a rule, villains in Venice were punished, "sed tamen eos qui in vestram non alterius perniciem machinantur." Nor, moreover, could all those who committed crimes be called villains, "neque qui aliquando iniuste egit, iniustus: potest quispiam scelere prodesse, neque plecti ut sceleratus; et sceleratus, qui nunquam nobis profuerit, poena affici" (p. 226 f.). Poggio, in other words, took for granted that the Venetian nobility pursued a kind of "realpolitik." On this subject, see also Poggio's letter to P. Tommasi, 1446, ed. Tonelli, vol. 2, p. 331 [ed. Harth, vol. 3, p. 35]: "Ego nihil contra nobilitatem scripsi, ut ille [*scil.* Qurini] temerarie somniat, sed contra falsam multorum opinionem nobilitatis."

222 "contra nobilitatem." Cf. Lauri Quirini, *De nobilitate contra Poggium Florentinum, Lauro Quirini umanista,* p. 74. The treatise follows a letter/tract addressed to P. Tommasi, about whom see n. 223 below. See moreover, on the chronology of the dispute, ibid., pp. 43 ff.

223 "solvere neque explicaare rationem"; "enigma insolubile." Cf. "Laurus Quirinus, Franciscus Contarenus, Nicolaus Barbus et socii Petro Thomasio prestantissimo phisico suo S. P. D.," *Lauro Qurini umanista,* pp. 71 and 73.

224 "Maior est enim nobilitatis ratio, quam a disertis tractari possit." Cf. L. Quirini, *De nobilitate,* ibid., p. 76; and also Poggio's letter to P. Tommasi, summer 1446, ed. Tonelli, vol. 2, p. 331 [ed. Harth, vol. 3, p. 36].

225 "utrum ne forte aliqua casuque fortunae erroneo, an consilio nutuque divino magistratus et rerum gubernacula dentur." Cf. "Ad Beatissimum D. N. Nicolaum V Pontificem Maximum Michael Canensis de Viterbio humillimus servulus de ipsius laudibus et divina electione," ed. M. Miglio, *Storiografia pontificia del Quattrocento* (Bologna, 1975), pp. 211 f.: On Canensi, cf. ibid., pp. 63–118; and also Fubini, *Papato,* pp. 332–34.

226 "Cum animus, bonis imbutus artibus se ipsum audierit . . . , ex bonis quibuscumque rebus quae optima sunt secutus fuerit; si a moderatione, constantia, maturitate, si a prudentia non secesserit . . . Nullum certe enim, ut sane Iunius ille Aquinas excla-

mat, numen abest si sit prudentia." Cf. ibid., p. 212. The reference is to Juvenal *Satires* 10.365 ("abest," which stands for "habet," is a reading actually existing in manuscript tradition; cf. edition by P. De Labriolle–F. Villeneuve [Paris, 1964], p. 137). Juvenal's citation is significant in this context insofar as it occurs in Lactantius, where he denies that it should be licit for a Christian to refer to fortune ("Fortuna ergo per se nihil est.") Cf. *Divinae institutiones* 3.29.1 and 17: "Fortunae vocabulum sibi inane finxerunt: quod quam longe a sapientia sit remotum, declarat Iuvenalis his versibus: 'Nullum numen habes si sit prudentia. Nos te/ Nos facimus, Fortuna, deam caeloque locamus.'" See on this Lactantius's edition and commentary by L. Friedlaender (Amsterdam, 1962), p. 366.

227 *De varietate fortunae*, pp. 25–36 [*Opera omnia*, vol. 2, pp. 527–38]. We read now the disquisition in the guise of a dialogue between A. Loschi and Poggio inside book 1, between the discussion on the Roman ruins (added at a later time) and the historical narrative proper, which begins with Tamburlain's exploits (anticipated in a letter to Leonello d'Este, 17 August 1436, cit. above, n. 135). It seems quite likely that, rather than being a connecting passage, it was originally the introductory prologue to the first draft of the work (the actual books 2 and 3.) Consider especially in this connection the suitable rhetorical cadence of the exordium ("Multa, inquam, Antoni, et audivi et legi de hac fortuna eiusque potestate," etc.). The passage, in fact, explains in its conclusion the author's main purpose of treating contemporary events episodically, almost as a corollary to the lengthier considerations on fortune, which explains the title of the "history" and from which the narrative flows.

228 Cf. *De varietate fortunae*, p. 27 [*Opera omnia*, vol. 2, p. 529]. Poggio states he makes use of the *Expositio in Physicam*, of which his own annotated copy still exists in Biblioteca Nazionale Centrale di Firenze, Conv. Soppr., J V 42 (cf. *Catalogo*, pp. 22 f., n. 17, and table II/b). On the Aristotelian and Thomistic conceptions of fortune, cf. T. Litt, *Les corps célestes dans l'univers de Saint Thomas d'Aquin* (Louvain, 1963), pp. 214–19. On the issue, and the entire discussion in general, see furthermore I. Kajanto, "Fortuna in the Works of Poggio Bracciolini," *Arctos. Acta Philologica Fennica* 20 (1986): 25–57; in particular p. 28: "He was quoting from the medieval Aristoteles Latinus, in places almost verbatim."

229 Aristotle, *Physique*, ed. and trans. H. Carteron (Paris, 1926), p. 19.

230 "dispositione superna ad id inclinante nos licet inscios." Cf. *De varietate fortunae*, ibid. On the subject, cf. Litt, *Les corps célestes*, p. 216: "Mais ce qu'il a surtout ajouté 'proprio marte' aux considérations d'Aristote sur les événements fortuites, c'est l'affirmation de leur indépendance par rapport aux corps célestes," the opposite, clearly, of what Poggio had asserted. Poggio, on the other hand, seems to keep his comments deliberately vague, avoiding the distinction between fortune and celestial influence (or perhaps better, including in the term "fortune" everything that transcends the human capacity for foresight). It should be specified in the end that neither the theory of the concurrence of causes nor that of celestial influences is found in Aquinas's explanation of the *Physics*.

231 "Est enim profecto aliud quiddam, quam definiatur ab istis, hoc quod appellatur a vulgo fortuna, longe lateque extra metas ab eis constitutas exercens imperium suum,

de qua citius addubitare possum, quam certam proferre sententiam." Cf. *De varietate fortunae*, ibid. See also Kajanto, *Fortuna*, p. 33: "From a philosophical point of view, Poggio's disquisition of the true nature of Fortune is a disappointment. Apart from the confusion of ideas in some places, none of the three interpretations is finally accepted. The Aristotelian definition of Fortune (*tyckhe*) as chance, or coincidence, is most clearly rejected. But no choice is made between the idea of the classical authors of fortuna as *vis divina quaedam* and the Christian subsuming of *fortuna* under divine Providence."

232 Ioannis Ioviani Pontani, *De fortuna, Opera omnia soluta oratione composita,* prima pars (Venetiis: in aedibus Aldi et Andreae soceri, 1513), ff. 264–309. On this issue, see F. Tateo, *Astrologia e moralità in Giovanni Pontano* (Bari, 1960), pp. 123–49; M. Santoro, *Fortuna, ragione e prudenza nella civiltà letteraria del Cinquecento* (Naples, 1967), pp. 23–65.

233 Cf. Pontano, *De fortuna*, f. 264 v: "Fortunae nomen apud omneis gentes divulgatum est adeo, ut docti etiam viri consentiant. . . . de fortuna erat hominum opinio, quae vis esset ea, quodque tum bona tum mala plurima obiicerentur"; and Poggio, *De varietate fortunae*, p. 25: "Multa . . . audivi et legi de hac fortuna eiusque potestate ab historicis, poetis, oratoribus, multa plura sermone hominum celebrantur, omnia fere humana ditioni fortunae subicientium . . . , quam secundam exoptant, adversam execrantur, . . . adeoque haec opinio inolevit, ut ab ea divitias atque opes largiri . . . putent; neque huic opinioni vulgo tantum creditur, sed doctissimorum et sapientissimorum virorum voces astipulantur."

234 *In octo libros Physicorum Aristotelis expositio*, ed. P. M. Maggiolo (Turin, 1954), p. 108, § 217: "Assignat rationem eorum quae de fortuna dicuntur. Et primo eorum quae dicta sunt a philosophis antiquis de fortuna; secundo eorum quae ab hominibus vulgaribus de fortuna dicuntur."

235 "sed firmum quid ac stabile, diuque in multis rebus ante praemeditatum." Cf. *De varietate fortunae*, p. 27.

236 "Inconstans est [*scil.* fortuna], inordinata, varia, repentina. Contra vero, quid natura ipsa ordinatius, constantius, certius?" Cf. *De fortuna*, f. 256 r.

237 "cum omnes certo consilio suscepto, nihil insperato, nihil praeter intentionem sint consecuti." Cf. *De varietate fortunae*, p. 28.

238 "an non prudentia humanarum est actionum omnium dux et magistra? . . . Adversatur igitur fortuna intelligentiae, cuius alumna est prudentia." Cf. *De fortuna*, f. 256 r.

239 "Quare fortuna sit natura quaedam"; "naturae impetum esse cuiusdam." Cf. *De fortuna*, ff. 278 v, 279 r.

240 "Defensio fortunae et naturae adversus eorum accusatores." Cf. *De fortuna*, f. 296 r.

241 Doren, *Fortuna*, pp. 121 ff.; Patch, *The Tradition of Goddess*, p. 218; Patch, *The Goddess*, pp. 23 ff.

242 C. Landino, *De vera nobilitate*, ed. M. T. Liaci (Florence, 1970), p. 46: "Nam quicquid agimus, gerimus, facimus, quo veluti via quadam ad finem, quem nobis proposuerimus, deduci possimus, id philosophi officium appellant. . . . Dignitatem autem dicemus excellentiam quandam, quam ex eo officio consequimur, qua cultu quodam observantiaque atque veneratione digni sumus." Cf. Dante *Convivio* 18.5: "Che lo piè del'albero, che tutti li altri rami comprende, si dee principio dire e cagione di

quelli, e non quelli di lui; e così nobilitade, che comprende ogni virtude, sì come cagione effetto, comprende molte altre nostre operazioni laudibili, se dee avere per tale, che la vertude sia da ridurre ad essa." It must be added that the idea of nobility as the final degree of perfection stemmed from Thomistic philosophy, as we see exemplified in the great treatise by G. Peraldus, *Summa virtutum et vitiorum* (bk. 1, 5: "De vera nobilitate"), precisely the title later taken up by Landino. Cf. *Enciclopedia Dantesca*, vol. 4, p. 58 (see n. 214 above). On Landino's work, with the introduction to the edition by M. T. Liaci, see Tateo, *Tradizione e realtà*, pp. 396–419.

243 "quasi splendor quidam ex virtute progrediens qui suos possessores illustrat"; "et sive sequentur exempla parentum, sive aliis exemplo se esse volent, adipiscentur veram nobilitatem"; cf. *De nobilitate*, p. 79. Cf. also n. 187 above.

244 *De vera nobilitate*, p. 39: "Verum, ut tandem universum hunc locum concludam, non ego ea ratione Venetos nobiles, quod a senatorio illius civitatis ordine originem ducant, appellaverim, sed plerosque ex illis, quod ita vivant iisque artibus excellant, ut iure suo nobiles appellari possint." See also pp. 45 f., with regard to Bartolo. According to his teaching, "nobilitatem non a sua origine, neque ab ea in qua sua essentia est, sed a legum positione deducit. . . . Et profecto bene institutae sunt leges, rectissimeque agent principes, si hominibus obscuriore genere natis, sed multis praeclarisque virtutibus insignibus, id veluti praemium esse velint, ut cum praeclare egerint nobilitatique ipsi suis actionibus sint, non dico nobilitate donentur—illam enim iam ipsi sibi pepererunt—sed suo privilegio ab aliis nobiles et haberi et appellari iubeant, non quia ea appellatione nobiles fiant, sed ut testimonium nobilitati afferant." For another contemporary case of an implicit debate with Poggio, see Bartolomeo Platina's *De principe* (1470; ed. G. Ferraù [Palermo, 1979]). Here the dispute over nobility is taken up (cf. pp. 28 f., 73–76), but also and especially with it, the theme of the *De infelicitate principum,* which gives the title to a special section, where Poggio is mentioned as "nescio quem" (pp. 87–88), and where "le posizioni di Poggio sono riprese ed in parte arricchite o confutate" (p. 18). The presence of Poggio in Platina's discussion is still more appreciable than is noted by the albeit attentive editor: the section *Contra avaritiam,* for example, takes up at length arguments and citations from Poggio's homonymous dialogue (pp. 128–34). Nevertheless, of course, the negative qualities find in Platina an adequate balance in the proper expounding of the positive ones, with the equipment of definitions and *exempla,* as was typical of such courtly precepts.

245 Cf. the privilege, by a bill of the Medici Balìa, 24 October 1434; see Walser, pp. 349–51 [*Opera omnia,* vol. 4, pp. 335–55]; the stipulation of the marriage with Vaggia Buondelmonti, on 19 January 1436, ibid., p. 353. The consequential character of these two acts, which is not observed by biographers, does not seem to be accidental. On the Buondelmonti family, cf. Martines, *The Social World,* pp. 210–14; and R. Bizzocchi, "La dissoluzione di un clan familiare: I Buondelmonti di Firenze nei secoli XV e XVI," *Archivio storico italiano* 160 (1982): 3–43.

246 "Quae omnia . . . soli scientiae, doctrinae, litteris accepta referre debemus." Cf. letter to Nicholas V, 26 August 1449, ed. Tonelli, vol. 3, p. 14 [ed. Harth, vol. 3, p. 98]. Cf. also letter to Benedetto Accolti, 6 May 1447, ed. Tonelli, vol. 2, pp. 340 f. [ed. Harth,

vol. 3, p. 46]: "Habemus pontificem virum doctissimum atque optimum. . . . Sed imperium difficile suscepit multis in rebus conturbatum et, quod est difficilius, egenum. Itaque distrahitur tanto rerum turbine ac varietate, ut neque sibi neque amicis vacare queat. . . . Credo declinabit a moribus multorum quibus carior pecunia quam virtus fuit. Principia quidem sunt optima et, ut spero, non erit alienus a priori vita: quanvis difficillimum sit in principatu servare modum, et amicorum priorum meminisse." This, quite clearly, is an illustration of the theme of the "Oratio ad Nicolaum V," written in the very same time (it is dated, according to an authoritative manuscript, 1 May 1447; cf. *Catalogo*, p. 30, n. 37); cf. also n. 111 above.

247 Cf. letter to John Carvajal, cardinal of S. Angelo, 6 April 1454, ed. Tonelli, vol. 3, p. 95 [ed. Harth, vol. 3, p. 193].

248 "absque triumphorum insigniis . . . optarem: bonitas per se ipsam lucet." Cf. letter to Bartolomeo Rovarella, archbishop of Ravenna, 1452, ed. Tonelli, vol. 3, p. 477 [ed. Harth, vol. 3, p. 144]; Walser, p. 283, grasps perceptively the meaning of these elusive words. On the pontificate of Nicholas V and the relative ideology, cf. the survey articles by C. Vasoli, "Profilo di un papa umanista: Tommaso Parentucelli," *Studi sulla cultura del Rinascimento* (Manduria, 1968), pp. 69–121; and J. B. Toews, "Formative Forces in the Pontificate of Nicholas V," *The Catholic Historical Review* 54 (1968–69): 261–84.

249 According to the only reference in Poggio's correspondence, the *Contra hypocritas* (dedicated to Francesco Accolti) was written around November 1417. Walser, p. 244, misunderstanding the identity of one figure—the bishop of Rimini in the work is not Bartolomeo Malatesta, but his predecessor Cristoforo of San Marcello, dead in 1444—extended the date of composition to 1448; cf. my *Introduzione alla lettura del "Contra hypocritas,"* p. 58. The process of Bernardino's canonization began the year after his death and was concluded on 24 May 1450, silencing old criticisms; cf. L. Valla, *Collatio Novi Testamenti,* Redazione inedita a cura di A. Perosa (Florence, 1970), p. xxxv. Not even Poggio, of course, took up his attacks on Bernardino; but his animosity against the Observant friars, who recognized him as their most prestigious leader, has, if possible, grown even more bitter than in his writings of 1428–1430.

250 Cf. the letter to Pietro of Noceto, autumn 1453, ed. Tonelli, vol. 3, p. 76 [ed. Harth, vol. 3, p. 189]. It refers with spitefulness to the favor Valla found in papal curia, being listed for the nomination as apostolic secretary by Nicholas V. With his *De miseria,* Poggio would emulate Valla's own anticlerical tracts, as well as the satires of Filelfo (another enemy of Poggio, now aiming at the pope's favors), given that these means granted them good rewards. On the work, cf. Walser, pp. 305 ff.

251 "Te vero, Sigismunde, oro obtestorque . . . hanc nostram disputationem (si qui forsan in eam malivoli invidique impetum facere conarentur) tuendam suscipias auctoritate tua." Cf. *De miseria humanae conditionis, Opera,* p. 112. These words, normally recast into the text, are found in the guise of an addition in the margin of the early copy of the tract, in Biblioteca Medicea Laurenziana, cod. Plut. 76, 52, f. 35r, precisely at the beginning of bk. 2 (cf. *Catalogo,* pp. 38 f., n. 57). The addition follows the probings at Sigismund's court at the end of 1455 and beginning of 1456, in order to obtain the consent for the dedication. See on the subject the letter to Roberto Valturio of

Rimini, summer 1456, ed. Tonelli, vol. 3, p. 223 [ed. Harth, vol. 3, p. 404]: "Bis iam ad te scripsi me addidisse ad libros nostros ea verba, quae desiderabas, ut nullus invidus aut malivolus titulum libri [scil. the dedication] posset immutare, misique ad te quae addita a me erant." Cf. also Walser, p. 307.

252 Cf. letter to Pietro del Monte, spring 1456, ed. Tonelli, vol. 3, p. 216 [ed. Harth, vol. 3, p. 394]; and also the pathetic "Conclusio" of the *Facetiae, Opera*, p. 491: "Hodie cum illi diem suum obierint, desiit Bugiale, tum temporum tum hominum culpa, omnisque iocandi confabulandique consuetudo sublata."

253 Calixtus III's renewal of his nomination as apostolic secretary on 20 April 1455 could perhaps be interpreted as a compensation for Poggio's complaints, cf. Walser, p. 393 f. [*Opera omnia*, vol. 4, pp. 397 f.]. Poggio, however, would not forgive Calixtus for his extension of the college of apostolic secretaries, in which, among others, Valla had actually found a post; cf. the late *Vitae quorundam pontificum*, ed. L. Duchesne, p. 559 [*Opera omnia*, vol. 2, p. 792]: "Hic omnia curiae officia pervertit . . . , secretarios ad quinquaginta fecit, in quos notarios et operarios et nullius doctrinae plurimos coniecit, honestissimumque officium sua stultitia decoravit."

254 "Difficile enim est hoc tempore satyram non scribere." Cf. letter to Pietro del Monte, Florence, spring 1456, ed. Tonelli, vol. 3, p. 216 [ed. Harth, vol. 3, p. 394].

255 "Pogius rabula": cf. Desiderii Erasmi Roterodami, *Opus epistolarum*, ed. P. S. Allen, vol. 1 (Oxford, 1906), p. 409 (letter to a Christopher Fischer, 1505).

256 Cf. *De varietate fortunae*, p. 63 [*Opera omnia*, vol. 2, p. 565]: "vir dignus prioribus saecu-lis, non in tyranni ut plerique nostrorum, sed in regios mores se componens"; and *Historiae Florentini populi*, ed. G. B. Recanati, p. 154 [ibid., p. 250]: "Princeps fuit per-liberalis magnique animi, ad regios mores se componens . . . Id in eo culpatur, quod fidem et promissa ex utilitate traditur servasse, quod vitium commune cum multis egregiis bello ducibus fuit; sed ea laudanda prae caeteris est virtus, quod omnium doctrinarum artiumque viros eximios ad se, tamquam egregiorum hominum re-ceptaculum, vocavit summoque in honore habuit." A similar praise of Giangaleazzo was written, very close to the time and place of the composition of *De varietate for-tunae*, by another Florentine in the papal curia, L. B. Alberti, *Della famiglia*, bk. IV (ed. R. Romano, and A. Tenenti [Turin, 1969], p. 329): "era cupidissimo de' virtuosi e amantissimo de' buoni, e padre della nobiltà."

257 *Lamenti de' secoli XIV e XV,* [ed. A. Medin] (Florence, 1883), p. 36: "son quel vagho e venusto fiore / Che ò gran parte di Nettuno e di Teti / E sotto i miei decreti / In terra tengho scetro e monarchia, / E sotto mia balia / Quasi tutta Toscana reggho e tengho" ("Risposta" to the "Canzone fatta per chonte di Poppi"). Cf. also the cir-cumstantiated chronicle by Neri Capponi, *La cacciata del conte di Poppi ed acquisto di quello stato pel popolo Fiorentino*, in Muratori, *R.I.S.*, XVIII (Milan, 1731), cols. 1217–30.

258 *De varietate fortunae*, p. 109 f. [*Opera omnia*, vol. 2, pp. 611 f.]. Poggio's letter to Fran-cesco Guidi of Battifolle, winter 1442–43, ed. Tonelli, vol. 2, pp. 276 f. [ed. Harth, vol. 2, pp. 421 f.], in which he protests against false reports, according to which he would have written "nonnulla quae vergerent in dedecus nominis tui," asserting his own devotion, "except in matters of public concern" ("excepta patriae causa"). It is possible that Poggio's excuse refers to an early circulation of the *De varietate*, but at

the same time it illuminates his sincere regret at the fall of the family ("documentum praebuit nihil perpetuum aut firmum in bonis humanis esse"). Even the *Florentine Histories*, pp. 350 f. [*Opera omnia*, vol. 2, p. 446] make reference to the family of the Guidi counts: here the fall is attributed to the "temeritas" of Francesco, who takes sides with Filippo Maria Visconti, "ignarus respublicas, optimis praesertim fundatas legibus, diuturniores unius hominis vita esse solere."

259 "Semper ad peiora mobilem." Cf. *Historiae*, p. 343 [*Opera omnia*, vol. 2, p. 439]; and above all ibid., p. 266 [p. 362], on the conclusions of the debate between Rinaldo degli Albizzi and Niccolò da Uzzano over the siege of Lucca, where, as in his letters from this period, the condemnation for entering into war is repeated: "tamen, ut saepissime contigit, melior pars a maiori superata est"; cf. Wilcox, *The Development*, p. 140; and n. 126 above.

260 Letter to Carlo Marsuppini, 13 June 1448, ed. Tonelli, vol. 2, pp. 361 f. [ed. Harth, vol. 3, p. 62]. Poggio laments his fate, "quod me in patria omnium molestissima ac laborum et sudoris plena nasci voluit . . . , ut incertus sim ubi sit senectutis quies futura."

261 Cf. *Historiae*, pp. 140 f. [*Opera omnia*, vol. 2, pp. 236 f.], where the memory of the Florentines' spontaneous contributions for the wars of defense against Giangaleazzo provides the opportunity to deplore the loans and extraordinary tributes, extorted by the leading citizens for self-interested motives: "At hodie eo redacta civitas est, ut cum viginti aut triginta aureorum milia cogenda sunt, aut versura comparetur pecunia, aut ad extraordinaria tributa recurrant, quod iniquum est pessimumque exigendae pecuniae genus et abominandum, atque ab his excitatum, quibus potior est res privata quam publica, quique opes sibi vendicant per aliorum calamitatem, ipsi eiusmodi tributi onere expertes." The accusation also reappears in connection with the covert private support given to Niccolò Fortebraccio in his raids on Lucca: "Alii quorundam civium ambitionem cupiditatemque, quibus bella usui erant opesque eorum aliorum damno augebantur, plus aequo valuisse tradunt, Nicolaumque privati cuiusdam civis consilio ad arma tyranno inferenda motum, cui confestim scriptum est, ut quod bellum antea sponte sua movisset et auctoritate populi Florentini administraret" (*Historiae*, p. 266 [p. 326]). The passage alludes mainly to Neri Capponi; cf. G. Cavalcanti, *Istorie fiorentine* (Milan, 1944), p. 160: "E' si diceva che Niccolò (Fortebraccio) aveva cominciata a guerra sotto il favore di Neri di Gino"; but cf. also n. 126 above. On the traditional charge that the *ottimati* were growing rich on the interests from the wartime loans, cf. A. Molho, *Florentine Public Finances in the Early Renaissance, 1400–1433* (Cambridge, Mass., 1971), pp. 187–92.

262 "potentiores ac civitatum principes illarum [legum] vires trasgrediuntur." Cf. *Historia tripartita, Opera*, p. 48 f.: "Ut vero descendamus ad nostra, nonne Lombardiae duces, Veneti, Florentini multique praeterea aliena appetendo rapiendoque crevere?" As it can be seen, here the "cupido dominandi," differently from in the semi-official context of the *Historiae* (cf. Wilcox, *The Development*, p. 136), was in Poggio's eyes not only an attribute of sovereign lords.

263 "nisi profluvio pecuniarum nostrarum." Cf. letter to Niccoli, Rome, 28 May 1423, ed. Tonelli, vol. 1, p. 89 [ed. Harth, vol. 1, p. 64].

264 "Illud certe mirandum videri debet, in tot bellorum inhexaustos sumptus tantam
 pecuniam suppeditatam, cum per tot continuos quibus arma viguerunt annos non
 suo sed conducto milite sit libertas defensa, neque solum nostrates sed exterae quoque gentes regesque sint magna vi pecuniae in suum auxilium excitati." Cf. the
 "Proemium," in Fubini, *Umanesimo e secolarizzazione*, pp. 301 f.

265 "Florentini bella populi tum repulsa tum illata"; ibid., p. 301. On the argument
 in general, see my essay "Umanesimo e società civile in Poggio Bracciolini," in
 R. Fubini, *Quattrocento fiorentino: Politica diplomazia cultura* (Pisa, 1996), pp. 221–34.

266 Cf. letter to Carlo Marsuppini, 13 June 1448, and to P. Tommasi, summer 1454, in
 Walser, p. 530 [*Opera omnia*, vol. 4, p. 534]: "Cupiebam civis vester fieri et domum
 apud vos parare, quae filiorum meorum in vestra republica quies et receptaculum esse
 posset . . . ; sed postea quam in patriam sum vocatus illa cogitatio effluxit ex animo,
 et ad alia mentem converti." Poggio had, moreover, already shown his own uncertainties with regard to public service at the time when L. Bruni was proposed for the
 Florentine chancellery, urging him to look after his own private dignity ("in quo
 maxime servatam fuisse dignitatem tuam"; cf. letter to Bruni, Rome, 28 December
 1427, ed. Tonelli, vol. 1, p. 216 [ed. Harth, vol. 2, p. 81]).

267 "ut mihi viderer non civis sed hospes quidam et novus accola in patriam venisse." Cf.
 letter to Francesco Condulmer, Florence, 30 June 1453, ed. Tonelli, vol. 3, p. 57 [ed.
 Harth, vol. 3, p. 153].

268 Cf. letter to Guarino, 18 June 1456, ed. Tonelli, vol. 3, p. 223 f. [ed. Harth, vol. 3,
 p. 405], in which, suspicious of civic corruption, he resolves to send him his son:
 "Nullo in loco tanta eius aetatis est virtutis incuria." Poggio expressed the same concern in a gloss to his own copy of Aristotle's *Ethics*: "Ideo mali in Florentia plures
 propter malam in pueris disciplinam" (cf. *Catalogo*, p. 22, n. 16).

269 Cf. Vespasiano da Bisticci, *Le vite*, vol. 1 (Florence, 1970), pp. 547 f. For all this, see
 my essay cited n. 265 above; and also *Catalogo*, pp. 16, 62 f.

270 Cf. Vespasiano da Bisticci, *Le vite*, pp. 548 f.: "e se non fusse istato Cosimo che poteva
 assai in lui, che mitigò lo sdegno, lo faceva pigliare qualche strano partito." Cf. also
 the invective "In fidei violatores," *Opera omnia*, vol. 2, pp. 891–902. Note the expressions: "Quidam qui rei publicae patronos et eius utilitatis auctores haberi volunt
 (p. 891); "Factio perversa est nominanda" (p. 897); "Tyrannis est ista perversitas, quae
 non publicae sed privatae consulit utilitati" (p. 902), etc. A tract such as *Contra fidei
 violatores* was the sign of Poggio's break with the city's establishment, and it must be
 presumed that it had serious consequences for the unhappy vicissitudes of his heir,
 Jacopo.

271 "ut Veneti faciunt"; "administretur iustitia et iuste vivatur." Florence, State Archive,
 Consulte e Pratiche, 54, f. 159r (7 November 1457). On Machiavelli's role, cf. Rubinstein, *Il governo di Firenze sotto i Medici*, (Firenze, 1971), p. 114.

272 Cf. the oration "In laudem rei publicae Venetorum," *Opera omnia*, vol. 2, pp. 925–37;
 and the introductory note, ibid., pp. 919–24. It seems not unlikely that, disappointed
 in his motherland, Poggio went back to yearn for the safe port of Venice, as he did
 in the letter to Tommasi of 1454 (cf. n. 266 above).

273 On the copyist signing the copy in Biblioteca Nazionale di Firenze, MS. Magl. XXVII,
 65, Giovanni di Ubaldino degli Stagnesi, cf. *Opera omnia*, vol. 2, pp. 919 f. In 1464

he transcribed a copy of Frontinus's *Stratagemata* "pro clarissimo iuvene Zenobio de Dietisalvis" (Biblioteca Medicea Laurenziana, MS. Strozz. 66); on 3 November 1470, the same Zenobi wrote from Rome to his father Dietisalvi di Nerone (then in Ferrara): "Piacemi lo Stagnese sii costi . . . , che mi pare persona da trarne fructo" (Archivio di Stato di Milano, Sforzesco, Potenze Estere, 280; the letter deals with various conspiracies of the political exiles among anti-Medici partisans); afterward this figure, brought into the circle of Lorenzo de' Medici, lent himself to intelligence and espionage work on Lorenzo's behalf. Cf. the letter from I[oannes] S[tagnesius] to Lorenzo, Ferrara, 2 July 1471, ASF, Mediceo avanti il Principato, XXVII, 355, autograph; and the "postscripta," 3 July, ibid., XXVII, 400 bis; cf. also A. Cappelli, "Niccolo di Leonello d' Este," *Atti e Memorie della Deputazione per le provincie modenesi*, 5 (1870), p. 433, doc. XI.

274 Cf. *Opera omnia*, vol. 2, pp. 922 f.; *Catalogo*, pp. 13, 57 f., n. 103; the entry by C. Vasoli, *Dizionario Biografico degli Italiani*, vol. 13 (1971), pp. 638 f.; N. Rubinstein, "An Unknown Letter of Jacopo di Poggio Bracciolini on Discoveries of Classical Texts," *Italia medioevale e umanistica* 1 (1958): 383–400; L. Michelini Tocci, "Poggio Fiorentino e Federico da Montefeltro (con una lettera inedita di Jacopo di Poggio)," *Miscellanea Augusto Campana*, vol. 2 (Padua, 1981), pp. 504–36. See also, for Jacopo's involvement with the anti-Medicean conspiracy of 1466, M. Phillips, *The Memoir of Marco Parenti: A Life in Medici Florence* (Princeton, 1987), p. 203; and especially, for the republicanism of Jacopo, F. Bausi, " 'Paternae artis haeres': Ritratto di Jacopo Bracciolini," *Interpres* 8 (1988): 103–98.

275 Jacopo di Poggio Bracciolini, *Contra detractores*, Biblioteca Medicea Laurenziana, MS. Plut. 46, 2, ff. 71r–91r; cf. *Catalogo*, p. 58, n. 104. Thus, just as Poggio had complained that the "informants" "vindicare sibi volunt . . . prima loca apud dominos et eorum benivolentiam acquirere per deducus nostrum et infamiam" (*Opera omnia*, vol. 2, p. 715), Jacopo now denounces the attempt of the "detractors," "ut primum apud eos locum obtineant, aliis vero viam ad dignitates, ad honorem, ad gloriam eripere" (f. 77v). The *Contra delatores* was referring to an episode of convivial licentiousness, illustrated by Poggio in a letter to Bruni, 1 June 1424, ed. Tonelli, vol. 1, pp. 100–103 [ed. Harth, vol. 2, pp. 31–33]; and, retrospectively, to A. Loschi, ca. 1426, *Opera omnia*, vol. 4, pp. 597–600.

276 "Quorum tamen nihil nobis accideret, si aut principes quique rerum administrationem habent, quorum arbitrio vivimus et a quorum nutu salus nostra ac nostra omnia dependent, iusti, modesti atque prudentes essent." Cf. *Contra detractores*, ff. 82v–83r. Note also the bitter accusation of the detraction in Florence: "in patria nostra maxime dominatur, in qua multorum ineptissimorum hominum secta nullis meritis, neque ulla virtutis umbra, sed probis et bonis detrahendo, bonorum praemia ereptum eat, illisque iniunctissime insimulando invidiae subicere conetur, ne pro honoribus debitis poenis ab illis, si rem publicam gesserint, afficiantur" (ff. 83v–84r).

277 "Unde plerosque insignia virtutis etiam sine ulla virtutis umbra, clarissimis sanctissimisque viris posthabitis ac reiectis, fortunae ludibrio assecutos videmus, qui, si seposita illa persona se ipsos aestimandos praebuerint, facile illorum stuporem cognoscere liceret." Cf. ibid., f. 85r.

278 "Nos more nostro haud aegre feremus ad convivia accersiri, in quibus ob istorum

reprehensorum contumeliam libere colloquemur." Cf. letter to A. Loschi, ca. 1426, *Opera omnia,* vol. 4, p. 600.

5. *An Analysis of Lorenzo Valla's* De Voluptate

This chapter was originally presented in 1979 as a paper at the "Società pavese di Storia Patria," at the invitation of Professor Emilio Gabba. I delayed its publication for various reasons, not the least of which was an awareness of my considerable variance from trends long prevalent in scholarship on Valla, and thus of the need to justify more thoroughly and with more immediately verifiable evidence my argument. On one point there should be no further debate: the state of research on Valla no longer permits generalizations nor the annexation of the author as a more or less emblematic figure in ideological trends (be they lay or confessional, theological or philosophical). This requires us not only to avoid making unilateral and categorical statements about Valla but also to reestablish reliable links between his own works. Most of all we must reconsider the origins of Valla's propositions in order to determine their relationship to the context in which they were written, and not how they were taken up later and compared to various other ideological contexts, from the time of Erasmus up to the present day. In this sense, a study that takes as its starting point the milieu of Pavia and the composition of the *De voluptate* could have a significance beyond the specific issue at hand, and I have tried to honor this task with additional research, which is documented in the notes.

1   For the purposes of this chapter, at least, the studies essential to the reconstruction of Valla's biography are: L. Valla, *Antidotum in Facium,* ed. M. Regoliosi (Padua, 1981); *Epistolae,* ed. O. Besomi and M. Regoliosi (Padua, 1984) (in citing the letters I refer to the series number of the letter itself; in the absence of such a citation, I refer to the substantial commentary provided by the editors). Fundamental for ideological topics is the edition of the philosophical treatise, *Repastinatio dialecticae et philosophiae,* ed. G. Zippel (Padua, 1982) (this includes both the first version, as indicated by the title, and the third: *Retractatio totius dialecticae cum fundamentis universae philosophiae,* later abbreviated respectively to *Repastinatio* and *Retractatio*); on this subject, see also C. Trinkaus, "Lorenzo Valla's Anti-Aristotelian Natural Philosophy," *I Tatti Studie: Essays in the Renaissance* 5 (1993): 279–324. Also relevant is the *Defensio quaestionum in philosophia,* ed. G. Zippel, "L'autodifesa di Lorenzo Valla per il processo dell'Inquisizione napoletana (1444)," *Italia medioevale e umanistica* 13 (1970): 59–94. The standard old edition, not yet completely replaced, is Valla's *Opera,* published in Basel in 1540 (and reprinted in Turin in 1962). The text of the dialogue referred to in this chapter is the following: L. Valla, *De vero falsoque bono,* ed. M. De Panizza Lorch (Bari, 1970); hereafter this work will be cited in the abbreviated form *Dvb.* The same edition reappears, together with an English translation and new introduction, in *On Pleasure, De voluptate* (New York, 1977). Sometimes I will refer to the dialogue by its original title, *De voluptate,* whenever this chapter focuses on the time when the text was composed; the title of subsequent versions, according to what Valla himself states (cf., for example, *Retractatio,* p. 92), is consistently *De vero bono,* and not that

drawn from the first line of the text, as it appears in the title of some manuscripts and hence in De Panizza Lorch's edition. The recent work of M. De Panizza Lorch, *A Defence of Life: L. Valla's Theory of Pleasure* (Munich, 1985), was not published in time for me to use. Finally, this essay is linked with chapter 2 in this volume; see also my other essay, "Note su Lorenzo Valla e la composizione del "De Voluptate," *I Classici nel Medioevo e nell'Umanesimo: Miscellanea filologica* (Genoa, 1975), pp. 11–57.

2 Cf. E. Nasalli Rocca, "La famiglia di Lorenzo Valla e i piacentini nella curia di Roma del secolo XV," *Archivio storico per le province parmensi*, 4th ser., 9 (1957): 225–51; and also *Epistolae*, pp. 337, 355.

3 See De Panizza Lorch, "Introduction," *On Pleasure*, pp. 16 ff.; and *Antidotum II in Pogium*, *Opera*, p. 352.

4 On the *Comparatio*, cf. S. Camporeale, *Lorenzo Valla: Umanesimo e teologia* (Florence, 1972), pp. 89–100. From Valla's few indirect references, it is not possible to determine the precise nature of this text. As he himself said, it was written with the intention to emulate (see *Antidotum II in Pogium*, p. 352: "tecum et cum omnibus secretariis de facundia certabam, quippe *De comparatione Ciceronis Quintilianique* conscripseram"). It is, nonetheless, clear that neither here nor in any other context did he mean to make a comparison between the two authors; his intention, rather, was to evaluate the efficacy of their pedagogical treatises. In this sense the Cicero compared to Quintilian's *Institutio*, (a text in this time only recently recovered and circulated in its entirety) was the institutional Cicero of the rhetorical textbooks (the so-called *Rhetorica vetus* and *nova*). The adoption of these texts (often with commentaries) was substantially increasing from the late thirteenth-century school up to Gasparino Barzizza and even to Guarino himself (see J. O. Ward, "From Antiquity to the Renaissance: Glosses and Commentaries on Cicero's *Rhetorica*," *Medieval Eloquence: Studies in the Theory and Practice of Medieval Rhetoric*, ed. J. J. Murphy (Berkeley, Los Angeles, and London, 1978), pp. 25–67). We might hypothesize an extention of Valla's youthful writing in a commentary he wrote later on *Rhetorica ad Herennium* (which is also lost), where he expressed doubts about the authenticity of Cicero's authorship (cf. *Antidotum In Facium*, pp. xxx, lxiii, 388). Moreover, where Valla boasts of being "idem ego . . . qui praeposui in *Commentariis*, quos in Ciceronem Quintilianumque composui, Quintilianum Ciceroni, Demostheni atque ipsi Homero" (*Epistolae*, n. 16, pp. 215 f.), he seems to contrast his own teaching to the typical scholastic method as illustrated by Barzizza, who unified the eloquence of prose and poetry into a single system of rules ("Quid mihi prodesset Cicero sine Prisciano et Terentio et ceteris poetis? Quid Priscianus sine Cicerone et Terentio? Quid Terentius sine Cicerone et Prisciano? . . . Quare non tunc est occupatus sensus circa plura, quia diversa, quando ea sunt unum"); cf. G. W. Pigman III, "Barzizza's Studies of Cicero," *Rinascimento* 21 (1981): 125. In other words, the *Comparatio* would seem to represent the first step toward Valla's criticism of the scholastic approach to grammar and rhetoric, one that would lead to his most significant innovations in the *Elegantiae*, where he tendentiously made use of Quintilian's treatise as a weapon for his own antischolastic bias. It was traditional to connect the teaching of rhetorics with that of ethics, and in particular as it was presented in Ciceronian *De officiis*: cf. Pigman, pp. 123–63, and L. A.

Panizza, "G. Barzizza's Commentaries on Seneca's Letters," *Traditio* 33 (1977): 297–358. See also, for an example, C. Colombo and P. O. Kristeller, "Some New Additions to the Correspondence of Guarino of Verona . . . ," *Italia medioevale e umanistica* 8 (1965): 239–42. This concern, in turn, represented for Valla a transition to his subsequent criticisms of ethical teaching in the *De voluptate.*

5 See *Epistolae*, pp. 115 f. Still fundamental to an understanding of the circumstances surrounding these events is R. Sabbadini, "Come il Panormita diventò poeta aulico," *Archivio storico lombardo,* 43, pt. 1 (1916), pp. 5–27.

6 Cf. R. Maiocchi, *Codice diplomatico dell'Università di Pavia* (Pavia, 1913), bk. 2, pt. 1, p. 247; and on Seneca, see *Memorie e documenti per la storia dell'Università di Pavia* (Pavia, 1878), p. 156; R. Sabbadini, "Briciole umanistiche, IV," *Giornale storico della letteratura italiana* 18 (1891): 228–230 ("Nel tempo che dimorò a Pavia e a Milano ebbe molta dimestichezza col Panormita, e fu anzi il Panormita che lo fece venire colà"); E. Spadolini, "Un poema inedito di Tommaso Seneca da Camerino," *Le Marche illustrate* 2 (1902): 3–27; G. Resta, *L'epistolario del Panormita* (Messina, 1954), p. 237. A. Corbellini, "Note di vita cittadina e universitaria pavese nel Quattrocento," *Bollettino della societa pavese di storia patria* 30 (1930): 35, observes the peculiarity of Panormita's position: he was taken on in 1429 with a salary of four hundred florins, compared to the sixty florins paid to Barzizza. It seems that instead of actually teaching, Panormita used his lofty position as court poet to try to gain substantial control over the workings of the Studio; and if an anonymous invective wrongfully accused him of claiming the title of "Studii Papiensis . . . cancellarium" (R. Sabbadini, *Ottanta lettere inedite del Panormita* [Catania, 1910], pp. 33 f.), he does, nonetheless, appear before the prince as a kind of union representative for professors who were claiming payment in arrears (cf. R. Maiocchi, "Spoglio d'archivio," *Bollettino storico pavese* 2 (1894): 329–33, document of 10 May 1431).

7 "positus in Rotulo porrecto per Rectorem Iuristarum." Cf. Maiocchi, *Codice diplomatico,* p. 293; and *Epistolae,* p. 119. On university teaching conditions, see D. Bianchi, "La lettura d'arte oratoria dello Studio di Pavia nei secoli XV e XVI (1376–1550)," *Bollettino della società pavese di storia patria* 13 (1913): 151–72. On Sacco's relations with humanist circle, see Panormita's letter to Cambio Zambeccari, November 1429, in Sabbadini, *Ottanta lettere,* p. 105; and also Resta, *L'epistolario,* p. 236; C. Colombo, "Altri inediti guariniani," *Italia medioevale e umanistica* 10 (1967): 219–57.

8 "quasi obsidione quadam liberatus sum." Cf. F. Pontarin and C. Andreucci, "La tradizione del carteggio di Lorenzo Valla," *Italia medioevale e umanistica* 15 (1972): 205–8; *Epistolae*, n. 1, pp. 132 f. (Valla to Antonio of Rho); n. 1 a, pp. 133 ff. (Antonio of Rho to Valla); and also ibid., p. 121.

9 *Dvb*, p. xxxiv (and *On Pleasure,* pp. 16 f.). According to the fictional events in the dialogue, Niccoli had come to Rome "ob indulgentias, ut vocant, romanorum pulvinarium" (ibid., appendix 1, p. 143). This setting is clearly in keeping with his own role as defender of Christianity; but at the same time it contains a hint of irony if compared to Panormita's remarks in a letter to G. Lamola, 8 December 1427, where he announces his own arrival in Rome, alluded to also in *De voluptate:* "Romae sum. Quam, inquis, ob causam? Non quidem ut Romae religiosior fierem—Deus enim et

Romae benefacientibus et ubique est, neque is sum qui dentes, ossa et vestimenta sanctorum hominum adorem sed animos eorum divinos et coeli pulcritudine gloriaque pro virtutibus ac fide donatos —, sed ut convenirem, viserem atque salutarem Bartholomeum pontificem [i.e., B. Capra, the bishop of Milan], virum primarium Caesarisque nostri [i.e., F. M. Visconti, the duke] legatum tunc ad summum sacerdotem" (Sabbadini, *Come il Panormita*, p. 22). Nor had the real Niccoli (whom Panormita had met in Florence) failed to incur the reproaches of Ambrogio Traversari for his neglect of the religious precept: "Neque enim fero amicissimum hominem, evi iam gravem, sacris litteris apprime deditum et eruditum plures iam annos sacrosanctam non attigisse alimoniam; quia, nisi sepe suscitetur ac firmetur, fides nostra inter seculi temptationes fatiscit ac deficit" (cf. G. Mercati, *Ultimi contributi alla storia degli umanisti: Fasc. I: Traversiana* (Vatican City, 1939), pp. 46 f. Finally, despite the Stoic role Valla attributed in *De voluptate* to Leonardo Bruni, the third important speaker, he nonetheless introduced a concealed citation of the little work by Bruni himself, *Oratio Heliogabali ad meretrices*, "opus sane philosophicum non ex Zenonis disciplina, sed ex intimo Epicuri sinu depromptum," according to the author's own words (letter to Niccoli, 7 January 1408; cf. H. B. Gerl, *Philosophie und Philologie: Leonardo Brunis Übertragung der Nikomachischen Ethik in ihren philosophischen Prämissen* (Munich, 1981), pp. 156, 304; and also Luiso, *Studi,* pp. 41, 46; *Dvb,* p. xxxiv.

10 Cf. chap. 3 above; and also Marsh, pp. 55–77. The affinities with *De avaritia* are evident both in the structure and in implicit citations in Valla's dialogue. In terms of structure, the two works have in common a tripartite form, corresponding in some sense to the degrees of rhetorical persuasion (*docere, delectare, movere*), the first of which is represented by the more rigidly doctrinaire assumptions (in Poggio, the condemnation of avarice; in Valla, the "Stoic" propositions); the second by a controversial paradox (the utilitarian reevaluation of avarice in Poggio, the developments in the Epicurean's argument in Valla); and the third in the final speech of a largely edificatory nature by the Christian speaker (Andreas of Constantinople in Poggio, Niccoli in Valla). On the implicit references to Poggio, for example cf. *Dvb* 2.22.9, p. 89, where the arguments in support of "avaritia" as useful "ad vitae cultum et ad earum rerum quibus utuntur homines facultatem, ad opes ad copiam" etc., are a direct reference to the central theme of Antonio Loschi's speech in Poggio. Cf. chap. 3 above, and also n. 116 below.

11 Panormita worked on Valla's behalf (as it appears also allusively in the dialogue's context) as a mediator among the Florentine groups which presumably Valla knew only indirectly. The Florentine ambience, especially represented by Niccoli and Carlo Marsuppini, proved an essential point of reference for the young Valla. In fact, at the beginning of 1428, supported by Panormita, he sent Marsuppini his first work, the *Comparatio Ciceronis Quintilianique* (see Sabbadini, *Come il Panormita,* p. 24; *Antidotum in Facium,* p. 373). Later, in the course of the debate with Poggio, he remembered that he had been inspired by Niccoli in his attack on scholasticism, of which Boethius was for him both a forerunner and a symbol: "cum . . . eius coniunctissimus Nicolaus Nicoli, vir non minimae auctoritatis, Boetium sit appellare solitus excolaturam bonae doctrinae, ut nemo mirari debeat si cum Boetio de linguae latinae

proprietate contendo" (*Antidotum II in Pogium*, p. 292). Valla's dialogue thus reflected the radicalism of the Tuscan circle, which, however, was represented in Rome and closely connected to humanist culture there. It is nevertheless clear, despite the persistent confusion over the issue (see M. De Panizza Lorch, "The Presence of Rome and Milan in Lorenzo Valla's *On Pleasure*," *Umanesimo a Roma nel Quattrocento*, ed. P. Brezzi and M. De Panizza Lorch (Rome, 1984), pp. 191–210) that, according to all documentary and internal evidence, from its first version the work was conceived in Lombardy, putting an imaginary event into an idealized historical setting that reveals both its author's cultural inspiration and his desire to be coopted into the elite of the humanist movement in the footsteps of Panormita.

12 Cf. especially "Praemissio ad translationem Ethicorum Aristotelis," *Humanistisch-philosophische Schriften*, p. 79, where he attacks the confusion in scholastic terminology between "bonum" and "honestum" ("ita tria maxime quae in philosophia versantur—'bonum,' 'utile,' 'honestum'—in unum confundemus"); and also *Isagogicon moralis disciplinae*, ibid., pp. 20–41, where, in keeping with the same principle, he cautiously puts forward a reevaluation of utilitarianism under the aegis of the Aristotelian teaching, combined eclectically with the Stoic and Epicurean ones. Valla openly acknowledges the importance of Bruni's version of the *Nicomachean Ethics*, citing it in *Dvb* 2.28.2, p. 75, and making Bruni responsible for his own understanding of "voluptas" in *Defensio*, p. 83: "Siquidem nescio qui homines imperiti, quos merito Leonardus accusat, transtulerunt Aristotelem non latine sed barbare, pro 'voluptate' dicentes 'laetitiam'" etc. Bruni had actually restored "voluptas," in contrast to the "vetus interpres" who had translated *edoné* as "delectacio": cf. Gerl, *Philosophie und Philologie*, p. 172. It seems to me of particular importance, however, that the title *De vero bono*, which ever since the first version had been presented as an equivalent and alternative title to *De voluptate* (". . . siquidem de vero bono, quam eandem voluptatem esse placet, in hoc opere disputamus," p. 151), is likewise taken out of Bruni's version of Aristotle. Here, in fact, *tò kat'alethéian agathòn* ("secundum veritatem bonum" in the literal version of Grossatesta) is rendered "verum bonum," in contrast to *tagathòn* ("the good"), which is translated as "summum bonum" (ibid., p. 165; see *Nicomachean Ethics* 3.5.1114b: "choose the good according to truth"; and also *Aristoteles latinus*, XXVI, 1–3, fasc. quartus, ed. L. A. Gauthier (Leiden, 1973), p. 420). In short, Bruni represents to Valla a direct point of reference in his plea for a new humanistic philosophical language, while at the same time providing a worthy term of comparison for new and original solutions.

13 "Quanto enim evidentius, gravius, magnificentius ab oratoribus illa disseruntur quam a dialecticis quibusdam squalidis et exanguibus disputantur!" Cf. *Dvb*, pp. 15, 157 (cited as it appears in the first version.) On the topos contrasting rhetoric and dialectic, cf. Cicero *Academica posteriora*, 28.91; *Rhetorica ad Herennium* 2.11.16; Quintilian *Instituto* 12.2.7–14.

14 Cf. *Epistolae*, pp. 115–18.

15 "librum illum tuum, quem eloquentia, doctrina et arte divinum multi audivimus, multi testantur." Cf. Pontarin and Andreucci, *La tradizione*, p. 207; *Epistolae*, n. 1a, pp. 133 f.

16 Maffeo Vegio is brought in here as Panormita's competitor for court poet. In 1430–31 he tried his hand with the epic, dedicating the poems *Convivium deorum, Astinax,* and *Vellus auream* to Filippo Maria Visconti; cf. A. Sottili, "Zur Biographie Giuseppe Brivios und Maffeo Vegios," *Mittellateinisches Jahrbuch* 4 (1967): 226.

17 On Antonio da Rho, see *Apologia, Orazioni,* ed. G. Lombardi (Rome, 1982), Introduction, pp. 5–38; and also, for his relationship to Valla, M. Regoliosi, "Due nuove lettere di Lorenzo Valla," *Italia medioevale e umanistica* 25 (1982): 161–64. On Guarino and his links with Sacco and Vegio, see Colombo, *Altri inediti . . .* vol. 2, *Guarino e gli amici pavesi dal 1430 al 1433,* pp. 232–45. On Valla's attempts to ingratiate himself with Guarino (who, with his own authority, had previously sanctioned another controversial work, Panormita's *Ermaphroditus*), see *Epistolae,* pp. 125–27; and also Colombo, *Some New Additions . . .* vol. 1, *Guarino e gli amici di Bologna e Firenze nella corrispondenza del 1426,* pp. 213–323.

18 On Brivio, a doctor in decretals and a disciple of Barzizza, see Sottili, *Zur Biographie,* pp. 219–29. The Berneri ("de Berneriis") were a family from Alessandria. It included Maestro Gerardo, a doctor in the arts and medicine at Pavia, and Giovan Maria, the owner of a codex in which are preserved writings of Lombard humanists, including the correspondence between Valla and Antonio of Rho (cf. *Epistolae,* pp. 70 f.). On the device of Poggio, see chap. 2 above, and n. 10 above.

19 Piccinino, and even more so Decembrio, were the leaders of the court group hostile to Panormita, who took advantage of the disgrace of his protector, Francesco Barbavera, in 1432 (cf. the entry by N. Raponi, *Dizionario Biografico degli Italiani,* vol. 6 (1964), pp. 141–44.) On the link between Valla and the Bossi family, Francesco, bishop of Como, and his nephew Antonio, see *Epistolae,* p. 118; and also the panegyrical passage on his clan in *Dvb* 3.23.2, p. 123.

20 For this event, see the exposition in *Epistolae,* pp. 122–27. It is still not entirely certain if Valla edited the new version of the dialogue while in Lombardy. The first version, *De voluptate,* had been produced in a kind of edition sponsored by Panormita (cf. *Antidotum in Facium,* p. 372), according to a procedure to which Valla would resort repeatedly afterward, relying in particular on the help of Giovanni Tortelli. This edition, however, must have circulated in narrow circles (when stripped of its rhetoric, Antonio of Rho's statement, cited in n. 15 above, was probably intended to suggest that the work was known more from hearsay than from actual knowledge). It is surely possible that the new edition from Pavia was prepared during his sojourn in the city (until March 1433), as the editors of the *Epistolae* claim (p. 123), on the basis of Valla's own testimony: "in libris *De vero bono* in ea urbe conditis." The drawing up of a work ("condere"), however, must not be confused with the process of publishing ("edere"), which is not always straightforward and immediate. This probably explains Valla's "promotional tour" to Florence and Ferrara in September 1433 and the warnings that his adversaries, Panormita and Poggio, issued to Guarino (ibid., pp. 126f.). It would have been impossible for Valla to circulate a work like *Dvb* without taking precautionary measures, something that would remain a chronic concern for him throughout his career.

21 Unless otherwise indicated, this analysis refers to the final text of the *Dvb,* as it ap-

pears in the critical edition. The English translation by M. De Panizza Lorch, *On Pleasure,* has been a reference point.

22 *Dvb* 1.2.2, p. 5: "Quae autem sunt bona? Nimirum qualia sunt quae pertinent ad honestatem, ut iusticia, fortitudo, temperentia." Note the absence of prudence at the beginning of the series of cardinal virtues, which is otherwise presented in its traditional order, according to Cicero *De officiis* 1.5.15. Cf. on this issue *Repastinatio* 1.14, §§ 11–12, pp. 411f., where in connection with *De officiis* 2.9.34, Cicero is accused of incoherence: "Quod fateri mihi videtur Cicero . . . fortasse non satis constanter ille quidem, sed tamen vere inquiens: 'Prudentia sine iustitia nihil valet ad faciendam fidem. . . .' Hic ego non video quemadmodum Cicero prudentiam separet a versutia, calliditate, malitia."

23 *Dvb* 1.3.7, p. 8.

24 Ibid., 1.15.1, p. 21: "Voluptas est bonum undecumque quaesitum, in animi et corporis oblectatione positum"; and ibid., 1.17.1, p. 23: "Quae dixi externarum rerum ea iccirco bona appellantur, quod animo et corpori, ex quibus duobus constamus, voluptatem parant."

25 Ibid., 1.18.1, p. 23: "Nunc autem de corporis bonis, quorum praecipuum sanitas est, proximum pulchritudo, tertium vires et deinceps reliqua" etc.; cf. also n. 114 below.

26 Ibid., 33.1–2, p. 34: "Illae autem quatuor quae virtutes appellantur, quas vos honestatis vocabulo coinquinatis . . . , non aliud quam ad hunc finem perveniunt. . . . Prudentia . . . , ut commoda tibi prospicere scias, incommoda vitare. . . . Continentia: ut una aliqua oblectatione contineas quo pluribus et maioribus fruaris. . . . Iustitia: ut tibi inter mortales benivolentiam, gratiam commodaque concilies. . . . Nam modestia, quam quidam a numero quatuor excludunt, quantum ego quidem intelligo, nihil aliud est quam conciliatrix quaedam auctoritatis inter homines et benivolentiae." Cf. on this point *Repastinatio* 1.14, § 19, p. 414: "Restat 'modestia' quam quarto numerant loco. Hanc Panetius, Cicero, Ambrosius, tanti viri tamque eruditi, nequiverunt satis distingui a reliquis tribus . . . Mihi vero videtur partim prudentia, partim esse iusticia seu fortitudo." Aside from the personal identification of "modestia" with "fortitudo," the series of virtues exemplified here, in contrast to the list cited in n. 22, is inspired by Christian treatises, where the order is variable and where occasionally the principle virtue, according to the classic scheme, is replaced by a corresponding lesser virtue (for example, "continentia" in place of "temperantia"). Moreover, the pattern proposed here, *mutatis mutandis,* of "prudence, temperance, justice, and fortitude," had been handed down especially in treatises inspired by Augustine and Bonaventure, where "prudentia" and "temperantia" were the virtues opposed to temporal good, apparent or superfluous; "iustitia" and "fortitudo" were opposed respectively to the "malum perversum et adversum"; cf. O. Lottin, "La théorie des vertus cardinales de 1230 à 1250," *Mélanges Mandonnet: Études d'histoire littéraire et doctrinale du Moyen Âge,* vol. 2 (Paris, 1930), pp. 233–59 (especially p. 240); and also É. Gilson, *Saint Thomas moraliste,* 2d ed. (Paris, 1974), pp. 342–46.

27 *Dvb* 1.44–45, pp. 38–41.

28 Ibid., 2.1.2, p. 45: "Agamus itaque primum de fortitudine, deinde de aliis virtutibus si res postulabit," etc.; and ibid., 13.3, p. 60: "ex quibus omnibus colligitur omnem

gloriam ad finem pertinere voluptatis, sicut omnem infamiae fugam ad evitandam animi molestiam."

29 Ibid., 2.15.1, p. 62: "Quid autem est virtus? Bonum, inquies, non propter aliud sed propter se expetendum et suapte natura laudandum. At quid est bonum? Sustantiane an actio, an qualitas? Dices actio. Sed quae actio? Virtutis, inquies, et honestatis. At ego nescio quid sit honestas et virtus." On this point cf. the classic definition in Cicero *De inventione* 2.53.159: "Quod aut totum aut aliqua ex parte propter se petitur, honestum nominabimus. . . . Est igitur in eo genere omnes res una vi atque uno nomine complexa virtus. Nam est animi habitus, naturae, modo atque rationi consentaeus." On the Christian and Thomistic assumption of this concept, see É. Gilson, *Lo spirito della filosofia medioevale,* 2d ed. (Brescia, 1969), p. 420; and Gilson, *St. Thomas,* pp. 160 ff. The criticism that Valla formulates here is closely linked with the developments in the *Repastinatio,* where "prudentia" is excluded from the number of virtues (1.14.8, pp. 411 f.), and the concept of moral "habitus" is challenged, ibid., § 32, p. 418: "Nec fere habitus est in virtute ut est in virtutis scientia ceterisque in doctrinis et artibus, neque in ipsis artibus dispositio est et habitus, ut peripateticis placet, sed prope infiniti gradus."

30 *Dvb* 2.15.6, p. 63: "Quae autem maiora bona et quae minora sunt, difficile est pronuntiare, praesertim quod mutantur tempore, loco, persona et ceteris huiusmodi."

31 Ibid., 28.5, p. 76: "Plato dixerat . . . duas esse in animo voluptates, alteram expetendam alteram fugiendam. . . . Aristoteles duas et ipse voluptates facit, unam in sensibus et quandam aliam in mente. At ipse non intelligo, cum unum et idem nomen sit, quo pacto possimus facere rem diversam" etc.

32 Ibid., 2.28.8–10, p. 77. The polemic is, of course, directed at Aristotle's ideal of contemplation ("ait . . . hoc maximum probari in contemplativa summam inesse felicitatem, quod deos maxime existimamus felices ac beatos esse, quorum beatitas est ipsa contemplatio"). As he continues his discourse, however, the Epicurean interlocutor conducts his rebuttal of the Stoic by using the same arguments employed by the Academician, Cotta, against the Epicurean, Velleius, in Cicero's *De natura deorum:* "Virtus autem actuosa, et deus vester nihil agens: expers virtutis igitur, ita ne beatus quidem" (1.40.110). One passage, which Valla later suppressed (*Dvb* Appendix II, pp. 144 ff.), underlined how paradoxical would be the conception of the gods as alien to the moral life of human beings, while on the other hand humanity was the only object of their contemplation: "Quid enim si genus humanum intercidat facietis? An felicitate vacabitis?" (§ 1). Aristotle's teaching ("semper fuerunt homines . . . et semper erunt") had not been supported with evidence ("nulla fides, nullum argumentum est"): on the contrary, it had been contradicted by the invention and progress of the arts, to such an extent that it legitimized the conjecture "semper non futuri sint fieri potest" (§ 2). Therefore, in turn, man would be held to divine contemplation only while abstracting from his own natural faculties ("Adeo nos ipsi mortales pro nostra pravitate infinito magis tenemur illis contemplandis . . . quam nostris virtutibus. . . . Eos plus laudo quam contemplor. Nisi forsitan libet suspicari quarundam virtutum alienarum a nostris operationem apud deos esse" (§ 3). The text that was approved afterward simply put into relief the sacreligious consequences of

this teaching ("At deos nescientes dicere et quotidie discentes profanum est," § 10, p. 77).

33 Ibid., 2.30.5–12, pp. 82 f.: ". . . dum ea verbis probant quae non faciunt, ipsa illa quae faciunt improbant" etc.

34 Ibid., 2.31.7, p. 87: "Quod si nobis Elysios campos repromitterent, stultissimum putarem certa pro incertis reliquere. . . . Haec igitur bona corporis que indubitata sunt, quae nunquam in alia vita recuperari possunt, quamdiu licet . . . elabi non sinamus."

35 Ibid., 3. praef., § 5, p. 92: "Primum ut Raudensis, cuius partes nunc sunt, Catoni Vegioque respondeat, deinde pro epicureis contra stoicos sententiam ferat, tunc ad confirmationem transeat causae christianae, vere voluptatis verique boni; postque de Paradiso, ubi sedes est veri boni, transigetur."

36 Ibid., 3.3.4, p. 94: ". . . utrasque partes honestatis et voluptatis et approbandas dico et improbandas. Approbandas quidem quia honestas et item voluptas optima res est; improbandas autem quae aliter accipiendum est quam vestrae voluere rationes."

37 Ibid., 3.4.6, p. 96: "Quod igitur virtus erit? Certe si eius nullum invenirem nomen, tamen sufficere deberet si dicerem complures res esse que appellationibus carent, nec id modo in lingua nostra quae inops, sed etiam in lingua graeca quae locuples est . . . (§ 8). Quin tribuis [*scil.* Aristotle] sua quibusque [virtutibus] nomina, sua tempora, suae vices? Nec enim iidem sumus, immo nec esse possumus." Here the criticism of the doctrine of "habitus," (on which see n. 29 above) is implicitly confirmed. On the notion of "qualitas" in Aquinas, as "the means by which virtue adheres to its subject," cf. Gilson, *St. Thomas,* p. 166; on the Occamistic implications of the doctrine Valla expounds here, cf. Zippel, "Introduction," *Repastinatio,* p. lxxxvii.

38 *Dvb* 3.4.14, p. 98: "Ego vero alia et veriore . . . ratione ostendi quod vitium cui virtuti sit magis contrarium . . . (§ 23, p. 100). Nam virtutes et vitia non ea ratione dignoscuntur quia sunt in infimo aut in medio aut in summo; sic enim quanta virtus quantumque vitium, non an virtus sit an vitium dignoscitur." The substitution outlined here of an intensity of virtue or vice for the Aristotelian criterion of the ratio between the mean and extremes corresponds to the formulation in the *Repastinatio* in which the virtues are reduced to "fortitude" alone ("reluctatio quaedam contra aspera et blanda;" cf. 1.14.16, p. 413). Fortitude, precisely, such as its opposite, feebleness ("imbecillitas"), the very cause of sinful actions, is recognized by its affective nature, directed toward a utilitarian end: "Quae cum ita sint, satis liquet fortitudinem (idest virtutem) rem per se minime expetendam, cum sit plena laboris, plena solicitudinis, plena sudoris ac sanguinis . . . ; quae per se mala sunt, quia molesta et dura toleratu, quia tamen ad victoriam tendunt, bona dicuntur" (§ 23, p. 415).

39 *Dvb* 3.4.25, p. 100: "Insumma, omnia et recte fieri possunt et prave . . . (§ 29, p. 101). Tanta est virtutum vitiorumque vicinitas ut inter se diiudicare non sit impromptu . . . (§ 30, p. 102). Cum itaque tanta sit in iudicandis hominum actibus ambiguitas, iniquum est dubia in deteriorem interpretari partem." Cf. on this issue Cicero *De inventione* 2.53.165: "propter se autem vitanda sunt non ea modo quae his [virtutibus] contraria sunt . . . , verum etiam quae propinqua videntur et finitima esse, absunt autem longissime. . . . Sic unicuique virtuti finitimum vitium reperietur, aut certo iam nomine appellatum . . . , aut sine ullo certo nomine."

40 Ibid., § 31, p. 102: "in ipsorum, non in nature crimine ponendum est."

41 Ibid., 3.5.2, pp. 102 ff.: "Quod te sentire equidem credo neque honestum constituisse solum bonum, quia solum sit, sed quia solum dignitatem hominis attingat, alterum vero non tam hominis quam bruti proprium videri voluisse . . . ; tu [*scil.* Stoice] quoque vicissim fateare esse alterum quoddam bonum praeter honestatem. . . . Nisi placet de verbo disputare, ut aliud sit bonum aliud propositum, aliud expetendum aliud eligendum et similia . . . (§ 4). Satis est ut hominis voluntas sua sponte ad bonum propensa sit." In the *Repastinatio* this issue is treated under the item, "Quid sit anima hominis et bruti," pp. 408 ff. It is here that Valla rejects the concept of a distinct human "animus," insofar as it represents a different faculty from the "anima" common to animals. The qualities of mortality and immortality are what distinguish the soul of "the man from that of the brute": "mortalis in brutis, immortalis in homine." What distinguishes their memories, powers of reason, and wills is not a matter of substance but rather of degree ("nec tam carere beluas, quam parvam habere"), while even man is attributed with "istinctus," instinct ("quasi impetus qui etiam in homines cadit," §§ 1 and 2).

42 *Dvb* 3.7.2, p. 106: ". . . cuius ratio ad pervertendos animos magis apposita. . . . Dixisti post dissolutum hominis corpus nihil postea relinqui, quod quidem philosophorum plurimi ut dixerunt ita quoque senserunt . . . (§ 4). Similis est anima hominum, inquis, animae brutorum. . . . Et tamen hoc mortale est, illus aeternum. . . . Tu comparasti actionem cum actione, ego substantiam cum substantia" (cf. also n. 41 above). On the concept of substance in Valla, cf. Zippel, "Introduction," *Repastinatio,* p. lxxxvii, who argues that Valla appropriates "la concezione puramente negativa e 'connotativa' di Occam." Cf. also ibid., pp. 363 f.: " 'Substantia' a 'sub stando' est appellata, quae vel per se stat nullis adminiculis fulcta, vel quae accidenti seu qualitati substat atque subsistit, non quasi illi subiaceat sed quia illam contineat. Exemplum nullum dari potest, quia non apparet ut qualitas et actio."

43 *Dvb* 3.7.7, p. 107: "cur mirum in tuo sermone de nostra religione silentium, quasi supervacua quadam et ex philosophorum praeceptis efficta et formata?"

44 Ibid., 3.8.2, p. 108: "Post fidem et spem tertius est locus caritatis, magistrae omnium virtutum, id est amoris in Deum et proximum." Compare this to the canonical passage in Augustine *De Moribus Ecclesiae Carthaginiensis* 1.15.25, where the ancient cardinal virtues are reduced to the single principle of "caritas": "Quod si virtus ad beatam vitam nos ducit, nihil omnino esse virtutem affirmaverim nisi summum amorem Dei. Namque illud quod quadripartita dicitur virtus, ex ipsius amoris vario quodam affectu . . . dicitur. . . . Sed hunc amorem non cuiuslibet sed Dei esse diximus, id est summi boni, summae sapientiae, summae concordiae"; cf. Gilson, *Lo spirito,* pp. 428 f., pp. 439 f.; and Lottin, *La théorie,* p. 234 and passim. Consider, however, the statement Valla makes before the one cited above, in which he reestablishes the symmetry between the cardinal and theological virtues by reducing them to a single principle: "Ubi sunt qui virtutes propter se dicunt expetendas? Ne Deo quidem sine spe remunerationis servire fas est."

45 Ibid., 3.8.4, p. 108: "Pugnare cum vitiis tormentum et mors est. Et hanc philosophi aiunt esse vitam beatam?"

46 Ibid., 3.8.7, p. 109: ". . . nam Sadducei, veluti non Moysem sed Aristippum legissent, negabant non solum resurrectionem sed etiam angelum et spiritum esse" (cf. Acts 3. 7–8).

47 Ibid., 3.9.2–3, p. 110: "Nostrum autem honestum qui christiani sumus illud ipsum est . . . , nec propter se expetendum utpote durum, asperum, arduum, nec propter utilitates quae terrenae sunt, sed gradum facit ad eam beatitudinem, qua sive animus sive anima exonerata his membris mortalibus apud rerum parentem a quo est profecta perfuitur (§ 3). Quam beatitudinem quis dubitet aut quis melius possit appellare quam 'voluptatem' . . . , ut in Genesi 'Paradisus voluptatis.'" On this point, cf. *Defensio*, p. 84.

48 *Dvb* 3.10.1–2, pp. 110 f.: "Nam ea duplex est: altera nunc in terris altera postea in coelis . . . ; altera mater est vitiorum, altera virtutum . . . (§ 2). Neque vero deest in hac vita probabilis quaedam voluptas et ea maxime que venit ex spe futurae felicitatis" (the Italian translation by Radetti gives "un piacere probabile," but here "probabilis" is used in the meaning of "worthy," as Valla paraphrases Cicero *De officiis* 1.29.101: "omnis autem actio vacare debet temeritate et neglegentia, nec vero agere quicquam cuius non possit causam probabilem reddere; haec est enim fere descriptio officii." Immediately before this statement, Cicero writes, "duplex est enim vis animorum atque naturae: una pars in appetitu posita est . . . , altera in ratione, quae docet et explanat quid faciendum fugiendumque est." This reinforces my belief that Valla had this Ciceronian statement in mind, making it an essential point of reference. Cf. also further on, n. 68.

49 *Dvb* 3.12.3, p. 112: "At virtus quidem et vitium actiones sunt, felicitas vero atque infelicitas qualitates, res etiam effectu ipso inter se longissime distantes. . . . Quin etiam, si recte aestimemus, ne bonum quidem virtus dicitur, nisi per metonimiam sive hypallagen, ut domus, ager, divitiae bona sunt quia bonum parant." On this point cf. *Retractatio* 1.10.69, pp. 95 f.: "non ipsa [*scil.* beatitudo sive felicitas] est bona actio, ut Aristoteles ait, nonnihil deceptus loquendi consuetudine . . . (§ 72). Nam hoc bene agere non est virtutis neque in nostra manu situm verum in fortunae et Dei, cum possim bene agendo tamen male habere." Valla's criticism is directed at Aristotle's notion of happiness as an "activity of the soul in conformity with a perfect virtue" (*Nicomachean Ethics* 1.13.1102a).

50 *Dvb* 3.13.2, p. 114: "Nam beatitudo nostra non est ipsemet Deus, sed a Deo descendit."

51 "Amatio ipsa delectatio est, sive voluptas sive beatitudo sive felicitas sive caritas, qui est finis ultimus et propter quem fiunt cetera." Cf. ibid., § 2, p. 114. See also further on, §§ 3–7, pp. 114 f.: "Quare non placet mihi ut dicatur Deus propter se esse amandum, quasi amor ipse et delectatio propter finem sit et non ipsa potius finis. Melius diceretur Deum amari non tanquam causam finalem sed efficientem. . . . Ceterum in libris sacris non reperimus Deum amandum propter se sed tantummodo amandum" etc. This entire passage is added in the third version in a way that corresponds closely to *Retractatio*, pp. 89 f., § 53: "Amor qui nos ad fortiter aggrediendum patienterque tolerandum impellit, non habet ille quidem finem ad quem tendat, sed causam unde procedat; et iccirco non placet mihi cum dicitur 'Deum amandum propter se,' quasi quis aliquem amet ob finem. Amandus est Deus ob efficientem causam, non finalem;

quia creator, quia bonus et cetera huiusmodi, non autem ob remunerationem . . . (§ 54). Neque aliud est amor quam delectatio. . . . Neque enim quis ob aliquem finem delectatur sed ipsa delectatio est finis" etc. Here Valla is answering precisely the accusations brought against him; cf. *Defensio*, p. 86, § 6. The controversial subject was actually Augustine, *De doctrina christiana* 1.27. On the scholastic application of the notion of efficient cause to the creation *ex nihilo*, at which Valla possibly hints here, cf. É Gilson, "Avicenne et les origines de la notion de cause efficiente," *Atti del XII Congresso di filosofia*, vol. 9 (Florence, 1960), pp. 121–30. On the other hand, in keeping with Valla's customary attempt to juxtapose definitions of Christian and ancient origin, it is almost certain that he had especially in mind Cicero *De officiis* 3.33.116: "Atque ab Aristippo Cyrenaici atque Annicerii philosophi . . . omne bonum in voluptate posuerunt virtutemque censuerunt ob eam rem esse collaudandam, quod efficiens esset voluptatis."

52 *Dvb* 3.16.1–4, pp. 117 f.: "Igitur, ut ad rem veniamus, omnis hic locus, ut ego quidem sentio, quadrifariam distribuendus est: primum quanta sit in hac vita calamitas, secundum quam exigua iucunditas, tertium post mortem quanta mala sint malis, quartum quanta bona bonis . . . , nisi . . . vestra sapientia mihi moderaretur, apud quam satis abundeque erit de ultimo dicere . . . (§ 2). Haec, ut dixi, transeo. Nemo est qui non haec [*scil.* mala] vel suo experimento intelligat . . . (§ 3). De tertio multa mihi ad dicendum suppeditaret oratio, si apud imperitam atque immoratam concionem habenda esset . . . (§ 4). Cum vero apud vos optimos atque doctissimos viros sermo sit, de hac re silentium agam. Non extimescunt generosi animi leges, non suppliciis propositis deterrentur, sed praemiis invitantur" etc. On this aspect see also D. Marsh "Struttura e retorica nel *De vero bono* di Lorenzo Valla," *Lorenzo Valla e l'umanesimo italiano: Atti del convegno internazionale di studi umanistici* (Padua, 1986), pp. 311–24 (especially pp. 320 ff.).

53 Ibid., 3.19.1, p. 120: "Quae quidem aenigmata et allegorias siquis excutere et ad liquidum perducere velit, frustra nimirum laborabit." On this issue, cf. J. H. Bentley, *Humanists and Holy Writ: New Testament Scholarship in the Renaissance* (Princeton, 1983), pp. 62 f.

54 Ibid., 3.20.1, p. 121: "Opereprecium tamen erit ut imaginari temptemus. Nam cum excogitaverimus optimum quendam beatitudinis . . . statum . . . , debet intelligi quantum pro illo annitendum sit, cuius ne minimam quidem partem complecti mens humana sustineat." The passage is modeled on a rhetorical device described by Quintilian *Instituto* 9.2.41: "Non solum quae facta sunt aut fiant, sed etiam quae futura sint aut futura fuerint imaginamur." Cf. on this point P. H. Schryvers, "Invention, imagination et théorie des émotions chez Cicéron et Quintilien," *Rhetoric Revalued: Papers from the International Society for the History of Rhetoric,* ed. N. Vickers (Binghamton, N.Y., 1982), pp. 45–57.

55 *Dvb* 3.21–25; cf. 25.2–3, p. 130: "Iam tibi urbs illa beatorum civium atque ipsius Dei, illa Hierusalem mater nostra apparet in mediis coeli campis (§ 3). An requiris ut qualis est illa describam? Nimirum ab *Apocalypsi* Iohannis mutuandum est" etc. Cf. also *Epistolae*, n. 5, p. 147: "Non enim visum est in hac materia poetice loqui, sed ut nonnulli doctissimi sanctissimique fecerunt." On the apocalyptic representations,

adopted here in his own way by Valla, and also on the image of celestial blessedness, cf. Gilson, *St. Thomas*, pp. 61–64; *La Gerusalemme celeste: Catalogo della mostra 'La dimora di Dio tra gli uomini' (Ap. 21–23), Immagini della Gerusalemme celeste dal III al XIV secolo*, ed. M. L. Gatti Perer (Milan, 1983) (with articles by various authors and a detailed bibliography).

56 Cf. on this point M. Fois, *Il pensiero cristiano di Lorenzo Valla nel quadro storico-culturale del suo ambiente* (Rome, 1969), pp. 636–39; M. De Panizza Lorch, in *Dvb*, pp. xviii, 148 f., and "Introduction" to *On Pleasure*, pp. 27 f.; Fubini, *Note*, pp. 23, 55 f. At least at the current stage of research, we can hypothesize Valla's influence on "libertine" and Epicurean trends of thought more from censuring statements than from positive ones, which were eventually echoing Valla's thought. However it is noteworthy that Badius's edition (cf. below, n. 71) was such a success that an inventory of humanist writings in a Parisian bookstore in 1529 listed, among other texts of Valla, five copies of the *De voluptate*; cf. H. Busson, *Le rationalisme dans le littérature française de la Renaissance*, 2d ed. (Paris, 1971), p. 157; and also on the issue, M. Gauna, "Les épicuriens bibliques de la Renaissance," *Association Guillaume Budé, Actes du VIIIe Congrès* (Paris, 1969), pp. 685–95 and also pages 626, 698; J. Wirth, " 'Libertins' et 'Épicuriens': Aspects de l'irréligion au XVIe siècle," *Bibliotèque d'Humanisme e Renaissance* 39 (1977): 601–27.

57 *Dvb*, praef., pp. 1–3, § 4: "ego e contra planum faciam non nostris, sed ipsorum philosophorum rationibus nihil cum virtute gentilitatem, nihil recte fecisse."

58 Fois, p. 128.

59 J. E. Seigel, *Rhetoric and Philosophy in Renaissance Humanism* (Princeton, 1968), pp. 144–60; H. B. Gerl, *Rhetorik als Philosophie: Lorenzo Valla* (Munich, 1974), pp. 88–191. It is worth remembering that the title *Dialecticae disputationes* was assigned by a sixteenth-century editor (cf. Zippel, "Introduction," *Repastinatio*, p. xxxviii), whereas Valla regarded it as "opus dialecticae et philosophiae" (cf. *Epistolae*, n. 11, p. 172). To consider Valla only in relation to a rhetorical or rhetorico-dialectical tradition would be misleading. This constitutes in fact a major reason for misunderstanding Valla's thought, as the scholars I just cited well exemplify: cf. my essays "Umanesimo ed enciclopedismo: A proposito di contributi recenti su Giorgio Valla," *Il pensiero politico* 16 (1983): 251–69; "Contributo per l'interpretazione della 'Dialectica' di Lorenzo Valla," *Rivista storica italiana*, 110 (1998): 119–43 (also in my book *L'umanesimo italiano e i suoi storici*, pp. 184–207); and also P. Mack, "Valla's Dialectica in the North: A Commentary of Peter of Spain by Gerardus Listrius," *Vivarium* 21 (1983): 57–72; Mack, *Renaissance Argument: Valla and Agricola in the Tradition of Rhetoric and Dialectic* (Leiden, 1993). A view of the question and its related bibliography is given by M. C. Leff, "Boethius' 'De differentiis topicis,' Book IV," *Medieval Eloquence*, pp. 3–24.

60 Gerl, p. 181; and in general chap. 2: "Die Kritik am Rationalismus und der Entwurf der Philosophie des Gemeinsinns: *De voluptate*," pp. 97 ff.

61 L. A. Panizza, "Lorenzo Valla's *De vero falsoque bono*, Lactantius, and Oratorical Scepticism," *Journal of the Warburg and Courtauld Institutes* 41 (1978): 76–107.

62 Ibid., p. 86; cf. further R. H. Popkin, *The History of Skepticism from Erasmus to Descartes*, 2d ed. (Berkeley, 1980); Ch. B. Schmitt, *Cicero Scepticus, A Study in the Influence*

of the "Academica" in the Renaissance (The Hague, 1972). According to Schmitt, there exists no verifiable evidence of an "outbreak of skepticism" (p. 48) in the first part of the fifteenth century. Valla is no exception to the rule. The Skeptical argument that the philosophical systems, in contradicting themselves, undermine themselves in turn is actually taken up in a specious way, in order "to use an author against himself" (Panizza Lorch, "Introduction," *On Pleasure,* p. 11). Actually, in regard to Lactantius, Valla shows himself to be anything but congenial (cf., for example, Zippel, Introduction, *Repastinatio,* p. cxii f.; and here further on). In general, on Ciceronian skepticism, see M. Ruch, "La 'Disputatio in utramque partem' dans le Lucullus et ses fondements philosophiques," *Revue des études latines* 47 (1969): 310–15 ("elle vise à la construction d'une vérité orientée non vers la domination, mais le Bien, selon l'aspiration suprème du platonisme").

63 Panizza, "Lorenzo Valla's *De vero falsoque bono,*" p. 107.

64 *Dvb,* praef., § 7, p. 2: "Licet ad refellendam et profligandam stoicam nationem omnes libri pertinent, tamen primus voluptatem solum bonum, secondus philosophorum honestatem ne bonum quidem esse ostendit, tertius de vero falsoque bono explicat."

65 On Quintilian's linking of ethics and rhetoric (considerably different, quite obviously, from Valla's) and the various ways in which it was transmitted in the medieval school, cf. Ph. Delhaye, "L'enseignement moral au XXIIe siècle," *Medieval Studies* 11 (1949): 77–99; and also, for general background, A. D. Leeman, "The Variety of Classical Rhetoric," *Rhetoric Revalued,* pp. 41–46; B. Vickers," Territorial Disputes: Philosophy Versus Rhetoric," ibid., pp. 247–66. On Lactantius and his strategy of transposing ancient and, in particular, Ciceronian values into Christianity—certainly not in the specious and antiphilosophical sense that Valla pretended—cf. also V. Loi, "I valori etici e politici della Romanità negli scritti di Lattanzio," *Salesianum* 37 (1965): 65–132; A. L. Fischer, "Lactantius' Ideas Relating Christian Truth and Christian Society," *Journal of the History of Ideas* 43 (1982): 355–77. On the contrary, Valla typically stands firm in his juxtaposing a "true" and a "false good," which represents a combination of the "false" and "true wisdom" of Lactantius's apologetics (*Divinae Institutiones,* bks. 3–4), of the "de veritate ac falsitate" of dialectical tracts (cf. Cicero *Academica posteriora* 28.91: "Dialecticam inventam esse dicitis veri et falsi quasi disceptatricem et iudicem"); and, lastly, of the "true good" of Aristotelian ethics (insofar as it is distinguished from the theleological "sommum bonum"), on which see n. 12 above.

66 "Si quis forte ex amicis . . . hunc admiratus titulum . . . a me postulet quaenam mihi libido incesserit scribendi de voluptate, . . . sic accipiat, me . . . hosce . . . libros maluisse 'De voluptate' inscribere . . . quam 'De vero bono,' quod poteram, siquidem de vero bono, quam eandem voluptatem esse placet, in hoc opere disputamus"; "quod verum, quod solum, quod voluptatem esse dicimus"; "alterum in hac vita, alterum in futura." Cf. *Dvb,* p. 151. See also above, chap. 2.

67 M. De Panizza Lorch, " 'Voluptas, molle quodam et non invidiosum nomen': Lorenzo Valla's Defence of 'voluptas' in the Preface to his *De Voluptate,*" *Philosophy and Humanism: Renaissance Essays in Honor of P. O. Kristeller,* ed. E. P. Mahoney (Leiden, 1976), pp. 214–28 (especially p. 217); and also *On Pleasure,* pp. 32–35. It should be added, however, that this analysis is weakened by its failure to recognize the Ciceronian origin

of the expression (cf. n. 76 below). In her recent interpretation of the dialogue, *A Defense of Life: Lorenzo Valla's Theory of Pleasure* (Munich, 1985), pp. 27 ff., 40, the author maintains that Valla had changed the introduction and the title in consideration of its more austere cultural context, because of the "discovery of a new content in the old word 'voluptas.'"

68   "Voluptas duplex est, altera quidem recta, altera vero prava." Cf. *Defensio*, p. 82, § 1. On Valla's consignment of a copy of book 3 of the *Dvb* to Pope Eugenius IV in 1434, cf. *Epistolae*, pp. 141 f. Cf. also n. 48 above.

69   "et duae voluptates tenendae sunt maxime." Cf. R. Sabbadini, *Cronologia documentata della vita di Lorenzo Valla* (Florence, 1891), pp. 66 ff. (*Opera*, vol. 2, pp. 372 f.); and *Epistolae*, pp. 125, 135 ff. On similar reservations—which Valla nonetheless circulated as praises—voiced by Bruni and Traversari, cf. chap. 2 above.

70   "Neque enim arbitraris par esse ut res tam longe inter se diversas eodem omnis vocabulo [*scil.* volputas] complectamur, ut si bonum et malum virtutem quispiam appellare velit, cum tamen aliud bonum sit, aliud malum." Cf. ibid.

71   *Dvb*, pp. xv f., xxix f.; *On Pleasure*, pp. 27 f.; Fubini, *Note*, p. 23. On Petit, cf. A. Renaudet, *Préréforme et Humanisme à Paris pendant les premières guerres d'Italie*, 2d ed. (Paris, 1953), p. 618. The date of this edition is 1512.

72   "nullum verbum inveniri potest quod magis idem declaret latine quod graece *edoné* quam voluptas. Huic verbo omnes qui ubique sunt . . . duas res subiiciunt: laetitiam in animo commotione suavi, iocunditatem in corpore." Cf. *Dvb* 1.15.1, p. 21, where this Ciceronian statement is quoted.

73   "At ipse non intelligo, cum unum atque idem nomen sit, quo pacto possimus rem facere diversam. Atque eo quidem magis, quod omnis voluptas non tam corpore sentitur quam animo, qui corpus moderatur: quod, ut opinor, sensit Epicurus." Cf. *Dvb* 2.28.5, 76; and n. 31 above.

74   Cf. C. Vicol, "Cicerone espositore critico dell'epicureismo," *Ephemeris Dacoromana: Annuario della Scuola Romena di Roma*, 10 (1945), pp. 157–347 (especially pp. 281, 319); and also P. Grimal, "L'épicurisme romain," *Assoc. G. Budé, Actes*, pp. 146 ff.; A. Michel, "L'épicurisme et la dialectique de Cicéron," ibid., pp. 393–411. It is typical that Valla captiously attributes Cicero's semantic distinctions to the Scholastics' lack of skill (cf. n. 12 above).

75   *Dvb* 1.10.3, p. 14: "Et M. Tullius quaecumque in philosophia vellet disputare sibi permisit libere loqui in nullam sectam obstrictus, idque praeclare" (cf. Cicero, *De natura deorum* 1.5.10: "Non enim tam auctoritatis in disputando quam rationis momenta quaerenda sunt"). Cf. also A. Michel, "La philosophie en Grèce et à Rome de . . . 130 à 250," *Histoire de la Philosophie*, vol. 1 (Paris, 1969), p. 813 (Encyclopédie de la Pléiade); Michel, "Cicéron et les sectes philosophiques: Sens et valeur de l'éclectisme académique," *Eos, Commentarii societatis philologae Polonorum* 7 (1967–1968): 108 f.; and further, Michel, "Éclectisme philosophique et lieux communs: À propos de la diatribe romaine," *Hommages à Jean Bayet*, ed. M. Renard and R. Schilling (Brussels, 1964), pp. 485–94.

76   "voluptuaria, delicata, mollis disciplina"; "invidiosum nomen, infame, suspectum." Cf. *De finibus bonorum et malorum* 1.11.37; and ibid., 2.4.12. See also Cicero *Acade-*

mica posteriora 45.138: "invidiosum nomen voluptatis." This last passage is particularly important because, distancing himself from the *Carneadia divisio* (which had influenced the complex scheme of the *De finibus*), Cicero introduces into such a context a more simplified version, attributed to Crisippus: "testatur saepe Chrysippus tres solas esse sententias quae defendi possent de finibus bonorum—circumcidit et amputat multitudinem—: aut enim honestatem esse finem aut voluptatem aut utrumque . . . ; ita tris relinquit sententias quas putet probabiliter posse defendi" (cf. Michel, *L'épicurisme,* pp. 401 f). It can be assumed that Valla, who also actually "circumcidit et amputat multitudinem," took his inspiration for his threefold scheme from here, with the concurrence, as we will see, of the Christian development of the Skeptic teaching, as proposed by Augustine (cf. also nn. 92 and 97 below.)

77 "Habetis veram brevemque de virtutibus diffinitionem. Inter quas non ita erit voluptas, ut contumeliosissimum hominum genus garriunt, tanquam meretrix inter bonas matronas, sed tanquam domina inter ancillas." Cf. *Dvb* 1.34.1, pp. 34 f. See in this connection, Cicero *De finibus* 2.4.12: "Quid enim necesse est, tamquam meretricem in matronarum coetu, sic voluptatem in virtutum concilium adducere?"

78 Cf. Fubini, *Note,* pp. 34 f.: and more generally, G. Radetti, "L'epicureismo nel pensiero umanistico del Quattrocento," *Grande antologia filosofica,* vol. 4 (Milan, 1964), pp. 839–961.

79 "argumento sunt tortuosissimae et perplexissimae de officiis quaestiones philosophorurm diversa sentientium." Cf. *Dvb* 1.47.1, 41. See, in this regard, Cicero, *De officiis* 1.2.4–6: "Nam cum multa sint in philosophia et gravia et utilia accurate copioseque a philosophis disputata, latissime patere videntur ea quae de officiis tradita illis et praecepta sunt . . . ; (§ 6) neque ulla officii praecepta firma, stabilia, coniuncta naturae tradi possunt nisi ab iis qui solam, aut ab iis qui maxime honestatem propter se dicant expetendam. Ita propria est ea praeceptio Stoicorum, Academicorum, Peripateticorum, quoniam Aristonis, Pyrrhonis, Erilli iam pridem explosa sententia est. . . . Sequimur igitur hoc quidem tempore et hac in quaestione potissimum Stoicos, non ut intepretes, sed, ut solemus, ex fontibus eorum iudicio arbitrioque nostro, quantum quoquo modo videbitur, hauriemus."

80 "Licet quod suum non erat sibi arrogaverunt, dicentes utile ab honesto manare, cum interim nomen officiorum, quod proprium erat alterius partis, et nostrae quoque impartierunt." Cf. *Dvb* 2.32.9, p. 89. See, in this connection, Cicero *De officiis* 3.28.101: "Pervertunt homines quae sunt fundamenta naturae, cum utilitatem ab honestate seiungunt. Omnes enim expetimus utilitatem ad eamque rapimur nec facere aliter ullo modo possumus. Nam qui est qui utilia fugiat? Aut quis potius qui ea non studiosissime persequatur? Sed quia nusquam possumus nisi in laude, decore, honestate utilia reperire, propterea illa prima et summa habemus, utilitatis nomen non tam splendidum quam necessarium ducimus." Further on, in order to avoid all Epicurean implications, Cicero distinguishes the notion of "utilitas" from that of "voluptas": "sin autem speciem utilitatis etiam voluptas habere dicetur, nulla potest esse ei cum honestate coniunctio. Nam, ut tribuamus aliquid voluptati, condimenti fortasse non nihil, utilitatis certe nihil habebit."

81 Cf. n. 28 above.

82 "sed tamen mallem ut [Marcus Tullius] non tanquam philosophum se illa tractare maluisset sed tanquam oratorem" Cf. *Dvb* 1.1.3, p. 14 (and n. 75 above).

83 Cf. Michel, *La philosophie*, p. 809; and also, more extensively, Michel, "Rhétorique et philosophie dans les traités de Cicéron," *Aufstieg und Niedergang der Römischen Welt: Geschichte und Kultur im Spiegel der neueren Forschung*, ed. H. Temporini, vol. 3 (Berlin, 1973), pp. 137–208.

84 M. Testard, "Introduction" to Cicéron, *Les Devoirs*, 2d ed. (Paris, 1974), p. 58.

85 Cf. Michel, *Rhétorique et philosophie*, p. 145. The author, with regard to Cicero's discussion with the Stoics, mentions *De finibus* 4.20.57: "cumque omnis controversia aut de re soleat aut de nomine esse"; and also ibid., 4.26.72: "Cur igitur, cum de re conveniat, non malumus usitate loqui?"

86 "magnum opus profecto et arduum, et haud scio an magis audax quam aliquod superiorum" Cf. *Dvb*, praef., § 5, p. 2. See in this regard Augustine *De civitate Dei*, praef.: "magnum opus et arduum"; and also Lactantius *De opificio Dei* 20.4: "Magnum opus videor polliceri"; on this, see Panizza, "L. Valla," p. 91.

87 Cf. Fois, *Il pensiero*, pp. 95–167, 574 ff.; Ch. Trinkaus, "L. Valla: Voluptas et Fruitio, Verba et Res: "a chapter in his book *In Our Image and Likeness: Humanity and Divinity in Italian Humanist Thought*, vol. 1 (London, 1970), pp. 103–70; and also Trinkhaus, "Il pensiero antropologico-religioso nel Rinascimento," *Il Rinascimento: Interpretazione e problemi* (Bari, 1979), pp. 105–47 ("Valla introduces the most complete synthesis of patristic-Christian ideas, especially Augustinian, and classical rhetorical language and theory," p. 146).

88 Cf. Testard, *Saint Augustin et Cicéron*, vol. 1, *Cicéron dans la formation et dans l'oeuvre de Saint Augustin* (Paris, 1958), pp. 247 f. According to Augustine, the Academicians were intent on arguing against the Epicureans and the Stoics, whereas "God was the author that Platonics were lacking." See also, Schmitt, *Cicero Scepticus*, pp. 29–33.

89 Cf. Augustine *De diversis quaestionibus* 83.31; cf. Delhaye, *L'enseignment*, pp. 92 f; and R. Tuve, "Notes on the Virtues and Vices, Part I," *Journal of the Warburg and Courtauld Institutes* 26 (1963): 264–303; and also Tuve, *Allegorical Imagery: Some Medieval Books and Their Posterity* (Princeton, 1977), pp. 62 f.

90 Cf. Cicero *De inventione* 2.53; and nn. 4 and 29 above.

91 Cf. H. I. Marrou, *Sant'Agostino* (Milan, 1960), p. 85. See in this connection Augustine *De doctrina christiana* 1.7 (3.3): "Res ergo aliae sunt quibus fruendum, aliae quibus utendum, aliae quae fruuntur et utuntur. Illae quibus fruendum est nos beatos faciunt; istis quibus utendum est tendentes ad beatitudinem adiuvamur et quasi adminiculamur, ut ad illas quae nos beatos faciunt pervenire atque inhaerere possimus"; and also *De diversis quaestoribus* 83.30: "Omnis itaque humana perversio est, quod etiam vitium vocatur, fruendis uti velle atque utendis frui; et rursus omnis ordinatio, quae virtus etiam nominatur, fruendis frui et utendis uti." This is the basis for the scholastic dogmatization: "ille tres [*scil.* virtutes] theologicae distinguuntur penes frui; iste scilicet quatuor cardinales, penes uti" (cf. Lottin, *La théorie*, p. 255).

92 Cf. nn. 76 and 91 above.

93 This, in fact, was one of the principal charges brought against Valla in the Inquisition's trial; cf. *Defensio*, § 7, p. 86.

94 Cf. n. 51 above.

95 "nec differre 'frui' ab 'amare' probat idem [*scil.* Augustinus], alibi dicens: 'frui est ali-
cui rei amore inhaerere propter se.' 'Adhaerere' autem 'amore' et 'amare' idem est;
'propter se' ex consuetudine philosophorum dixit, non ex rei natura, ut testatus sum.'
Cf. *Retractatio* 10.62, p. 93. Valla discusses here the passages of Augustine mentioned
in n. 91 above. In a previous passage of the *Retractatio,* § 59, p. 92, Valla refers to
fruitio in these terms: "Hanc [*scil.* delectationem] quidam recentiorum (*sic!*) appellant
'fruitionem,' qui est actus percipiendae voluptatis, quia verbum 'voluptari' . . . non
habemus"; and in the *Defensio,* § 7, p. 86: "Qui tantopere amplectuntur hoc nomen,
"fruitio," non video qua certa auctoritate nitantur (*sic!*). Immo partim ex errore nata
est haec opinio, quod credunt 'frui' pertinere tantum ad res divinas, cum apud auctores linguae latinae fere nunquam reperiatur in hunc modum, et apud sanctos in-
differens sit, non modo divinorum humanorumque sed etiam boni operis et mali."
As it can be seen, Valla's self-defense trespasses in a rather disconcerting way to the
level of provocation or, rather, of jest.

96 "de duabus sectis . . . omnium nobilissimis." Cf. *Dvb* 3.7.1, p. 106; and, in this connection, Acts 17.18–20. So far as Valla's taste for referring to ancient Christian disputes
in Acts is concerned, cf. also n. 46 above.

97 "Quid ergo? Iam constitutis ante oculos nostros tribus, Epicureo, Stoico, Christiano,
interrogemus singulos. Dic, Epicuree, quae res faciat beatum? Respondet: voluptas
corporis. Dic, Stoice: virtus animi. Dic, Christiane: donum Dei." Cf. Augustine *Sermones* 150.7. § 8. On the basic value of this passage, cf. Gilson, *Lo spirito,* p. 393; and
also M. Spanneut, "Le Stoïcisme et Saint Augustin," *Forma futuri: Studi in onore del
cardinale Michele Pellegrino* (Turin, 1975), pp. 896–914 (especially p. 900).

98 "sed tamen eius [*scil.* virtutis] cura atque amor perquam raris beneficio ac peculiari
dono naturae concessus est; plurimis autem eiusdem naturae malignitate non aliter
denegatus, quam quod monstruosos, debiles, vitiatos corpore videmus. Excaecavit
mentes hominum quae illuminare debebat, ne lucem sapientiae contemplentur." Cf.
Dvb 1.5.7–8, p. 10.

99 Cf. Cicero *De natura deorum* 3.27–28. On this subject, see J. Beaujeu, "Les constantes
religieuses du scepticisme," *Hommages à Marcel Renard,* ed. J. Bibauw, vol. 2 (Brussels, 1969), pp. 61–73. In Cicero's dialogue the Epicurean Velleius declares himself in
agreement with the Skeptic's arguments: "ita discessimus, ut Velleio Cottae disputatio verior, mihi Balbi ad veritatis similitudinem videretur esse propensior" (ibid.,
3.40.95).

100 "iis solis consuluit quos bona ratione donavit, quos videmus, si modo ulli sunt, esse
perpaucos;" "quod multi eorum beneficio perverse uterentur"; "sic istam calliditatem
hominibus di ne dedissent! Qua perpauci bene utuntur, qui tamen ipsi saepe a male
utentibus opprimuntur, innumerabiles autem improbe utuntur, ut donum hoc divinum rationis et consilii ad fraudem hominibus, non ad bonitatem impertitum esse
videatur." Cf. Cicero *De natura deorum* 3.27.70; ibid., 28.70, and 30.75.

101 Romans 11.6–7: "Si autem gratia, iam non ex operibus: alioquin gratia iam non est
gratia. Quid ergo? Quod quaerebat Israel, hoc non est consecutus; electio autem
consecuta est; ceteri vero excaecati sunt"; and Ephesians 1.17–18: "Ut Deus . . . det

vobis spiritum sapientiae et revelationis in agnitione eius: illuminatos oculos cordis vestri, ut sciatis quae sit spes vocationis eius." Cf. on the subject Marrou, *S. Agostino,* pp. 98 ff.; P. Brown, *Agostino d'Ippona* (Turin, 1971), pp. 328–72.

102 "quod . . . infelicissimum vitium est, quia excaecatur, unde illuminare debuit." Cf. R. Tuve, "Notes on the Virtues and Vice, Part II," *Journal of the Warburg and Courtauld Institutes* 27 (1964): 47. On Peraldus, see A. Dondaine, "Guillaume Peyraut, vie et oeuvres," *Archivum fratrum Praedicatorum* 17 (1948): 162–236. Note that the argument of Valla's Stoic speaker, concerning the far greater number of vices than virtues, although referred to Aristotle's doctrine of "mediety," is really related to scholastic treatises, which had classified Augustinian traditions of ethical teachings within an Aristotelian framework. Theological moral thought, unlike Aristotle, perceived virtues as the stronghold of the soul "contra vitia"; and vices, in turn, were subdivided into various "species," precisely as the Dominican Peraldus did in his definitive treatise. On the subject, see Lottin, *La théorie;* and S. Wenzel, "The Seven Deadly Sins: Some Problem of Research," *Speculum* 43 (1968): 3–22 (especially pp. 12 f., 19 f.). It is worth noting, however, that Valla's assertions could be also supported by a reading of *Nichomachean Ethics* 2.6.1106b, in the current version by Grossatesta, ed. Gauthier, 2.056b: "Adhuc peccare quidem multis modis est."

103 Cf. L. Valla, *Dialogue sur le libre-arbitre,* ed. J. Chomarat (Paris, 1983), p. 10. The essential reference on this issue in late scholastic period is still P. Vignaux, *Justification e prédestination au XIVe siècle: Duns Scot, Pierre d'Auriole, Guillaume d'Occam, Gregoire de Rimini* (Paris, 1934). With regard to explaining Valla's position, the following should be noted: (a) the fundamental importance throughout the debate of the notion, according to its classic formulation in Peter Lombard's *Sententiae,* of "infused habit" as a condition of the capacity to love God; (b) the corrosion of such a concept in Occam, and his criticism of intellectualistic and Platonic positions on the issue: "nullus habitus reddit aliquem ex natura habitus delectabilem, nisi quia causatur ab actu acceptabili" (p. 106); (c) Gregory of Rimini's rigid readings of Pauline and Augustinian doctrines, also in reaction to the aforesaid assumptions, which he charged with Pelagianism; and his related intention of reestablishing a positive theological tradition, weakened by nominalist reasoning. Cf. also D. Trapp, "Augustinian Theology of the XIVth Century . . . ," *Augustiniana* 6 (1956): 146–274; and J. W. O'Malley, "A Note on Gregory of Rimini: Church, Scripture, Tradition," *Augustinianum* 5 (1965): 365–78. The Occamist teachings thus appear to be not so much the inspiration as the premise for Valla's arguments, which in turn must be considered against the backdrop of reacting institutional currents, aimed at a confirmation of the positive tradition.

104 Legitimate doubts are expressed by P. Mesnard, "Une application curieuse de l'humanisme critique à la théologie: l'Éloge de Saint Thomas par Lorenzo Valla, *Revue Thomiste* 55 (1955): 155–76 ("On ne saisit bien comment se fait, dans son système, le rencontre entre la nature et le grâce," p. 164); see also G. Farris, "Teologia e paolinismo in Lorenzo Valla," *Studium* 7 (1973): 671–83. Generally speaking, of the two most fundamental themes in Paul's letters—the opposition of "Christ wisdom of God to the vain wisdom of the world" as in 1 and 2 Corinthians, and the opposition of "Christ justice of God to the justice that men pretend to merit by their own

efforts," as in Galatians and Romans (cf. *La Bibbia di Gerusalemme,* 2d ed. [Bologna, 1982], p. 2405)—the first is taken up by Valla and emphasized at will, whereas the second is intentionally ignored. For a typical example, cf. *Epistolae,* n. 13, p. 204.

105 "Videre enim licet a primis statim annis pueros defluere potius ad vitia gulae, lusus, deliciarum, quam tollere se ad decus atque honestatem: odisse castigationes, amare blanditas; fugere praescriptiones, sectari lascivias." Cf. *Dvb* 1.5.1, p. 8; and ibid., 3.5.4, p. 103: "Satis est ut hominis voluntas sua sponte ad bonum propensa sit"; "corporis bonum, quod intellegunt, id petunt." See also Augustine *Confessions* 10.21; and Marrou, *S. Agostino,* p. 81.

106 Cf. S. Floro di Zenzo, *Un umanista epicureo del sec. XV e il ritrovamento del suo epistolario* (Naples, 1978), pp. 57–66; Garin found an anonymous version of this text different from the one published by G. Santini in 1899 (cf. Garin, *La cultura filosofica,* pp. 87–92), which bears the title quoted here, and which Floro di Zenzo identified as the original version, modified later with various stylistic revisions. More recently two other copies appeared. For the first, cf. *Epistolae,* pp. 65 f.; and W. Irtenkauf and I. Krekler, *Die Hss. Der Würtembergischen Landesbibliothek Stuttgart,* vol. 1, pt. 2 (Wiesbaden, 1981), pp. 94 f., where MS. Poet. et philol. 4, 29, ff. 90v–96r is described. The second was discovered by M. C. Davies in MS. Harl. 3568, ff.167v–170v of the British Library. On this basis Davies has produced the critical edition of Raimondi's tract: "Cosma Raimondi's Defence of Epicurus," *Rinascimento* 27 (1987): 123–39. Hence it results that the version edited by Garin is isolated with respect to the remaining manuscripts, which confirm the stylistic improvements of the Berliner code (the one of Santini's edition). Returning to Stuttgart's ms., it was written, according to the description by W. Irtenkauf (p. 127), "in an Italian humanistic hand of the second quarter of the century" and later came into possession of the German humanist Dietrich von Plieningen, who obtained it in Ferrara. Originally untitled, the text bears the later title of "Guarini responsio ad quidam (*sic!*) qui Epicurus (*sic!*) damnabat" etc.; the codex mainly contains letters of Poggio and Guarino. Analogously, MS. Laur. Ashbur. 267 (Garin's text) contains writings of Guarino, together with the *Isagogicon* of Bruni and verses by Panormita, and comes from Verona. There is reason, therefore, to suppose that Guarino had a hand in the presumably anonymous transmission of Raimondi's work and that it was no accident that it came by way of Verona and Ferrara.

107 Cf. nn. 12 and 78 above. See also, in general, A. Michel, "À propos du souverain bien: Cicéron et le dialogue des écoles philosophiques," *Hommages à M. Renard,* vol. 1, pp. 610–21. Note that as a preliminary statement in his examination of various philosophical schools, Cicero damns Epicurean conclusion, Bruni rehabilitates it, and excludes in his own turn the academic Platonism that inspired Cicero's analysis: "Nam vulgus . . . philosophorum, qui absurda dicebant, iam pridem auditores scholaeque ipsae respuerunt. Hae restant disciplinae [*scil.* Peripatetics, Stoics and Epicureans] quae aliquid dicere videantur" (cf. Fubini, *Note,* pp. 26f.). Raimondi's approach is still more radical, by overturning Cicero's statement in Epicurus's favor.

108 Cf. Radetti, *L'epicureismo,* p. 854; Fois, *Il pensiero cristiano,* p. 125, and my *Note,* pp. 35–46.

109 "quem suis omnibus libris tantopere extollunt et celebrant." Cf. Floro di Zenzo, p. 59; Garin, *La cultura filosofica,* p. 89; Davies, p. 133.

110 "ut quidam magni auctores tradunt." Cf. *Dvb* 2.7.1, p. 51. On the exemplum of A. Regulus in ancient and Christian writers, cf. in general P. Monat, "Introduction" to Lactance, *Institutions divines, Livre V* (Paris, 1973) ("Sources chretiennes," 204–05), pp. 40 f.

111 Cf., for an extensive treatment of this issue, M. Perrin, "Introduction" to Lactance, *L'ouvrage de Dieu créateur,* ed. M. Perrin (Paris, 1974) ("Sources chrétiennes," 213–14).

112 "Ad haec vero probanda unde potius ordiar quam ab illa una omnium rerum principe et institutrice natura, cuius in quaque re verissimum semper putandum est iudicium? Haec igitur cum hominem fabricaretur, ita illum undique adhibito quasi artificio expolivit, ut aliam nullam ob rem fabricatus videatur, nisi ut omni voluptate potiri et iucundari posset." Cf. Floro di Zanzo, p. 61; Garin, p. 90; Davies, p. 135. On the theme, see Cicero *De natura deorum* 2.56.140: "Ad hanc providentiam naturae tam diligentem tamque sollertem adiungi multa possunt, e quibus intellegatur quantae res hominibus a dis quamque eximiae tributae sint"; and Lactantius *De opificio Dei* 1.11: "homo ipse . . . , non a Prometheo fictum, ut poetae loquuntur, sed a summo illo rerum conditore atque artifice Deo, cuius divinam providentiam perfectissimamque virtutem nec sensu comprehendere nec verbo enarrare possibile est"; ibid., 2.1: "Dedit enim homini artifex ille noster ac parens Deus sensum atque rationem, ut ex eo appareret nos ab eo esse generatos, qui ipse sensus ac ratio est."

113 "Sensus ei plures dedit quam varios, quam distinctos, quam necessarios, ut cum voluptatum genera essent plura, nullum relinqueretur cuius ille particeps non foret." Cf. ibid. (n. 112 above). On the subject, Cicero *De natura deorum* 2.57.142: "Quis vero opifex praeter naturam, qua nihil potest esse callidius, tantam sollertiam persequi potuisset in sensibus?"; the statement is followed by the description of the sense organs and their rewards: sight, hearing, smell, taste, touch; Raimondi follows the same order and concludes, remarking, "Itidem de odoratu reliquisque sensibus iudicandum est quibus tamquam instrumentis voluptatem animus et sensit et percipit." Valla only hints at, and almost equalizes, touch with sight (cf. *Dvb* 1.20, p. 26: "Haec de aspectu quidem et tactu dixi, idque tantum de uno genere").

114 "Quemadmodum Lactantius . . . manifestissime ostendit in eo libro quem 'De Opificio' inscripsit." Cf. *Dvb* 1.10.1, p. 14. Note the more elaborate celebration of the senses in the order we know: sight (and, therefore, beauty, sexual attraction, etc.), hearing (and the pleasures of music and eloquence), taste, and lastly smell, which is defined as "the last of the senses" ("de ultimo sensu;" cf. *Dvb* 1.26.1, p. 32). This detail is important: Cicero had written (*De natura deorum* 2.58.145): "Narium item et gustandi et quadam ex parte tangendi magna iudicia sunt"; Raimondi had omitted through a praeterition the last two senses ("de odoratu reliquisque sensibus"; cf. n. 113 above). All this may provide an evidence that Valla had been led back to Cicero's text through the suggestion provided by Raimondi's tract.

115 Cf. letter from Milan, 15 January 1429, in Floro di Zenzo, p. 46: "Tu velim ut me ames et certior me de redditis acceptisque litteris pro tua diligentia facias Panormitam quoque"; and repeated again in his answer to Vegio: "Satis mihi erat, si unius

tui ipsius praedicatione niterer. . . . Cum vero alterius quoque poetae commendatio accesserit, summam prope ingenii consecutus gloriam videor, qui vestrum duorum, quorum maxima in scribendo est auctoritas, laude perfruar. Nec mehercle miror Panormitam, plurimis ipsum abundantem ornamentis, liberaliter aliquid in me conferre, praesertim in quem prolixa et lauta mea fuerit liberalitas" (p. 47).

116 "tanquam fucus labores apum devorans in alvearia tua mutatis quibusdam verbis furtim coniecisti." Cf. B. Facio, *Invectivae in Laurentium Vallam*, ed. E. I. Rao (Naples, 1978), pp. 92 f.; and L. Valla *Antidotum in Facium* 4.10.4, pp. 371f. It is worth transcribing the entire passage: "Librum 'de summo bono' te scripsisse gloriaris qui quidem a patruo tuo, docto homine, ut accepi, conditus fuit; quem tanquam fucus labores apum devorans in alvearia tua, mutatis quibusdam verbis, furtim coniecisti, quamquam in furto deprehensus es, cum forte Antonii Lusci, qui in eo opere a patruo tuo inducebatur, nomen delere forte oblitus esses." Taken literally, the accusation seems absurd: Scrivani, as Valla readily points out, never wrote anything; the reference to Loschi, who in the Roman setting of the dialogue is said to be absent because he was sick ("ut Pogius nuntiaverat," p. 144), is no less puzzling; and there is something of a contradiction in the fact that the book, "a patruo tuo . . . conditus," would not be signed by Valla immediately but recast in another context, "in alvearia tua." Facio's accuses, therefore, must be understood in a context of allusions, deliberately distorted, not to one but rather to a series of facts (the *mafia* warning was an ancient custom indeed). Lorenzo had tried in vain to be taken on among the papal secretaries, and here his failure is emphasized with remarks that the post belonged to his uncle and was not his parasitically. The reference to Loschi evidently aims not so much at the historical personage as at the character and his well-known speech in the literary context of Poggio's *De avaritia*, of which obvious references in Valla's *De voluptate* are easily recognizable (cf. n. 10 above). So it remains to explain Facio's allusion to a text recast "in alvearia tua mutatis quibusdam verbis," which can be nothing else but Raimondi's letter, of which Panormita, the one who had inspired Facio's *Invectiva*, was surely well aware.

117 Cf. letter to Antonio of Rho, "Cosmae Raimundi exhortatoria ad fratrem Antonium Raudensem ut librum cudat de imitationibus eloquentiae," c. 1428–1429, in Floro di Zenzo, pp. 41–43. Raimondi's letter has been preserved as a preface to the *Imitationes* by Antonio of Rho; cf. Lombardi, "Introduction" to Antonio da Rho, *Apologia*, pp. 30 f.

118 Cf. G. Federici Vescovini, *Astrologia e scienzia: La crisi dell'aristotelismo sul cadere del Trecento e Biagio Pelacani da Parma* (Florence, 1979), pp. 372 ff.

119 Cf. F. Adorno, ed., "Catonis Sacci Originum liber primus in Aristotelem . . . ," *Rinascimento* 2 (1962): 157–201 (especially p. 166): "Iam pauca dicamus de ridicula illa voce et auctoritate quae in cunctis gymnasiis celebratur: Philosophus, inquiunt, mundum esse aeternum dixit, quia sine ratione apud aristotelicos eius valet auctoritas, ut de Pythagora legitur." Adorno has noted a similarity of concepts in the prefaces of the *Origines* and in Valla's *Repastinatio* (the modesty of Pythagoras in contrast to the scholastic conceit of "ipse dixit," etc.). Although the works were written around the same time, in my opinion these similarities are evidence that Sacco's came first; Valla

would later refer to it, but with a completely differing approach. Valla, moreover, directly contrasts the guiding concept of the *Origines* in a passage of *De voluptate* he later omitted (cf. n. 32 above). In a discussion of the Aristotelian doctrine of the world's eternity, he states that on the belief that men had always existed, "nulla fides, nullum argumentum est." In other words, in spite of a common anti-Aristotelian concern, Valla invalidates Sacco's etymological argument.

120 "Sed mihi non certum mea post sit clade peracta / vita ne venturos intuitura dies." Cf. G. Mercati, *Opere minori* . . . (Vatican City, 1937), p. 106. On the letter about Joan of Arc, see now also P. Gilli, *Au miroir de l'Humanisme: Les représentations de la France dans la culture savante italienne à la fine du Moyen Âge* (Rome, 1997), pp. 90–92.

121 At the beginning of his *Defensio Epicuri* (n. 106 above), Raimondi presents himself as a man "gravioribus multoque difficilioribus studiis occupato (nam, quod profiteri me non pudet, astrologicis disciplinis assidue operam impertior;)" and at the same time as an ancient follower of Epicurus: "cum Epicuri, viri omnium sapientissimi, auctoritatem et sententiam maxime semper assecutus sim." There is a real similarity between these arguments and those stated a century or more later in French libertinism; cf. Gauna, *Les épicuriens bibliques;* F. Joukovsky, "L'épicureisme poétique au XVIème siècle," *Ass. G. Budé, Actes,* pp. 639–675.

122 Cf. Chomarat, Introduction to *Dialogue sur le Libre-arbitre,* p. 10: "un acte de confiance."

123 Cf. Floro di Zenzo, pp. 58 f; and Garin, p. 88: "Ne quis vero quibus temporibus de his disputem ignorare me existumet, hac tota disputatione intelligi illud volo, me hic de illa simplici veraque philosophia, quam theologicam appellamus, nunc non agere, sed de hominis humano bono quaerere et de opinionibus ipsorum inter se hac de re dissentientium philosophorum." This was essentially the same position taken by L. Bruni, who reprimanded Valla for having trespassed into the sphere of theology, since, in Aristotelian terms, he intended for Valla to limit himself to a consideration of man in this life: "nam post mortem non est homo amplius" (Sabbadini, *Cronologia,* p. 65; cf. also n. 69 above).

124 *Elegantiae* 5.30: " 'Fides' enim proprie latine dicitur 'probatio.' . . . Religio autem christiana non probatione nititur sed persuasione, quae praestantior est quam probatio. . . . Qui persuasus est plane acquiescit, nec ulteriorem probationem desiderat."

125 M. Luther, *Discorsi a tavola,* ed. L. Perini (Turin, 1969), p. 53: ". . . Disputa bene sul libero arbitrio. Ha trovato la purezza nella pietà e insieme nella cultura. Erasmo l'ha trovata solo nella cultura, ma si fa beffe della pietà." In Valla, nevertheless, the dilemma is not conceived in terms of a contrast between Scripture and tradition: in the eyes of the author of the *Annotationes in Novum Testamentum,* Scripture itself was already tradition.

126 Cf. *Antidotum II in Pogium, Opera,* pp. 362 f. According to Valla, King Alfonso had stopped the trial by making a transparent allusion to the tract on the Donation of Constantine: "se scire aiebat quid illos ad hanc rem induxerat dixitque palam de alio opere meo." This is ignored by W. Setz, *Lorenzo Valla Schrift gegen die Konstantinische Schenkung* (Tübingen, 1975); on this work, cf. my review in *Studi medievali,* 3a ser., 20 (1979): 221–28. See also R. M. Grant with D. Tracy, *A Short History of the Interpre-*

tation of the Bible, 2d ed. (London, 1984), pp. 100 f.; and my essays: "Lorenzo Valla tra il Concilio di Basilea e quello di Firenze, e il processo dell'Inquisizione," *Conciliarismo, Stati nazionali, inizi dell'Umanesimo* (Spoleto, 1990), pp. 287–310 (also in Fubini, *L'umanesimo italiano e i suoi storici*, pp. 136–62); "Contestazioni quattrocentesche della Donazione di Costantino," in *Costantino il Grande dall'Antichità all'Umanesimo*, ed. G. Bonamente and L. Fusco, vol. 1 (Macerata, 1992), pp. 385–431.

127 Cf. Zippel, *Defensio*. Of the twenty-six charges to which Valla responds, the first ten directly concern the dialogue; the other ones relate to various other works ("Aliae quaestiones propter quas sum accusatus," pp. 88 ff.).

128 I cite only two examples of contemporary authors who participated in this same bold and unconventional atmosphere of culture and can be characterized by a common leaning toward utilitarianism. L. B. Alberti, in his little tract *De iure* (1437), excludes *honestas* from the sphere of law, just as Valla did from that of ethics, insofar as it is subordinate to necessity ("necessitati vel coniuncta est honestas vel paret"), and makes the ancient classifications of virtues relative through a quite utilitarian standard of proportioning its values. In this text we find actually a utilitarian interpretation of the *exemplum* of Attilus Regulus, which would seem to have been borrowed from Valla: "Hoc enim Regulum sensisse possumus interpretari . . . , nam plus apud eum valuit diuturnae atque sempiternae infamiae vitatio quam paucorum dierum acerbitatis" (cf. C. Grayson, "Il 'De iure' di Leon Battista Alberti," *Tradizione classica e letteratura umanistica: Per Alessandro Perosa*, ed. R. Cardini [Rome, 1985], vol. 1, pp. 173–94, especially pp. 181, 185). Aeneas Silvius Piccolomini, of whose personal and literary relationship with Valla there is documentary evidence (cf. *Epistolae*, pp. 235 f.), seems to have taken the suggestion for his comedy *Chrysis* (1444) from the *De voluptate*. Valla, in fact, had recommended as a literary subject not only famous women but even immodest ones, "ut appareat ipsas etiam Thaidas, Chrisidas, Bachidas . . . , si modo pulchrae sint, non excludi a gloriae dignitate" (*Dvb* 2.12.1, p. 59). The Epicurean reflections in one monologue of the play, about the vanity of tombs (*Chrysis*, ed. E. Cecchini [Florence, 1968], vv. 187–88: "Quid gloria vanius / sepulchrali?"), are actually taken from *Dvb* 2.11.1, p. 54: "Sed remittamus Curtium ad sepulchrum suum . . . Nam quid ad defunctum pertinet id cuius sensum non habet?" (cf. also *Dvb*, apparatus, p. 175).

129 On the *De vitae felicitate* (1445–46) and on the intentions of its author ("semper aspernandos et fugiendos existimavi qui hanc voluptatem vel summum in vita bonum vel felicitatem homini conferre videntur"), cf. *Antidotum in Facium*, pp. xxxiii, lxvi. On Bartholomaeus Platina's *De falso et vero bono* ("Veritati tamen stoici appropinquare magis visi sunt, qui in virtute, quae ad felicitatem via est, solum bonum collocarunt"), cf. L. Pastor, *Storia dei papi . . .* , 2d ed. (Rome, 1961), vol. 2, p. 322; C. Del Bravo, "Giovanni Bellini in relazione al Valla," *Annali della Scuola Normale Superiore di Pisa*, ser. 3a, 13 (1983): 695. But see especially the most recent edition: B. Platima, *De falso et vero bono*, ed. M. G. Blasio (Roma, 1999) (Edizione nazionale dei testi umanistici, 3).

130 Letter from November 1453 in M. C. Davies, "Niccolò Perotti and Lorenzo Valla: Four New Letters," *Rinascimento* 24 (1984): 143: "Quem enim habeo inter omnes

homines te cariorem? . . . quod te meorum operum defensorem cum vita defunctus fuero aut solum aut primum destino. . . . Nam ceteri fere aut non possunt aut nolunt" (also in Davies, "Lettere inedite tra Valla e Perotti," *L. Valla e l'umanesimo italiano,* p. 104).

131 Cf. Maiocchi, *Codice diplomatico,* p. 283; Corbellini, *Note,* pp. 261 ff. ("Regissol statua Papiensis in magistros theologos"); and also Z. Volta, "La facolta teologica nei primordi dello Studio generale di Pavia," *Archivio storico lombardo,* ser. 3a, 10 (1898): 282–316.

132 "qui hostem philosophorum me appellarant." Cf. *Antidotum in Facium* 4.13.29, p. 393.

133 Cf. M. Speroni, "Lorenzo Valla a Pavia: Il 'Libellus' contro Bartolo," *Quellen und Forschungen aus italienischen Archiven und Bibliotheken* 59 (1979): 452–67. See the critical edition of Valla's tract in M. Regoliosi, "L'epistola *Contra Bartolum* del Valla," in *Filologia umanistica per Gianvito Resta,* ed. V. Fera and G. Ferraù, vol. 2 (Padova, 1997), pp. 1501–71.

134 "posteros interpretes, Bartholum et alios." Cf. D. Maffei, *Gli inizi dell'Umanesimo giuridico* (Milan, 1956), pp. 41 f.; and now, the more extensive discussion by M. Speroni, "Il primo vocabolario giuridico umanistico: Il 'De verborum significatione' di Maffeo Vegio," *Studi Senesi* 88 (1976): 7–43. Valla's work is dated to the end of February; Vegio's preface is precisely dated 15 March.

135 Cf. Speroni, "Il primo vocabolario giuridico," pp. 8 and 21.

136 Ibid., pp. 15 f: "Maffeo Vegio può essere considerato l'iniziatore dell'antitribonianesmo in senso stretto." Vegio's text is cited in Maffei, *Gli inizi,* p. 42: "quod non aliunde evenisse arbitror quam Tribuniani causa, a quo absumptis Iureconsultorum libris necesse fuit oriri tot difficiles quot in Iure sunt contrarietates."

137 Cf. D. R. Kelley, *Foundations of Modern Historical Scholarship: Language, Law, and History in French Renaissance* (New York and London, 1970). In pp. 19–50 there is an extensive and important discussion of Valla.

138 "utinam integri forent, aut certe isti non forent qui in locum illorum etiam Iustianiano vetante successerunt." Cf. *Elegantiae latinae linguae* 1.3.praef., *Prosatori latini,* p. 608.

139 P. Vaccari, "Lorenzo Valla e la scienza giuridica del suo tempo," *Archivio storico per la province parmensi,* 4th ser., 9 (1957): 253–66. Vaccari, *Storia dell'Universita di Pavia,* 2d ed. (Pavia, 1957), p. 72.

140 Vaccari, "Giovan Pietro de' Ferraris e la 'Practica Papiensis,'" *Contributi alla storia dell'Università di Pavia pubblicati nell'XI centenario dell'Ateneo* (Pavia, 1925), pp. 307–25. See also in general M. Sbriccoli, *L'interpretazione dello Statuto: Contributo allo studio della funzione dei giuristi nell'età comunale* (Milan, 1969), pp. 90–101.

141 "quam de utili et inutili transigere, nihil de honesto?" Cf. *Dvb* 2.23.1, p. 69. The passage represents a studied upsetting of *Digesta* 1.1.1: "iustitiam namque colimus et boni et aequi notitiam profitemur . . . , bonos non solum metu poenarum, verum etiam praemiorum quoque exhortatione afficere cupientes." On theoretical premises of this issue see *Repastinatio* 1.14.13–14, pp. 412 f: "Separatam tamen volo a 'iure' 'iusticiam.' Est enim 'ius' scientia recte agendi et suum cuique tribuendi, et, ut iurisconsulti quidam aiunt, 'ars aequi et boni.' 'Iusticia' vero non scientia neque ars, sed actio bona,

recta et aequa. . . . Porro ius, id est scientia sive ars sive prudentia, praecedit, iusticia sequitur. [§14] Neque ab 'iusticia' 'ius,' quemadmodum aliqui volunt, sed ab 'iure' 'iusticia,' seu rei rationem quam demonstravi seu nominis etymologiam intuendam putes, dicitur."

142 Cf. Lactance, *Institutions divines, Libre V,* pp. 59 ff.; and E. Heck, "Iustitia civilis-iustitia naturalis": À propos du jugement de Lactance concernant les discours sur la justice dans le 'De re publica' de Cicéron," *Lactance et son temps: Recherches actuelles. Actes du IVe Colloque d'Études Historiques et Patristiques* (Chantilly, 21–23 September 1976) (Paris, n.d. [1978]) ("Théologie Historique," 48), pp. 171–84.

143 "quod miserationem nobis natura communem cum ceteris animalibus dedit, sicut iram, spem, odium, dolorem, gaudium, cum virtutes non dederit." Cf *Dvb* 2.21.4, p. 66. On this issue, cf. H. Pétré, " 'Misericordia': Histoire du mot et de l'idée," *Revue des études latines* 12 (1934): 376–89.

144 "Verum et virtus quid sit adversa ei malitia detegit, et aequitas fit ex iniqui contemplatione manifestior." Cf. Quintilian *Institutiones* 12.1.35. On "aequitas" as an "élément fondamental de la *tractatio* des controverses, qui s'oppose aux conclusions du droit strict," cf. J. Cousin, "Quintilien et la notion d' 'aequum,' " *Hommages à M. Renard,* vol. 1, pp. 260–67.

145 *Dvb* 2.32.10, 89: "Nec multum abfuit ab opinione mea academicus ille Carneades, qui impune nec stoicos nec peripateticos reformidans pro iusticia et contra iusticiam disserebat . . . Si vero more aliorum utrum verius esset asserere potuisset, haud dubito partem utilitatis fuisse probaturum." Cf. also Marsh, pp. 68 f.

146 "ius naturale dicere, quod natura omnia animalia docuit, ridiculum est"; "atque ideo nocendi imbecilliori animali, spoliandi, occidendi, quis ius esse dixerit?"; "quasi illius scriba"; "toties novam legem appellant, non ab aliquo legislatore unam legem, sed ab infinitis interpretibus legum infinitas leges esse iudicantes." Cf. *Elegantiae* 4.48.

147 Cf. O. Besomi, "Un nuovo autografo di Giovanni Tortelli," *Italia medioevale e umanistica* 13 (1970): 95–137; *Epistolae,* pp. 189 ff. On the issue in general, see also my note: "La coscienza del latino, Postscriptum," *Umanesimo e secolarizzazione,* pp. 55–75 (not in this volume).

148 Cf. Bianchi, *La lettura d'arte oratoria,* pp. 157 ff; an additional bibliography in *Epistolae,* p. 39.

149 "Ea nanque est argumentorum inculcatio, ea exemplorum redundantia, eaque rerum earundem repetitio, is flexus orationis quidquid occurrit more vitium apprehendentis, ut an inutilius sit an turpius nesciam." Cf. *Dvb* 2.praef. § 2, p. 43.

150 On this topic, see the very detailed research by A. Sottili, "Università e cultura a Pavia in età viscontea-sforzesca," *Storia di Pavia,* vol. 3, pt. 2 (Milan, 1990), pp. 359–451.

Index

⸻⸻

Naples, 123, 166–67
Nelli, Francesco, 48, 200
Neoplatonic philosophy, 121
Neroni, Dietisalvi, 138
Niccoli, Niccolò, 25, 56, 58–59, 69–70, 83, 102, 106, 109, 128, 142
Nicholas V, pope, 7, 111, 124, 128–29, 134–35, 167
Novati, F., 45

O'Brien, Emily, vii
Observance, friars of the, 66, 69, 113
Oliari, Bartolomeo, 182
Olivi, Pietro di Giovanni, 81
Oppel, J. W., 81–82, 84

Padua, 47, 141
Panizza, L. A., 150
Panormita, Beccadelli Antonio, 104, 141–44, 163, 166, 172–73
Papal court, 5, 59, 70, 91–92, 138, 140–42
Papia: *Lexicon* entitled to, 23
Paul of Tarsus, Saint, 107. *See also* Sacred Scripture
Pavia, 142–43, 167; University, 141, 144, 163, 169, 172–73
Pazzi conspiracy, 138–39
Pelacani, Biagio, 163
Pelagius, 159
Peraldus, Guglielmus, 159
Perotti, Niccolò, 167
Peter, Saint, 107
Petrarch, Francis, 1–7, 12, 17–18, 24, 26, 34, 46–49, 51–53, 55, 57, 59, 64–65, 74, 77, 84, 86, 90–91, 95–100, 109, 124, 154; *Africa,* 54; *De viris illustribus,* 48–49, 54, 98; *Familiares,* 19, 20, 48, 50–51, 54, 75, 84; *Rerum Memorandarum libri,* 49, 53–54; *Rime,* 18; *Secretum,* 74–75, 97, 106; *Seniles,* 50
Petworth, Richard, 101, 125
Philelphus. *See* Filelfo, Francesco
Piacenza, 140–41
Piccinino, Francesco, 144

Pius II, pope, 91
Pizolpasso, Francesco, 3, 7
Platina, Bartolomeo: *De falso et vero bono,* 166, 297; *De principe,* 268
Plato, 52, 64, 82, 96, 100–101, 121, 145, 147, 153, 165
Plautus, Titus Maccius, 76
Plinius, C. Secundus, the Older, 131
Plutarch, 111
Poliziano, Angelo, 7
Pontano, Giovanni, 7, 73, 92, 118, 129–33
Popkin, R. H., 150
Premierfait, Laurent de, 121–23
Pseudo-Chrysostom, 81, 84
Pythagoras, 164

Quintilian, Marcus Fabius, 5, 29, 37, 73, 77, 143, 150–51, 170–71
Quirini, Lauro, 6, 128

Raimondi, Cosma, 1, 161–65, 172
Ramakus, Gloria, vii
Rasini, Baldassare, 173
Regulus, Marcus Attilius, 63, 161–62
Riario, family, 139
Ricasoli, Carlo, 69
Ridolfi, Antonio, 195
Rinuccini, Cino, 98
Robert of Anjou, king of Naples, 52
Robert of Bavaria, emperor, 137
Rome, 36–38, 40–41, 44, 51, 71, 90, 115, 140–43; Roman empire, 31, 40, 135. See also *Corpus Juris Justinianei*
Rustici, Cencio, 11, 72, 82, 84, 140

Sacco, Catone, 141, 143, 148, 168; *Origines,* 163–64, 172
Sacred Scripture, 4, 45–46, 147–48, 150; Acts, 157; Apocalypse, 148; Matthew, 81; St. Paul, 58, 63, 84 106–7, 155, 157, 159–60
Salutati, Coluccio, 20–26, 45–47, 55, 94–98, 100, *De laboribus Herculis,* 62, 76
Salviati family, 139

Riccardo Fubini is Professor of Renaissance History at the University of Florence.

Martha King is the translator of Grazia Deledda's *Reeds in the Wind* and *Elias Portolu* and the editor of new *Italian Women: A Collection of Short Fiction.*

Library of Congress Cataloging-in-Publication Data
Fubini, Riccardo.
[Umanesimo e secolarizzazione. English]
Humanism and secularization: from Petrarch to Valla /
by Riccardo Fubini ; translated by Martha King.
p. cm. — (Duke monographs in medieval and Renaissance studies)
Includes bibliographical references and index.
ISBN 0-8223-3002-4 (cloth : alk. paper)
1. Latin literature, Medieval and modern—Italy—History and criticism.
2. Italy—Intellectual life—1268-1559.   3. Humanism—Italy.   4. Bracciolini,
Poggio, 1380-1459—Criticism and interpretation.   5. Petrarca, Francesco,
1304-1374—Influence. I. Title. II. Series.
PA8045.I6 F83   2002   144'.0945—dc21   2002010477